OLD MASTERS

# Old Masters

## *Great Artists in Old Age*

Thomas Dormandy

Hambledon and London
London and New York

Hambledon and London

102 Gloucester Avenue
London, NW1 8HX

838 Broadway
New York
NY 10003-4812

First Published 2000

ISBN 1 85285 290 9

A description of this book is available from the
British Library and from the Library of Congress.

Typeset by Carnegie Publishing,
Lancaster LA1 4SL

Printed on acid-free paper and bound in
Great Britain by Cambridge University Press

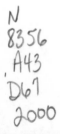

# Contents

# Illustrations

## Text Illustrations

# Acknowledgements

First, my thanks and love, as always, to Liz: without her there would be no book. I also want to thank all the Dormandys who have read this book at various stages of its long gestation and have given me such wonderful support. I am grateful to my artist friends, Richard Robbins and Leslie Smith, for their help and comments; and to my friend and colleague Robert Morgan for his great skill and kindness. Lucky is the author who can work with an editor as inspired and inspiring as Martin Sheppard; I am also grateful to others who have helped me at Hambledon and London, especially Rachel Moss, Eva Osborne and Catherine Sheppard.

The author and publishers would like to thank the following for permission to reproduce illustrations: Mme Dina Vierny and ADAGP (Plate 20); The Bridgeman Art Library (Plates 3, 4, 13, 15, 16, 17, 18); The British Museum (Plate 5 and Page 2); The Paul Getty Museum, Malibu, California (Plate 9); The Kunsthistorisches Museum, Vienna (Plate 1); The Louvre (Plate 6); The Metropolitan Museum, New York (Plate 10); The Minneapolis Institute of Arts, Minneapolis, Minnesota (Plate 8); The Munch Museum, Oslo/Munch-Ellingsen Group/DACS 2000 (Plate 20); The Prado, Madrid (Plates 2, 7 and Page 180); Tate Britain (Plate 12).

*In Living Memory of S. D.*

From the age of six I was in the habit of drawing all kinds of things. Although I had produced numerous designs by my fiftieth year, none of my work done before my seventieth is really worth counting. At the age of seventy-three I have come to understand the true forms of animals, insects and fish and the nature of plants and trees. Consequently, by the age of eighty-six I will have made more and more progress, and at ninety I will have got significantly closer to the essence of art. At the age of one hundred I will have reached a magnificent level and at one hundred and ten each dot and each line will be alive. I would like to ask you who outlive me to observe that I have not spoken without reason.

Hokusai (1834)

# Introduction

"The Master is very old", Albrecht Dürer wrote to his friend Willibald Pirckheimer from Venice in 1505, "but he is still the best in painting." [1] The Nürnberger was thirty-four and in his own country already celebrated as a great artist. He was not unaware of this. Nor was he easily overawed. But, though this was his second visit to Venice, he still marvelled at its riches. He noted, not without a touch of envy, the esteem in which its artists were held. True, the boasting of Venetians about their unique constitution could try the patience of a saint; but, in fairness, they had much to boast about. Yet it was neither wealth nor politics which impressed Dürer most. By then Giovanni Bellini had been First Painter to the Republic for forty years; and his workshop was famous. It was, as always, teeming with young talent. Several were slightly impatient to step into the master's shoes. They would, they assured the visitor, surpass Bellini. The First Painter had been a great innovator in his time, but his style was getting a little old-fashioned. Some of the pupils were a trifle patronising to the visitor too. Coming from the artistically backward north, there was much for him to learn. Dürer preferred to form his own judgement; and what he saw left him in no doubt. The master was still unsurpassed. Even today Dürer's judgement can be faulted in only one respect: its faintly valedictory tone was premature. True, the master was old. Seventy-one? Seventy-three? Or even seventy-five? Renaissance artists seem to have been less exercised by their exact dates of birth than are authorities on their times and lives today. Whatever the exact number of years, he was a little tremulous and had a tendency, as have many old people, to take on more than he could deliver. But it was during the ten years *after* Dürer's visit that Bellini was to paint some of his loveliest and most prophetic works.

Dürer's comments on Bellini are sometimes quoted to illustrate the quirkiness of old age. In the same vein, it is sometimes recalled that Titian painted some of his greatest *poesies* in his seventies. Hokusai at eighty-five begged the gods for another ten years of life: he had, he claimed, only just learnt

[1] Pirckheimer, like the artist, was living in Basel at the time. See K. Lange and F. Fuhse, eds, *Dürers schriftlicher Nachlass* (Halle, 1893).

how to hold a brush. Michelangelo was still chipping away at his blocks of marble at almost ninety. Such morsels of information are usually imparted and received as evidence of the freakishness of human nature, as improbable as the four-year-old Mozart's pretty minuets or the ten-year-old Ovid's wailing in faultless hexameters at the other – and more familiar – extreme of life. But how freakish were the old ages of Bellini, Michelangelo, Titian and Hokusai?

No chronological age is probably more creative than any other; but less is known about the creativity of great artists in old age than about their creativity in youth, maturity or even childhood. Monographs which lovingly explore parents, grandparents, aunt, uncles and second cousins often wrap up their hero's sunset years in a paragraph or two. This is odd – or perhaps not. "We arrive as novices at every age of our life", Sébastien de Chamfort observed.[2] It is a profound truth. Novitiate implies ignorance. No twenty-year-old has ever fully understood a forty-year-old and no forty-year-old has ever properly understood a seventy-year-old. Every self-respecting writer likes to write about things he understands – or thinks he understands. Art historians are no exceptions. Hence there are hundreds of books – some excellent – about the childhood and youth of famous artists and virtually none about their old age. There is also often a disturbing air about the last creations, an element of mystery about their appeal and even more about their faults. Neither the appeal nor the faults are easy to categorise or explain. Perhaps they are best left alone.

There is yet another reason for this neglect. Few preconceptions are so deeply ingrained as those which surround old age; and no others exercise a firmer grip on people's minds. For centuries both to doctors and to laymen the term has meant (whether or not consciously) the sum total of a large number of disease processes lumped together in modern medical jargon as "degenerative". Much is known about their symptoms, signs and pathology; nothing about their causation. What is certain is that they start insidiously, quite early in life, and progress slowly but irreversibly. Sooner or later all organs and systems in the body are affected; but, because their relative degree of involvement varies, no two people age in exactly the same way. Some of the changes are nevertheless both constant and relevant to the art of old age – or to the art of old age as it is generally perceived.

To paint a great – or even passable – picture, or to carve a modest-size statue, needs more than artistic afflatus. It needs muscle strength, nervous control, stamina, dexterity, reasonable eyesight, powers of coordination, a tolerable memory, clarity of thought. To a lesser or greater degree all these accomplishments – and many others – diminish in men and women in their

---

[2] S.-R.-N. de Chamfort, *Maximes et pensées*, i (Paris, 1778), p. 436.

seventies, eighties and nineties. And it is no more than common sense to postulate that when so many, perhaps most, components of a complex process decline, then the complex process itself must do so too.

Yet there is another way of looking at ageing. Not only individuals but also cells and molecules and even non-living artefacts age. Only their pattern of ageing is different. A stainless steel pin driven across a bony fracture site will last for many years, usually much longer than the recipient. But, depending on its molecular structure and the stresses and strains put on it, it will ultimately snap. Structural engineers call this "metal fatigue". When structural engineers use biological terms, such as fatigue, one can be fairly certain that they have no idea what they are talking about. What the pin will *not* do is to show anything that remotely resembles tiredness. It will not bend or wobble or develop any of those long drawn out mental or physical ailments associated with wear and tear, fatigue and ageing. Even a few seconds before it snaps it may seem perfect. Then the moment arrives and it dies.[3]

This has given doctors and biologists food for thought. The idea of ageing as the sum total of chronic degenerative diseases can be turned upside down. Perhaps there is a mysterious process one can for convenience call "ageing" of which the obvious and familiar degenerative changes – greying of the hair, cataracts, loss of stamina, inability to remember the names of one's nearest and dearest – are but the symptoms and signs.[4] Indeed, they are perhaps only a few of the symptoms and signs. There may be others. And some of the others may be positive. Such positive characteristics might account for the odd, at times contrary, behaviour of artists like Bellini, Michelangelo, Titian and Hokusai. They might even explain the unexpected new heights reached in their artistry. That, in short, is what the present book sets out to explore.

---

[3] Contrary to fable and legend, where the prolongation of life almost always entails the prolongation of youth, even in living organisms ageing and life-span are only tenuously related. (The Cumaean Sybil disastrously forgot this. She asked Apollo for as many years of life as there are grains of sand on the seashore without asking to be allowed to retain her youth for the same length of time.) Life-span is probably encoded in the genes of every species and every individual; and nothing short of genetic engineering will ever be able to change it. This is almost certainly not true of ageing, whatever it is.

[4] There are several theories as to what kind of a process ageing is; and it is possible to retard ageing in insects and perhaps other animals by drugs without necessarily affecting their life-span. (A dedicated entomologist can distinguish between a youthful and an elderly insect as easily as the reader could distinguish between a youthful and elderly entomologist.) See, for example, I. Emerit and B. Chance (eds), *Free Radicals and Ageing* (Basel, 1992); T. L. Dormandy, "Free Radicals in Pathology and Medicine", *Advanced Medicine*, 22, ed. D. R. Triger (London, 1988).

PART ONE

# Artists in Old Age

Michelangelo Buonarroti (1475–1564), *Madonna and Child*, after 1560. Possibly Michelangelo's last drawing. (*British Museum*)

# 1

## *The Age of Creation*

Titian was a great painter at thirty, forty, fifty and sixty. Was he still a great painter at seventy, eighty and perhaps ninety?[1] And, if he was, was he the *same* great painter? Similar questions could be asked about other artists who lived into their late seventies, eighties and nineties. A surprising number did; and their names are familiar.[2] The answers are less so.

Scholarly books and exhibition catalogues usually date individual works of art. They also give the date of birth of the artists. But few readers calculate (often across the daunting mathematical barrier of a turn of centuries) the age of the artist that corresponds to any particular work. The biological significance of the two dates, the *age* of creation, is therefore lost. Of course a few instances of artists creating great works in old age are comparatively well known. Some may recall Bellini and Titian, others Michelangelo and Hokusai, as the old-age wonders of art history. But what about Donatello, Tintoretto, Hals, Bernini, Claude, Chardin, Turner, David, Goya, Corot, Ingres, Rodin, Renoir, Monet, Maillol, Munch, Nolde, Kandinski, Bonnard and Matisse? All produced remarkable works in their last years, even if the late creations are less famous than those of their maturity; and the list could be extended to the more recent past and include artists still living and vigorously at work. The freakish suddenly begins to look like the norm, the exception like the rule.[3]

There is more than one way to confirm or disprove such impressions.

[1] Estimates of Titian's date of birth have varied between 1477 (based on the Florentine writer Raffaello Borghini) and 1490 (based on Titian's friend, Lodovico Dolce). See C. Hope, *Titian* (London, 1980).

[2] See Table, below, p. 5. It is surprising not only in relation to what is known about human life expectancy in past centuries, but also compared to the longevity of great composers. Of course some great composers lived to an old age – Schütz, Haydn and Verdi come to mind – but one cannot compare the creations of young and old Mozart, young and old Schubert, young and old Chopin; and even "late Beethoven" was only fifty-six. Have the fumes of linseed oil and turpentine mysterious life-prolonging properties?

[3] "There are no exceptions to a rule", Sherlock Holmes said. "If there are exceptions it is no longer a rule." He was of course perfectly right, as always; but the Holmesian definition makes birth and death the only rules of human behaviour. Norms, by contrast, imply exceptions, accounting for the infinite vagaries of human nature and destiny.

Statistics are often held up today as the supreme, even the only, way to solve problems relating to human behaviour.[4] Sometimes, sadly, the trappings are mistaken for the substance. To prove or disprove a statistical relationship, the variables must be measurable with roughly equal accuracy. Chronological age is one of the most accurate, if not necessarily the most meaningful, measurements in medicine and biology. That is why it is so widely used and even more widely misused.[5] Creativity, by contrast, is one of the least measurable ones.[6] Correlating the two statistically is therefore likely to give unreliable or even misleading results. But such warnings ignore the lure of correlation coefficients, standard deviations and that queen of twenty-first-century sirens, the two-tailed t test.[7] Attempts to correlate have been numerous; and the results have been interesting, though rarely in the way intended.

H. C. Lehman's ground-breaking book, *Age and Achievement*, is replete with graphs, tables and all the paraphernalia of mathematical rigour.[8] Obviously based on meticulous research, it covers a wide range of creative activities – philosophy, medicine, music, literature, politics, science, industry and business among others. The chapter dealing with the visual arts alone looks at sculpture, architecture, etching, oil painting and water-colour painting systematically and in turn. On sculpture, "when every effort to ascertain the ages at which the most noted sculptors of ancient Greece executed their best sculptures proved fruitless",[9] the author turned to a more contemporary academic work, *The History of American Sculpture*, by Lorado Taft.[10] Unlike the unhelpful Greeks, "this listed the 262 best sculptures of the sixty-three most famous American sculptors, now deceased ... together with the date of execution of their works".[11] With such a database the writer was able to construct a statistical production curve, representing "the average number of best works executed during each five-year period of the sculptors' lives".[12]

---

[4] This is a comparatively new development. Fifty years ago the editor of the *Lancet* looked askance at the idea that anything to do with medicine could have a mean or any kind of deviation, let alone standard.

[5] The root of ageism in all its nefarious manifestations.

[6] Even its definition is difficult. Most writers on the subject seem to equate it with success or achievement, neither a true alternative but both more easily measurable.

[7] Supplemented, as they usually are, with mystifying symbols, boldly arching curves and sturdy histograms.

[8] H. C. Lehman, *Age and Achievement* (Princeton, New Jersey, 1953).

[9] Lehman, *Age and Achievement*, p. 83.

[10] L. Taft, *The History of American Sculpture* (New York, 1925).

[11] Lehman, *Age and Achievement*, p. 84.

[12] Ibid., p. 85.

*Great Artists who Lived to the Age of Seventy-Five or Over**

| | | Age at death |
|---|---|---|
| Donatello (Donato di Niccolò di Betto Bardi) | 1386–1466 | 80 |
| Uccello, Paolo | 1397–1475 | 79 |
| Della Robbia, Luca | 1400–1482 | 82 |
| Piero della Francesca | 1415–1492 | 77 |
| Bellini, Giovanni | 1430–1516 | 86 |
| Cranach, Lucas, the Elder | 1472–1553 | 81 |
| Michelangelo Buonarroti | 1475–1564 | 89 |
| Titian (Tiziano Vecellio) | 1487–1576 | 89 |
| Tintoretto (Jacopo Robusti) | 1518–1594 | 76 |
| Hals, Frans | 1581–1666 | 85 |
| Bernini, Giovanni Lorenzo | 1598–1680 | 82 |
| Claude Gelée (Lorrain) | 1600–1682 | 82 |
| Chardin, Jean-Baptiste-Siméon | 1699–1779 | 80 |
| De La Tour, Maurice-Quentin | 1704–1788 | 84 |
| Goya, Francisco José de Goya y Lucientes | 1746–1828 | 82 |
| David, Jacques-Louis | 1748–1825 | 77 |
| Hokusai, Katsushika | 1760–1849 | 89 |
| Turner, Joseph Mallord William | 1775–1851 | 76 |
| Ingres, Jean-Auguste-Dominique | 1780–1867 | 87 |
| Corot, Jean-Baptiste Camille | 1796–1875 | 79 |
| Rodin, Auguste | 1840–1917 | 77 |
| Monet, Claude | 1840–1926 | 86 |
| Renoir, Pierre-Auguste | 1841–1919 | 78 |
| Maillol, Aristide Joseph Bonaventure | 1861–1944 | 83 |
| Munch, Edvard | 1863–1944 | 81 |
| Kandinski, Vasili | 1866–1944 | 78 |
| Nolde, Emil (Emil Hansen) | 1867–1956 | 89 |
| Kollwitz, Käthe | 1867–1945 | 78 |
| Bonnard, Pierre | 1867–1947 | 80 |
| Matisse, Henri | 1869–1954 | 85 |

* For details of inclusions and exclusions, see below, pp. 8–10.

(A whimsical secondary peak between seventy-five and eighty could be discounted when it was discovered that J. Q. A. Ward completed three big contracts at the age of seventy-seven but using three youthful assistants.) The peak of the production curve was demonstrated to be between forty and forty-five years of age.

Like his foray into ancient Greece, Lehman's initial attempts to correlate creative oil painting with the age of artists proved disappointing. The production curve based on the number of mentions of fifty-three individual works by thirty-two painters in oils in two separate guidebooks to the Louvre was erratic.[13] Yet the method had been painstaking, "a point [having been] assigned to each painting each time it was mentioned in one of the two publications".[14] The totals harvested from the two books were counted separately but the tallies were added, "since it could be assumed that paintings mentioned in both books possessed greater artistic merit than those referred to by only one".[15] Undeterred, the author then embarked on a monumental task. Sixty-two art histories, all by recognised authorities, were scoured, "since the one painting by a given artist cited most frequently had to be regarded as that particular artist's best painting".[16] The composite list obtained yielded an impressive 5684 paintings by 305 deceased artists. Among them, sixty-seven could be classified as "indubitably major since they were mentioned at least five times in the sixty-two books".[17] (Minor but still significant artists were mentioned more than twice but less than five times.) Production curves could then be plotted; peaks could be identified; and mathematical conclusions drawn. They established that the maximum creativity in oil painting of recognised major artists – that is the age when they produced "most of their best works in oil" – was forty-nine years.

Such exercises shed welcome light on the average life-span of major artists.[18] They may also suggest the age when they were most prolific. Most usefully, they illustrate an extraordinary change in taste over a relatively short period of time. Even allowing for the fact that the most recent art history consulted had been published in 1937 (partly perhaps to allow the artists mentioned time to die), it is surprising that not a single painting by Manet or Courbet,

---

[13] F. Hayward, *The Important Pictures in the Louvre* (London, 1927) and M. K. Potter, *The Art of the Louvre* (Boston, 1904).

[14] Lehman, *Age and Achievement*, p. 84.

[15] Ibid., p. 85.

[16] Ibid., p. 85.

[17] Ibid., p. 87.

[18] Since no allowance was made in establishing the peak period of creativity for the life-span of the artists, the two had to be related. A peak creativity at ninety could not have been derived from the calculations since few of Lehman's "top" artists lived to that age.

let alone Monet, Pissarro, Cézanne or Van Gogh, is included among the sixty-seven top scorers.[19] Charming as Millet's *The Gleaners* is, few today would place it ahead on artistic merit of any work by Raphael, Titian, Velasquez or Rembrandt, while Gainsborough's *Mrs Siddons* and Hobbema's *The Avenue*, both lovely paintings, would not today be rated among the "top five" in the history of art. But what works would be? Only a researcher in the grip of statistical fury would try to compile such a list.

Searching for citations in textbooks does not of course exhaust possible statistical approaches; but ultimately all depend on assigning numerical values to works of art. Impersonal objectivity is one of the merits of statistics and such evaluations can never be either impersonal or objective. "Creativity Quotients" (CQs) have also been devised and used in investigating normal populations. Ominously modelled on "Intelligence Quotients", they analyse a combination of mental functions (such as "fluency", "flexibility" and "originality") according to a complicated key. Some work using this method has shown that among ordinary people in Scandinavia creativity does not significantly deteriorate between sixty and seventy.[20] Such approaches often reflect favourably on the creativity of the investigators, less convincingly on those investigated. Theoretically, and with small adjustments, it could be applied to dead artists. But nobody, it seems, has tried to measure the CQ of Michelangelo or Goya.

The limitations of the statistical method do not make the questions unanswerable.[21] Adopting a historical approach, one can instead look at a selection of great artists spread over five centuries and half a dozen countries. Some can be used as illustrative case histories, others can be seen collectively from different angles. What happened to their creative genius in old age? Did it decline? Or stagnate? Or reach new heights? Of course the result may show that there was *no* general pattern: what was true of some artists was

[19] Inevitably perhaps, the scorecard is headed by the *Mona Lisa*.

[20] For example, E. Anderson, "Creativity in Old Age: A Longitudinal Study", *Age and Ageing* (1990).

[21] The knee-jerk condemnation of any method other than statistics by medical and behavioural scientists as "anecdotal" and therefore unreliable makes little sense: at least 90 per cent of current medical knowledge is based on anecdotal evidence. To try to re-establish statistically that the bark of the willow tree has painkilling properties, that fresh fruit juice can prevent scurvy, that the outlook for life of the common cold is good, and that the prognosis of gunshot wounds through the heart is bad, would be foolish. Nobody doubts the anecdotal evidence on which these statements – like the vast bulk of medical science – rests. Much recent medical lore, by contrast, which purports to rest on mountainous statistics is deeply suspect. This is not to suggest, of course, that statistics are bad and anecdotes are good. It is simply to assert that both have their scope, their limitations and their rules.

not true of others. But the findings are more likely to reflect the realities of art in old age than Herculean mathematical labours. What the historical approach needs are a few ground rules in selecting the case material.

First and most obviously, the selection should not be targeted to prove or disprove a preconception.[22] Secondly, a few boundaries have to be defined. The creativity of great artists in old age can clearly be assessed only in great artists who lived to be old. But how old is old? The meaning of the term has always been as elusive as the meaning of beautiful. It may also have meant different things in sixteenth-century Venice, seventeenth-century Holland, eighteenth-century France and nineteenth-century Japan.[23] A chronological age of seventy-five has, nevertheless, been regarded as elderly in most places and in most periods. It has therefore been chosen as the lower age limit for inclusion. Any such cut-off point entails losses. This one excludes such excellent painters as Mantegna, Murillo, Pissarro, Tiepolo and Vuillard, all of whom died in their *early* seventies. Fragonard, who died five months before his seventy-fifth birthday, slips through the net. Yet even lowering the age limit to sixty-five would have excluded Rembrandt – he was sixty-three when he died in 1669 – a giant in what most of his contemporaries probably regarded as venerable age.

There is a second ground for exclusion. The late works of living or recently dead artists often arouse fierce controversy; and passing trends and private passions tend to be at their most distorting. Was Picasso in his eighties and nineties at the peak of his creativity? Or was he, as he himself declared (but surely with his tongue in his capacious cheek), painting worse every day? The assessment of artistic merit is always fallible, but perhaps a little less so after the lapse of a generation or two. Artists who are still alive and those who died after 1955 have therefore been excluded. This exclusion was also at times frustrating. Apart from Picasso, the original culprit, it eliminated interesting painters and sculptors like Miró, Kokoschka, Chagall, Manzù, Arp, Archipenko, Dali, Henry Moore, Diego Rivera,

---

[22] Since there was no preconception, this was an easy condition to fulfil; but a certain bias in the choice of the illustrative case histories may nevertheless be admitted. All the long-lived artists listed in the table have been the subjects of detailed, sometimes inspired, monographs and thousands of learned articles; but the old ages of the chosen ten – Tintoretto's rather than Michelangelo's, Hokusai's rather than Turner's, Renoir's rather than Monet's, and Maillol's rather than Rodin's – are perhaps fractionally less familiar. The lives not included among the case histories are briefly reviewed in the Biographical Appendix, below, pp. 319ff.

[23] The difference was less, though, than is sometimes assumed. The life expectancy *at birth* was of course much shorter in times past – less than thirty years in mid Victorian England – but at fifty it was probably only a few years shorter than it is today; and at seventy it may have been longer.

Rouault, Dufy, Hopper, Brancusi and Braque. All lived and worked into their late seventies, eighties or nineties but died within the last forty-five years.

A few great artists who lived to be over seventy-five and have been dead for over forty-five years had to be excluded for a variety of other reasons. Illnesses or political repression rarely stopped long-lived painters and sculptors from working; but sometimes the obstacles were insuperable. Maurice-Quentin de La Tour, who died in 1788 aged eighty-four, was the greatest pastellist of his age, perhaps of any age.[24] He was also one of those rare geniuses (Corot was another) who seem to have been universally loved: by his family, by his *petite amie* Mlle Fell, by Mme de Pompadour and her circle, by the old guard of Versailles, in the theatre and even by his fellow artists.[25] But he became a harmless lunatic at the age of fifty and spent much of his last thirty years roaming his native St-Quentin, embracing the trees and telling them that their sufferings would soon be over.[26]

Physical handicaps too were treated by most great artists as challenges to be overcome rather than as reasons for abandoning their chosen vocation; but complete blindness – as distinct from severe visual impairment – is incompatible with painting. Degas lived to eighty-three but he was totally blind for the last eight years of his life; and his friend and most gifted pupil, Mary Cassatt, went blind after a cataract operation ten years before she died in 1926, at the age of eighty-two.[27]

In a different way the uniquely repellent character of large chunks of twentieth-century history makes a fair assessment of the late development of some artists difficult or impossible. Käthe Kollwitz was the supreme chronicler of the tragic destiny of women in an age tolerant only of

[24] Others, like Degas, created splendid works in chalks but it was not their chief medium. Unfortunately, pastels still tend to be patronised as a "minor" art form, and Maurice-Quentin de La Tour is not as widely celebrated as he deserves to be. The more honour to the Banque de France for putting his self-portrait on the old 50 franc banknote and the more shame on the Louvre for still mislabelling his brilliant portrait of Voltaire as a self-portrait.

[25] Chardin was a friend, of whom he drew or painted (whichever term is proper for pastels) a charming portrait.

[26] He left his considerable fortune to various local charities, including a still flourishing school of art. Many of his best works are preserved in the museum in St-Quentin dedicated to him. See C. Debrie, *Maurice-Quentin de La Tour* (St-Quentin, 1991).

[27] Her reputation has suffered from the widespread notion that women who like to paint mothers and children (especially women artists born in the United States to great riches) cannot be taken seriously. Her finest paintings are wholly unsentimental and combine the superb linear simplicity of Japanese art at its best with the immediacy of the Impressionists. In her last years she exercised a decisive influence on the formation of many of the best private collections of paintings in the United States.

intolerance.[28] In the 1930s, when she was in her sixties, the Nazis expelled her from artistic associations and forbade dealings in her work. Some of her sculpture in public collections was destroyed, other pieces were withdrawn from view and subsequently lost. She could have emigrated but, like her friend Barlach (whom she drew unforgettably on his deathbed), she feared that this would bring retaliation on her family. Her studio with much of her sculpture and unpublished prints and drawings perished in the bombing of Berlin in 1943. She died in 1945, aged seventy-eight, on the Moritzburg estate of Prince Ernst Heinrich of Saxony near Dresden.[29] She was one of the greatest artists of the twentieth century, perhaps still insufficiently recognised, but it is impossible to compare her work in old age with the creations of her youth.

No less limiting is the occasional lack of raw data, especially about the old age of artists of the distant past. The Italian Renaissance was not the beginning of European art but it was the beginning of European artists as named and therefore traceable individuals. Donatello was Donatello, not the Master of Florentine *putti*. Michelangelo was Michelangelo, not the Master of the Sistine Chapel. But the change was slow and gradual and this is reflected in the volume of personal details available about them. The ailments of the masters' decline – if decline they did – was still usually nobody's business. A few examples may serve to make the point.

For centuries Piero della Francesca was barely a footnote in standard art histories. It was the generation reared on Cézanne and steeled by the rigours of Cubism which raised him to the status of a cult figure. He was seventy-seven or older when he died in 1492;[30] but his last known works, *The Madonna of the Duke of Urbino* and the unfinished *Nativity*, date from his fifties. He may then have lost his eyesight. He may have been seduced by science.[31] Perhaps his creative genius declined. Nobody knows.[32] A different kind of uncertainty surrounds the old age of Luca della Robbia.[33] He too is at last being recognised as one of the most abundant and innovative artists of the Italian Renaissance, not just as a clever potter of charming ornamental ware; and it is known that he was active in the family workshop until shortly before

[28] She was born Käthe Schmidt in Königsberg in East Prussia into a deeply religious though nonconformist Lutheran family. In 1891 she married Dr Karl Kollwitz, a district physician in Berlin. They shared strong socialist convictions and a deep moral purpose.

[29] Where some of her last drawings remain. See E. Prelinger, *Käthe Kollwitz* (London, 1992).

[30] Many current estimates of the age of Renaissance artists are based on tax returns or similar documents, probably no more tabernacles of the truth in fifteenth-century Florence or Venice than in twenty-first century London or New York.

[31] In his old age he wrote two learned tomes on the science of perspective, one of the most exciting discoveries of his generation.

[32] See R. Lightbown, *Piero della Francesca* (New York, 1992).

[33] See J. Pope-Hennessy, *Luca della Robbia* (London, 1965).

his death at the age of eighty-two.[34] But beyond a few doubtful attributions, and contrary to some pontifical pronouncements, it is impossible to separate with certainty most of his late works from the creations of a gifted brood of younger della Robbias.[35] On perhaps a slightly lower level, Paolo Uccello died in 1475 at the age of about seventy-nine; but only one creation attributable to his old age is known, the *Night Hunt*, now in the Ashmolean Museum in Oxford.[36] It is a lovely work, suffused with poetry, an old man's remembrance perhaps of the nocturnal mysteries of childhood; but it is not quite enough to trace the artist's progress late in life.

One encounters similar – and even greater – difficulties north of the Alps. The portraits of Lucas Cranach the Elder still bring the circle around his friend Martin Luther vividly to life. He also perfected the slightly gawky nude which many modern connoisseurs find more alluring than most Latin Venuses. But, though he lived to be eighty-one, no fully authenticated works of his survive from later than the 1520s, when he was still only in his fifties. (The self-portrait in the Uffizi in Florence is almost certainly a tribute by his son, the younger Lucas, as are the rather crude wood-cut illustrations of the Bible, for long attributed to the father and sometimes cited to illustrate his supposed decline in his dotage.)[37] The fate or whereabouts of the much-acclaimed portrait of Titian, undoubtedly painted by the elder Lucas during the Venetian master's visit to the imperial court at Augsburg, surely the stuff of art-historical dreams, remains unknown.

[34] The workshop in fact became more a factory, dispatching large consignments of della Robbia ware to faraway lands like Poland and Portugal. (The nineteenth-century English della Robbia ware was attractive but no relation.)

[35] Especially his gifted nephew, Andrea della Robbia, another long-lived artist possibly of the first rank. But Luca's most resplendent heraldic device or *stemma*, showing the arms of King René of Anjou, can be dated with fair certainty to his seventies; and the *Lady's Portrait* in the Bargello in Florence, the embodiment of Florentine elegance, is almost certainly a late autograph work.

[36] Vasari included him among the second wave of "illustrious painters ... who raised the arts from their medieval slough of barbarism", but he was also the first to strike the faintly patronising note that has stuck to the artist ever since. "Uccello's preoccupation with perspective and the truthful rendering of nature was estimable and instructive; but he sometimes tried too hard and the strain shows." See G. Vasari, *Le vite de' più eccellenti pittori, scultori ed architectori*, edited by G. Milanesi, 9 volumes (Florence, 1906), ii, p. 104. True or not, his panoramic battle-scenes commemorating an engagement of the utmost historical insignificance but known as *The Rout of San Romano* (now separated into three panels, in London, Paris and Florence) are a joy to museum-weary eyes; and his *St George* in the National Gallery, London, is an unique representation of the dragon as a lady's pet being taken for a promenade.

The original purpose of the *Night Hunt* is still uncertain – it may have been the predella of a lost altar-piece. See M. Angelini, *Paolo Uccello*, translated by L. Pelletti (London, 1985).

[37] See M. Friedländer and J. Rosenberg, *The Paintings of Lucas Cranach* (London, 1992).

Beyond objective or at least verifiable facts, there was one criterion for inclusion which is neither objective nor verifiable. The long-lived artists to be studied had to be of the "first rank". Outside philistine totalitarian regimes, a contribution to history of the twentieth century,[38] no such ranking can ever command universal approval. At their most inspired, artists of the second, third and no rank have created and still create masterpieces as sublime as any art-historical landmark. Conversely, some of the works of famous names which command obscene prices at auction are breathtakingly feeble.[39] Nor is the present study aimed at exploring artistic creativity in old age in an arbitrarily defined sub-species of "genius". The reason for focusing on artists of the first rank has been purely practical. Even great artists were usually men and women of little social consequence. Compared to popes, emperors, religious reformers and (usually a little more discreetly) bankers and business entrepreneurs, they wielded no power, and their comings and goings were therefore of little interest to anybody outside their immediate family and circle of friends. This has always made the writing of artists' biographies a hazardous enterprise. The difficulties multiply with artists of the lower rank, or considered by later generations to be of a lower rank, and therefore of even less general interest. More importantly, the works of artists widely regarded as "great" are more easily accessible. Most museums nowadays can exhibit only a fraction of their holdings; and, while many make admirable efforts to rotate their display and show from time to time little-known works by little-known artists, they are less likely to keep their Titians and Davids under permanent wraps, even the creations of the famous artists' off days, than the products of little-known contemporaries, however sparkling. This is even more true of reproductions. Art books nowadays can be wonderfully well printed, lavish and informative, but most seem to be about Monet (and a handful of currently fashionable names). Works about the less fashionable have to be searched for.

Accessibility matters to the writer as much as to the reader. Assigning merit or the lack of it to a work of art always involves a personal element. This is even more so when comparing the works of a single artist at different

---

[38] Earlier authoritarian regimes of various kinds from Alexander the Great (or before) to Napoleon were often vile but rarely philistine.

[39] "Ranking" becomes progressively more difficult as one approaches the present, another reason for the forty-five year embargo on artists included in the case material. Should one have crossed the Rhine more readily to look at the last works of that excellent artist, Max Liebermann (who died in 1937, aged eighty-eight)? Or taken the Channel boat from Dieppe back to England and followed the career of Walter Sickert (who died in 1942, aged eighty-two)? Or made the even shorter crossing to Dublin and allowed oneself to be dazzled by the last creations of Jack Yeats (who died in 1958, aged eighty-six)?

periods of his or her life. With artists whose works are accessible (at least in reproduction) this does not matter – or does not matter much. Of course the writer hopes that his readers will agree with his assessments, or at least see what he is trying to say, but he is not asking them to accept his pronouncements as holy writ. No writer on art can subscribe to the doctrine that good or bad in art is simply a matter of taste, but taste does come into it; and about accessible works readers can dismiss the writer's taste as perverse, jejune, infantile or worse. This is extremely comforting.

# 2

# *Tintoretto*

Tintoretto was the last in a succession of long-lived artists whose lives spanned a hundred and sixty years, the golden age of Venetian art.[1] The first, Giovanni Bellini, half-brother of Gentile and son of Jacopo,[2] grew to manhood in a city at the height of its imperial power. Its possessions on the mainland shifted kaleidoscopically (as did most land frontiers in Renaissance Italy),[3] but a fleet of 300 ships, manned by 36,000 of the world's best seamen, controlled the sea-routes to the east and with them Europe's trade in dyes, sugar, spices, drugs, precious stones, silks, cottons, silverware and other luxury goods, including a small but profitable market in slaves.[4] Venetian merchants had penetrated the ancient caravan routes of Central Asia and were welcome among the nomadic tribes of the Steppe.[5] The city's wealth was both legendary and real. Only in the arts and letters did it lag behind not only ancient rivals like Florence, Rome and Naples but also pitifully ramshackle places whose ducats were the laughing stock of the Rialto. There was of course no shortage of works of art and precious manuscripts in Venice: even the houses of ordinary citizens sometimes contained them. But they had been bought – or at any rate acquired – abroad. Not surprisingly, educated people on the mainland regarded the Queen of the Adriatic with envy but also with a trace of condescension: she was rich, indecently so, but also vulgar, philistine and barren. It was the workshop of Giovanni Bellini, more than any other single enterprise, which changed this perception.

For fifty years Virgins and sacred conversations flowed from that workshop.[6] They may seem monotonous, even boring subjects; but no two of

---

[1] See J. Steen, *Venetian Painting* (London, 1989); J. Martineau and C. Hope (eds), *The Genius of Venice* (London, 1983). Tintoretto means "little dyer". His real name was Jacopo Robusti. His father was a dyer of silks, a much valued skill and craft.

[2] Both were celebrated and excellent painters. Mantegna married Giovanni Bellini's sister.

[3] At times Venetian territory extended to the foothills of the Alps in the north and to Bergamo in the west.

[4] Both Cyprus and Crete were under Venetian rule, as were much of the Dalmatian coast and trading outposts as far as the Black Sea and the Persian Gulf.

[5] The source of precious furs, lovingly painted by both Titian and Tintoretto.

[6] He became First Painter to the Most Serene Republic at the age of thirty-five, and remained in this prestigious post till his death in 1516 in his mid eighties.

these magical pictures are the same. Except in one respect. Whether the Virgin is enthroned in a cool architectural setting or against the verdant countryside of the Veneto, her remoteness from human strife makes her immediately accessible to human prayer; and grave and poised, the saints around her – the scholarly Jerome, the beautiful Catherine, the compassionate Francis, the brave St George, and many others – conduct their sacred conversations in civilised silence.[7]

By the time Bellini died, his pupil and successor as First Painter to the Republic had been waiting in the wings for some time.[8] Titian had arrived in Venice from the periphery of the city's mainland empire at a moment never to recur.[9] To generations of Venetians the accumulation of wealth had been an overriding concern. But aspirations change. To the generation that reached manhood around 1500, spending money suddenly became as attractive as hoarding it;[10] and the appeal of spending it on such frivolous and speculative ventures as art seemed irresistible. The names of Titian's first patrons are mostly lost; but their likenesses – young, handsome, arrogant, self-assured – and the ample charms of their wives and mistresses now grace the walls of the world's most famous galleries.[11]

Then as today, the young set trends and those of their elders who did not want to be thought of as elders eagerly followed. The great Bellini's dignified quarter-length portrait of the reigning Doge continued to radiate the wisdom and sobriety of past centuries;[12] but Titian was thirty and the future belonged

[7] See R. Pallucchini, *Giovanni Bellini* (Venice, 1949); G. Robertson, *Giovanni Bellini* (London, 1968). See also below, Chapter 21, pp. 289–90, 294–97.

[8] Despite gathering storm clouds both in the east and the west, the city had blossomed in splendour since Bellini's youth. St Mark's Basilica was about to receive its crowning glory, the "Gothic Crown" of marble pinnacles, the Doge's Palace was nearing completion, and new palazzi and churches were rising everywhere.

[9] His birthplace, Pieve de Cadore in the foothills of the Dolomites, was part of the Venetian empire at the time. A chapel in the small but lovely local church is still dedicated to St Tiziano, a somewhat obscure third-century Alexandrian martyr. See R. Pallucchini, *Tiziano*, 2 volumes (Florence, 1969).

[10] Historians tend to seek a cause for such changes; but the answers are usually ingenious rather than convincing. Perhaps even making money palls after a few hundred years.

[11] *The Man in the Blue Sleeve* in the National Gallery in London is perhaps the best of the surviving ones. Was it a self-portrait? A kind of publicity still to demonstrate the young artist's brilliance to potential customers? Considering that well over half of his known portraits from the time when he was painting the Habsburgs, the Gonzagas, the Estes and the Medicis are lost, it seems not unreasonable to assume that many more have disappeared from the years when he was painting the city's *jeunesse dorée*.

The most complete catalogue of Titian's surviving works is H. E. Wethey, *The Paintings of Titian*, 3 volumes (London, 1969–75).

[12] *Leonardo Loredan*, now in the National Gallery, London.

to him. Accidents and circumstances helped. The plague carried off Giorgione, his friend but also his only serious rival; another rival, Sebastiano Luciani, later known as del Piombo, took himself off to Rome.[13] The republic's foolish imperial ambitions on the mainland, always a drain on its resources, were shattered at Agnadello in 1509.[14] Older citizens grieved over the defeat, but the young probably sighed with relief. Paradoxically, wealth which is slowly dwindling is usually spent more ostentatiously than wealth which is still accumulating; and young Titian was as ostentatious a genius as anyone could wish. His new *Assumption* in the church of the Frari was the biggest altarpiece ever painted. Its scale and sweep stunned many of the friars who had commissioned it: for good or ill, it turned their plain Gothic pile into a tourist attraction.[15] Soon the young man was courting princesses and cardinals rather than the city's golden youth: in Bologna he painted his first papal portrait; and his other exalted sitter, the Emperor Charles V, reverently picked up his brushes from the floor.[16]

It has often been said or hinted that, as his fame spread, Titian made discreet attempts to push Bellini aside. This is unlikely and for a reason that merits a brief digression. Venice is probably the most written about (let alone painted) city in the world, but the unique place traditionally occupied by old men in its social structure is rarely noted. The background is partly

[13] He was tempted by a well-paid sinecure in the pontifical mint: hence the nickname by which he is known today. He never quite fulfilled his early promise after the move.

[14] Half of Europe combined in the League of Cambrai to check Venice's imperial ambitions on the mainland. It was perhaps the most crushing defeat of the republic before her final demise three centuries later; but, by skilfully exploiting the inevitable rivalries among the victors, she regained most of her lost territories within a decade. From then on it was Venice's diplomatic skill, rather than her military might, which was widely feared and respected.

[15] Santa Maria Gloriosa dei Frari, to give the church its proper name, was and is the collegiate church of the Lesser Franciscan Friars. Apart from Titian's two great altar-pieces, by the end of the century it contained Donatello's *St John* and one of Bellini's celestial Madonnas, as well as half a dozen masterpieces by della Quercia, Vivarini, Bassano and others. Titian's and Canova's tombs, by contrast, are no more than respectable.

[16] The artist's response has not been recorded: perhaps he liked painting with his fingers or even his beard. But there is no doubt that the two men hit it off almost from the start. (The first meeting in Parma had been mismanaged.) The Emperor was impressed by the Venetian's luscious nudes and dignified Madonnas: better still, unlike most artists whose services were continually pressed on him, one more uncouth than the other, Titan was a man of the world and as polished as a courtier. Titian may also have appreciated a prince who recognised quality but did not pretend to know more about tone values and complementary colours than a professional. The artist was granted the rank of a Count Palatine and made a Knight of the Golden Spur. His letter patent gratifyingly described him as a new Apelles (none of whose paintings actually survive) and was, even more gratifyingly, put under a contract and paid a handsome retainer.

biological and partly historical. Biologically, despite the wet and windy climate which many expatriates find trying, Venetians have always lived long, many remaining vigorous into their eighth, ninth and tenth decades. Male inhabitants of the city still have a longer life expectancy at twenty than those born in any other province of Italy and probably anywhere in Europe. Historically, the constitution and tradition combined to eliminate or mitigate the feuds between generations, a constant theme elsewhere in Europe. Venice was not of course a modern democracy any more than was Pericles's Athens, but any attempt by individuals to gain absolute power and found a dynasty was staunchly and by and large successfully resisted. In the service of the state there was usually room for both the young and the old. Doges were mostly elected in their sixties and seventies;[17] and, in so far as Venice had individual heroes, they were the great patriarchal doges who guided its destinies in moments of crisis. There was the magnificent Sebastiano Zeani, elected at seventy-five, who brought to an end decades of war between emperors and popes in 1177. There was Enrico Dandolo, elected in his eighties and almost completely blind, who personally led the terrible assault of the crusaders of the Fourth Crusade on Constantinople on 9 April 1203. Andrea Contarini, also in his eighties, guided the republic through perilous decades of war with Genoa. Leonardo Loredan (immortalised by Bellini) was elected at seventy-four, Antonio Grimaldo at eighty-three, Michaelo Steno at seventy-eight, Tommaso Mocenigo at seventy-three and Antonio Venier in his eighties: all presided over the state in testing times.

It was in this mould that the unique succession of great Venetian masters – Bellini, Titian and Tintoretto – continued to paint into their seventies and eighties; and they were not the only ones. Jacopo Bassano died in 1628 in his eighties, having painted some of his best works in his last years; Lorenzo Lotto died in 1556 aged seventy-eight; Palma Giovane died in 1628 aged eighty-four; Rosalba Carriera died in 1758 aged eighty three; Gianbattista Tiepolo died in 1770 aged seventy-six; Canaletto died in 1768 aged seventy-two; Longhi died in 1785 aged seventy-six; Guardi died in in 1760 aged seventy, Piazetta died in 1754 aged seventy-six; and Giandomenico Tiepolo died in 1804 aged seventy-eight. All, even Rosalba who went partially blind, continued to work until the end. (Tintoretto's rival, Paolo Veronese, died comparatively young, in 1588, aged sixty.) A similar list could be compiled of the great Venetian architects and musicians; but perhaps one should end this almost random selection with Angelo Roncalli, born of Venetian stock

---

[17] As were popes; but there was rarely the scramble for lucrative offices by a rapacious kinship which followed the sacred conclaves in Rome. The office of doge was a drain on the holder's personal fortune.

in the formerly Venetian city of Bergamo and elected as a stop-gap pope at eighty-four. His pontificate as John XXIII (1958–63) was a turning point in the history of the Christian churches.

The third artist in the succession made no attempt to step into his master's shoes amongst royalty and the cosmopolitan elite; but, if he lacked Titian's social graces, Tintoretto did not lack the older man's ambition.[18] "Titian for colour and Michelangelo for design", he is said to have scribbled on the wall of his cell-like room in Titian's workshop;[19] and a more daunting task he could hardly have set himself. In the event he learnt a little – but not too much – from both his models and then created his own distinct artistic personality.

Tintoretto is not a painter who instantly wins admirers wherever his pictures are shown. The pictures may not be his best. One need not go to Venice to admire Bellini or Titian. Many of their most successful creations were collected in their lifetimes by princes and prelates and are now dispersed around the world. To succumb to Tintoretto – or even to be repelled by him – one has to travel to his native city. On his first visit there the twenty-three-year-old John Ruskin, an admirer of the purity of the middle ages and the early Renaissance, fully expected to be repelled. A few days later he wrote home: "I have been perfectly prostrate these last few days after my first acquaintance with Tintoret's *Crucifixion* ... but then I feel that I had got introduced to a being on a planet 1,000,000,000 miles nearer to the sun, not a mere earthly painter." [20]

Tintoretto painted the work which established his reputation in 1547, a year when Titian was away from the city.[21] *St Mark Rescuing a Slave* is a bravura

[18] Among important monographs devoted to Tintoretto's life and art are F. Osnaston, *The Art and Genius of Tintoret* (London, 1915); P. de Vechi, *Opera completa del Tintoretto* (Milan, 1970); F. Valcanover and T. Pignatti, *Tintoretto*, translated by S. Gilbert (Geneva, 1956); H. Tietze, *Tintoretto: The Paintings and Drawings* (New York, 1948).

[19] R. Palucchini, *La giovinezza del Tintoretto* (Milan, 1950); O. Benesch, "Titian and Tintoretto: A Study in Comparative Criticism", *Arte Veneta*, 12 (1958), p. 21.

Though the famous dichotomy is undoubtedly of sixteenth-century origin, Tintoretto's authorship is doubtful. But it does epitomise his artistic roots. Michelangelo's creations were well known in Venice from engravings and strongly influenced Tintoretto's early work. But *colorito* in contrast with *disegno* cannot mean colour alone. Michelangelo's colouring could be brilliant; Venetian colours, even allowing for the fact that many Venetian pigments aged badly, could be muddy. It is more likely to indicate freedom in the application of colour, that is brushwork. This in Venice had priority over all else.

[20] Quoted in J. Evans, *John Ruskin* (London, 1954), p. 65. Give or take a few million miles, the young traveller from Surrey got it about right.

[21] Titian always favoured his other star pupil, Veronese.

performance in more senses than one:[22] it still tends to evoke from visitors something between a gasp and a giggle. But Tintoretto was not painting for visitors. Venetians loved it – as they still do. St Mark was their saint;[23] and here, as always, Tintoretto spoke their language.[24] It was rumoured that the ambitious young man bribed some of his fellow apprentices to let themselves be strung up to the ceiling of Titian's workshop in a cage so that he could get the head-first plunging figure of the saint right. If he did, it was an act of youthful inexperience: soon he would conjure up celestial acrobatics far more implausible without the need for ropes and pulleys.

After the success of St Mark, Tintoretto was never short of official or unofficial commissions. He was cheap compared with Titian (and even with his rival Veronese) – ludicrously so per square yard. Paradise, which he painted for the main hall of the Doge's Palace after the disastrous fire of 1577, was reputed to be the largest oil painting in the world.[25] The windows of some of the old Gothic churches of the city had to be blocked out to accommodate his canvases.[26] But scale was only part of his appeal. Surprise was another, and breathtaking virtuosity. Spectators were struck dumb by his dramatic contrasts, broken vistas, sudden jumps into space, unearthly lights and flashes of spectral colours.[27]

[22] It tells of how the saint's timely intercession saved the life of a slave who had been condemned by his owner, a Provençal nobleman, to be blinded and have his limbs broken on a wheel in punishment for venerating the saint. The episode had rarely been commemorated before, perhaps because of the technical difficulty of showing a holy figure swooping down from, rather than up to, Heaven.

When some elderly members of the Scuola di San Marco expressed their strong disapproval of the "violence" depicted, Tintoretto unhooked the painting in a huff and threatened to take it home. But this only made him more popular with the younger set and wiser counsels eventually prevailed as they usually did in Venice.

[23] His attribute, the winged lion, is everywhere in Venice and wherever Venice ruled on Terra Firma. A series of mosaics in St Mark's Basilica tells the original story of the Evangelist's martyrdom in Alexandria and how his remains were miraculously discovered and transferred to Venice (in the ninth century), as predicted to him by an angel when, in his wanderings, he had found temporary refuge on one of the then still uninhabited islands of the Venetian lagoon. In later paintings he is usually shown as a dignified figure, holding an inkhorn, a reference to the legend that he acted as St Peter's amanuensis. Tintoretto painted several scenes of the saint's life and named his eldest son in his honour.

[24] He was the only one of the supreme Venetian masters who was actually born in the city.

[25] It was deliberately surpassed by the huge "cooperative" canvas painted under the auspices of Robert and Sonia Delauney for the Railway Palace of the 1937 Paris Exposition Universelle.

[26] As in Tintoretto's own parish church, the lovely Santa Maria dell' Orto.

[27] L. Rudrauf, "Vertiges, chutes et ascensions dans l'espace picturel du Tintoret", in Proceedings of the 18th International Congress on the History of Art, Venice, Arte Veneta, 10 (1956), p. 279; C. Gould, "The Cinquecento at Venice: Tintoretto and Space", Apollo, 96 (1972), p. 32.

In his mid forties Tintoretto embarked on the task that would occupy him – on and off – for the best part of three decades. He won the fiercely contested commission to decorate the public rooms and assembly halls of the Scuola Grande di San Rocco. His competitors hinted at backstage intrigue and dirty tricks. Of backstage intrigue one can be reasonably certain: it was the lifeblood of the Most Serene Republic. Family connections also helped. Shortly before winning an earlier commission from the Scuola Grande di San Marco, Tintoretto had married Faustina, the daughter of the *guardian grande*, Marco Episcopo. It proved to be a long and happy union, blessed with many lucrative commissions as well as with a brood of gifted children. But dirty tricks one doubts. Tintoretto was an astute businessman; but he was also a devout Christian and supremely confident with good reason in his own talent.[28]

The school of San Rocco, like the other five Venetian *scuole grandi*,[29] was not an educational but a charitable institution, financed and administered by laymen under the benevolent auspices of the church. The organisations dated back to the time of the Crusades when even hard-headed businessmen felt that some of the stupendous loot that accrued to Venice from these holy enterprises should be invested in good deeds. They blossomed and multiplied as the city prospered and came to occupy an important position in public life. The republic's constitution was a matter of immense pride to its citizens, but it was of such diabolical complexity that few claimed actually to understand it.[30] To a great extent social stability depended not on written laws but on the unofficial contribution of these charitable foundations. They helped the poor and the sick, protected the interests of individual trades and professions, supported the weak and the needy among the non-Venetian communities (ignored by the constitution but crucial for the city's prosperity), maintained schools, orphanages, alms-houses and old sailors' homes, and in the case of San Rocco's, financed

[28] Tintoretto is said to have secured the commission by presenting the governors of the Scuola not with preliminary plans and sketches as had been stipulated but by the finished oval canvas of *The Glorification of St Roche* for the ceiling.

[29] The two most prestigious ones were the Scuola Grande di San Marco and the Scuola Grande di Santa Maria della Carità, for which Titian painted his *Presentation of the Virgin*. There were also numerous *scuole piccoli*.

[30] Though it left power in the hands of a comparatively few patrician families – less than a thousand individuals in a city of some 150,000 – it proved remarkably effective against arbitrary government. No doubt the system had its faults, but whenever and wherever a non-monarchical constitution was planned or discussed – in England, Holland, Pennsylvania or New Jersey – it was Venice, and not Lucca, Genoa or the Swiss Confederation, which was held up as a model to emulate.

hospitals.[31] They also, of course, like the livery companies of the City of London, provided a dignified setting for convivial gatherings and the transaction of informal business. Their patronage of the arts was comparatively recent and was occasionally criticised both outside the confraternities and by some of the brethren.[32] It was partly inspired by the Catholic Reformation, a spiritual movement, now barely remembered, which flourished in Venice for longer than anywhere else in Europe.[33] It fuelled a mystical, sometimes ecstatic faith, exalted direct communication between the faithful and Heaven, and, incidentally, promoted poetry, music and the arts. The unashamed opulence of Venetian religious painting is sometimes taken as a manifestation of extreme worldliness, but this is a misinterpretation: Tintoretto's late art was as spiritual as Fra Angelico's. In contrast to the Jesuit-led Counter-Reformation, the Catholic Reformation was also resolutely tolerant;[34] another Venetian tradition. (There was never any scope in Venice for the fanatical zeal of a St Ignatius or the austerities of a Calvin: the Jesuits were actually expelled in the year of Tintoretto's death.)[35] In the turmoil

[31] The Scuola di San Rocco was a comparatively recent foundation and named after St Roche or San Rocco of Montpellier, who spent much of his life seeking out rather than escaping from outbreaks of the plague and tending the sick and the dying. He died in Piacenza in 1327 and his remains were brought to Venice in 1485. He was venerated throughout Europe and many hospitals were named after him.

[32] They were more than once investigated for spending funds on building and art patronage rather than on charitable works.

[33] The spiritual bedrock of the movement (sometimes referred to as the "Italian" Reformation) was salvation through faith alone. It was not far removed from the slightly later doctrines of Luther and the Protestant (or "German") Reformation; and it was the earnest hope of many Catholic prelates and lay thinkers that it would purify the church "from the inside". As Michelangelo expressed it in one of his great sonnets dedicated to Vittoria Colonna: "Through the Cross, through blood and sweat / With spirit ever more burning for trial / And not with idle wishes and sluggish deeds / Should man serve his True Lord ..." At the Councils of Pisa and the Lateran in 1511 and 1512 it was still backed by many churchmen and theologians grouped together in the Oratory of the Divine Love; but it began to crumble in the face of the more militant (though theologically no more radical) German Reformation. By the mid century most of its supporters were beginning to be investigated for heresy in Rome and sought refuge in Tintoretto's Venice, where they were still welcome.

[34] To the Jesuit inspired Counter-Reformation the Catholic Reformation was as suspect and heretical as Protestantism.

[35] The power struggle between the republic and Pope Clement VIII Borghese towards the end of Tintoretto's life was the last occasion when Venice emerged triumphant as the champion of religious tolerance. As Doge Marino Grimani memorably put it when accused by the Pope of being "a Calvinist in disguise": "What is a Calvinist? We are Christians as good as the Pope himself and as Christians we shall die, whether the Pope likes it or not." In countless allegories painted by Tintoretto (and other Venetian artists) the republic appears often, usually in the company of the Virgin and saints; the church as such never.

of the religious wars the Catholic Reformation was doomed; but it survived long enough to animate Tintoretto's last masterpieces, just as it inspired the incandescent late sonnets of Michelangelo.

Vasari wrote that Tintoretto's ambitious projects for the Scuola more than once raised conservative eyebrows. They probably did.[36] But most of the time the confraternity and their chosen artist worked in harmony.[37] Some at least of the brethren must have realised that their headquarters, one of the few ugly buildings in Venice,[38] was being transformed into an artistic shrine. On the other side, for a reasonable if far from princely stipend (which, however, was at least regularly paid),[39] Tintoretto could paint what he wanted and how he wanted. It is true that some of the walls were badly lit and awkwardly shaped; but such constraints worried him less than they would have worried Michelangelo or Raphael. More important, there were acres – or so it must have seemed – of surfaces to cover.

The work began with twenty-seven huge canvases for the walls and ceiling of the Sala dell' Albergo, where the governing bodies of the confraternity, the *Banca* and the *Zonta*, regularly met. They mostly depict scenes from the Passion, culminating in the cataclysmal vision of the Crucifixion. After an interval of a few years the artist was commissioned to resume his labours with twenty-five paintings for the Upper Hall, showing episodes from both the Old and the New Testament. His invention was inexhaustible: the seemingly unconnected subjects express the faith of the Catholic Reformation in the continuity between the world of the Prophets and the miracle of the Redemption. Then came the eight canvases of the Lower Hall, illustrating events leading up to the birth of Christ and those of His childhood. No subjects had been painted more often and by better artists; but there is not one among these tumultuous images which, in a kind of spiritual frenzy, Tintoretto did not reinterpret, almost reinvent. His *Adoration of the Shepherds* on the end wall of the Upper Hall, one of the most formalised and unchanging scenes of Christian iconography, takes place at two levels in a huge broken-down barn. An unearthly glow penetrating through the

[36] Quoted in F. Valcanover, *Jacopo Tintoretto and the Scuola Grande of San Rocco* (Venice, 1983), p. 10. At one of the meetings of the governors, a certain Zani de Zignioni declared himself ready to donate fifteen ducats on the understanding that the work should *not* be assigned to Tintoretto.

[37] The artist himself became a brother in 1576.

[38] Antonio Abbondi, known as Scarpagnino, was mainly but not entirely responsible for the façade. It has an almost Victorian profusion of fluted columns, figured capitals, inlaid coloured stones and little carved animals, including at least one elephant. The building was not finished until four years before Tintoretto started his decoration of the interior.

[39] In contrast to payments by the state which were regularly in arrears, the Scuola paid him in advance.

rafters alights unpredictably on bales of straw, a few hens, a surprised peacock, a basket of fruit and a cow, as well as angels, shepherds and a woman of uncertain function, perhaps a midwife. At the lower level there is a kind of controlled chaos, Tintoretto's speciality. At the upper level there is awe-struck stillness, if the word "stillness" can ever be used in connection with Tintoretto. None of the figures in isolation (except perhaps the cow) is solid enough to create a space to breathe in; and the contrasts in colour are arguably too bright to generate atmospheric perspective. Yet the conception works. Indeed it can be guaranteed to fire even the most torpid post-prandial imagination.[40]

Vasari disapproved as he had disapproved of Titian; and Tintoretto's critics, including it was said the great Michelangelo, deplored the tendency of Venetian artists to paint without "composing".[41] The critics had a point but their criticism was also beside it. To Tuscans painting was an intellectual concept executed with paint on canvas. With the great Leonardo the work often never got much beyond the concept stage. To Vasari this in no way detracted from its greatness. To Tintoretto, and one suspects to most Venetians, it would have seemed a lamentable waste of time and effort. So was obsessively detailed planning. For all his gigantic enterprises Tintoretto left behind hardly any preliminary sketches. Perhaps they have been lost. More likely, he made few.[42] He was, after all, not building domes which had to defy complicated physical laws. He was not even chipping away at costly pieces of marble. What had been painted could always be repainted, or over-painted, both of which he probably did often. One can imagine him a day or even an hour before the unveiling – or a year later – wiping off a column, raising a limb, lighting up a face, curling a lock or adding a figure or two. There is an unalterable rightness about the best Florentine paintings of the period. It is wholly lacking from the late works of Tintoretto. In the schoolmasterly phrase, even his greatest pictures could be improved. Only it would need another Tintoretto to do the improving.

These vast undertakings did not monopolise the master's time. Like all good Venetians, he hated leaving the city – a journey to Mantua is his only recorded journey on *Terra Firma* – but his fame spread and in his sixties and

[40] Valcanover, *Jacopo Tintoretto and the Scuola Grande of San Rocco*; C. de Tolnay, "L'interpretazione dei cicli pittorici del Tintoretto nella Scuola di San Rocco", *Critica d'arte*, 7 (1960), p. 341.

[41] "Composing" seems a better translation of *disegno* than "designing".

[42] During the restoration works in the early 1970s Tintoretto's sketches on the canvases were revealed by infrared photography . These showed the figures in the nude, the artist gradually defining and redefining his composition on the canvas itself rather than on preliminary drawings on paper.

seventies commissions began to trickle in from distant lands. The mad Emperor Rudolf II in his fairytale castle in Prague wanted allegories which would combine scientific with sexual titillation.[43] The legend of the *Origin of the Milky Way*, whether a brainchild of the Emperor or suggested to him by the learned antiquary Ottavio Strada,[44] was hardly a set-piece in the master's repertory; but he obliged. And if he could call to prayer the devout, he could also celebrate, when required, carnal pleasures. As his beautiful and apparently weightless Juno starts up from her bed of clouds, her naked flesh shimmers entrancingly; and the whole group – peacock, Jupiter, the infant Hercules and assorted *putti* – becomes imbedded in the azure sky pierced by the new stars.[45] What, one wonders, did the Imperial Astronomer in Prague, the famous but sadly misused and overworked Johannes Kepler, think of this representation of the Heavens.[46]

There was also a constant demand for portraits. These still tend to be unfavourably compared to Titian's. Of course Tintoretto was not a fount of invention like the older master. Nor did he try to convey the *braggadocio* of an earlier age. How could he? Times were changing and nowhere was this more keenly felt than in Venice.[47] Conflicts more bloody than anyone could have imagined fifty years earlier were tearing Europe apart and threatened,

[43] The great-grandson of the mad Joanna, and a cousin of Philip II, he succeeded to the Austrian domains of the Habsburgs and the imperial title in 1570. He inherited all the weirdness and some of the brilliance of his ancestors. He was the greatest collector of his day and the most eccentric of any day, filling his castle with *objets d'art*, gold plate, jewellery, coins, stuffed and live animals, clocks, telescopes and other scientific instruments, alchemical rubbish, mummies, anatomical preparations, books, maps, holy relics and scientific curios as well as magnificent paintings by amongst others, Tintoretto. He was forced to abdicate in 1611 a year before he died, aged sixty.

[44] Rudolf's learned antiquary and dealer, the sitter to one of Titian's last portraits, a masterpiece, and to a slightly less distinguished one by Tintoretto – the Vollard of his day.

[45] Jupiter wanted to guarantee the immortality of Hercules, his son by the mortal woman Alcmene, by holding up the infant to drink from the breast of his sleeping wife, Juno. Waking suddenly, the unsurprisingly surprised Juno spilled her milk in two streams, one giving rise to the Milky Way in the sky and one to the lilies on earth.

[46] The great astronomer, a tragic figure, was forced to spend much of his time casting horoscopes for the Emperor and his Court, including the royal stallions.

[47] The Turkish advance in the east and the discovery of the sea routes to India and the Americas in the west threatened Venice's position as the commercial link between Asia and Europe. But there was more to the change in the prevailing mood. Just as generations of Europeans in the twentieth century would look back on the shots fired in Sarajevo in 1914 as the end of the "Good Old Days", so in the Italy of the sixteenth century the event that shattered people's optimism was the Sack of Rome by the troops of a Holy Roman Emperor under a Christian commander in 1527. The religious schism and economic depression merely compounded the gloom, just as the rise of the totalitarian regimes did in Europe in the twentieth century.

from time to time, even to engulf the republic. No one expected them to be peacefully resolved any more.[48] Tolerance itself was going underground. Yet, keeping within the constraints of official portraiture, Tintoretto in his old age created something startlingly new.

The ancient and the venerable were often commemorated in Renaissance Italy; but nowhere had the genre become so formalised as in Venice. Though patriarchs like Admiral Pesaro, Gabriele Vendramin or Vincenzo Cappello expected to be represented as repositories of infinite wisdom and bottomless experience, this was never allowed to detract from their appearance of in-destructible and youthful vigour. Many even in their seventies and eighties chose to be painted sporting full armour or at least clutching some item of martial gear. And even if they allowed themselves to be portrayed ever so slightly bowed under the responsibilities of their high and usually multiple offices,[49] the sparkle in their eyes and the firmness of their stance (even in prayer) left spectators in no doubt that they were both capable and willing to continue to carry the burden for many years yet; indeed, God willing, indefinitely. At seventy-six Doge Andrea Gritti in Titian's portrait fairly bursts with energy. Doge Francesco Venier shortly before his death at seventy-five (and already showing signs of a wasting disease) is nevertheless fully in command. And Doge Alvise Mocenigo, a mere stripling at seventy-three, in the last of Tintoretto's votive pictures, looks positively street-wise. In the case of aged ecclesiastics a hint of sanctity was allowed – but even that must not suggest any weakening of their grip. Cardinal Pietro Bembo at seventy-five looks rejuvenated by the arrival of the long-coveted red hat in Titian's portrait, certainly not a day older than fifty. Cardinal Guido Lorenzini at seventy-eight could be mistaken in Tintoretto's early portrait for one of his grandsons (of whom he had many). Seventy-six years have clearly not blunted the evil cunning of Paul III Farnese in Titian's masterly triple portrait. And if Julius II della Rovere (in Titian's copy of Raphael's

---

[48] For some decades earnest efforts were made on both sides of the religious divide to heal the breach. Erasmus of Rotterdam was the hero of the conciliators and even in Spain his works remained widely read until the 1530s. But as Protestantism advanced and the Counter-Reformation arose in opposition, the religious wars became the bloodiest conflict to divide Europe before the First World War. The poison spread far beyond the confines of religion. Tens of thousands of witches were burned by both Catholics and Protestants; the blood laws of Spain anticipated the racial lunacies of the twentieth century; and, for the first time, torture became part of the European judicial process. (It had of course been widely practised before but never judicially codified.) Toleration found fragile refuge in such islands of sanity as Venice and in the Netherlands of Frans Hals.

[49] Jacopo Pesaro, one of Titian's earliest and most generous patrons, was a millionaire businessman as well as Grand Admiral of the Venetian fleet and Bishop of Paphos in Cyprus.

original) has lost some of the lustiness of youth,[50] the steely malice of the mouth belies any suggestion of battle-fatigue.

It was left to Tintoretto in his own old age to break this vaguely reassuring but fraudulent mould. His *Old Senator* is among the first commissioned formal portraits of an aged magistrate to show a profound awareness of too many years in office. No longer is this a cause for self-congratulation. It has become a burden. And this is not a pose, the conventional sigh about the heaviness of the mantle. The drawn features, the flabby hands and the slightly stupefied expression are almost shocking in their truthfulness. And their message is not about power and glory but the whispered prayer: Nunc dimittis.[51]

Such unceasing and varied activity could not of course have been sustained without the support of a workshop. There were four or five prestigious ones in Venice in Tintoretto's day, each different. Titian's, the largest, was under the day-to-day supervision of his elder son, the worthy and hardworking Orazio, and the apprentices there spent most of their time copying the master's early works. His *Magdalen* in particular (with bosom exposed or covered according to taste) was still a bestseller in lands as distant as Poland and Portugal. The master would put in brief appearances, add a brushstroke here, make a suggestion there. These would always be received with deference: his signature was already worth a fortune. Veronese's workshop was known to be high-spirited, even rowdy, and had the fastest turnover of apprentices. But Tintoretto's was the most sought after. His pupils did not spend their time copying the master's early paintings: there were always new commissions to complete. Large tracts of the work for San Rocco's and the Doge's Palace were undoubtedly done by them but always under the master's watchful eye. He was known as a hard taskmaster but a sound teacher. Two of his sons, Domenico and Marco, became successful painters in their own right; while his eldest daughter, Marietta, was not only the apple of his eye but also said to be the most talented of the siblings.[52]

Tintoretto was in his seventies when he painted *The Slaughter of the Innocents*, one the greatest and most terrible of his San Rocco canvases; but he did not reach his peak at the Scuola. By the time he was finishing there, he

[50] He was the last pope to lead his troops on horseback into battle as well as the only one to be hit on the head with a broomstick by an enraged genius (Michelangelo espying him peeping at the unfinished ceiling of the Sistine Chapel).

[51] The portrait (now in the Irish National Gallery, Dublin) was not the only one of its kind. There are similar ones in the Prado in Madrid, the Kunsthistorisches Museum, Vienna, and the Royal Collection.

[52] R. Gallo, "La famiglia di Jacopo Tintoretto", *Ateneo Veneto*, 128 (1941), p. 73.

was already negotiating with the chapter of San Giorgio Maggiore. The lovely church and monastery complex had been designed by his old friend, Antonio Palladio, and in 1589 it was nearing completion.[53] In its graceful and uncomplicated lightness, with its huge windows and cool reflecting surfaces, it was as Venetian as were the creations of Tintoretto; but the two styles were at the opposite ends of the spectrum. Where Palladio was tranquillity, Tintoretto was pandemonium. Today any fine art commission would warn prospective patrons against trying to marry such incompatibles. Fortunately, none was available in sixteenth-century Venice. No combination of opposites has ever proved more successful.

The theme of *The Last Supper* had been stirring in Tintoretto's mind for decades. The earliest version was among the first canvases he sold. At least two more were produced, largely by the workshop, in later years. The scene is also dramatically depicted on one of the walls of San Rocco's. None of these can compare with the painting in San Giorgio. Tintoretto's last *Last Supper* is not a frugal take-away meal in the tradition of Leonardo's famous but dull refectory picture; but nor is it a gorgeous panorama of a feast in the manner of Veronese. The dusky atmosphere is lit by a blazing oil lamp (as well as by mysterious sources outside the canvas). The air above the table is filled with insubstantial angelic forms. The foreground is a riot. A sideboard groans under dishes which suggest a banquet. Male and female servants scurry around. Dogs sniff at the baskets of food. Bottles of wine stand in readiness on the marble-tiled floor. The Apostles sit, stand, pray, exclaim in wonderment and recoil overcome with emotion. Christ stands two-thirds up the table, just off-centre, a diminutive figure compared to the bulk of the servant attending to a gigantic tureen. By every rule in the rule-book it should add up to an unholy, even blasphemous shambles. Perhaps it would have done fifty years earlier, even in Tintoretto's hands. But rule-books did not legislate for Tintoretto in his seventies. The profanity of the setting only serves to intensify the mystery of the sacrament. Fascinating as the incidental details are, they do not distract from the central act. Canonical as well as critical niggles are silenced by the perception of a miracle.

[53] For most of his life Palladio (who died in 1580, aged seventy-two) was employed on the mainland only, building villas and country mansions for the Venetian nobility, while Sansovino, Titian's friend, reigned unchallenged in the city. But after Sansovino's death (in 1570, aged ninety-one), Palladio was commissioned to build his two masterpieces in Venice: the monastic complex of San Giorgio Maggiore and the church of the Redentore (where Venice still annually celebrates her deliverance from the plague of 1576). He was a great admirer as well as a friend of Tintoretto and, by all accounts, a man of charm, learning and humility. Both he and Tintoretto were accomplished amateur musicians.

In contrast to the great nocturnal scene, the companion work, *The Gathering of Manna*, is bathed in calm morning light and silvery reflections. The pulsating blues and shades of rose of the garments of the Israelites hark back to the first cycle of biblical scenes in San Rocco's. But there is a more nervous profusion of ideas, with perhaps an excess of agricultural implements cluttering up the foreground, possibly an indication of God's prodigality. It is not entirely successful.

Both canvases were completed shortly before the master's death; but neither was his last. "Being sound, by the grace of God, in mind and intellect but infirm in body", Tintoretto wrote in May 1594 in the preamble of his last testament, "I commend my soul to the Eternal God, Our Saviour Jesus Christ and the Glorious Virgin Mary".[54] Jesus and Mary are also the main characters of his last painting. By the time he had finished the two canvases for the main church, the coffers of the Order were empty; but for the modest sum of seventy ducats the artist agreed to paint a *Deposition* (Plate 3) of token size for the chapel of the dead. There it remains, stopping visitors in their tracks, still comforting the bereaved. In the foreground the lifeless body of the Redeemer is held up by a group of mourners. In the middle ground the Virgin swoons, overcome with grief. Behind her Golgotha looms up indistinctly against the sunset. The whole could be totally fragmented. What unites it is the play of light. It emanates from different directions as if illuminating a stage. Yet the whole is the opposite of stagy. Harsh metallic hues alternate with soft off-whites, creating a continuous sense of movement.[55] But there is also peace. The deed has been accomplished. Only a year or two earlier Tintoretto had painted a mysterious, full-frontal self-portrait and even inscribed it with his name: "Jacobus Tentoretus Pictor Venetius F".[56] Among Christ's mourners in his last picture one recognises the old man who kneels at the side of the dead Christ in reverent piety. The hair wreathing the forehead and the round curling beard are the same.

---

[54] Osnaston, *The Art and Genius of Tintoret*, p. 342.

[55] In response to Aretino's sneer that Tintoretto neglected colour, Tintoretto is said to have replied that the finest colours could be bought ready-made on the Rialto. It has been received wisdom to compare him as a colourist unfavourably with Titian; but Tintoretto's colours in his lovingly restored last paintings are magical though quite unnatural. To say that he was less of a colourist than Titian is like saying that El Greco was less of a colourist than Velasquez, or that Gauguin was less of a colourist than Monet.

[56] It may have been a farewell gift, as one guidebook to the Louvre suggests, but to whom and on what occasion?

# 3

# *Hals*

Professional critics are usually remembered for their critical aberrations. Théophile Thoré, better known by his adopted name of W. Bürger,[1] is the rare exception. Born in Paris in 1807, he became a political journalist during Louis-Philippe's tepid reign.[1] He helped to man the barricades in 1848, was forced to flee and, during ten peripatetic years, returned to his first love, art history. In 1857 he visited the Great Art Treasures exhibition in Manchester. By fluke rather than selection, and because the paintings were in the collection of one of the exhibition's sponsors, two works by Frans Hals were included among the exhibits. The catalogue, replete with biographical hyperbole, referred to him laconically as "a Dutch painter of portraits of the Seventeenth Century".[2] To Bürger the paintings were a revelation.[3]

To say that for two hundred years Hals had been forgotten would be an exaggeration. His "unblended brushstrokes and his slapdash execution, clear reflections of a wanton and feckless character", were regularly held up as warnings to students. "He was", Reynolds pontificated in one of his *Discourses*, "not without ability to portray strong individual characteristics, but alas, he could never join to this the most difficult and most important part of the art of painting, a patience to carefully *finish* what he had often correctly planned and begun."[4] Bürger looked and saw better. "Here", he

---

[1] As Citoyen Thoré he edited the brilliant but short-lived daily, *La Vrai Republique*. In exile he adopted the pseudonym W. Bürger (chosen for its suggestion of supranational citizenship). After the amnesty of 1859 he returned to France but continued to use his pseudonym until his death in 1869, aged fifty-eight. In addition to rediscovering Hals, he was also among the first to appreciate the genius of Vermeer and strongly supported the Impressionists in their early struggle. An admirable man.

[2] *Catalogue of the Art Treasures of the United Kingdom Collected at Manchester in 1857* (London, 1857).

[3] W. Bürger (T. Thoré), *Trésors de l'art en Angleterre* (Brussels, 1860).

[4] Sir Joshua Reynolds, *Works* (London, 1981), p. 68. Hals's unsavoury reputation originally derived from an almost totally inaccurate but widely plagiarised biographical essay in J. Houbraken's compendium on Dutch art published sixty years after Hals's death. It contained the invented episode of Van Dyck, the polished court painter, meeting Hals and being so impressed by the astonishing facility of the Haarlemer that he tried to rescue Hals from the "dissipations of tavern life" and whisk him off to England. In reality the two painters probably

wrote, "is one of the freest and boldest masters of any school of painting, an impetuous and eccentric genius who was to Rembrandt what Tintoretto was to Titian".[5] The review launched the obscure Dutch artist on his posthumous career; but the man who unwittingly clinched his reputation was Richard Seymour-Conway, fourth Marquess of Hertford.[6]

An unframed and begrimed *Portrait of a Gentleman* was offered at auction in Paris in 1865 and was expected to fetch a few hundred francs.[7] Even this would have been wildly optimistic had it not been rumoured that Baron Alphonse de Rothschild had taken a fancy to the gentleman's lace collar. He was in fact more interested in a pair of cowscapes by van Helms; but he gave his agent the usual *commission illimité* to acquire the portrait as well. But the sale also attracted an eccentric English milord who, looking as if he had just emerged from under one of Paris's less hospitable bridges, calmly bid into the thousands and then into the tens of thousands. At 50,000 francs the Rothschild agent lost his nerve and the picture was knocked down to the Marquess of Hertford.[8] The event made unflattering headlines in Paris and London: the London *Times* in particular lost no time in displaying its uncanny prescience, forecasting that the painting would "soon disappear into an underground vault of one of Lord Hertford's many mansions never to emerge therefrom, a sad fate for so dashing a gentleman". But the purchase was the sensation of the season. To be hailed as a genius by a penniless journalist of reputedly socialist leanings was one thing. To be

never met. The passage is reproduced, translated by M. Hoyle, in the *Catalogue to the Frans Hals Exhibition* (London, 1989).

[5] W. Bürger (T. Thoré) "Frans Hals", *Gazette des Beaux Arts*, 24 (1868), pp. 218 and 435.

[6] The Seymour-Conways, descended (more or less) from Edward Seymour, Duke of Somerset, brother of Jane Seymour, Henry VIII's third queen, had devoted their energies and marriages during the centuries between the Tudors and Queen Victoria to amassing one of the largest fortunes in England. Among their other possessions, they were among the largest and most absentee landlords of Ireland, owning about 60,000 acres in County Antrim alone. (At the height of the great famine Peel persuaded the third Marquess to visit his estates for the first time. He stayed for three days for which he was rewarded with the Garter but not with the dukedom which, Hertford felt, was his due.) Both the third and fourth Marquesses were ravenous collectors: the Wallace Collection, which Sir Richard Wallace, the fourth Marquess's illegitimate son, bequeathed to the nation, contains only a fraction of their hoard.

[7] The sitter for *The Laughing Cavalier* has never been identified, nor is it known who gave him the name by which he is known. Millions have found his impudent good looks irresistible. Among his dottier admirers, Baroness Orczy claimed that she instantly recognised in him a forebear of Sir Percy Blakeney, the Scarlet Pimpernel.

[8] The agent, as he was soon to discover, lost his job as well. Baron Alphonse de Rothschild was one of the second generation of the ennobled French Rothschilds. All his family were avid collectors.

bought by an English milord for a fortune was another.[9] By the time President Eisenhower was discovered by an enterprising *Washington Post* journalist painting *The Laughing Cavalier* by numbers, triggering off the biggest painting boom in history, the Hals industry had been in full swing for a century.[10]

The bare biographical facts have never been difficult to establish. Hals's parents came to Haarlem with the exodus of Protestant tradesmen from Antwerp after the city had surrendered to the Duke of Parma in 1585.[11] The elder Hals was a clothmaker.[12] In 1627, at the age of twenty-eight, Frans enrolled in the painters' Guild of St Luke;[13] and he remained a member – not always paid up – for the rest of his life. Apart from a year as a junior warden, he never held office. He married into one of Haarlem's rich brewing families and had two children by his first wife,

[9] F. S. Jowell, "The Rediscovery of Frans Hals", in the *Catalogue to the Frans Hals Exhibition* (London, 1989), p. 78. The painting was first publicly exhibited at the Whitechapel Gallery (for the edification of the more deserving of the London poor) in 1872.

[10] According to A. F. Mohun, by the end of the 1960s there were more people painting in California than there were people in Renaissance Italy.

The term "industry" does not cover the researches of several Hals scholars of great distinction. Apart from the comprehensive monograph by S. Slive, *Frans Hals*, 3 volumes (New York, 1970–74), there have been several notable works on the artist, including W. von Bode and M. J. Binder, *Frans Hals: sein Leben und seine Werke* (Berlin, 1914); N. S. Trivas, *The Paintings of Frans Hals* (London, 1941); C. Grimm, *Frans Hals: Entwicklung, Werkanalyse, Gesamtkatalog* (Berlin, 1972); and H. P. Baard, *Frans Hals*, translated by George Stuyck (New York, 1981). *The Catalogue of the Frans Hals Exhibition at the Royal Academy of Arts, London*, edited by S. Slive, contains several important contributions on different aspects of Hals's art and its social background.

[11] In 1576 Antwerp with the other Catholic provinces joined the Revolt. Gradually, however, these southern provinces made their peace with Philip II and in 1585 Antwerp surrendered to Parma. Under William the Silent and his son, Maurice of Nassau, the North continued its struggle; and, by 1598, the year of Philip II's death, it was on the threshold of independence. Antwerp never recovered its former commercial pre-eminence.

P. Geyl's volumes on Dutch history, *The Revolt of the Netherlands* (London, 1960) and *The Netherlands in the Seventeenth Century*, Parts I and II (London, 1961 and 1962) still provide a most detailed and readable historical and social background to Hals's life. See also Jonathan Israel, *The Dutch Republic: Its Greatness and Fall* (Oxford, 1995).

[12] One of the emigrant business community from which the pioneers of modern capitalism were drawn. But Hals the elder was not in the class of Jan de Willem, founder of the Dutch East India Company, or Louis de Geer, who supplied the armies and fleets of Gustavus Adolphus of Sweden.

[13] Both in Protestant and Catholic countries painters' guilds were named after the Evangelist, traditionally a painter and a doctor, whose intercession members of the guilds solicited, often successfully.

Anneke.[14] She died young. He married again and had another eleven children.[15] Several of his sons became painters.[16] He died at the age of eighty-five, an inmate of the old people's almshouse in Haarlem. His second wife survived him. But these bones had to be fleshed out and art historians set to it with occasionally excruciating zeal.

Little has ever been established about Hals's personality, his loves, his hates, his friends, his beliefs, his politics, his sex life or his working practices. He never became a celebrity like Rembrandt,[17] and he hardly set foot outside Haarlem. He wrote few letters and he did not, so far as is known, paint members of his family. But the Netherlands in the first half of the seventeenth century was not only the most civilised but also the most litigious country in Europe. The two were in fact related. Not the autocratic whim of kings but written contracts relentlessly pursued regulated daily life. Nowhere else were public records so meticulously kept, judicial proceedings more faithfully recorded, debts more assiduously collected. Few today would wish to be remembered on the basis of third reminders or proceedings in the magistrates' courts for parking offences. Yet something like such a fate befell the rediscovered Hals.

His first daughter was born a fortnight after his wedding: a shot-gun marriage obviously.[18] In 1880 the proceedings of a case were unearthed recording Hals's court appearance accused and found guilty of drunkenness and wife-beating. Not till forty years later was it discovered that at the time of the offence Hals had no wife to beat: he had not yet remarried after the death of Anneke. Further archival digging revealed that the offender was another Frans Hals. It was too late to salvage the painter's tattered reputation. More than once Hals had been taken to court for being late in paying tradesmen's bills. He was obviously not only a soak and a wife-beater but also untrustworthy in his business dealings. Nor was he a sound committee man: his contributions to the affairs of his guild were deplorably few and his absences numerous. His first-born, Sara, had been sent to a House of Correction after giving birth to her second illegitimate child.[19] "It was hardly

---

[14] There is a certain amount of mystery about this marriage. Anneke's guardian was her rich uncle, Job Gijblant, a prominent member of the city council, and her aunt was a Huydecoper, one of Amsterdam's rich patrician families and godmother to Hals's first child. But relations soon cooled and none of her family attended Anneke's funeral.

[15] He may have had more. The births of babies who died before being baptised were not registered.

[16] None of their works have been identified.

[17] Rembrandt was twenty-five years younger but survived Hals only by three years.

[18] As were many marriages in Holland in Hals's day (but this is seldom mentioned). About 30 per cent of all births were illegitimate.

[19] Her offence was not to reveal the name of the father and she remained in the House of

surprising, given her home background", one academic biographer sagely commented. And an imbecile son had to be maintained in an asylum at public expense.[20] The Hals industry could never decide whether their man should be pitied, censured or both. "Dissolute and reckless as he was", another authority ruminated, "one nevertheless weeps for him in his destitution." Did the lachrymose professor, one wonders, ever look at Hals's pictures?[21]

No great painter ever took such obvious delight in his artistry or displayed his skill with such swank. His range was extraordinarily narrow. "He never painted Christs, annunciations, angels, crucifixions or resurrections: he never painted nudes, voluptuous women or mouth-watering still-lives", the young Vincent van Gogh wrote to his brother Theo in 1888, "but what he painted

Correction for only ten days. There is a record of her marriage to a sailor in Amsterdam three years later. Her good character on that happy occasion was attested to by two ministers of the church.

[20] For some reason this has been raked up by every Hals biographer as casting a further adverse reflection on him. It was no doubt a tragedy, as it would be in any family today; but the only comment one might otherwise hazard is that nowhere else in seventeenth-century Europe would an imbecile boy have been the subject of such public concern.

[21] In contrast to such commentators, many practising artists have hailed Hals as one of their inspirations. After Bürger's pioneering advocacy, the opening of the Halsmuseum in Haarlem was a milestone. Courbet, Manet, Monet, Jongkind, Daubigny, Mary Cassatt and Alden Weir were among the early visitors. "I am now a visitor in Haarlem", the last-named young American wrote home, "a town I revere! The birthplace of Frans Hals! How to describe this wonderful man of genius is more than I know, but let me say that of all the art I have seen so far I place him next to Titian if not ahead of him." See D. W. Young, *The Life and Letters of J. Alden Weir* (New Haven, 1960), p. 62. Max Liebermann too venerated Hals above all other Dutch painters and copied several of his works. Sargent was a great admirer, as was Whistler. The latter, already gravely ill, made a last pilgrimage to Haarlem in the summer of 1902. According to his companion, the sight of the row of Hals's works made him forget his illness and he wandered down the line from the early to the late works, discussing them excitedly, envisaging Hals's relations with his sitters, how he "divined their character". In his enthusiasm he crept under the railing to get closer to the painting but was ordered back again. Then the chief attendant intervened, impressed by the enthusiasm of the "great painter" and even helped him to a chair. "From that moment on there was no holding him back – he went absolutely into raptures over the old women, his exclamations of joy coming out now at the top of his voice, now in the most tender, caressing whisper ... 'Oh what a swell he was, can you see it all? How he realised character! ... Oh, I must touch it!' and he moved tenderly over the face of one of the old women [almost certainly one of the Regentesses of the Almshouses]. They say he was a drunkard, a coarse fellow, but don't you believe it ... Just imagine a drunkard doing those beautiful things!" See E. Robins and J. Pennell, *The Life of James Whistler*, 2 volumes (London, 1908), p. 287. Whistler's companion had to drag him away fearing that the artist might collapse in his excitement. The scene is vividly recaptured by F. S. Jowell, "The Rediscovery of Frans Hals", in the *Catalogue of the Frans Hals Exhibition* (London, 1989), p. 76.

is worth as much as Dante's *Paradise* and all the Michelangelos and Raphaels and even the Greeks." [22] What he painted was in fact portraits.[23] More specifically he painted everybody who was anybody in the prosperous and orderly Dutch city of Haarlem.[24] On top of the social heap were the oligarchs of the city council, rich brewers to a man.[25] They appear staid, solid and dignified, their ladies ostentatiously unglamorous. There was the old Catholic nobility, disbarred from public office but still prominent in the professions.[26] There were the rich merchants, many trading with exotic lands, often on the edge of bankruptcy but also of fabulous wealth. There was an academic elite – preachers, doctors, teachers and scholars. And there were well-to-do tradesmen and artisans, including fellow artists. All make their appearance on canvas and it seems that one has met them all.

But Hals also painted nobodies – in so far as anybody was a nobody in the closely integrated society of the Netherlands of his day. He painted a merry rommel-pot player surrounded by urchins shrieking with delight, actors, fishermen, market women and a crazy inmate of the municipal asylum. The rector of the Latin school of Leyden left a pen-portrait of the artist at sixty-five. "He surpasses all others", the rector wrote, "with his superb technique, uniquely his. His paintings are imbued with such force and vitality that he seems to defy nature himself with his brush ... His portraits, so numerous as to pass belief, are coloured in such a way that they seem to live and breathe." [27] They do indeed, even after three centuries.

Yet he never lacked detractors. The insolent facility of his brushwork often led to the charge of superficiality. Was he superficial? Of course. Surfaces are what painting is all about. He did not, like Rembrandt, try to penetrate his sitters' souls; and his portraits are arguably the better for it. Perhaps the only soul a man can penetrate is his own; and uniquely among great portraitists, indeed among great painters in general, Hals never painted

---

[22] V. van Gogh, *The Complete Letters*, 3 volumes (London, 1958), p. 342.

[23] In his younger days even his landscape settings were painted by professional landscape painters.

[24] Only about half his sitters known from portraits have so far been identified. The only international celebrity he painted was René Descartes. See P. Biesboer, "The Burghers of Haarlem and their Portrait Painters", in the *Catalogue of Frans Hals Exhibition* (London, 1989), p. 32.

[25] In 1618 Prince Maurice of Nassau sacked the entire city council and stacked the new one with his supporters. Hals served as a principal portraitist to this new elite (like the Olycan family), all devout Protestants. It is inconceivable that they would have employed a disreputable drunkard.

[26] Non-membership of the city council was in fact the only disability suffered by religious minorities.

[27] Quoted by Slive, *Frans Hals*, p. 453.

a self-portrait.[28] He painted what other people looked like. Only fools believe that they can read a character from a face; but the quest is perennially fascinating. What secrets lie behind the malevolent grin of the crazy old woman *Malle Babbe*, infinitely more interesting than the smile of the *Mona Lisa*? Is it in fact malevolent? Or cheerfully welcoming. But where? Hell, perhaps. One does not really want Hals to provide all the answers.

Even the earliest of his portraits are so accomplished that it is easy to call him, even to think of him as, unchanging. This is a charge often levelled at great artists.[29] It is rarely justified. Hals in fact never stopped experimenting and advancing. Step by step he discovered every trick of the modern portrait painter's art. In his fifties he began to make use of shifting focus. It makes one almost hear the twang and clatter of the buffoon's lute. In his sixties he introduced the quick sideways glance. It still stops casual amblers in museums. What has suddenly distracted the attention of the sitter? Usually it is something just outside the frame of a Hals portrait. Poses and gestures grew simpler but more original every year. He first painted his friend and patron, Willem van Heythuysen, when they were both in their thirties. The rich merchant stands proudly upright, his right hand resting on a magnificent ceremonial sword. Hals made a lightning sketch of the same man twenty years later.[30] The sitter is older, more pensive and more interesting.[31] The pose in the first portrait is a well-tried formula. That in the second is unprecedented. The chair is tipped back and the right leg rests indecorously on the left knee. It was as serious a breach of polite manners as yawning in public would be today.[32]

Hals was seventy when he painted his pair of portraits of Stephanus Geraerdts and his young bride. She is walking away from him – but looking back. Is she offering him the rose in her hand? Challenging him to follow her? Or just laughing at her teddy-bear of a husband? Comfortably ensconced in his armchair – or perhaps not so comfortably – he raises his hands towards her with a sheepish grin. There is warmth and gaiety in the exchange of glances and gestures – but also tension.

[28] It has been suggested that he appears inconspicuously in his group portrait of the St George's Militia, with which he may have been loosely associated. A copy by an unknown artist of what may have been a self-portrait is in the Clowes Fund Collection in Indianapolis. See W. R. Valentiener, "The Self-Portraits of Frans Hals", *Art in America*, 13 (1925), p. 148.

[29] Corot has been another frequent target.

[30] M. Boot, "Über Willem van Heythuysen, seinen Nachlass und die symbolische Bedeutung des Porträts von Frans Hals", *Pantheon*, 29 (1973), p. 420.

[31] Whether a great portrait of the past was a good likeness is always difficult to decide, but less so in the case of artists, like Hals, who painted the same sitters more than once at different times of their lives. Applying this test confirms contemporary testimonials that he achieved astonishingly good likenesses.

[32] According to Lomazzo's popular sixteenth-century guide to etiquette.

Hals was the greatest painter of fabric of his age and one of the greatest of any age. Nothing was beyond him: the subtle transparencies of lace, the modulations of silk, the voluptuousness of velvet, the shimmering of taffeta, the glow of old leather. The few brushstrokes with which he recreated them – often no more than an abstract zig-zag of highlights – are optical miracles. In youth and middle age he revelled in vivid colours. As he grew older and his textures became simpler, black emerged supreme; or rather blacks. Van Gogh reckoned that by the time he had reached his seventies Hals had twenty-seven different blacks: black for modesty, black for sobriety, black for dignity, black for glamour, black for old age, black for boldness, black for polish, black for seduction, black for grief and many blacks for mourning.[33]

Group portraits as a genre present special problems. Apart from having to assemble the sitters harmoniously and with due regard for hierarchical relationships – no Adonis of a young subaltern must steal the show from the paunchy old colonel – the artist faces a conflict of priorities. Should he try to portray a clutch of competing egos? Or should he attempt to convey a corporate sense of purpose and mood? From the vantage point of posterity (no longer agitated by the feud between one of the junior wardens and the deputy treasurer), neither Rembrandt nor Hals always got it right.[34] The roistering companies of civil guard officers whom Hals painted in his forties have many bravura touches; but his attempts to portray both civic decorum and bibulous bonhomie were not always successful. The *Regents of the St Elizabeth Hospital*, a grave but unpompous group of mature men, which he painted at sixty-seven, is nearly perfect: a concerto in black and white. But as profound human documents no group portrait by Hals or any other artist, not even by Rembrandt, can touch the pair which Hals painted at the age of eighty-four and eighty-five.

The worst fatuities of Hals lore still encrust the *Regents and Regentesses of the Old Men's* and *Old Women's Almshouses*. Even Bürger, one of Hals's most perceptive and admiring critics, misinterpreted the paintings, referring to the artist as "the old lion ... defeated by poverty, imprisoned in this refuge for old men", and mistook the regents for glorified prison-warders.[35] Eugène Fromentin, another influential admirer and second only to Bürger among critics responsible for Hals's rehabilitation, wrote in sorrow about Hals's "receding virtuosity", "remote intimations of his past power".

---

[33] V. Van Gogh, *The Complete Letters* (London, 1958), p. 376.
[34] A. Riegl, *Das Holländische Gruppenporträt* (2nd edn, Vienna, 1931).
[35] W. Bürger, "Frans Hals", *Gazette des Beaux Arts*, 24 (1868), p. 437.

His hand is no longer there. He displays instead of paints; he does not execute, he daubs; the perceptions of his eye are still vivid and just, the colours entirely pure ... it is impossible to imagine finer blacks or finer greyish whites ... but you find no longer either consistency of design or of execution ... the heads are an abridgement ... the hands of no importance ... The touch is given without method, rather by chance, and no longer says what it would say. Everything is wanting, clearness of sight, surety in the fingers ... The painter is three-quarters dead.[36]

From such misguided but affectionate laments, it was but a step to modern fantasies. The fact that both Hals and his wife were supported by the institutions "shows the level of dire poverty – virtually the gutter – to which sixty years of dissipation had reduced the artist".[37] "Technically he was past it, no longer able to wield his cheerful brush." [38] John Berger provided hilarious television entertainment by deliberately dismissing factual research as "mystification" and expatiating on "the destitute old painter who has lost his reputation ... wreaking his vengeance on his tormentors for the indignities he had to suffer".[39] Masterpieces do not need interpretation; but they deserve better than such distortion of their historical background.

What made the early seventeenth century the golden age of the Protestant Netherlands was neither the country's wealth nor its military and naval victories. These were of course justifiable sources of satisfaction. The country was rich because its people were industrious, ingenious and, in an expanding world, possessed of the right mixture of prudence and enterprise. At terrible cost they had rid themselves of the tyranny of foreign kings. They had learnt to distrust divine rights. But no denizen of the twenty-first century needs reminding how easily wealth and power can create a spiritual desert. What saved Hals's Netherlands from such a fate was the tradition of Dutch Humanism and the character of the Dutch Reformed Church. The two were often in conflict, and the tension between them – as well as changing circumstances and a shift in international power – eventually brought the country's golden age to an end. But they were also complementary and they continued to nourish Hals's art.[40]

---

[36] E. Fromantin, *The Old Masters of Belgium and Holland*, translated by M. Robbins (New York, 1963) (first published in Paris as *Les maîtres d'autrefois: Belgique, Hollande*, in 1876), p. 321.

[37] G. Schomberg, *Hals von Haarlem* (Munich, 1954), p. 214.

[38] M. Schapiro, "Hals in Old Age", *Art*, 4 (1962), p. 23.

[39] J. Berger, *Ways of Seeing* (London, 1972), p. 13.

[40] To present the cultural and social panorama of a distant age is difficult. S. Schama, *The Embarrassment of Riches: An Interpretation of Dutch Culture in the Golden Age* (London, 1987), is a bold attempt but not, one hopes, the last word on the subject.

The essence of Dutch Humanism was a reverence for the dignity of man as an individual. It was a reverence which was not conditional on wealth, strength, power or even virtue. It was every individual's birthright, that of a simpleton as well as a genius, a beggar as well as a millionaire, a woman as well as a man's, and a sinner as well as a saint. It had been luminously propounded though not of course invented by Erasmus of Rotterdam; and, almost miraculously, it survived in his own country (and a few other citadels of reason) during some of the bloodiest and most bigoted decades of European history.[41] It helped to create a society which clearly distinguished between right and wrong but which was also determinedly tolerant. No Catholics were tortured in Delft. No witches were burnt in Haarlem. There was no ghetto in Amsterdam. No homosexuals were pilloried in The Hague. No whores were flogged in Rotterdam. And no scientists were muzzled in Utrecht. Tobacco was officially condemned but no hysterical lobby clamoured for its suppression. Heavy drinking was deplored but not forbidden.[42]

The social message of the Dutch Reformed Church was different but equally clear. It rejected the Franciscan ethos which had for centuries exalted poverty as the only safe passport to Heaven. It endorsed Calvin's reinterpretation of the divine prohibition on usury.[43] Far from being inherently sinful, the accumulation of wealth by hard work and careful husbandry was recognised as a Calvinist virtue. But this was not budding capitalism at prayer. Wealth was not an end in itself, nor indeed a passport to Salvation. It was a means of fulfilling the divine ordinance of the prayerful performance of good deeds.

In human society such noble precepts are never fully realised and the

[41] Other such islands were Venice, Henri IV's France and to some extent Elizabethan England.

[42] Only a profoundly confident society could afford such luxuries and it was too good to last. By the end of the seventeenth century and during most of the eighteenth, as trade declined and military and naval reverses as well as devastating floods poisoned the political and social atmosphere, the great Dutch cities became more and more like other urban dung-heaps in Europe. Yet, the tradition of tolerance, the golden legacy of a golden age, remains alive in Dutch culture today – and long may it flourish.

[43] Calvin argued that Deuteronomy 23:19 was not intended to be universal but applied only to Hebrews. Hals's contemporary in Holland, Claude Saumaise, went so far, in his remarkable book *On Usury*, as to maintain that charging interest was actually necessary for salvation. But permitting interest on loans was only one reason – and not the most important one – for the economic success of Protestant countries in Hals's day. At least as important was the relative freedom from clerical interference in the daily life of Protestant citizens. The religion of the rich Haarlemmers whom Hals painted was intense but private: they read the scriptures for themselves, believed in the worthiness, even sanctification, of lay life and exalted the married state and the family but viewed anything resembling canon law with suspicion.

Netherlands of Hals was no earthly paradise. But a concern for one's fellow men – especially of course for one's fellow citizens – and a deep spiritual need to channel wealth into good works was widespread and genuine. Foreign visitors (like Descartes) gasped at the sums collected in Sunday boxes even in modest country churches. But such munificence was not a purely religious obligation. It was at the heart of civic life, binding together the givers and the beneficiaries.[44] Charitable institutions were not Victorian poor-houses or twenty-first-century geriatric wards but the pride of every self-respecting Dutch city. The great orphanages of Amsterdam and Haarlem were show-pieces; and to be maintained by one of the civic almshouses was no social stigma, let alone a sign of physical degradation. The sums which Hals and his wife received are in fact known, and allowed him to stand as guarantor in his last year for a debt incurred by one of his sons-in-law. It was certainly enough to maintain Hals and his wife in modest comfort.[45] They were in their eighties and he had been an industrious citizen of Haarlem all his life. Indeed, he was still in demand as a painter. Contrary to tearful romancing and diatribes against stony-hearted capitalists, there is no reason to believe that he was not cherished and there is ample evidence that he was.[46] To lament that so great a genius did not spend his last years, like Salvador Dalí, in a Mediterranean château kept alive by medical science at its most officious, may tell us something about western society at the turn of the millennium but nothing about Hals and early seventeenth-century Haarlem.

There were also other, more local circumstances which imprinted themselves on the last great pictures. Haarlem reached its peak of prosperity in the 1640s. For almost fifty years both the textile and the brewing industry, the mainstays of the city's wealth, had been booming. But both overreached themselves. Haarlem beer and Haarlem cloth continued to be valued for

---

[44] Public charities were in fact an important and perhaps still insufficiently recognised feature of Baroque Europe in general; but nowhere did they flourish as splendidly as in the Protestant provinces of the Netherlands. They embraced the care of cripples, the homeless, the mad and the leprous, as well as the sick and the old; and the *Heilige Geist* institutions, financed mainly by lotteries, were specifically dedicated to non-Calvinists.

[45] There is an embarrassment of riches of inane passages in the Hals literature but one may serve as an illustration. "Hals was over eighty and utterly destitute. Most of his life he had been in debt. During the hard winter of 1664 he obtained three loads of peat on public charity, otherwise he would have frozen to death." See J. Berger, *Ways of Seeing* (London, 1979), p. 14. Apart from the well-documented consignment of peat (and there are many old age pensioners in London today in unanswered need of such charity), not a single statement in this passage is supported by evidence.

[46] The two group portraits were commissioned separately, and there was no reason why the second should not have been entrusted to another artist had the sitters been dissatisfied with the first. This was never even discussed.

their quality but ceased to be competitive. This had a knock-on effect. As breweries closed and clothmakers became insolvent, wealthy Haarlemmers began to invest in businesses in Amsterdam, now the richest city in Europe. This was inevitably followed by an exodus of tradesmen and the service industries. Many of the city's younger artists left.

This was not all. In 1664, the year before Hals was commissioned to paint his last pictures, the city was struck by the worst outbreak of the plague in its history. As many as a third of the population may have perished, and probably a quarter of the households were left without a breadwinner. The burden which fell on the municipal charities nearly bankrupted them. There could have been few among the Regents and Regentesses who had not themselves suffered personal loss, perhaps personal illness. Whatever made them carry on in their posts, it was surely not vanity. The notion that Hals set out to mock them – "to wreak his vengeance" – shows ignorance of the historical background. The city and the almshouses survived the plague as they had survived the devastating Spanish siege two generations earlier; but the end of the epidemic was not a moment for jollification, for Hals to wield "his cheerful brush". For the city council the commissioning of the picture was clearly an act of homage and remembrance. For the artist it was also perhaps a time of summing up.

There are almost no props: even the few which had originally existed – cushions, swags of drapery, the Burgundy-coloured tablecloth – have been lost by the darkening of the paint.[47] Also gone is the swashbuckling bravado with which in years gone by Hals would have conjured up yards of lace, coloured silk and rich brocade. But nowhere did his brush fumble: it had lost none of its sureness of touch. The starched whites still dazzle even if the blacks have lost some of their modelling. For the faces Hals used a kind of personal shorthand – as did the aged Titian, Goya and Rembrandt – the detached brushstrokes combining breadth and strength. Of course some of the characters are comical: nothing to the young and fit can be so risible as illness, deformities and the decrepitude of old age.[48] The face of the Regentess on the right has a Parkinsonian stillness. The suggestion that the Regent, whose large slouch hat barely covers his long lank hair, is deliberately and cleverly shown to be inebriated has achieved canonical status in Hals mythology.[49] The idea has no foundation; nor would a disquisition about

[47] Suggested by a few old engravings. See H. P. Baard, *Frans Halsmuseum* (Munich, 1967).

[48] John Berger's close-up of two of the Regentesses on the television screen must have raised many a guffaw.

[49] Wearing the hat at an extreme rakish angle may look stupid today but was the height of *chic* among men at the time, as shown in several other contemporary paintings – such as the *Portrait of a Man* by an unknown artist in the Fitzwilliam Museum in Cambridge.

half a dozen unprovable but infinitely more likely diagnoses. But, more poignantly than a cart-load of moralising vanitas pictures, the eleven faces convey the fragility of the human condition. Or, more accurately, the eleven faces and the eleven pairs of hands.

Hands had always been the main sub-plot in Hals's portraits. One recalls the hand of the flute-player, pointing a well-turned phrase, the cheerfully raised hand of the merry drinker, the tender hand of the nurse offering an apple to the child in her arms, the hand of the scholar marking a place in his book, the intertwined hands of lovers. The long, thin, almost transparent right hand of the Regentess on the right is simply and hauntingly immobile. It was probably Hals's last hand and it was his greatest.

# 4

## *Chardin*

Chardin would surely be every intelligent castaway's desert island painter.
He was not the greatest of all artists – the frivolity of such a suggestion would
have irritated him – but he would be the most companionable. His
comely kitchen maids would be a source of endless delight without arousing
unseasonable passions. His children – so grave and yet so innocent – would
lift the gloom in moments of dejection. But, above all, one would never tire
of the becalmed splendour of his apples, peaches, nuts, grapes, squashy
pomegranates, succulent melons, jars of olives, bunches of onions, game
pies, cheeses, terrines, golden brioches and – glory of glories – baskets of
wild strawberries. His art was entirely without idiosyncrasy, exaggeration
and excess. He had no religious or antireligious axe to grind, no slick
psychological messages to impart, no instant social comments to make. So
many negatives may make him sound dull. But he was never – or almost
never – dull.

His career almost exactly coincided with the reign of Louis XV.[1] That
reign, in the opinion of most historians, was not a success. After an auspicious
but deceptive start, there was waste, incompetence, frivolity and drift.[2]
But there was also incomparable elegance. Nothing more could be asked
from a salt-cellar, a mustard pot, a fan, a commode, a chair, a wall-paper,
a *fauteuil*, an escritoire, a soup tureen, a snuff-box, a toilet service, an
inkstand, a bracket clock, a pack of cards, a silk bodice or a chocolate cup
than the restrained perfection lavished on them by the craftsmen who worked

---

[1] Christened Jean-Baptiste-Siméon, Chardin was born in Paris in 1699 and was apprenticed
to the Guild of St Luke at thirteen. He died in 1779, aged eighty. Louis XV was born in 1710
and was five when he succeeded his great-grandfather, Louis XIV (who had reigned for an
unsurpassed seventy-two years, surviving both his eldest son and his eldest grandson). Louis
XV died in 1774, aged sixty-four.

[2] The King's uncle, the debauched but intelligent Philippe d'Orléans, acted as Regent, not
incompetently, until his death in 1723. Power then passed to the quiet but capable Bishop of
Fréjus, Cardinal Fleury. He presided over two prosperous decades until his death in 1743,
aged ninety. After that Louis assumed the role of prime minister himself – in what little time
he could spare from more enjoyable pursuits.

for Madame de Pompadour.³ Of course the Chardins never aspired to hob-
nob with royal mistresses. The artist's father, a respected Parisian cabinet
maker, supplied royal residences with billiard tables; but the son probably
went to Versailles only once.⁴

Yet on a more modest scale, the life style of hardworking Parisian craftsmen and artisans matched the elegance, if not the opulence, of the Court.
They lived in solidly built town houses which were neither too big nor too
small for a well-ordered family of five or six and two or three servants.
Their rooms were uncluttered, airy and well-proportioned. The central
gutters in the streets stank a little in the summer; but at the back the windows
usually looked out onto pleasant courtyards or well-kept gardens. Church,
school, shops and workplace were usually within walking distance; and
during the walk one could still be refreshed by the balmy air of the Ile de
France. The dresses of both men and women were the last European fashion
to combine prettiness with comfort; and the hair-styles were charming.
Above all, the objects they handled in their daily lives – furniture, dishes,
cutlery, craft implements, musical instruments, books and toys – had a *belle
tournure*, a kind of well-bred shapeliness, that pleased the eye and served
their purpose in equal measure. Even in scholarly books the tableware
Chardin used and painted is sometimes described as "porcelain" or even as
"Meissen". In fact, the painter and his friends had no more use for porcelain,
even Sèvres, than they would have had for gold knives and forks. The bowls,
tureens and pitchers in Chardin's paintings are made of the most beautiful
and yet most homely ware ever brought to perfection by European potters
– the faïence of Rouen, Sceau, Strasbourg, Marseille, Montpellier, Nevers
and countless other smaller faïenceries.⁵ Of course none of this explains

---

³ Mme Le Normant Etoiles (née Jeanne-Antoinette Poisson), created Marquise de Pompadour, was one of the King's more enjoyable pursuits. An ambitious little beauty, her charm
and wit (which even her enemies conceded) had won over such crusty intellectuals as Crebillon,
Fontanelle and Montesquieu even before she became the King's official mistress in 1745. She
was then twenty-four. She retained this position for only five years – the King's taste in bed
inclined increasingly to a younger age group – but she remained Louis's closest and most
influential confidante until her death twenty years later (perhaps from tuberculosis). She was
execrated by those who never met her but loved by many of those who did (including
Maurice-Quentin de La Tour). But she was no model of thrift: after her death two notaries
took a year working full time to draw up a provisional catalogue of her personal possessions.
⁴ A younger brother, Jules, continued to run the family workshop after the father's death.
It folded during the Revolution.
⁵ Tin-glazed earthenware was brought to France from Italy – the name derives from Faenza
– and reached its peak of perfection in Chardin's lifetime. The famous faïenceries and countless
smaller ones produced everything from rough kitchenware to services worthy of any aristocratic
table. (They were given a boost by Louis XIV who, in 1700, ordered all silverware to be melted
down to help finance his disastrous wars.) Many of Chardin's pictures show examples of

Chardin's genius; but nor is it possible to imagine that genius blossoming in any other setting.[6]

There is a quality in Chardin's work which seems to compel unbounded admiration for the man. This is unusual. Nobody in his right mind would write a business reference for Rembrandt or Titian, however greatly one admired them as artists, Yet Thoré, the Goncourts, Balzac, Proust, Gide, Giacometti, Picasso and Lucian Freud, none of them starry-eyed about the relationship between genius and middle-class morality, have described Chardin as modest, good-natured, generous, upright and humane, a man of unfailing good sense: in short the embodiment of that French paragon, the *honnête homme*.[7] He was especially admired in times when yuppiedom was rampant (as it was at the ends of the nineteenth and twentieth centuries): "in the midst of a period stuffed with every kind of jerky innovation, narcissistic blurting and trashy 'relevance'", Robert Hughes wrote in 1981, "one is reminded by Chardin that lucidity, deliberation, probity and calm are still among the chief virtues of artists".[8] There was indeed much to admire about him – and, above all, he was fortunate in his obituarist.[9]

---

faïence at its loveliest. The disadvantage of the ware was the relative ease with which the glaze (which did not fuse with the body) chipped; and by the end of the century it was largely replaced by hard-paste porcelain and (in the lower price range) Wedgwood's creamware.

[6] The ambience is well described in K. Scott, *The Rococo Interior: Decoration and Social Spaces in Early Eighteenth-Century Paris* (London, 1995); T. E. Crow, *Painters and Public Life in Eighteenth-Century Paris* (London, 1985); and M. Baxendall, *Shadows and Enlightenment* (London, 1995).

[7] Perhaps the nearest equivalent in French to the English "gentleman".

Proust wrote a characteristically perceptive and complicated piece, "Chardin et le coeur des choses" in 1895 which was not published until 1954, in the *Figaro littéraire*, 27 March 1954, p. 5. In an interview with the *International Herald Tribune* of 6 December 1995, p. 20, Lucian Freud is reported to have said: "Even as a painter I'm not technically aware of what he is doing, any more than you notice the vocal timbre of someone who is telling you something that is very important." See also P. Rosenberg and H. Prigent, *Chardin* (London, 2000).

[8] R. Hughes, *Nothing if Not Critical* (London, 1990), p. 96.

[9] Charles Nicolas Cochin the Elder and then the Younger were secretaries to the Académie and Chardin's close friends as well as engravers. (In France, as in England, the income of painters largely depended on the sale of prints based on their paintings. Conversely, a stable of good or at least fashionable painters was the livelihood of engravers.) Almost all biographies of Chardin are based, often word for word, on the long, detailed and wholly adulatory obituary written by the younger Cochin shortly after the artist's death, *Essai sur la vie de M. Chardin* (1780), published by Charles de Beaurepaire in *Précis analytique des travaux de l'Académie des Sciences, Belle-Lettres et Arts de Rouen*, 78 (1875), p. 417, translated by E. McCarthy and reprinted in M. Roland Michel's comprehensive modern biography, *Chardin* (New York, 1996).

Among other modern biographies and monographs on Chardin are G. Schefer, *Chardin* (Paris, 1904); K. Garas, *Chardin* (Budapest, 1963); G. Wildenstein, *Chardin*, English edition

Having got himself, by a series of "innocent ruses" (according to his admiring friend and business partner, the younger Cochin), admitted to the Académie Royale,[10] as a "talented painter of fruit and animals", he hardly ever missed a monthly meeting.[11] Nor was he, like many dedicated committee men, a mere nodder. There is never a shortage of volunteers in such assemblies for escorting royal parties or upholding the dignity of the institution at civic banquets. But for the endlessly tedious chores of day-to-day administration there is rarely a jostle of contenders. For such tasks *notre bon confrère Chardin* was the man. Hardly a meeting passed without him being requested, charged or delegated to visit an ailing but not particularly popular colleague to express the warm good wishes of the president and council (the choice and purchase of a not too extravagant present being usually left to his discretion); to enquire into the reasons for the disappointing results achieved by a class of students; to draft citations for prizes and medals to be distributed by the president; to express the gratitude of the Académie for the infinitely gracious gift of a Prince or Princess of the Blood (to be conveyed by the president); to thank (personally) less exalted donors; to report on a new range of paint brushes; to condole with members' widows and report on their possibly straitened circumstances; to argue with lawyers about ambiguously worded bequests; to report on criminal charges (no doubt groundless) brought against eminent colleagues; to propose ways of improving the lamentable state of the members' kitchen at a reasonable cost;

revised and enlarged by D. Wildenstein (Oxford, 1969); P. Rosenberg, *Tout l'oeuvre peint de Chardin* (Paris, 1983); P. Conisbee, *Chardin* (Oxford, 1986); G. Naughton, *Chardin* (1996); and catalogues accompanying the Chardin exhibitions in the Grand Palais, Paris, edited by P. Rosenberg and S. Sylvie (Paris, 1999) and the Royal Academy of Arts (London, 2000).

[10] The Guild of St Luke was the trade association of painter decorators dating back to the middle ages; and it was as an apprentice to Nicholas Coypel that Chardin spent some time in Fontainebleau in refurbishing the château. The guild lost most of its power in the art world and almost all of its social prestige with the foundation of the Académie Royale de Peinture et de Sculpture in 1650. According to Cochin, Chardin was twenty-nine when two of his still lives, *The Rayfish* and *The Buffet*, attracted the attention of two academicians at the annual open-air exhibition of paintings in the Place Dauphine (known as the *Salon de Jeunesse*). They offered to sponsor his admission to the Académie without the usual examinations and, "overcoming his innate modesty", Chardin accepted. The story does not quite ring true, although under the Regency the Académie had lost some of its numbing rigidity. But what were the "innocent ruses"?

[11] The proceedings of the Académie in Chardin's lifetime were published in eleven volumes between 1875 and 1892: *Procès verbaux de l'Académie Royale de Peinture et de Sculpture, 1648–1793*, edited by A. de Montaiglon in Paris. Apart from being written with a literary grace to which no modern company secretary could aspire, and recording more leisurely meetings – they usually lasted a whole day interrupted by a sustaining repast of eight or nine courses – they have the timeless air of committee minutes.

or to warn – politely but firmly – the ancient and honourable Guild of St Luke to desist at once from their usurpation of the functions and privileges of the Académie Royale. Having denounced the *concierge d'affaires* for mismanaging the funds, who but Chardin could be elected to the newly created post of treasurer? And when the squabbles seemingly inseparable from the hanging of works at the annual Salon [12] became too much for the Marquis de Marigny,[13] who but Chardin could have been appointed to undertake the task on a regular basis? [14]

Such exertions did of course earn their modest rewards. By the mid century Colbert's undeclared aim in founding royal academies had long been achieved: the livelihood of all but a handful of privileged artists, scientists and writers now depended on the pensions, perks, bounties and benevolences which flowed or trickled down (or, more frequently, did not) from on high.[15] Royal manna did not make Chardin corrupt or conspicuously rich. He was a slow worker – he rarely completed more than fifteen or twenty small canvases in a year – and still lives and genre scenes were cheap compared with history paintings and portraits. His pictures sold quickly and to prestigious buyers,[16] but special gifts and emoluments were therefore welcome, as was a well-appointed grace-and-favour residence in the Louvre.[17]

No less important was Chardin's ability to ensure that his paintings and those of his friends received due prominence at the Salon.[18] Not

[12] The annual show derived its name from the *Salon Carré* of the Louvre where the first exhibition was held. Later the venue proved too small and the exhibitions moved to other locations, but the name stuck and was adopted in many languages.

[13] He was a brother of Madame de Pompadour and cast in the same mould of easygoing charm.

[14] The title was *tapissier* and the work was quite demanding.

[15] The declared aim of the Académie was to raise the status and promote the prosperity of artists. As in the case of the other royal academies, its true purpose was to bring potentially troublesome groups of subjects (artists, writers, philosophers, scientists and suchlike) under the control of the King. It was under the effective rule of the Superintendent of the King's Buildings and the King's First Painter.

[16] Early purchasers of Chardin's work were the Margravine of Baden, the Comte de Tessin, Chancellor Maupeou and the Prince de Conti. His later genre scenes were snatched up by Frederick the Great of Prussia, Catherine the Great of Russia and the Prince of Liechtenstein. The only British collector was Dr William Hunter, surgeon obstetrician to Queen Charlotte, who bought *The Scullery Maid* and *The Cellar Boy* from the artist on a visit to Paris. They are still the glories of the Hunterian Collection in Glasgow.

[17] It was still a royal palace but untenanted by royalty since the Court moved to Versailles. Chardin's rooms and studio were a spacious maisonette of at least six rooms on two floors. It was rare for a painter of still lives to be given this privilege.

[18] It was the main showcase for selling works. In the 1760s about sixty exhibitors showed about 400 exhibits. The number of visitors daily was about 700–800 over a period of two to three weeks.

unexpectedly, his tireless efforts were not always appreciated. Greuze complained that the hanging arrangement invited unfavourable comparisons between his and Chardin's superficially similar offerings.[19] Oudry spluttered at having his dead fowl murdered for a second time by having it hung too near the ceiling.[20] Peronneau faded into a second-rate pastellist when shown next to Chardin's friend, Maurice-Quentin de La Tour.[21] The accusations never stuck, but at times even Diderot, Chardin's devoted admirer, tut-tutted.

Chardin's private life was overcast for some years, though (once again in the words of his admiring obituarist, the younger Cochin) he bore his trials with exemplary fortitude. His first wife, the mother of his only son, died when the boy was five.[22] He married again, a widow of some means. They were well matched in thrift. In 1757 the son, Jean-Pierre, came of age and was in law entitled to a share of his mother's estate. "With his usual clarity and exactitude",[23] Chardin drew up an account not only of the medical, funeral and legal expenses arising from his first wife's illness and death but also of his expenses in feeding, clothing, lodging and educating his son over the previous twelve years, not forgetting doctor's fees and the cost of medicine on the occasion when, at the age of eight, the son had suffered from a severe inflammation of the bowels.[24] Thereupon "the ungrateful son denounced his father in violent and abusive language ... leaving the father with no choice but to obtain a state scholarship for the ungrateful offspring to study art at the French Academy in Rome".[25] The arrangement, however generous, did not work out well. The director of the Academy soon reported that, while he could detect gratifying signs of the father's "transcendent talent"

[19] Jean-Baptise Greuze had, by the 1750s, established himself as the most popular painter of sentimental genre scenes in Europe; prints of his paintings sold by the thousand while Chardin's sold by the hundreds. Greuze was also quick and prolific and an accomplished self-promoter. One would therefore take little notice of his whinges if Diderot, one of Chardin's admirers who thought little of Greuze, had not himself written that "Monsieur Chardin must stop playing tricks: he has no need of a foil". See D. Diderot, *Salons, 1765* (Oxford, 1960), p. 683.

[20] Jean-Baptiste Oudry was an excellent and popular painter of still lives of dead game as well as the designer of some of the grandest hunting tapestries for Beauvais and the Gobelins. Within his deliberately limited field he had little to fear from Chardin; but there was no love lost between them.

[21] Jean-Baptiste Peronneau was a gifted pastellist whose misfortune it was to be constantly compared to Maurice-Quentin de La Tour. His application for a studio in the Louvre was turned down; and he suspected Chardin's hand. He may have been right.

[22] He commemorated her in one of his loveliest early genre scenes, *A Lady Taking Tea*, now in the Hunterian Collection in Glasgow.

[23] Cochin, *Essai sur la vie de M. Chardin*, p. 9.

[24] This hair-raising document is still extant.

[25] Cochin, *Essai sur la vie de M. Chardin*, p. 12.

in the son, he could detect none of the father's no less celebrated application and industry. On the way home the son was kidnapped by pirates, or so a ransom note informed the father. Chardin refused to pay, prudently perhaps since the son soon turned up in Paris unharmed. But a few weeks later he was off again, this time as a member of the entourage of the Comte de Paulmy, ambassador of France to the Holy See. He never made it to Rome. He died in Venice, probably by his own hand.[26]

Chardin's image as a man has always been the product of his art rather than of biographical research. He was not an innovator; but "he elevated the modest genre of still life to one of the loftiest and most astounding pinnacles of art".[27] The Goncourts were right even if their breathless prose is out of keeping with Chardin's style or personality. He advanced slowly but continuously. Many of his paintings from his thirties and forties centre on dead game, and still exploit memories of the drama of the chase. They are accomplished; but Chardin was not by nature a dramatist. But with *The Jar of Olives*, painted when he was sixty-three, he reached one of the peaks the Goncourts would celebrate a hundred years later. His more perceptive contemporaries did so at the time. Diderot wrote in one of his reviews:

> If I were to destine my child for a career in painting it is to Chardin's *Jar of Olives* that I would direct him ... "Copy that for me", I would tell him, "and copy it again!" But how obtuse! Nature would be no more difficult to copy ... These olives are really separated from the eye by the water in which they float; all you have to do is to take those biscuits and eat them; open the Seville orange and squeeze it; take those fruit and peel them ... Yet how could I even think of destroying such beauty! O Chardin! It is not white, red and black pigments that you mix on your palette, not even the very substance of the objects you paint. It is air, light and shadow ... Your magic defies understanding.[28]

Beside innumerable technical felicities, these late still lives have the capacity to induce a sense of almost physical well-being, a joy at the beauty of simple objects.

[26] The circumstances are obscure. Jean-Pierre did in fact exhibit some pictures in Paris and Diderot praised his work; but none of it is known to have survived. See P. Rosenberg, "La mort du fils de Chardin", *Archives de l'art français*, 29 (1988), p. 17.

[27] J. and E. Goncourt, *L'art du XVIIIe siècle* (Paris, 1859–75), was the result of twenty years' dedicated labour and became a landmark in the appreciation of eighteenth-century French art. Chardin was discussed in the second volume, published in 1864. The quotation here and below are from the 3rd edition (Paris, 1909), i, p. 126.

[28] D. Diderot, *Salons, 1765* (Oxford, 1960), p. 683. Among his many accomplishments, Diderot was the virtual founder of modern art criticism: his reviews of the annual *Salons* were witty, biting but also admiring when he felt so inclined. Most of his judgements were "sound" even in the light of later art criticism; and some were inspired. Four volumes have been splendidly edited by J. Seznec and J. Adhémar (Oxford, 1957–67).

But it was not only objects. In his fifties Chardin added genre scenes to his repertory; and they are as lovely as his fruit and game pies. His subjects were ordinary housewives, children, domestic servants (still part of the extended family) in a world which was neither too poor nor too rich for comfort, and in which everybody had their allotted place. Except perhaps, if one accepts Chardin as one's guide, the master of the house. He never appears. He is obviously the provider and one cannot doubt that in due course he will make his entry and be received with due deference, warmth, even perhaps love. But men tend to make a mess in well-ordered middle-class homes and disarray made no part of Chardin's scenes.

The absence of adult males from the artist's cast has led to some half-hearted and not a few half-witted attempts to present him as a social warrior, a harbinger of female emancipation. But suggestions that "kitchen maids and ordinary housewives felt grateful seeing themselves represented by a famous artist, perhaps encouraged to think of themselves as equals" might just as well have been written about the dead hares and partridges of the youthful still lives.[29] Yet it would be bigoted to deny these faultlessly composed and beautifully painted late genre scenes social significance. The unsigned entry on *Femmes* in the great *Encyclopédie*, the bible of the Enlightenment, contrasts their role as "featherbrained coquettish playthings, still alas so prevalent in the highest strata of society" with what should be their real place,

> occupying their days in running their households, ruling their husbands with forbearance, their children with tenderness, their servants with kindness ... their houses the homes of religious feelings, of filial piety, of conjugal love, of maternal tenderness, of order, of inner peace, of untroubled sleep and health ... economical and settled, averted from uncontrolled passions and wants ... emanating a gentle warmth and pure light which illuminates and brings to life all that is around them.[30]

This ideal may seem a little over the top today, and may not command the unreserved approval of politically correct twenty-first-century social scientists; but in Chardin's day the *Encyclopédie* expressed revolutionary, not reactionary sentiments; and he echoed these sentiments in such wonderfully quiet and intelligent (as well as beautiful) works as *The Morning Toilet, A Good Education, Return from the Market* and *Saying Grace* – just as Fragonard's scintillating brush, at about the same time,

---

[29] J.-P. Moreau, *Art revolutionnaire du 18e siècle* (Paris, 1932).

[30] *Encyclopédie*, vi, quoted by J. Morley, *Diderot and the Encyclopedists* (London 1886), p. 358. The celebrated *Encyclopédie* was published over a period of twenty-one years, 1751–72, in Paris, under the general editorship of Diderot and D'Alembert in twenty-eight volumes.

immortalised contemporary women as the featherbrained and coquettish –
but oh how delectable – playthings so severely and justly censured by the
Encyclopedists.

The smooth surface of Chardin's industrious and modestly successful life
began to show alarming cracks as he progressed through his sixties. At
sixty-five, under some pressure from his colleagues, he resigned his treasurer-
ship of the Académie. A few months later he relinquished all responsibility
for superintending the hanging of pictures at the Salon. Then he was prevailed
upon to vacate one of his rooms in the Louvre to make way for a younger
artist. There were unwelcome changes in the higher echelons of the art
world. The dissolute but charming de Marigny was succeeded by the Comte
d'Angiviller as Superintendent of the King's Buildings (effectively Minister
for the Arts) and Jean-Baptiste-Marie Pierre was appointed first painter to
the King.[31] Pierre regarded the Chardins as "worthy but grasping". There
was probably some truth in this. The correspondence between the elderly
couple, the Minister and the Court Painter does not make edifying reading.
"You have long been enjoying free quarters and the largest allowance available for an artist of your class ... The most senior and highest ranking
officers are receiving salaries of 500–800 livres, whereas at your urgent insistence I have already raised yours to 1400." In Pierre's and D'Angiviller's
defence (in so far as they need it), the correspondence took place against a
darkening economic background – at least where the state's finances were
concerned.[32]

The more worrying development was Chardin's declining health. An
aura of golden age perfection clings to the craft methods of the Age of the
Enlightenment. Aesthetically it is well deserved. After the burnished glow of
eighteenth-century ormolu one recoils from crude Victorian or Second
Empire imitations. Even chipped and crazed, the creamy glazes of Chantilly

---

[31] Pierre was a good though distinctly sub-Chardin painter of genre scenes: his *Old Man
and Young Maid*, now in the Hermitage in St Petersburg, was the sensation of the Salon of
1767. His dislike of the Chardins became obsessional and was clearly inspired partly at least
by envy; but his comments in a letter written to Joseph-Marie Vien a few days after Chardin's
death are worth quoting as an antidote to the chorus of admiration (probably somewhat
exaggerated) that has been Chardin's posthumous reward over the past 150 years: "That man
was so puffed up with the little bit of tawdry fame he got from Cochin's protection that it
went to his head and he could not bear being demoted to council member [from treasurer].
Scarcely able to read or write his name, he wrote voluminous letters in friends' hands, moving
heaven and earth to insist he should not be compromised ..." Quoted by Rosenberg and
Prigent, *Chardin*, p. 98, who immediately add that "Chardin's responses show him to be a
man of wit and character, and, above all, someone always ready to spring to the defence of
his art". Perhaps the truth lay somewhere between the two.

[32] *La Déluge* was not far off.

and St-Cloud easily eclipse the dishwasher-proof gloss of modern ceramics. Despite the ravages of time, the colours of Chardin's largely home-made oil paints are still more vibrantly alive than yesterday's acrylics. But there was a dark side to this splendour. Almost every eighteenth-century master of ormolu who lived into his fifties must have ended his life "mad as a hatter" with mercury poisoning.[33] The mere listing of the chemicals Chardin used in grinding and mixing his paints would induce a state of shock in a modern Health and Safety Inspector. It is surprising how long the hearts, lungs and livers of Chardin's contemporaries withstood the chemical insults heaped upon them.[34] He began to have violent attacks of breathlessness in his sixties; and by his early seventies the mere proximity of organic solvents made him acutely ill. He was not a versatile artist; and it was his technique with oil paints that was widely admired. What saved him from ending his life as an invalid and perhaps a pauper was the introduction to France, a generation earlier, of a new and beguiling medium.

In its refined form (in which it could rival both oil paint and water colour) pastels were the invention of the Venetian lady artist Rosalba Carriera. She began experimenting with them as a child, one of three gifted daughters of a poor shopkeeper, and, at twenty-three, caused a sensation with her charming portrait of the mistress of Count Fernando Nicoli of Bologna. Over the next twenty years her workshop became one of the most highly patronised in Europe; the more remarkable since, as a good Venetian and a dutiful daughter, she refused to travel.[35] It was the death of her father and the fabled wealth of Pierre Crozat which eventually persuaded her to venture abroad and to make Paris her first destination.[36] Every circumstance combined to

[33] The term originated in the eighteenth century when hatters had to work their felt in a haze of hot mercury vapour. Like workers in ormolu, they almost invariably developed chronic mercury poisoning by middle age, characterised by uncoordinated movements, a balletic gait and the uttering of involuntary and incoherent exclamations. They were a familiar sight in the streets of London and Paris.

[34] Despite the lavish use of such potentially noxious heavy metals as lead, cobalt and cadmium, industrial poisoning among artists was apparently rare. Even Chardin's allergy may have been due to non-specific dust rather than organic solvents. Apart from the spectacles perched on his nose (which seem to be quite strong), there is no evidence that he suffered from lead poisoning, or amaurosis (blindness) due to lead, as has been studiously copied from book to book.

[35] In recognition of her services to art she was the first woman to be elected to the Accademia di San Luca of Venice in 1705, when she was thirty.

[36] Pierre Crozat, Baron de Thiers, was a somewhat mysterious self-made businessman who became one of France's richest men. He also became an avid collector and patronised Chardin among others.

make the visit a resounding success.[37] She arrived at a time when the Regent and his court were furiously dismantling the rigidities and pomposities of the previous reign; and the new medium – light, quick, and elegant – could have been invented for them. From the moment her elegant portrait of the young King was unveiled, the grandees of Versailles, as well as the debauchees of the Palais Royale, queued up to place commissions with her. Her success with fellow artists was no less spectacular. Brushing aside their own constitution, the Académie made her an honorary member and invited her to set up a new course devoted to her technique. By the time she left (amid tearful farewells and promises to come again),[38] the new medium had taken root; and two of its greatest practitioners were to flourish in France over the next fifty years.

The first, Maurice-Quentin de La Tour, was five years younger than Chardin; but by the time they met – both were then in their twenties – the younger man had already been through more scrapes, escapades and changes of fortune than the older would pack into a lifetime. He was handsome, witty and charmingly eccentric, and for twenty-five years the most sought-after portrait painter in France.[39] Chardin sponsored his membership to the Académie and, despite their diametrically opposed temperaments, they remained firm friends. But of course, so long as Chardin abstained from portraits and pastels, they were in no sense rivals. To do so was no hardship for the older man. He was not by nature an experimenter and the idea of challenging an established star of Maurice-Quentin's lustre would have horrified him. Indeed, despite his growing allergy to oils and the possibility that pastels might offer an escape route, he would never have become the

[37] She arrived in Paris in 1720 aged forty-five, still a fine figure of a woman, accompanied by her mother, her unmarried sister, a maid, a cook, a fiercely mustachioed bodyguard and mountainous luggage. Among the last a specially constructed leather trunk contained over five thousand chalks (soon to be known as pastels) specially made for her in Rome. She stayed for a year and a half.

[38] She never did return: indeed she left Venice only once after her trip to Paris, to go to Vienna at the pressing invitation of the Emperor, Charles VI. But she continued to work and her reputation remained undimmed both as an artist and as a person of charm and generosity. She developed bilateral cataracts in her late seventies and two operations were only partially successful. She died in 1758, aged eighty-three.

[39] At different times in his life and in different documents he spelt his name in at least four different ways, the confusion being aggravated by the greater fame of his near namesake, Georges de La Tour (1593–1652). There was also a more obscure eighteenth-century painter who called himself François-Xavier Latour. The spelling adopted here follows the suggestion of C. Debrie, Maurice-Quentin's biographer and curator of the museum dedicated to him in St-Quentin. See *Maurice-Quentin de La Tour* (St-Quentin, 1991). Among others he painted the only known portrait of Chardin in middle age (other than the self-portraits and an uninspired engraving by Cochin). It is now in the Louvre.

second greatest exponent of the medium had Maurice-Quentin not gone mad at the age of fifty. By the time Chardin had to abandon oil painting to stay alive, his erstwhile colleague was a harmless lunatic.

Portraits were not an entirely new departure for Chardin. He had tried to establish himself as a portraitist in his forties and fifties, mainly for financial reasons, but with scant success. The critics ignored his first attempts. When he persisted, they openly expressed their disapproval. Commissioned portraits were the jealously guarded professional enclave of a few, not to be entered by painters of dead hares and cabbages. Resignedly Chardin returned to his old métier of still lives and domestic scenes. But in his seventies, experimenting with a new technique, he felt free to paint what he liked. He was no longer trying to become fashionable or to make a killing. The sitters he chose were his wife, friends, servants, himself – people of no social consequence. Nor did he make any attempt to conform to conventions of pose, dress and background. The idea of flattering such sitters or commemorating their virtues and accomplishments was laughable. Of contemporary critics only Diderot welcomed the venture, and even he did so with a shade less than his usual enthusiasm. Others expressed their admiration at the "tenacity" of a sick old man approaching eighty but perhaps wished that he would retire gracefully.

It was left to the Goncourts and Thoré a hundred years later to make up for this tepid reception. "Go to the Louvre", the Goncourts urged their readers,

> and look at the two portraits in which this veteran progenitor of a mighty oeuvre depicts himself [Plate 6] and his wife. What astonishing images! The work is so violent and so passionate, the density, the hammerings and dabbings, the scratches, the thickness of the chalk, the strokes spread with such freedom, the boldness which marries seemingly unmarriagable tones ... the assurance with which he throws colours onto the paper in all their harshness and which yet, as we step back a few paces, blend, fuse and become luminous ... and then, amazingly, we have before us real living flesh with its creases, pores and sheen and the soft bloom of a healthy skin.[40]

The Goncourts deserve much credit for rediscovering Chardin at a time when eighteenth-century French painting was unfashionable, but Chardin's skin in his late seventies did not have "a healthy bloom" and he was too honest an artist to disguise it.

Chardin's portraits in pastels – or "studies of heads" as he called them in order not to provoke the portraitist Mafia – are astonishing, even if they do not show the same throwaway insights as Maurice-Quentin's sketches. They do not in fact exploit the special qualities of the medium – lightness and

[40] J. and E. Goncourt *L'art du XVIIIe siècle* (Paris, (1859–75), i, p. 128.

spontaneity. Thoré called them "oil paintings executed in pastels; but executed with what astonishing mastery! ... They compress a lifetime's study even if the study was in a different genre. One would be tempted to describe them as 'still lives of people' if they were not so intensely alive." [41] But so were Chardin's still lives of fruit and bread.

Of course the output of his last years was small even compared to the modest size of his oeuvre in his physical prime. But what do numbers matter at this level of artistry? The last pastels are rarely reproduced and may be neglected in standard art histories. His *Head of an Old Woman* in the Musée des Beaux-Arts in Besançon has been compared to Rembrandt's; but Rembrandt was Rembrandt and Chardin was Chardin and never more different than in their old age except in their complete mastery of their craft. Chardin at eighty could still portray youth and also childhood, showing its innocence, its confidence and its mischief in his *Young Girl* and *Young Boy*.[42] There is in those works not a trace of the saccharine that makes Greuze's portraits of the same age group so hard to take. They are simply, "comment le dire?", Diderot artfully pretended to search for the right words in his review of Chardin's last pastels. "Ah oui. La beauté tout simple." And of course they are quintessentially and gloriously French, just as Gainsborough's portrait of his daughters (painted about the same time) are unmistakably and gloriously English.

He was past eighty when he exhibited the *Portrait of a Young Lackey*, in the Salon.[43] He could still paint sitting down and with his swollen legs resting on a high stool, but he was too weak to attend in person when the King and his family visited the show on the eve of its official opening.[44] The painting enchanted Madame Victoire, one of the King's maiden aunts, and the painter's long-standing admirer.[45] She sent a message: Monsieur Chardin

[41] T. Thoré (W. Bürger) "Exposition de tableaux de l'école française, tirées de collections d'amateurs", *Gazette des Beaux-Arts*, 7 (1860) p. 258.

[42] Both are still in private collections. Pastels on paper are far more fragile than canvases; and more than one of Chardin's late works may have disappeared or may even have been deliberately destroyed during the Revolution.

[43] Together with four others, one of them his penultimate self-portrait. The others have not been traced with any certainty.

[44] Louis XVI had succeeded his grandfather, Louis XV, in 1774.

[45] As "a daughter of France" (that is a legitimate daughter of Louis XV), Madame Victoire was one of the four sisters whose exalted birth made them virtually unmarriageable. "Madame Victoire is the one who is tall and fat", Horace Walpole wrote, to distinguish her from Mesdames Adelaide, Sophie and Louise. She was also kindly and artistic: the young Mozart, whom she dandled on her knees during the Mozarts' visit to Paris, dedicated his sonatinas K6 and K7 to her. She survived the Revolution and died in Italy aged ninety-two. *The Young Lackey* was at that time still in her possession but has since disappeared.

must let her purchase it before it could be snatched up by another collector. "But no", the message came back, "Madame must accept it as a humble gift of the utmost insignificance, an unworthy token of an old man's profound gratitude and inexpressible bliss at having given Madame a moment's pleasure." "But no." "But yes." Of course in the end she accepted the gift; but next day the Comte d'Affry called on the artist to deliver a gold presentation box with Madame's portrait enamelled on the inside of the lid.

Royalty has its uses. Perhaps the present made up for the slights Chardin had suffered in his last years. "After the visit", the academician Renou reported back to his council, "our esteemed colleague, Chardin, was carried back to his studio to complete the self-portrait which he had begun but had nearly abandoned." [46] The swelling of his legs and thighs has now reached almost as far as the trunk, despite the application of leeches and cupping the day before.[47] But both he and Mme Chardin were cheered by Madame Victoire's gift and invited Renou to toast her good health in an excellent Burgundy. "Like Rousseau, he believed that a dying man should never seek to frighten or distress visitors. During his final days he continued to be shaved every morning." [48] His last painting was still on his easel, by all but his own exacting standards finished, when, few days later, he received the sacrament and died. "His passing", Cochin wrote, "was like the end of a beautiful day." [49]

Except in his art, and even there almost imperceptibly, Chardin was the least adventurous of the great artists; and almost all the stations of his long life can be encompassed today by a stroll lasting less than an hour.[50] Crossing and recrossing the river to observe chronology, one can inspect the site of the house in the Rue de Seine where he was born, pause before crossing at the corner of the Rue du Four where he spent his childhood, and perhaps have coffee in the Place Dauphine where (at the northern end, near the Pont Neuf) he first exhibited. Back on the Left Bank, one can look at the site of the house in the Rue Princesse which came to him in his second marriage, walk to the Institut where he became an assiduous attender of meetings, and admire the Neoclassical pile of St-Sulpice where he and his wife worshipped. Then it will be time to return to the Louvre where he lived and died, and lastly to say a prayer in the lovely church of St-Germain

[46] Quoted by J. Leclerc, "Les dernier autoportraits de Chardin", *Art français*, 3 (1947), p. 127.
[47] Whatever the underlying cause, he clearly died of congestive heart failure.
[48] C. N. Cochin, *Essai sur la vie de M. Chardin* (Rouen, 1875), p. 427.
[49] Ibid., p. 428.
[50] He never travelled further than Fontainebleau.

l'Auxerrois,[51] for centuries the parish church of the palace, where, on a fine spring day in 1779, he was buried. A Mass dedicated to the memory of artists is still celebrated there every year.

[51] Boucher, Nattier, the two Coustous, Coysevaux and the architects Soufflot, Gabriel *père* and Le Vaux are among those buried there in addition to Chardin. (Not mentioned in the guidebook is the fact that it was the bell of St-Germain which on 14 August 1571 gave the signal for the St Bartholomew's Day Massacre.)

# 5

# *Goya*

Sacred monsters were the contribution of the Romantic Age to Europe's bestiary. They were not common, either then or later, but they riveted the attention of their contemporaries and their memory lingered. They came in all shapes and sizes. Rousseau was an archetype. Beethoven, Napoleon and Byron were authentic examples. An Olympian himself, Goethe created in Faust the fictional prototype. In painting David displayed many of the essential traits. Goya surpassed him.[1] They were all not only and by definition monstrous but also unrepentantly so. "What do a few thousand lives matter to a man of destiny like me?", Napoleon asked Metternich. Byron was indeed mad, bad and dangerous to know and stoked with relish his evil reputation. Beethoven was a sharp-practiser in his business dealings and drove his nephew to suicide while bemoaning that his solicitude was insufficiently appreciated. David sent his former patrons, including "the pride of France, an ornament of science and the noblest of men", to the guillotine while uttering high-minded platitudes about universal brotherhood.[2] And Goya was, in modern parlance, a collaborator; and he could not have created the most horrific images of human degradation without a taste for it.[3] Many had physical deformities or terrible illnesses to match their characters but they never invited pity and rarely got it.

But they were sacred as well as monstrous. Napoleon's eagles carried

[1] Contrary to legend, the two almost certainly never met.

[2] He was referring to Lavoisier, whose praises he sang when he was being commissioned to paint the double portrait of the great chemist and his wife, now in the Metropolitan Museum, New York. The charges against Lavoisier were totally trumped up: his real crime was to expose Marat's scientific vapourings to the ridicule they well deserved.

[3] He had in his private collection a pile of drawings of couples making love, brigands stripping and raping women, naked men and women fighting, nuns and monks in obscene poses, and diseased and crippled figures; and, unlike the erotica of Titian, Turner, Ingres, Rembrandt and Rubens, much of Goya's has a strong sadistic element. (De Sade's *Justine*, published in 1791, had a wide circulation among wealthy collectors in Spain. Goya may have provided illustrations for it.) Far from wishing these sheets to be destroyed, as he approached death he specifically bequeathed them to his son, Javier. See F. Nördstrom, *Goya, Saturn and Melancholy: Studies in the Art of Goya* (Stockholm, 1962); S. Symmons, *Goya in Pursuit of Patronage* (London, 1988).

the lofty ideals of the French Revolution into the most obscurantist corners of Europe; and in the millions whom he sacrificed he also inspired selfless heroism.[4] Beethoven composed music that overwhelmed even those defrauded by him. Lord Byron inspired love in foreign lands as no Englishman of unblemished character had done before him or has since. David could transform the death of a mountebank into an icon.[5] On the stage Faust still calls forth purifying tears of joy. And Goya remains not only a great purveyor of horror but also the most liberating artist of the modern age. Their secret remains well kept. They were the first modern stars and mystery was part of their stardom. Many seemed to revel in self-revelation, but what they chose to reveal teases more than it enlightens. Goya's letters to his boyhood friend, Martin Zapater – "my dearest Martin", "Martin of my Soul", "Martin my best friend!" – are in turn boastful, exultant, despairing, depressed, indiscreet and abusive; but they rarely shed light on his innermost thoughts.[6] Even today, the more one strains to make sense of his actions, the more illogical they seem: he is admired – he remains the greatest painters' painter – but few claim truly to understand him.[7]

Francisco José de Goya y Lucientes was born in 1746 in a small village near Saragossa, the capital of Aragon. His father was a master gilder, his mother belonged to the impoverished Aragonese nobility. The Pious Fathers in Saragossa educated him free of charge. Then his gift for sketching caught the eye of a regional grandee, the Conde de Fuentes, and he was apprenticed to a local painter. One cannot see him excelling at washing brushes and priming canvases. After a brief apprenticeship and a stormy first spell in

---

[4] His charisma continued to inspire not just hero-worshipping Romantic youths; it also overwhelmed the world-weary cynicism of Heine, the patriotic distaste of Schumann and the Russianness of Chaliapin to produce, in the greatest recording of *Die beiden Grenadiere*, the perfect answer to those who still profess to disbelieve the Napoleonic mystique.

[5] Almost every detail of his *Marat Assassinated* was a calculated invention.

[6] See F. Goya, *Cartas a Martin Zapater*, ed. X. de Salas and M. Agueda (Madrid, 1982).

[7] His recognition in the English-speaking world has been comparatively recent. The Goya Exhibition, *Goya and his Times*, of 1963 in the Royal Academy of London, with an excellent catalogue, was an eye-opener to many. Notable contributions to the Goya literature today in English include T. Harris, *Goya: Engravings and Lithographs*, 2 volumes (Oxford, 1963); F. J. Sánchez Cantón, *Goya*, translated by G. Pillement (London, 1964); N. Glendinning, *Goya and his Critics* (London, 1967); D. B. Wyndham Lewis, *The World of Goya* (London, 1968); P. Gassier and J. Wilson, *The Life and Complete Works of Goya* (New York, 1971); J. W. Bareau, *Goya's Prints* (London, 1981); E. Harris, *Goya* (2nd edn, London, 1994); and J. Tomlinson, *Francisco Goya y Lucientes* (London, 1996). In German, the catalogue of the exhibition in 1980 in the Kunsthalle, Hamburg, *Das Zeitalter der Revolutionen, 1789–1830*, is wide-ranging and informative.

Madrid, he departed to Italy. There he won an honourable mention but no prizes in a painting competition in Parma and, more in character, attempted to abduct a novice nun from her convent in Rome. He failed. Back in Saragossa he obtained his first commission: to collaborate with Francisco Bayeu, painting the frescoes of the cathedral of the Madonna del Pilar. He also painted Bayeu's portrait − the first unmistakable Goya masterpiece − and married Bayeu's sister, Josefa.[8] He was to remain her devoted and unfaithful husband, capturing her quiet charm on canvas more than once and always affectionately.

In 1776 he began his climb to the top. He was invited by Raphael Mengs, Carlos III's artistic factotum, to join the recently reorganised royal tapestry manufactory as a designer.[9] He produced for them more than sixty cartoons over the next twelve years, a ravishing panorama of the Spanish Rococo in its autumnal glory.[10] But the sacred monster was never far below the surface. Weavers trying to reproduce the riches and subtlety of his palette returned *The Blind Guitarist* to Mengs, demanding simplification. Goya's answer was to send them an even more complex design, *The Fair of Madrid*. His treatment of his director and even of his royal master was no less cavalier. Mengs he ridiculed as a plodder. The King, who wanted carpets as well as tapestries, he ignored. Obstreperous artists were no novelty even in hierarchical Spain. What was new was the cult of sacred monsters. Once Goya's genius was recognised, his boorishness was greeted with squeals of delight.

The one who squealed loudest was Maria Teresa Caietana (to pick her three favourites from her numerous Christian names),[11] thirteenth Duchess of Alba in her own right.[12] She was beautiful, generous, artistic, sterile and,

[8] Francisco was one of three Bayeu brothers, all painters and of marginally more aristocratic descent than Goya. (The blood of no two families in Spain was of exactly the same shade of *limpieza*.) The portrait may have been painted after Francisco's death.

[9] After Murillo's death in 1681 (by falling off a ladder), the Spanish art world was dominated by three foreigners for a hundred years: Michel-Louis van Loo, Philip V's import from France; Gianbattista Tiepolo of the Venetian painting dynasty; and Anton-Raphael Mengs of mixed Saxon-Danish-Bohemian ancestry − the dullest of the three. His insipid artistry was redeemed by his many worthy enthusiasms, including his long-suffering patronage of Goya.

[10] See J. Held, *Die Genrebilder der Madrider Teppichmanufaktur und die Anfänge Goyas* (Berlin, 1971). Some of the pictures, such as the idyllic *Wine Harvest Time*, are of Goya and his extended family, including both Josefa and the Duchess of Alba.

[11] For those in search of a girl's name: Maria del Pilar Teresa Manuela Caietana Margerita Leonora Sebastiana Barbara Ana Joaquina Francisca de Paola Francisca de Asis Francisca de Sales Javiera Andrea Abelina Sinforosa Benita Bernarda Petronila de Alcantara Dominga Micaela Rafaela Gabriela Venancia Idylla Fernanda Bibiana Vicenta Catalina.

[12] She had been born in one of the vast Alba palaces in Madrid, only grandchild of the twelfth Duke of Alba, captain general and premier grandee of Spain, descendent of Alba, the butcher of Holland. Her mother, the Duchess of Huescar in her own right, was one of the

at times, more than a little crazy. She was also intermittently besotted with Goya, just as she was besotted with the little black girl she picked up at a country fair and treated as her daughter; a half-witted old friar who went into amusing epileptic fits; Pedro Romero, Spain's champion toreador; her pet monkey; and (if Goya's cartoon of her is to be believed) a swarm of occasional lovers. Goya made savage fun of her, showing her tearing her hair out or flying off on a cloud of easily recognisable grotesques, though few now believe that she was the clothed and naked Maya. Their exciting and excruciating relationship lasted till the Duchess's death at forty-two.[13]

But anything the Duchess of Alba possessed, her rival the Duchess of Osuña had to possess too;[14] and Queen Maria Luisa, who could never decide which of Spain's rival duchesses she abominated more, felt that she, together with her complaisant husband, Carlos IV, and her cherubic lover-in-chief, Godoy, Generalissimo and Prince of Peace, had to possess it first of all.[15] The result was a lucrative escalation of royal commissions, culminating in the great line-up of Aranjuez: the whole of the royal menagerie, complete with paramour and first artist, never to be surpassed in brilliance and brutality.[16]

country's leading bluestockings, not entirely uninfluenced by that textbook of advanced lunacy, Rousseau's *Emile*. Paintings by Correggio and Velasquez (now mostly in the National Gallery in London) adorned her nursery. At thirteen she was married to the Marquis de Villafranca, a long-nosed, melancholy-looking aristocrat and music lover, in Goya's portrait of slightly bilious complexion. Her thousands of servants adored her; and she left all her vast fortune to be distributed among them. The will was successfully contested by the King and Godoy and duly annulled. See J. Esquerra del Bayo, *La Duquesa de Alba y Goya* (Madrid, 1959).

[13] Her sudden death gave rise to persistent rumours of poisoning, not laid to rest (and even then not entirely) until her body was exhumed in 1945 by order of the then Duke of Alba. The findings were inconclusive but consistent with abdominal tuberculosis. The report was published by three pathologists, B. Soler, P. Piga and D. Perez y Petino, *La Duquesa de Alba y su tiempo* (Madrid, 1945).

[14] The salon of the Duchess of Osuña challenged in wit, sparkle, polish, corruption and excess any to be found in contemporary France (which meant anywhere in the civilised world).

[15] Carlos III, the most successful of Spain's Bourbon Kings and in many respects a model of the enlightened monarch, died in 1788. His son and heir, Carlos IV, portly, good-natured and dull, was one of history's most complaisant husbands. His Queen, also a Bourbon from Naples, was ungallantly described by the French ambassador as "a woman who concentrated more guile and perfidy in her person than anybody alive".

Godoy started his career as a cadet in the Queen's bodyguard known to Madrilleros as *los chocolateros*. He has had a bad press both as a person and as a statesman; but it was his bad luck to be pitted against Napoleon, and he was a good friend to Goya.

[16] There was never any need for the Kings and Queens of Spain to be represented as anything other than what they looked like: it was only parvenus like Napoleon who had to

How far Goya, the spoilt pet of duchesses, welcomed the French Revolution is uncertain. The news was probably overshadowed for him by a brief illness which left him totally deaf for the rest of his life.[17] It has been said that the impact of a sudden complete loss of hearing cannot be understood by anybody who has not experienced it. It has also been suggested that it may enhance visual acuity. There is no objective evidence for such a compensatory balance between the senses. Goya was approaching what must have seemed like the peak of a glittering career; and he was devastated. Yet six months later he was back at work. A few circumstances worked in his favour. He lived in a world which, despite distant rumbles from across the Pyrenees, was still rigidly ordered. If God in His wisdom had placed an amiable buffoon (or, as happened a few generations earlier, a gibbering idiot) on the throne of Spain to rule over His chosen people, it was not for His chosen people to question His wisdom.[18] And what was true of the King was also true of the King's servants. Deaf, dumb or demented, the King's first painter would remain the King's first painter until it pleased the King to dismiss him from that position. There was no question of that. It was also a world which, under a thin veneer of reason (always a mistrusted foreign importation in Spain), was still medieval. Its bigotry and superstitions may have irked a self-proclaimed rationalist like Goya; but it took physical deformities, disabilities and diseases in its stride. Goya was to be called *El Sordo*, the Deaf

be shown as demigods or indeed (by Ingres) as a reincarnation of Jupiter. Goya certainly made no effort. The lady with the luminous eyes staring like a malign owl is the Infanta Maria Josefa, the King's sister. The one whose face is turned away is the future bride of the Prince of Asturias, the future Ferdinand VII: her identity was still a state secret. Godoy is shown in the background, as is the artist. Only the children are charming, as always in Goya's paintings.

[17] In historical diagnoses the golden rule of clinical practice holds: common diseases are common while rare but interesting diseases are interesting but rare. But in Goya's case an eminent London ear nose and throat surgeon, Sir Terence Cawthorne, showed convincingly that his deafness was almost certainly due to a virus infection so rare that even other eminent London ear nose and throat surgeons had never heard of it. It is known by the name of those who first described it in modern times as the Vogt-Koianaghi or Vogt-Koianaghi-Harada syndrome, and may have been recognised by the Arabic physician Ali ibn Isa as long ago as 940 A.D. It can attack the eye as well as the ear and is sometimes accompanied by meningeal inflammation and may lead to post-encephalitic personality changes. See E. M. Pattison, "Uveomeningoencephalitis Syndrome", *Archives of Neurology*, 12 (1968), p. 197; T. Cawthorne, "Goya's Deafness", *Proceedings of the Royal Society of Medicine*, 55 (1962), p. 213. Goya's sight was severely affected during the acute phase of the illness but later improved, as did his attacks of giddiness.

[18] The last Habsburg King of Spain, Carlos II "The Bewitched", epileptic and feeble-minded, held Europe's predatory powers at bay for thirty-four years simply by staying alive. His long-awaited death was the signal for the outbreak of the War of the Spanish Succession.

Man, by all and sundry; but, if there was no compassion attached to the sobriquet, there was no stigma of strangeness attached to it either.[19] Life at its most ordinary was strange enough.

The ordeal did not pass without leaving a legacy. At forty-eight Goya embarked on a series of "cabinet pictures" – works for private enjoyment, not for public exhibition – which lampooned the superstitions, perversions and cruelties of the age with a new and blistering venom. Of course he had done it before: his depictions of witchcraft, torture and violence were already treasured by collectors. But there was a new bite to his latest etchings; and surprisingly, for nothing ages more quickly than satire, they remain as sharp as they must have been when first published. What made his irony so deadly is hard to pinpoint. He was less inventive than Bosch, less original than Hogarth, and without the burning indignation of Daumier or even (at their best) the German Expressionists. He was never really funny. His captions were uniformly banal. And many of his targets, the Inquisition among them, were sitting ducks by the time he squirted his poison at them.[20] But his gift for the flickering line, for the simple and yet sickeningly effective juxta-position of light and shade remains unique. In No. 17 of the *Caprichos* a pretty young woman is straightening her stocking. An old crone looks on. The caption merely says: "It fits nicely". Of course the image has given an erotic thrill to countless voyeurs before Goya (and since); but nobody before him had exploited it with his mastery.

> Goya, cauchemar plein de choses inconnus,
> De foetus qu'on fait cuire au milieu des sabbats,
> De vielles au miroir et d'enfants toutes nues
> Pour tenter des démons ajustant leurs bas.[21]

It inspired Delacroix but deeply shocked John Ruskin. Goya's monsters too had a special quality. What made them unbearable to Baudelaire was their naturalness. "They have been born, they are viable, they are even well-formed. All their contortions, all these bestial faces, all those diabolical grimaces are

---

[19] The suddenness of the onset of the illness was also probably preferable to a slow but inexorable progression; and, after the acute phase which must have been horrible, he was spared the ordeal of ghostly and insistent noises which plagued Swift, Beethoven and Smetana. But most important was undoubtedly the patient's robust faith in himself, which was strengthened rather than weakened by the ordeal.

[20] The Inquisition was effectively powerless by the last quarter of the eighteenth century. It was officially abolished in 1813 and its records were destroyed by the last Grand Inquisitor. The Duchess of Osuña, her fragile beauty and staunch Catholicism notwithstanding, was an avid collector of Goya's most scurrilous drawings.

[21] C. Baudelaire, 'Les phares' in *Les Fleurs de Mal* (Paris, 1857), p. 86.

us." [22] A first sight of a strange animal in the zoo can sometimes suddenly induce in visitors the same terrifying sense of recognition. Many of his prints mocked his closest friends and patrons. They loved it. When the Inquisition threatened to confiscate his plates, the King conferred immunity on them by buying the rights to publication. The much-mocked (and much-maligned) Godoy took time off from playing diplomatic games and leading the King's armies against mostly invisible enemies to learn a sign language, so he could converse with his favourite painter. One cannot see many modern generalissimos doing that.[23]

But time for the old regime was running out. In March 1808 a bewildered Carlos IV, his Queen and Godoy were summoned to Bayonne by Napoleon. The Emperor had aged badly: the once charismatic heir to the Revolution was now a gross, middle-aged bully. In calculated gutter language he berated his visitors for three hours.[24] Then he sent them packing.[25] The same day an army of 40,000 French guardians of the peace crossed the Pyrenees. A fortnight later the self-appointed deliverers of hag-ridden Spain entered Madrid. With Murat, the swaggering son of a Gascon innkeeper, and Berthier, dripping with jewels, at the head of an invincible army, they were a dazzling sight.[26] Or rather, they might have dazzled most capitals in Europe. But not Madrid. Within a month the most backward and formerly the most ill-governed of Napoleon's conquests was alight with rebellion.

---

[22] C. Baudelaire, *The Painter of Modern Life and Other Essays*, translated by J. Mayne (London, 1864), p. 192.

[23] For some years Godoy tried hard to pose as Napoleon's ally against their common enemy, England. The only result of this misconceived policy was that the Spanish as well as the French fleet was annihilated at Trafalgar. He also persuaded the King to purchase David's famous picture of Napoleon on horseback for the stupendous sum of 9000 reales payable in advance. (The picture was never delivered.) None of this deflected Napoleon's ire at what he represented as the wilful evasion by Spain of the unenforceable Continental Blockade against England.

[24] "What a pity that so great a man is so appallingly ill-mannered", Talleyrand famously remarked as he hobbled out of the imperial audience chamber after a similar tirade; but none of the Spaniards is known to have protested.

[25] Ferdinand VII gave a foretaste of his royal character when he fully collaborated with Napoleon in dethroning his parents and sending them and Godoy into exile. It did him no good. He too was summarily dismissed a few months later.

[26] Napoleon had no more dashing cavalry commander; but off the battlefield the marshal was a blockhead. In 1808 Napoleon, whose sister Caroline he married, made him King of Naples. During the Hundred Days (between Napoleon's first abdication and Waterloo) he unerringly backed the wrong side. In 1815 he mounted an expedition against the restored Bourbons of Naples. He was easily defeated, caught and shot.

Berthier too was of humble origin and became Napoleon's dependable quartermaster. He was created Duc de Neuchâtel but submitted to the Bourbons after Napoleon's first abdication. On hearing of Napoleon's return from Elba he committed suicide.

Goya was seventy-five when he recorded two events which had occurred eight years earlier and inscribed the canvases with the dates: 2 May and 3 May 1808. He had probably had a ringside view of the first.[27] A few days later he was taken round the site of the second, the Montana del Principe Pio, just outside the city. The first is a conventional Rubenesque battle scene, full of virtuoso detail but forgettable. The second is also conventional but, once seen, can never be forgotten. It is conventional because, ever since Assyrian sculptors carved into stone serried ranks of archers slaughtering their enemies, brute military force has always been represented by stylised, almost abstract repetition. This pattern has always contrasted with the disorderly huddle of the victims. In Goya's painting, as on the walls of Nineveh, the victors are perfectly aligned, totally disciplined, without a flicker of individual human interest – and deadly. The victims lie about like sacks of rubbish, defeated and futile. But not, in Goya's incandescent vision, completely futile. The death of the man whose white shirt ignites the scene is both a crucifixion and a resurrection. The message is not specifically Christian or even religious. It is a universal affirmation of the ultimate triumph of the individual against all the odds over dehumanised evil.[28]

Yet even sympathetic biographers, especially those writing in the shadow of the Second World War, have felt embarrassed by Goya's record after the

[27] At the time – Josefa was still alive – he occupied the first floor of a house on the corner of the Puerta del Sol and the Calle del Arsenal, now demolished.

A few weeks earlier the Madrilleros had heartily acclaimed the downfall of Godoy; but the godless French could never impress them with their swagger. On the morning of 2 May French cavalry descended the Calle de Alcala and drew a crowd. They found a travelling coach drawn up in front of the Royal Palace guarded by a military cordon. The realisation quickly dawned that the last member of the royal family still in Madrid, the Infante Francisco de Paula (the little boy standing between the King and Queen in Goya's Aranjuez line-up), was to be spirited away to join Napoleon's other "guests". That was not to be borne. The crowd surged forward. The French officer in command gave the order to fire. The first martyrs of the rebellion fell and died. In less than a hour the quarter was in an uproar. Murat ordered a detachment of Mamelukes to the scene. Some were cut to pieces by an assortment of homely but surprisingly effective weapons. More of the populace were trampled and killed. "Then I ordered a hundred people to be rounded up and shot", the marshal reported to his master, "before sitting down to my belated dinner. The country has been taught a salutary lesson." But it was not all the country that had been taught. Napoleon was soon left under no delusion.

[28] According to the guide to the Prado, the paintings were completed in 1814 but were not shown in public till 1870; but it is inconceivable that Manet did not see the Executions of 3 May, on his visit to Madrid in 1865, before he painted his own Execution of the Emperor Maximilian. Manet made his painting a personal rather than an universal human tragedy simply by separating one of the execution squad from the rest.

events of May 1808. His second great series of etchings, *The Disasters of War*, the most horrifying record of civil strife in art, leaves no doubt as to where his sympathies lay. In drawing after drawing it is his countrymen and countrywomen who are impaled, dismembered, raped, hanged and shovelled into mass graves – as indeed they were. There are no formal military engagements, no elegant skirmishes, no galloping cuirassiers. Nor does the artist spare any sympathy for the invaders. But while in the privacy of his studio he recorded the suffering of his people, in public he accepted lucrative commissions and even a decoration from King Joseph Bonaparte,[29] assiduously attending to his business interests, and even helping to select works of art from the Spanish royal collection to be dispatched to Paris as the spoils of war. (But outrage is confounded, as usual with Goya. Surveying the list, one has to conclude that he and his two fellow commissioners, Maella and Napoli, were either wholly without artistic judgement, which seems unlikely, or that they deliberately sabotaged Napoleon's wishes. Not one of the treasures of the royal palaces – not a Velasquez, a Titian, a Claude or a Rubens – was included.) He was in short a collaborator, the equivalent, if not of a Quisling or a Laval, at least of a Knut Hamsun or Ezra Pound; and his petition to the provincial government in 1814, after the French had been safely expelled, to be allowed to "perpetuate by means of my brush the most notable and heroic actions of our glorious insurrection against the Tyrant of Europe" is faintly nauseating. But there is no equivalence. This was still the age of sacred monsters; and, though Ferdinand VII, restored to his ancestral throne after Napoleon's fall, playfully admonished his favourite painter that he deserved to be garrotted, the artist was restored to his old position at Court at an increased salary.

Perhaps it is Goya's modernity which makes one forget that his Spain was not Nazi-occupied Europe and his victims were not the villagers of Guernica.[30] For generations the country had been ruled with staggering incompetence by a class above the law, with whom he had little reason to identify. But neither was he one of the ordinary people who in a heroic frenzy of xenophobia had risen against the invaders. Perhaps the most cruel and personally revealing sheet of *The Disasters of War* shows a corpse, already half decomposed, rising from the grave and bearing the message: *Nada* – Nothing. It was not for nothing though. Unbeknown to Goya himself, he was in his old age becoming one of a new breed of men – not yet of

[29] As an individual Joseph Bonaparte was neither cruel nor particularly greedy, and his lot as his younger brother's puppet was not an enviable one. He tried to please the Spaniards by establishing a new order (popularly known as the Egg Plant), which he also bestowed on Goya. His efforts were unsuccessful. He died in 1844, aged seventy-six, in Florence.

[30] Yet Goya was much in Picasso's mind when he painted his masterpiece.

women – who were emerging from the European undergrowth in the wake of the Napoleonic marches and countermarches: an international aristocracy of talent. From now on their voice would be heard in art, music and literature, faintly but insistently rising above the bleatings of reactionary politicians. Of course each proclaimed something slightly different in his own medium – Blake, Pushkin and Petőfi in poetry, Beethoven in music and Delacroix in painting – but they shared a deep unspoken conviction that, after their battles had been fought and won, there would be no more fawning on capricious princes, no more begging for archiepiscopal favours, no more courting of royal mistresses, and no more upholding of a degrading social order by the geniuses of the age. Sooner or later, they would celebrate and sometimes acknowledge their debt to Goya.

That lay in the future. In the present, life in Spain even for the King's First Painter was not easy. The French Bourbons had, in Talleyrand's famous phrase, learnt nothing and forgotten nothing. The same could not be said of their Iberian cousins. In obsequious captivity Ferdinand VII had forgotten nothing but had learnt many new tricks of misrule.[31] Soon the colonies in America, for centuries the only reliable source of income of the Spanish Crown, were in revolt; and in Spain itself there were ferocious uprisings. They were suppressed with a brutality which might have earned a disapproving *mou* even from Murat.[32]

Compared to such savageries, hardly less bloodcurdling than the disasters of the war against the French, the formalised slaughter of the bullring must have acted almost as a sedative.[33] In a series of etchings Goya, now in his late seventies, recorded its history and deadly skills as well as the mass hysteria which usually attended it. The *Tauromaquia* never attained the popularity of the *Caprichos* or *The Disasters of the War* and it is easy to see why. The format is small, the execution seemingly perfunctory, the overall effect almost tawdry. But by his eighth decade Goya was the complete master of etching. He understood as Rembrandt had before him, and perhaps only

---

[31] He spent the years between his deposition and his restoration in the charming Château de Valençay. His parents spent their not uncomfortable exile in various country villas in Italy, chosen for their hunting facilities.

[32] Even so, but for the armed intervention of Louis XVIII's French army under the Duc d'Angoulème, the King's nephew, the only successful military exertion of the Holy Alliance, combined with extravagant promises of a constitution (never to be kept), Ferdinand would have been toppled in 1823. After his successful campaign the Duc d'Angoulème reported to his uncle that Spain was "ungovernable".

[33] Bullfighting, a rite not a sport dating back to Moorish times, had been forbidden by both Philip V and Carlos III as dangerous; but it never disappeared. Although Goya incorporated a self-portrait in one of his bullfighting paintings, it is unlikely that he tried his luck in the bullring. But he was an addict and an aficionado.

Rembrandt, that the medium is the most heavily encoded of the visual arts and that, like all communications in code, it has to enlist the cooperation of the viewer. When that is forthcoming, the shapeless squiggles, scrapings, hatchings and blank areas can resolve themselves into deeply disturbing messages about life – or, in Goya's case, death. They encapsulate the waste and barrenness of individual destiny when pitched against overwhelming evil, but also the inevitable self-destruction of that evil. The work may leave some viewers cold and haunt others.

Eventually even the bulls failed in their anodyne duty. "I get so furious sometimes", the sickened artist wrote to Martin Zapater, "that I become unbearable even to myself."[34] In disgust – or self-disgust – he left his comfortable town house and withdrew, with only a manservant, to a kind of hermitage just outside the city boundaries of Madrid. The building, shielded by trees from intrusive eyes, was soon known to neighbours as the Quinta del Sordo, the Deaf Man's Cottage. Here he covered the walls of two rooms with the horrifying visions known today as the Black Paintings (Plate 7).[35] The meaning of some is still obscure; but that does not make them any less shocking.

> Suns sink on suns and systems crash
> Headlong, extinct, in one dark centre fall,
> And death and night and chaos mingle all.[36]

The first lethal fight between two men has been painted often enough. Goya alone, at his most horribly prophetic, painted what may prove to be the last: two men knee-deep in a quagmire, unable to move, bludgeoning each other to death in front of a landscape of total devastation.[37]

Goya was now an old man. In youth and triumphant middle age he had often mocked the infirmities and vanities of old age. He saw no reason to change his tune. Two wizened but still grinning and heavily made-up ex-beauties gaze into the mirror. Behind them hovers Father Time, broom in hand, smile on his face. "How's life?" And a bent, bearded eternal student hobbles along on two sticks. The sarcastic inscription echoes Michelangelo: "Aun aprendo", "Still I'm learning". But was he being wholly sarcastic? With Goya, one never knows. Grating self-contradictions were part of the inner core of sacred monsters. In the midst of the nightmare of the Black Paintings

---

[34] See Goya, *Cartas a Martin Zapater*, p. 178.

[35] See below, Chapter 18, pp. 256–57. See also P. E. Müller, *Goya's Black Paintings: Truth and Reason in Light and Liberty* (New York, 1948); and A. Malraux, *Saturne* (Paris, 1950).

[36] Erasmus Darwin, *Economy of Vegetation*, canto iv, lines 56–58.

[37] Described as "peaceful" by some Goya scholars.

he also painted his grandson, Mariano, conducting an imaginary orchestra, as happy and tender a portrait of a young man as Rembrandt's *Titus* or Renoir's *Coco*.[38] And the relentless and mordant mocker of priests and of all their mumbo-jumbo accepted a commission from the Pious Fathers of Madrid to paint a deeply felt altar-piece showing the last communion of the founder;[39] and he not only returned his payment to the monks but also added as a gift one of the most mysterious and spiritual *Agonies in the Garden* painted since Rembrandt. He also repainted some of the happy rustic scenes of his youth – a peasant girl with a pitcher, a knife-grinder, a blacksmith. The insouciance of youth and the Rococo charm have vanished but there is about these late recreations a simplicity and grandeur not seen before.

At seventy-six Goya also presented his medical adviser, Dr Arrieta, with his last *Self-Portrait* (Plate 8), showing himself in the grip of an attack of cardiac asthma.[40] It is one of the greatest medical documentaries ever painted. It is also a generous consolation piece to doctors who may feel hard done by when represented in art as incarnations of greed, pomposity and ignorance. Dr Arrieta was obviously not of that kind. Nor was he just a smart diagnostician and an effective prescriber of unguents and elixirs. As portrayed by Goya, he was something much rarer (then as now): a good doctor. The way he supports his patient, the look of kindly but controlled concern on his face, makes one feel that one would be glad to have him around in a serious illness. But more remarkable is the patient's portrayal of himself. No trained medical writer could better describe the agony of the illness. Yet nothing is exaggerated. The complexion is just slightly cyanosed and the posture of the upper body merely hints at the ineffectual effort of the respiratory muscles. The skin glistens with a light sheen of perspiration. The position of the head, the dishevelled hair, the slight parting of the lips and the fingers of the left hand plucking the bedclothes are perfect in their self-observation. So mesmeric are the clinical details that it takes time to realise that they are part of a great painting. The colours are dull in the light

[38] He had already painted a similarly affectionate picture of the foppish Javier, the only one of his and Josefa's four or five children to survive infancy.

[39] St Joseph of Calasance, a Spanish nobleman, who founded the Order of Pious Fathers (Piarists) in Rome in 1584 for the education of poor children. After a life of great hardship, borne with dignity, patience and faith, he died in 1648, aged ninety-two. The Order which educated Goya (and the present writer) still flourishes.

[40] The condition is related in name but not in cause to the more common bronchial asthma. Cardiac asthma is brought on by stagnant circulation in the lungs due to failure of the right ventricle of the heart to empty itself of blood. Whereas in bronchial asthma (due to spasms of the muscles of the bronchi) the difficulty is in expiration, in cardiac asthma it is mainly inspiration which becomes laboured. For some reason attacks of cardiac asthma tend to come on at night, as they did for Goya.

of an invisible source, perhaps an oil lamp reflected by a mirror; but, despite the limited range of tones, not just the skin, hair, eyes and lips but every scrap of material is alive. Shadowy faces loom up from the background. Family? Nurses? Ghosts in waiting? Never has a night seemed so long. Never has a caring arm around one's shoulder seemed so welcome. If there is anything to criticise here, it springs from foreknowledge. Looking at the painting today few doctors would give the patient more than a year or two to live, and those under constant medical supervision and a restricted lifestyle. In fact, Goya's sojourn in Bordeaux, his trip to Paris, several return trips to Madrid and some of his masterpieces still lay in the future.[41]

Goya's wife, Josefa, died during the French occupation in 1811. At seventy-four Goya invited Dona Leocadia Weiss, a distant relative and the estranged wife of a German merchant, to run his household and perhaps to warm his bed. The exact dates and details are uncertain; but it was during Señor Weiss's second petition for a separation that she presented him with a baby girl, Rosarito.

Four years later Goya applied to the King for six months' leave to take the waters in Plombières-les-Bains in the Vosges in France. He had no intention of going there: he was going into voluntary exile. Why? His motives remain obscure. He had, it is true, uncharacteristically revealed himself as a constitutionalist during Colonel Riego's abortive rebellion, but Ferdinand VII remained as stubbornly forgiving to his favourite painter as he was glassily vindictive to others. Goya's request was granted and his pension, payable to him in France, actually increased. But eighty is surely not the best age to start a new life in a new country, even for a fit man.[42] And Goya was far from fit. Nor had he any intention of following what must have been the unanimous advice of his doctors: a quiet life, no excitements, moderation in everything. A week after arriving in Bordeaux, exhausted after a taxing journey over the Pyrenees, he set out for Paris. "I fear the journey will be

---

[41] Apart from his last and greatest self-portrait, Goya's oeuvre brims over with medical interest. His portrait of Dr Peral, in the National Gallery, London, is a superb though discreet representation of Bell's palsy, the usually transient paralysis of the facial nerve and the consequent drooping of one side of the mouth and face (pace Stevie Smith's "Dr Peral / In a coat of Gray / Has a way / With his mouth / Which seems to say / A Lot / But nothing very good to hear ..." etc.).

In some of his *Caprichios* he also shows "grotesques" with missing or shortened limbs which exactly presage the deformities caused by the sedative thalidomide in one of the pharmaceutical disasters of the 1950s. Its survivors are still to be seen. Were the deformities in Goya's day a side-effect of some popular herbal remedy taken during pregnancy?

[42] Freud was eighty when he was forced to leave Vienna in 1938. He settled in London, where he died on 23 September 1939.

too much for him", his friend, the poet and schoolmaster Leandro Fernandez de Moratin wrote despairingly, "and we shall never see him again. He cannot even make his wishes known." [43] It was true: Goya had learned to lip-read in Spanish but he neither spoke nor could lip-read French. But he spent three months in Paris on his own, doing nobody knows what. Did he go to the Salon, probably the most memorable in the history of that dismal institution? [44] Did he meet an elderly, slightly down-at heels gentleman who liked to wile away long afternoons in the garden of the Tuilleries, watching children at their games and acknowledging the occasional passer-by who addressed him in Spanish as Your Highness? [45] Whatever he did, Goya was back in Bordeaux in October, not an invalid on his last legs but an artist bursting with creative vigour. In particular, he was anxious to try a new technique: lithography.[46]

Even in his last exile Goya became something of a twentieth-century prototype. Conveniently near the frontier (why is that always so important to elderly political exiles?), the city of Montaigne, with its neat squares, public gardens, superlative cuisine and classic wines, had become the haven (or, as they preferred to think, the future springboard) of wave after wave of Spanish exiles. There were republicans, legitimists, freemasons, clericalists, Catalonian

[43] A. Canellas López, ed., *Francisco de Goya, diplomatorio* (Saragossa, 1981), p. 236. Moratin was also one of Goya's last sitters. The brilliant portrait, another almost in black and white, is in the Museo des Bellas Artes in Bilbao.

[44] The works of Delacroix, Géricault and (from England) Constable and Parkes Bonington signalled the beginning of the Romantic Movement and the temporary eclipse of Davidian Classicism.

[45] Godoy had accompanied Carlos IV and his Queen to Rome and held the dying Queen's hand in 1819. The King was out hunting but died in the same year. Ferdinand VII's vindictiveness then forced Godoy to move to Paris, where he subsisted on a modest pension from Louis-Philippe. (Godoy was invited to live in England as a private citizen but he declined.) By the late 1830s public opinion in Spain had veered back in his favour and under Isabella II his titles and even some of his property were restored to him; but he died before he could return, in 1851, aged eighty-four.

[46] This was the truly revolutionary discovery of Alois Senefelder, a Bavarian playwright (born in Prague of Austrian parents) who was getting weary of copying out parts for his troupe. Providentially, the idea struck him not far from the Pappenheim-Kellheim district where the best varieties of lithographic stone (a sedimentary limestone belonging to the Oolite strata of the Jurassic system) are still quarried. The discovery, which combined the scope of the soft pencil, the crayon, the brush and washes with that of printing, turned him at thirty from an impecunious playwright into a prosperous printer. He died in 1834, aged sixty-three.

Lithography was taken up even more enthusiastically in France than in Germany: Delacroix, Géricault and the young Daumier were among the first to make use of it. Goya probably learnt the technique on his mysterious trip to Paris; but, since he was notoriously rude to anyone who wanted to teach him anything, he must have taught himself.

separatists, constitutionalists, ardent francophiles, rabid francophobes; bitter enemies in the past and, hopefully, again in the not too distant future; but united for the time being by their common hatred of the regime back in Spain. They would meet at the Café of Braulio Poch in the Rue de la Petite Taupe and drink not coffee but velvety *chocolat à l'Espagnole* and thump the table in indignation. They had plenty to thump the table about.[47] Occasionally joining in, but more often just reading their lips, would be the doyen of the expatriates, one who could still travel freely and was welcome in Madrid and who was still drawing a handsome pension from the ogre.[48] For some reason of his own he nevertheless preferred to live and soon no doubt die in exile.

Soon but not quite yet. There was still much to interest him in this world. Using the new lithographic process, he was drawing another bullfighting series. Unlike the *Tauromaquia*, *The Bulls of Bordeaux* were a gratifying commercial success. And standing close to the canvas and sometimes using a magnifying glass he continued to paint portraits, some of his best. His sitters were no longer kings and duchesses but sober bourgeois folk – a banker, a poet-schoolmaster, the engraver Gaulon, the architect Tiburcio Perez (in brilliant shirt-sleeves) and middle-class ladies *d'un certain âge*. Their preference for dignified black suited them and him. His last commissioned portrait, of Don Jose Pio de Molina, is ghostlike in its not-quite-finished state: a "Decomposition in Black and White" Whistler might have called it. But it was not quite his last painting.

Soon after settling in Bordeaux he had bought a house with a small garden in Dona Leocadia's name in the Rue de la Croix-Blanche.[49] Their relationship continued changeable, "like the April weather" as their friends reported, but no cloud ever obscured his love for Rosarito. And she promised to fulfil his high hopes, showing precocious gifts both in music and as a painter of miniatures.[50] The latter activity had an unexpected side-effect. Whether to encourage her or in paternal competition, he too embarked on a series of small paintings on ivory. This was a new departure, one of the few techniques

---

[47] In Spain 1823 marked the beginning of what many Spanish historians still refer to as the "most ignominious decade": years of revolt, oppression and butchery. Among those executed was Mariana Pineda, found guilty of no more than embroidering a revolutionary flag. (A hundred years later she became the heroine of Lorca's first play.)

[48] He continued to do so until he died. On his last visit to Madrid his request for an extension of his sick-leave was granted on condition that he should have his portrait painted by his successor as Court Painter, Vicente Lopez. The painting is now in the Prado, a respectable work even if not in Goya's class. Ferdinand's generosity was the more remarkable as Goya's portraits of him are among his least successful.

[49] J. de Félibien, *Goya à Bordeaux* (Bordeaux, 1967).

[50] She eventually became the drawing mistress of Princess Isabella, the future Isabella II of Spain. Sadly, she was carried off by a fever at the age of twenty-six. No work by her is known.

in art he had never tried before.[51] The products, none of them well-known, are brilliant "accidents" in the same way as are Emil Nolde's "Ungemalte Bilder" painted 120 years later.[52] But if they were accidents, they could have happened only to Goya in his ninth decade. Rosarito also modelled for his last painting. Set in the open air against a spring sky, *The Milkmaid of Bordeaux* is unlike any of the sombre late portraits. It is a burst of joyous colour, a return to the resplendent palette of his youth. Everything has changed. Nothing has changed.

His last illness was short. His grandson, Mariano, and his daughter-in-law arrived in time. "I can say no more than that such happiness has almost exhausted me", he wrote to his son, Javier. "May God grant that you should soon join them. My happiness will then be complete." He adored his family, worrying about them, promoting their careers, delighting in their every success.[53] Javier did not arrive in time to see his father alive; but Rosarito and Mariano were at his bedside when he died.

---

[51] He had painted some more conventional miniature portraits of his family on copper twenty years earlier to mark the wedding of Javier.

[52] E. Sayre, "Goya's Bordeaux Miniatures", *Boston Museum of Fine Arts Bulletin*, 64 (1966), p. 108. See also below, Chapter 19, p. 277.

[53] Mariano eventually lost his fortune by speculation, and died without an heir in 1874. Goya's last will was dated 1811 and Dona Leocadia probably had reason to complain of being left destitute.

# 6

# *David*

At dawn on 17 March 1815 Napoleon, former Emperor of the French, accompanied by fewer than a thousand men, sailed from his island empire of Elba.[1] Ninety-six hours later they disembarked at Golf Juan on the French Riviera. The local gendarmerie and then whole regiments sent to stop him fell in behind his eagles. No shot was fired. The Tricolour was hoisted in Grenoble. The *Marseillaise* called Frenchmen to arms in Lyon. At Auxerre Marshal Ney, who had vowed to bring back the beast in a cage to Paris, embraced his old commander.[2] Two weeks later the once-again Emperor of the French entered his capital amid scenes of frenzied jubilation.[3]

It was characteristic of Napoleon that in the turmoil of the Hundred Days, drafting a new constitution and preparing for his last all-or-nothing campaign, he found time to visit France's most famous painter in the artist's studio in Clichy. It was no less characteristic of Jacques-Louis David that his grumbles and grouches against the Napoleonic "bureaucracy" were instantly forgotten.[4] Tears ran down his cheek when his Emperor pinned to his chest the insignia of Commander of the Legion of Honour. All his life David had been a hero-worshipper. All his life his heroes had let him down. He was now sixty-eight and this was to be his last affirmation of faith. He was also to become, in name as well as in substance, First Painter

[1] After his first abdication, on 20 April 1814, Napoleon was allowed to retain his imperial title as well as being given sovereignty over the island of Elba. He was, in Rostand's words, "not a prisoner but".

[2] He was to be shot for his change of heart, one of the comparatively few victims of the second Bourbon Restoration. (He was probably offered a chance to escape but refused it.)

[3] The news of the landing took four days to reach Paris and another few days to sink in. When it did, Louis XVIII and his court fled.

[4] Oddly perhaps, the two most sparkling and revelatory artist biographies in English – D. B. Wyndham Lewis's *The World of Goya* runs a close second to Anita Brookner's *Jacques-Louis David* (London, 1980) – are about sacred monsters and succeed in making them almost attractive and entirely human. The latter was published in London in 1980. Other monographs about David include E. Delécluse, *Louis David: son école et son temps* (Paris, 1880); H. Rosenau, *The Painter Jacques-Louis David* (London, 1948); R. Verbraeken, *Jacques-Louis David jugé par ses contemporains et par la posterité* (Paris, 1973); and the *Catalogue of the Centenary Exhibition in the Louvre* (Paris, 1989).

of the Empire.[5] Enthusiastically he signed the *Acte Additionel* which "for all eternity" repudiated the Bourbons and was to be the bedrock of the new Napoleonic Empire. The signature committed him for life. The new Napoleonic Empire was to last for another sixty-two days and four hours.

After Waterloo, even before Napoleon's second formal abdication, the First Painter of the Empire fled to Geneva. He found the austere and windy Calvinistic city uncongenial. A year later he and his wife moved to Brussels. The capital of the Catholic Southern Netherlands was a haven of former Bonapartists.[6] To the younger generation the artist seemed a patriarch if not a fossil, but he was warmly received by his contemporaries. "You will never paint again, my dear David", wrote the former Napoleonic general, Riom de Gourlay, in cheerful welcome,

> any more than I shall ever command another artillery battery. But, like me, you will be able to reminisce in this charming city about the stirring events in which you have so signally participated. You will find both the cuisine and the theatre here excellent.[7]

The prophecy was off the mark, but about the stirring events of the past the general was right.

Jacques-Louis David was born in 1748 into a family of prosperous Parisian tradesmen. The Burons and Desmaisons, his mother's and his maternal grandmother's family, were the backbone of the future Third Estate: they knew their place in society but also their worth. They were thrifty, hardworking and law-abiding. An incurable romancer, David later claimed that he had been a rebel all his life. In fact, the maternal milieu was the only one in which he ever felt happy and relaxed.[8] He also liked to recall that he had been something of a child prodigy. This too was a distant approximation to the truth. He was twenty-one when he won a third prize in a painting competition of his *quartier*.

For several years he submitted a painting for the Grand Prix de Rome, an

---

[5] Perhaps he was also ever so slightly swayed by promised advancements for both his sons and his sons-in-law in the army and civil service.

[6] Napoleon had installed one of his brothers, Louis, as King of the Netherlands in 1805. He became the only imperial satrap who earned the respect and even the affection of a section of his subjects. The Congress of Vienna restored the House of Orange to rule over the whole of the Netherlands; but the Bonapartes and Bonapartists retained considerable popularity in the South, the future Belgium. Napoleon's death was marked with an official day of mourning in Brussels.

[7] J. Présson, *L'émigration Belge* (Paris, 1905), p. 34.

[8] His father was killed in a duel when Jacques-Louis was five; the circumstances are obscure. The boy was brought up by his mother's family. It was on the Buron side that he was related to François Boucher. Boucher helped him to gain admission to the Académie school.

essential preliminary at the time to a career in the arts. The subjects were rigidly prescribed, awe-inspiring titles of considerable length, drawn from obscure episodes of antiquity. (Obscure, that is, to the present illiterate age: to David – and later to Napoleon – Plutarch's heroes and heroines were instantly familiar.) At twenty-six he came second with *The Combat of Minerva and Mars*, now one of the worst paintings in the Louvre. The draperies flutter despairingly and Venus floats on a cloud like a punctured Zeppelin. David recognised his limitations and in later work eschewed celestial apparitions. Two years later he won the coveted prize with *The Physician Erasistratus Discovering the Cause of Antiochus's Illness.*[9] It was an advance on previous efforts but the pervasive sickly green suggests that, despite Erasistratus' diagnostic acumen, Antiochus's illness had not yet fully abated. At the comparatively advanced age of twenty-eight, he was ready to depart for Rome.

The Rome of the 1770s was a delicious mix of material and moral decay, seedy ecclesiastical pomp and cheerful brigandage. It was also an antiquarian boom town. The excavators were everywhere and splendid new (and occasionally recent) discoveries almost daily fanned the enthusiasm of collectors and the greed of the excavators. The former were mainly English milords on the grand tour, to Romans an almost supernatural source of riches. The latter were everybody who could move, from the barber in the shop on the corner to his Holiness and his kin in the Vatican. But the living arts too were catered for. Fashionable anatomists in luxuriously appointed dissecting rooms demonstrated the intimate workings of the human body to well-heeled visitors who might wish to continue where Praxiteles and Michelangelo had left off. The younger and less affluent chased after more nubile sources of inspiration.[10] There was weightier fare too. Classical scholars, led by the crushingly learned Johann Joachim Winckelmann, intoned about "edle Einfalt und stille Grösse", the very essence of *le grand style.*[11] And in the

[9] By holding the sick young's man's pulse the physician identified the patient's illicit love for his stepmother, Stratonice, as the cause of his physical decline. The subject was to be tortured to death by Ingres.

[10] The artist colony in Rome at the time of David's sojourn included Houdon, Clodion and Pierre Julien from France, Nollekens, Thomas Banks and James Barry from England, Benjamin West and Copley from America, Abilgaard from Denmark, Angelica Kauffmann from Germany and Fuseli from Switzerland.

[11] Winckelmann was the most influential of the local oracles. His great work on the art of Antiquity was written almost entirely before he left Germany and had much chance to see authentic examples. (He never travelled to Greece.) He settled in Rome in 1754, became Pontifical Librarian and was the moving spirit behind the first excavations of Pompeii and Herculanaeum. He was murdered in a robbery at Trieste on his way to meet Goethe in 1768, at the age of fifty-one. He was the archetype of the dedicated German art-historian whose influence on artists (as distinct from fellow academics) was almost entirely dire.

comparative solitude of numberless churches the work of the sublime masters of the past – or what little was still visible of their work under centuries of accumulated grime – could be admired and copied. The *pension-naires* of the French Academy were housed in some splendour on the Corso, their exquisite manners and mountainous debts equally admired. Most of them would look back on their sojourn in Rome as the happiest days of their lives. But not David. After only a few months he was collapsing in suicidal despair.

The immediate cause of his breakdown remains obscure (as the cause of such breakdowns still usually is). His duties were far from arduous. The newly appointed director, Joseph-Marie Vien, exercised a tepid tyranny over his charges but he was not ill-disposed to David.[12] The young man was also well-liked by his fellow *pensionnaires*: several would remain his friends for life. Apart from a small scar on his left cheek which left him with a slight speech impediment,[13] he was fit. He was not prone to unhappy – or even to happy – love affairs. But he would continue into old age to rail against the frivolity of the institution and bemoan its "lack of purpose". This was unfair. The French Academy in Rome had no formal teaching commitment: the *pensionnaires* were expected look around and teach themselves. In any case what David craved was not teachers but heroes. Of these in the last quarter of the eighteenth century there was a dearth, in Rome as elsewhere. David admired the technical virtuosity of his celebrated kinsmen, Boucher, but he held Boucher's style and choice of subjects in contempt.[14] He painted in Rome one of his few religious pictures, a passable altar-piece dedicated to St Roche, but his heart was not in that either.[15] The mission of artists was surely higher than to beguile the rich with pastoral frolics or comfort the poor with the deeds of kindly but ineffectual martyrs. Classical antiquity furnished glorious examples of men – and steadfastly supporting women – rising to heroic grandeur. No other subject was worthy of portrayal. Yet demand for such themes was slight; nor perhaps did David feel as yet equipped to do them justice.

[12] Vien was among Winckelmann's most devoted disciples and artistic victims. About his prim scenes of Olympian revels, Diderot remarked that no Greek maidens had ever aroused in him less desire to be their lover and a more fervent wish to be their uncle. Vien ended his life an imperial senator, his grizzled head bobbing up above Mme Mère in the great Coronation picture. He died in 1808, aged eighty-nine.

[13] It was the result of a fencing accident at school.

[14] Boucher was the friend and protégé of Mme de Pompadour. He died in 1762, aged sixty-four.

[15] It was commissioned by Marseille after one of the regular outbreaks of the plague but ended up in Dijon.

Back in Paris after two years, the Salon of 1781 was a breakthrough for a cohort of young artists dedicated to uplift.[16] Lagrenée was represented by *Fabritius Refuses the Presents of the Ambassadors of Pyrrhus*. Hallé chose to commemorate *Miltiades Tearing Down the Walls of his Property and Inviting the Populace to Share his Crops*. David's *Belisarius Refusing Alms and Being Recognised as the Blind Beggar*, a parable on Stoic virtues contrasted to the fickleness of the mighty, impelled Diderot to rhapsodies of praise.

> This young man works in the Grand Manner. He has a heart. His faces are expressive without being artificial, the attitudes are noble and natural ... He can draw. His colouring is harmonious without being garish.[17]

Everybody who mattered agreed with him. The painting was bought by the Duke of Saxe-Teschen. The Duc de Noailles ordered a copy. The Comte d'Artois (the future Charles X) ordered a new mythological composition.[18] With his next major work, *Andromache Mourning Hector*, David was admitted to the Académie and given a studio apartment in the Louvre. To furnish it he turned to a craftsmen friend of his Desmaison cousins, Monsieur Charles-Pierre Pécoul. Would the *maître* design for him a small alcove bed? But why a *small* alcove bed, Monsieur Pécoul expostulated? Why not a big one for two? – and promptly threw his daughter Charlotte into the bargain. With her came a respectable dowry; and David painted a superb pair of portraits of his parents-in-law. (He was always at his best painting people of the same social background as his own.) To crown his successes, he was commissioned by the King to paint *The Oath of the Horatii* for the royal apartments at Versailles.

Despair and hope, impatience with the present but ardent faith in the future, make a potent mixture; and every now and then in the history of most nations they ignite. The resulting fireworks rarely last long but they provide a grand spectacle. It happened in France in the years immediately preceding the Revolution. The *Horatii* has to be seen against this background of exploding stars. The historical episode, in so far as the episode had a historical basis, was far from heroic. That mattered not at all. What mattered was the painting. Three groups of figures are lined up against a sombre background of Doric columns and arches. Horatius *père*, sternly putting

---

[16] But the triumph was critical rather than popular. In popularity *le grand style* never supplanted *le petit style* of Boucher, Fragonard, Nattier and their many followers. Formidable as the Greek and Roman heroes looked on canvas, the delightfully fragile shepherds, shepherdesses, nymphs, *putti* and *amoretti* in their begarlanded and happily lascivious arcadias proved infinitely more durable.

[17] D. Diderot, *The Salon of 1781*, edited by J. Séznec and J. Adhémar (Oxford, 1967), iv, p. 231.

[18] To become one of David's best, *Paris et Helène*.

patriotic duty before paternal love, holds aloft three swords. His three sons face him in stark profile. Their eyes are flashing, or so one imagines. Their stance is resolute. Their right arms are raised in solemn oath. The women form a justly celebrated group: Camilla (who is going to lose either a brother or a lover) swoons in an exquisite arabesque of grief; Sabina weeps quietly; Lavinia cuddles two bewildered little Horatii. Louis XVI expressed dutiful rather than rapturous approval; but the Queen put her dainty foot down. The painting was stupendous but not for daily consumption. It should stay in the Louvre. She was of course right. But at that moment the image, even without understanding the story line, was exactly what the patriotic hearts of many Frenchmen craved. With it David entered history.

Other gruesome episodes of antiquity followed. Of such there was an almost unlimited supply. *Brutus Receiving the Bodies of his Three Sons whom He Had Sentenced to Death for Failing in their Duty to the State* was only marginally less impressive. Reality would soon parody such loathsome scenes with flesh-and-blood embodiments of Roman virtue like Robespierre and Saint-Just. But for the time being they were still no more than pleasantly spine-chilling evocations of the past, reassuringly heroic but no less reassuringly remote. David himself would still occasionally turn from such exalted subjects to paint more intimate domestic scenes. In 1785 he was commissioned to paint a double portrait of Monsieur and Mme Lavoisier.

There are many masterpieces in art which celebrate love, passion, ecstasy and even lust. There are not more than half a dozen which celebrate conjugal felicity.[19] This is one of them.[20] The great chemist is shown in his laboratory but his face is turned at his young wife. She leans on his chair in a pose of undemonstrative tenderness. Effortlessly David conveyed why the couple was so much admired. He was not only France's most distinguished scientist but also a *fermier general* or tax commissioner, a member of the most execrated group of royal functionaries. She was the daughter of another *fermier general*, even richer than her husband. But in an age in which corruption in the state service was the norm and private morality lax, nobody had ever impugned

[19] The Arnolfini marriage by Jan Van Eyck, Rubens' self-portrait with his wife, Isabella Brant, in the Honeysuckle Bower, Renoir's wonderful portrait of Alfred Sisley and his wife and, less well-known perhaps, the limewood relief of Joachim and Anne meeting at the Golden Gate by an unknown sixteenth-century master in Passau, Germany, nominate themselves.

[20] Antoine Laurent Lavoisier married the beautiful and accomplished Marie-Anne Paultz when he was thirty-eight and she was fourteen. She helped him with his researches and drew many of the illustrations to his monumental *Traité elémentaire de chimie*. The establishment of burning as a form of oxidation was only one of his many ground-breaking contributions to the natural sciences.

the honesty of Monsieur Lavoisier – he declined to be ennobled – or the virtue of his wife.[21] "An ornament of France", as David himself described him, he was also one of the country's leading patrons of the arts. Despite David's uncharacteristic protestations – "to paint Lavoisier is its own reward" – he was paid 7000 livres, twice as much as the King paid for the *Horatii*. In his acknowledgement, David expressed his undying gratitude and devotion: "I shall never forget your noble countenance and generosity of your spirit, genius of our age!" Six years later he was a vociferous member of the Committee of Public Safety which, on a ludicrously trumped-up charge, sent Lavoisier to the guillotine.[22]

Was David hypocrisy incarnate? None of those who knew him well thought so. He was a little dour by the polite standards of the Ancien Régime; but Talleyrand found him insufferably priggish rather than evil. His colleagues respected him for his hard work (if not always for his judgement) and his pupils revered him without perhaps following his precepts to the letter.[23] He was hard-headed in business matters; but nobody ever accused him of financial dishonesty. He was a devoted family man and strongly disapproved of those who strayed. Oddly perhaps, his murderous past seemed to trouble him not at all. "France was in a fever. In such times one does not know what one is doing", another regicide, François de Natter, assured him after Robespierre's fall. It seemed a satisfactory answer.[24] Baudelaire admired him as an artist and, apostrophised him, a little cryptically, as an "astre froid". His most perceptive modern biographer (and he has been extremely fortunate in his biographers) merely describes him as the "most fallible and human of artists". But if not a hypocrite, he was certainly naive. He railed against imaginary or minor misdemeanours while hero-worshipping real monsters. And he undoubtedly regarded his own dramatic depictions of Antiquity not as pleasing literary conceits but as authentic recreations of the past ready for instant emulation.[25]

The Revolution swept him along as it did millions of Frenchmen. Not many were swept quite so far. He never became a significant political figure; but in artistic matters he became more powerful than any royal superintendent of buildings and bridges had ever been. He designed official

[21] There is not a scrap of evidence for the allegations that David and Mme Lavoisier were lovers or even had a crush on each other.

[22] He was accused of having adulterated tobacco with water. His real crime was to have exposed the scientific vapourings of Marat.

[23] Gros and Ingres were the most prominent; but there were many others, including Fragonard's son, Evariste.

[24] The same explanation was frequently heard at the Nuremberg Trials. It did not wash.

[25] Brookner, *Jaques-Louis David*, p. 328.

costumes.[26] He stage-managed ceremonial occasions.[27] He abolished the old-style Académie.[28] These were, in the long term, enterprises of profound futility. But two deaths, neither in themselves of great historical moment, inspired him to create masterpieces.

On 13 July 1793 Jean-Paul Marat, gutter journalist, medical mountebank, darling of the Paris mob and one of the vilest creatures washed up by the tide of the Revolution, was murdered in his bath.[29] David, an ex-officio

[26] According to his friend, Talma, France's leading actor, it was David who stopped actors and later the general public from powdering their hair and who launched the revolutionary flowing hairstyle. (Robespierre was among the few who staunchly resisted the trend, continuing to wear his immaculately powdered wig to the end.)

[27] The grandiose revolutionary fêtes, substitutes for religious festivals and royal occasions, remained unsurpassed in banality till the twentieth century. The celebration of the Supreme Being, Robespierre's brainchild, was David's culminating assignment. The festivities began at 7 a.m. at the Place de la Bastille, where a crowd of about ten thousand – maidens in white, flag-waving patriotic citizens and revolutionary mothers with their broods – assembled to martial strains specially composed by Gossec. They were later joined by huge floats and chariots loaded with actors impersonating such diverse revolutionary personages as William Tell, Brutus, Cornelia, the mother of the Gracchi, Vercingetorix the Gaul and Benjamin Franklin. With frequent stops for sustaining free refreshments, stirring speeches and *tableaux vivants* depicting inspiring patriotic episodes from the past, the procession wound its way to the Champ de Mars where an artificial mountain, 300 feet high, had been erected in a matter of days by enthusiastic revolutionary volunteers. It was capped by a statue of Hercules (designed by David), a Tree of Liberty, and a tasteful assortment of floral allegories. The procession was received at the foot of the mountain by deputies of the Convention bedecked with flowers and carrying (among other necessities; it was to be a long day) three sheaves of corn each. More invigorating music and speeches followed, interspersed with more liquid sustenance and the ministrations of a specially recruited *corps de ballet*. As the last strains of the *Great Hymn to the Supreme Being* faded away, and to the tumultuous cheers of the befloreated and becerealled deputies, Robespierre himself emerged in a new and exquisitely cut blue coat, tricolour sash and plumed hat. After a short oration (by Robespierrean stand-ards), he set alight with a torch handed to him by David a cardboard effigy of "Atheism". From the ashes, and only slightly sooty, emerged another symbolic figure: this time a live young female, representing "Virtue".

[28] "We must expose the petty cruelty of that infamous body", he orated, "the tyranny and jealousy of its members which has long sought to crush all budding talent in the arts." Sadly, his impassioned denunciation could have been applied with equal justice to the Institut which was to exercise an even more doleful influence on French artistic life over the next hundred years. At a more practical level, David appreciated that, with the abolition of the monarchy, state religion and the aristocracy, new patrons were needed if artists were to survive. A Patriotic Jury was therefore elected by the Convention especially to distribute generous prizes among artists. To David's dismay, the prizes were all awarded to members of the Patriotic Jury.

[29] Born in Cagliari in Sardinia in 1743, he had studied medicine in Bordeaux and had practised in London before being awarded an M.D. degree by St Andrews University. He left Scotland under a cloud and, after several unsuccessful attempts to establish himself as a doctor or scientist in France, he applied his not inconsiderable journalistic talents to keeping the

admirer, inevitable stage-managed the lying-in-state and the funeral. The occasion did not pass without a hitch. The body's gracefully arranged right arm detached itself at the shoulder and had to be hastily replaced with a suitable limb from another body. (Of these there was a wide choice.) But the artist also commemorated the event with a painting. It is, unintentionally one has to assume, a deeply religious work. The martyred hero lies in a setting of monastic poverty. An unfinished letter in his left hand, accompanied by a bank-note, reads: "Give this money to the mother of five whose husband died for his country." Such charity makes the gaping wound under the collar-bone all the more shocking. But the picture is not an exercise in horror. "From now on", Baudelaire wrote many years later,

> Marat can compete with Apollo, for death, acting through David's brush, has kissed him with loving lips ... in that cold room with its cold walls, around the cold coffin of a bathtub there hovers an immortal soul.[30]

And on 23 November 1794, leaning out of Citoyenne Julien's window, David caught sight of the *ci-devant* Queen, Marie-Antoinette, on her way to the scaffold. Her husband had gone this way a few months earlier and her much-loved children had been taken away from her.[31] With a few strokes David drew the passing image on a scrap of paper. A dowdy middle-aged woman with shorn head and with her hands tied behind her back looks down impassively. It is impossible to analyse such a picture: it conveys everything or nothing.

The Terror ended abruptly and unexpectedly. On 9 Thermidor in Year III (27 July 1794) Saint-Just rose for the opening speech of the session in the Convention. The bloodbaths of the previous weeks had been horrendous: hundreds had been sent to the guillotine, humble citizens of no consequence as well as bearers of great names. Now there was a faint expectation in the air that, as a tactical move at least, Saint-Just would content himself with a few pious exhortations. But Saint-Just was not one for tactical moves. At once he launched into the denunciation of more traitors in the very heart of the Convention, a routine preliminary to their unmasking and inevitable

mood of the Paris mob at fever pitch. A painful skin condition obliged him to work in a hot bath. His murderess, Charlotte Corday, a well-bred young lady from Normandy, made no attempt to escape and went to the guillotine unbowed.

[30] C. Baudelaire, *Ecrits sur l'art*, 2 volumes (Paris, 1981), i, p. 342. In contrast to the literary scene in England, the great literary figures in France during the nineteenth century – Stendhal, Chateaubriand, Balzac, Baudelaire, Gautier, Flaubert, the Goncourts, Bourget, Proust and Zola among others – took a lively interest in the visual arts and wrote many inspired pages about artists.

[31] David had been one of interrogators of the young Dauphin (nominally Louis XVII after his father's beheadal).

journey to the guillotine. But he had hardly reached his first reference to the Tarpeian Rock when he was interrupted an obscure backwoods deputy, Billaud-Varenne. Quaking with fear but egged on by fellow deputies, he hesitantly questioned (no more) the wisdom of threats against members of the Convention. On earlier occasions such an unseemly interruption would merely have added another name to Saint-Just's list of vermin. Still unaccountably, Saint-Just hesitated as if considering the merits of the suggestion. Robespierre himself then rushed to the tribune and began to speak. It was too late. He was interrupted."To hear Citoyen Robespierre speak", another backwoodsman shouted, "one might think of him as a man of the rarest modesty. He never wants anything for himself but his will must always be done." It was hardly devastating wit, let alone reasoned argument. But it elicited a giggle, the giggle became a guffaw, and the guffaw grew into a roar. The laughter killed the Terror.

Next morning 152 of Robespierre's closest followers went to the guillotine. The sea-green incorruptible himself had to be dragged. He had tried to shoot himself during the night (or somebody had tried to shoot him); and France's most fastidious dresser had to be strapped to the plank bespattered with blood and screaming. Saint-Just died cool and composed.[32] Others followed. Only the pageant master of the Terror got away. He was saved by his constipation. Only two days earlier in the Jacobin Club he had publicly pledged his undying fidelity to Robespierre."Wherever you go, Citoyen Robespierre, I shall follow you … *Si tu bois la cigüe, mon ami, je la boirai avec toi!*" But no important matters relating to the arts had been scheduled for 9 Thermidor, and he had set the day aside for a *grande laxative*. In a rented room in the Rue Sauvage the news of his leader's fall did not reach him till the evening and he felt too drained to try to escape. Perhaps he was too depressed to try. But the country's new masters lost no time in demonstrating their staggering incompetence. The artist's name was near the top of the wanted list but nobody knew where to find him. Mme David professed both ignorance and indifference. He did not resurface and make an appearance in the Convention until a week later. He mounted a pathetic and unconvincing defence of himself; but, though it embarrassed his friends, the first flush of anti-Robespierrist fury had by then abated. But what about hemlock? Ah, but such things are said in the heat of the moment. Besides, and more importantly, many of those now jockeying for position had been too heavily implicated in the Terror to make much of an ill-judged hyperbole. The Prosecutor thundered in terms worthy of David himself – "cet usurpateur,

---

[32] Robespierre, who started his career as a lawyer in Arras, was thirty-six: Saint-Just, the scion of an impoverished noble family, was twenty-seven.

ce tyrant des arts, aussi lâche qu'il est scélérat" – but the specific charges against him were somewhat contrived. He was imprisoned in comparative comfort at the old Fermes Générales and then transferred to an apartment in the Luxembourg. His pupil Delécluse brought him paint and canvas and he painted his only landscape, a rather charming one. He also painted a surprising self-portrait. He looks younger than his forty-seven years except for the grey stubble on his cheeks and around his somewhat cyanosed lips. He made no effort to disguise the slight deformity of his mouth. The colours are aristocratic, the paint applied with great freedom. But what is most striking is the look of baffled honesty, deep hurt. Why is he here? What mistake has he made? What crime has he committed? Or rather, what mistake has he made that many others have not? But he was also regaining his self-confidence: with his old penchant for romancing he signed the canvas "J. L. David in vinculis". Also, on receiving a hamper of home-made delicacies, he made his peace with Mme David, whose distaste for the excesses of the Committee of Public Safety had led to a separation a year earlier. They remained a devoted couple for the rest of their lives; she was to survive him by only a few months. He was freed on 26 October, the day the Directory, France's new government, took office.

An orgiastic mood of merry-making swept over the country (or at least Paris) in the wake of the Terror. Presiding over it was the most venal regime France had ever experienced.[33] The country was still officially at war with half of Europe. It was bankrupt. Its troops, like its civilian employees, stole or starved. The Davids had no need to do either. The rich countryside of the Ile de France was still a short walk from the city walls; and Mme David had relations who were farmers and market gardeners. Also, surprisingly, people were still buying pictures: not a few, it seems, needed to be reminded that, somehow or other, they were still alive. Deprived of his hero, David did not suffer another nervous breakdown; but he was looking for a replacement.

The Corsican gunner was twenty-seven, newly wed and still General Buonaparte with an "u", when he assumed what his political masters confidently expected (and hoped) was a doomed army command.[34] A few weeks later he was leading his underfed, ill-equipped and bedraggled men across the Alps. Soon they were delivering crushing blows to Europe's best-fed

[33] The Directory was presided over by Paul Barras, a former Count turned Jacobin turned anti-revolutionary, a pillar of corruption and a cousin of the Marquis de Sade; and he alone remained in post from beginning to end. The Directory stayed in power until the coup of 18 Brumaire (9 November) 1799, when Bonaparte was declared First Consul. Barras, whom David loathed, was bought off with half a million francs

[34] He was born in 1769 in Ajaccio in Corsica.

army.[35] It was the beginning of a legend; and, fortunately, there was an artist at hand to commemorate it.[36] Fortunately, too, the recognition of genius was mutual. In fact, David had neither the stomach nor the talent to recreate the gore and exhilaration of indiscriminate slaughter.[37] He also had a regrettable tendency to paint heroic but lost battles, like Thermopylae. Who wanted those? Not General Bonaparte (now without an "u") and even less the Emperor Napoleon. But there was no need for David to paint *contre-coeur*: Napoleon had a brilliant stable of battle-scene painters.[38] What David was not merely good but by common consent the best at was grand ceremonial occasions. It chimed in with Napoleon's unerring sense of the theatre. The imperial coronation on 2 December 1804 was a monstrous display of *folie de grandeur*, but it impressed (even if it did not overawe) even such hardened cynics as Talleyrand.[39] The vast canvas showing the event took David three years to complete and entailed meticulous planning and dozens of preliminary portrait sketches. It was of course a propaganda piece which required some tampering with the facts. Napoleon's mother, the wonderful Letitia, refused to attend "the vulgar charade" but was painted in by the artist. David frequently sermonised about the truth and probably believed in what he preached; but abstract concepts were subject to practical as well as to purely artistic limitations.

[35] This was in many ways Napoleon's most dangerous and brilliant campaign. He broke all the rules of eighteenth-century warfare and made full use of his exceptional gifts of decisiveness, understanding of the terrain, willpower, quickness of mind, sustained effort and personal charisma. It was also the occasion of the first of the great Napoleonic battle-scene paintings. After much dilly-dallying, Josephine, recently wed, joined her husband on the campaign with David's pupil, Antoine-Jean Gros, in tow. The result was the picture of *Bonaparte on the Bridge of Arcola*, now in the Louvre.

[36] David painted his first portrait of Napoleon – unfinished – soon after their first meeting at a reception given by the dumbfounded Directory in honour of their conquering general. "Bonaparte is my hero", the artist enthused to Delécluse after the first sitting, "a man to whom in Antiquity people would have raised altars ... his head is big, beautiful, Greek."

[37] He never went near a battlefield but he did go to witness (a little reluctantly) the deaths of Danton and of Camille Desmoulins on the guillotine.

[38] Gros was one: his *Bonaparte among the Plague Victims in Jaffa* and his *Battle of Eylau* are masterpieces. Horace Vernet, scion of one of the most prolific French painting dynasties, was another.

[39] Having bullied the saintly if perhaps simple-minded Pius VII to travel from Rome to Paris to crown him Emperor, Napoleon snatched the crown from the pontifical hands and placed it first on his own head, as shown in many of David's preliminary drawings, and then on Josephine's. (It was later maintained by Napoleon's hagiographers that the charade had been prearranged with the pontiff. There is no evidence for this.) During David's exile an almost exact copy of the painting toured the United States and was a huge success. It established the work as an obligatory illustration in all history books.

In a celebrated rage Beethoven, on hearing of Napoleon's assumption of the imperial title, changed the dedication of his Third Symphony from "Bonaparte" to "Eroica"; but few of the ardent regicides and republicans of yesteryear in France (and indeed Europe) shared his outrage. To David and to many others the Emperor was not only a hero but also heir to the Revolution. There was some substance in this. Compared to the hereditary monarchies of continental Europe – their oppressiveness redeemed only by their *Schlamperei* – the Napoleonic empire was the embodiment of reason, enlightenment and hope. Or so it seemed at first. But Beethoven was of course right. The most spectacular military victories were still to come, but Napoleon's greatest achievements were already in the past.[40] The pomp and panoply of his coronation, so ably masterminded by France's greatest painter, helped to implant the seeds of corruption that ten years later would destroy the hero of the event and his Empire.

Until comparatively recently David's last years in exile have been widely regarded as a quiet epilogue, a period of artistic decline, inevitable perhaps both on grounds of age and of political eclipse, and not, when all is said and done, entirely undeserved. He was not, like his early *Belisarius*, blind and begging. Prints of his *Sabines* and other operatic tableaux were still selling briskly; and his devoted pupil, Baron Gros, and his two sons were faithfully looking after his business interests in France.[41] His fees as a portraitist remained exorbitant but were paid without demur by those who wanted only the best. As a former regicide and vocal Bonapartist to the last, he was inevitably *persona non grata* to the Bourbon Restoration; but Louis XVIII bore him no personal ill-will and admired him as an artist.[42] Until his short last illness his health was good: occasional "chills on the liver", requiring a slight adjustment of diet and a few weeks of taking the waters at a congenial spa, were acceptable trials of old age, bravely borne. His Belgian hosts were considerate and respectful.[43] Yet many felt that he had lost his drive. He

[40] The great legal codes and educational reforms, as well as the Concordat with the church, were all achievements of the Consulate. At the time of the coronation France was secure behind her natural frontiers for the first time since the outbreak of the Revolution.

[41] Gros made his peace with the Bourbons after Waterloo and was created a baron by Charles X on completing the decoration of the dome of the Panthéon. (The original design, showing the apotheosis of Napoleon, was easily adaptad into an apotheosis of the Bourbons.) But his late classicising pictures were received with undeserved derision and this, coupled with his miserable married life, drove him to suicide in 1835, aged sixty-four.

[42] The Duke of Wellington reported that the King, Louis XVIII, was "furious with David", but that may have been because David refused to take advantage of the proferred amnesty.

[43] His *Mars and Venus* was first shown at a public exhibition organised by the municipality of Brussels.

declined pressing and flattering invitations from the King of Prussia to settle in Berlin and become Director of Fine Arts there.[44] He refused financially tempting offers to visit the United States. Although he explained his reluctance to sign a petition for a royal pardon (which would have allowed him to return to France) by his disinclination to "humble himself" before the Bourbons, this was a piece of Davidian humbug. Both he and Mme David liked their comfortable house on the corner of the rue Willems and the rue Fossé-aux-loups. It was conveniently close to his studio and opposite the Théâtre de la Monnaie where he had his reserved seat which nobody else could use. He noted with approval that the streets of Brussels were cleaner than those of Paris. They were also less noisy. He relished the visits of his grandchildren but did not want them to be unduly prolonged.[45] He took little interest in political events in Paris (except for his disapproval of the monstrous proposal of levying a tax on prints); and he did not get entangled in labyrinthine emigré politics. But most surprising, and to most of his admirers hugely disappointing, were his paintings.

First, there were the portraits, many for long in private hands and jealously guarded. The image of the eminent antiquary Alexandre Lenoir has been described as "curiously shabby";[46] and so it is. But as a character study few works in David's earlier career quite match it. Henri-Amadée, Comte de Turenne, is shown as a supercilious toff, handsome and repellent. The former Abbé Emmanuel-Joseph Sieyès, by contrast, appears vulnerable and fragile, a great survivor but only just.[47] The two Bonaparte princesses, Charlotte and Zenaïde,[48] are huddled uncomfortably together almost smothered by a profusion of unsuitable accessories (Plate 9). They look frightened and yet cheeky, which is what they probably were, entirely lacking in that imperial aura with which David would have invested them ten years earlier. Mme Mongez in her double portrait with her husband looks a little frumpish and ill at ease, overawed perhaps by being immortalised by a great artist. None of these works is faultlessly painted but the evocation of personalities is mesmeric. But the real horror story is the triple portrait of Mme Isabelle Rose Tangry

[44] It was a remarkable offer from a King previously humiliated by Napoleon. But this was still the age of sacred monsters: great artists were above the law. The King even sent his brother, Prince Mansfeld, to try to persuade David.

[45] He rarely painted his family; but he did make a charming drawing of his daughter, Pauline-Jeanne, married to Baron Jean-Baptiste Jeanin, and her daughter, on one of their visits.

[46] By Anita Brookner in *Jacques-Louis David*, p. 235.

[47] Robespierre called him "the mole of the Revolution" and he does look a little molelike.

[48] They were the daughters of Joseph Bonaparte, former King of Spain. Their mother took them to Brussels where David gave drawing lessons to Charlotte. Both Princesses later married Bonaparte cousins.

and her two daughters.[49] It encapsulates a wordless domestic drama of will and submission, of determined old age in the mother and fading youth in the daughters. The dimensions of the painting are too small; but the meanness is part of the message. Neither gaoler nor victims have room to move, either physically or metaphorically.

Worse than the unvarnished portraits were the mythological compositons in what David himself described as his "novel style"."His Amor", wrote Edouard Miel about his *Amor and Psyche*, "is not even a handsome adolescent. He is a common-looking model with a cynical grin on his face, slavishly copied ... the whole is hardly credible as a work of a painter known and admired in the past for his noble and elevated style." [50] The Reverend Thomas Dibdin, who travelled to Brussels especially to see David's recent works, described them as being "in the worst possible taste". He was, like Miel, particularly repelled by *Amor and Psyche*. "Amor has the vacant countenance of an idiot ... dark squat and utterly inane. The lady lying on the bed is totally divested of drapery! Her bones and muscles are far too prominent. Her colouring is much too ruddy." [51] Count Jean du Plessis was a little more charitable."David's draughtsmanship is still admirable", he wrote to his father, an old admirer, "but you would grieve over his decline. He can no longer convey a message of heroic grandeur." [52] It did not occur to the letter writer that at seventy-four David might no longer wish to convey messages of heroic grandeur or indeed messages of any kind. He might be busy painting pictures because he liked painting them.

Of course there had always been two Davids. There was the sermonising ideologue, impressive at his best but even at his best slightly preposterous. Did his contemporaries really feel a frisson contemplating *Les Sabines*? [53] Many professed that they did but one has niggling doubts. Narrative paintings exist in time as well as in space. What excites, interests or horrifies is not just the moment depicted but also the imagined events leading up to it and, even more, the terrible happenings that must surely follow. The only happening one can envisage following most of David's grand historical tableaux

[49] The painting is sometimes referred to as *The Ladies of Ghent* because the name of the city appears on the envelope held by Mme Tangry. In fact, the women resided in Brussels. Some of the work was certainly painted by David's assistants, but he never disowned it.

[50] E. F. Miel, *Essai sur les Beaux-Arts* (Paris, 1817). Miel was a journalist and minor writer who became David's first biographer.

[51] T. F. Dibdin was an Irish Protestant clergyman, bibliographer and antiquarian. He wrote about David in *A Biographical, Antiquarian and Picturesque Tour in France and Germany* (London, 1821), ii, p. 54.

[52] Quoted in F. Duvachel, *David en exile* (Paris, 1904), p. 56.

[53] Usually translated as *The Rape of the Sabine Women*; but perhaps it should be *The Intervention of the Sabine Women*, as suggested by Anita Brookner.

is the fall of the curtain and a rush for refreshments. But there was another David. In the midst of his public labours he would dash off a drawing or a small painting whose only message was its own loveliness. Some were not discovered until his studio was cleared after his death. One of them, his portrait of Louise de Pastoret, was begun and left unfinished in 1793, the terrible year when mass executions became the order of the day. Mme de Pastoret herself was far from safe. None of this shows. Against the simplest of backgrounds, a young mother with her first-born in a cradle next to her pauses in her sewing and looks up.[54] Few painters have so beautifully captured the contentment of young motherhood.

Until David's last years, such moments had been rare. There had always been public duties to perform, exacting masters to glorify, lofty programmes to proclaim, historic moments to commemorate. As an exile in his last years he found himself without heroes or even villains, with no sermons to preach and no audiences to inspire, reprimand or exhort. As a young man the discovery might have crushed him. Now it came as a vast transforming relief."I had a good summer", he wrote to his son Eugène, "I enjoyed painting." [55] It was, on the face of it, not an earth-shattering statement from a man who for twenty-five years had been Europe's most famous and highest paid professional. But to David at seventy-four it seemed like an epiphany.

Of course not all his ventures were successful. The figures in *Venus and her Nymphs Disarming Mars* (described by Gros as a Homeric masterpieces) seem to have been modelled in coloured ice-cream. The nymphs have a fixed gaze and awful frizzy coiffure to match their convulsive gestures. Venus is a caricature of Ingres' *Grande Odalisque*.[56] The clouds and sky are an improbable powder blue. The overall effect is not so much ludicrous as provincial and dowdy. Most young artists embarking on a new venture commit such atrocities. The works usually fall by the wayside or are quietly destroyed. David's old-age indiscretions ended up in museums. But when David succeeded, he painted some of his loveliest pictures. They were, until recently, hardly known. Worse, many were known from feeble reproductions or grotesque engravings. The majority quickly passed into private collections; and the dismal verdict recorded for posterity by David's contemporaries (and inevitably copied from book to book) was no incentive to try to winkle them out. For once it was the market-place which brought enlightenment. The hype which accompanies the appearance of newly-discovered "lost" works by old masters in the salesrooms is usually self-defeating. Old masters had

---

[54] The infant, the future academician, senator and social climber was later painted by Ingres.

[55] J. David, *Le peintre Louis David, 1748–1825* (Paris, 1880), i, p. 68.

[56] The teacher had become a pupil. David certainly had a copy of Ingres' painting.

their "off" days (or weeks or months), like any artist; and, more often than not, the resurfacing of a such creations merely proves the fact. But the offer at auction in 1987 of *The Parting of Telemachos and Eucharis*, one of David's "rediscovered" Brussels paintings, was an eye-opener to many. Although the work illustrates a sad event, the parting of two young people in love under pressure from the elders, it lacks all sense of Greek tragedy. It is, despite the improbable tears in the hound's eyes, gentle, melancholic and sentimental. Yet it is not maudlin. Indeed, David had never used colours and graceful lines to better effect. Costumes and props are rendered with all his old mastery; the composition is simple but harmonious. But what makes the painting, like all his best works in old age, a revelation, is the inner conviction and persuasiveness of the sentiments expressed.[57]

In the long run artists can represent persuasively only what they understand. Well-rehearsed attitudinising may deceive contemporaries, as it may almost deceive the artists themselves, but it will rarely convince future generations. Conversely, genuinely felt sentiments, however old-fashioned or even trite, never pall. David was – or had been until his last decade – a hero-worshipper; but he had never been a hero. Nor, though he huffed and puffed heroically, did he have any real understanding of the heroic. What he understood were simple emotions like the sadness of parting, boy meets girl love, the joys of a happy marriage, the contentment of young motherhood, as well of course as the lark of a casual conquest. To portray these as truthfully as he did in his last years required as much artistry as the portrayal of super-human (or subhuman) virtue. He was an old man when this truth dawned on him; but the moment was worth waiting for.

[57] At auction the painting went to the Paul Getty Museum in Malibu, California, for $4,500,000. Sections of the French press waxed indignant, but one cannot help feeling that David would have approved.

# 7

# *Hokusai*

In 1603 the all-conquering Shogun, Ieyashu Tokugawa, moved the seat of his government to an insignificant fishing village, barely more than a hamlet, on the eastern seashore of Japan.[1] With him came droves of officials, their families, servants and hangers-on, soldiers, artisans, tradesmen, businessmen, priests, doctors, writers, beggars and courtesans. Thousands of builders and carpenters were imported to build palaces for the families of the 250 feudal lords who were to reside in the new capital as gilded hostages. Almost overnight Edo – today's Tokyo – became a city, spilling from seven hillocks into the surrounding marshlands.[2] Bridges spanned the rivers and the creeks, and over them moved an unending stream of humanity. There have been other capital cities rising from swamp or desert at the whim of an ambitious ruler; but never has the event marked so great and long-lasting a change in a country's history.[3]

For fifty years before the move there had been growing contact between Japan and the seafaring nations of Europe. Trade with the Dutch and the British flourished. Portuguese Jesuits came to preach Christianity and became a power in the land.[4] Japanese merchants sailed along the Chinese coast and

---

[1] The dualism between the Emperor, directly descended from the sun goddess, and an effective ruler runs throughout Japanese history. The title Shogun (*Sei–i tai-Shogun* or "barbarian-slaying great general") was first bestowed on Minamoto Yarimoto in 1192 and remained a more or less permanent office of varying importance. Tokugawa Ieyasu of the House of Minamoto secured the title in 1603, and his descendants ruled Japan in the name of shadowy Emperors until the Meiji Restoration of 1863.

[2] Edo was renamed Tokyo or Eastern Capital in 1868.

[3] Even the foundation of St Petersburg by Peter the Great did not alter the power structure of Russia; nor did it isolate Russia from the outside world for 250 years.

[4] The Jesuits from Portugal were soon followed by Franciscan and Augustinian friars from Spain. Although the number of missionaries never exceeded two hundred, there were nearly half a million Japanese Christians out of a total population of fifteen to twenty million by the end of the sixteenth century. They included several powerful feudal lords who propagated the faith with almost European ruthlessness. Nagasaki was overwhelmingly Christian and virtually ruled by the Jesuits. Trade with the Portuguese centred on Macao and was highly prized for the imported Chinese silks. Trade with the Dutch and the English brought the musket and gunpowder to Japan and was devoid of any missionary fervour. Indeed, neither the Dutch nor the English were regarded as Christians by their hosts, a view with which the

in the East Indies, and were poised to penetrate the Philippines and anticipate by a hundred years Captain Cook's discovery of Australia. It was also a period of warring clans, the rise and fall of territorial barons, and of bloody and by and large futile adventures on the Asiatic mainland.[5] All this was swept away within a decade by the Tokugawa shogunate. Ieyashu was a soldier and politician of genius and total ruthlessness. Rivals were subdued, bought off or destroyed. Christianity and its native supporters were crushed.[6] The Emperor was provided with adequate funds to maintain a shadowy court in the old capital, Kyoto, but his role was to remain purely religious and ceremonial. No territorial magnate could approach him without the permission of the Shogun. Foreign conquest was renounced; foreign travel was prohibited; and all foreigners, except for a small Dutch trade mission in Nagasaki, were expelled. Isolated from the outside world, peace descended on the Island Empire.[7] It continued for an unprecedented 250 years.

Jesuit Fathers heartily concurred. See C. Boxer, *The Christian Century in Japan* (Berkeley, California, 1951).

[5] China and its peripheral satellites presented a constant challenge to predatory adventurers. (To the Chinese the inhabitants of Japan, like all alien races, were a species of monkeys.) In 1592 a Japanese army of 200,000 men, assembled by the warlord Hideyoshi, invaded Korea, occupied Seoul and reached the Imjin river. The consequences might have been a dress rehearsal for the war 360 years later. The Chinese intervened – the Ming Emperors were feudal overlords of the Kings of Korea – and the war ended with the rout of the invaders.

[6] The first edict prohibiting Christianity was issued by Ieyasu in 1612 but was not rigorously enforced. But his son, Hidetada, recognised the faith as irredeemably subversive. More than a hundred European and thousands of Japanese Christians were martyred. In 1637 a popular uprising on the Shimbabara peninsula quickly assumed a Christian character. The castle of Hara was defended under Jesuit leadership for three months. In the final massacre 300,000 are said to have perished with invocations of Jesus, Mary and St James on their lips. Christianity thereafter totally disappeared from the country – or so it was believed for three hundred years. But American travellers in the early years of the twentieth century were amazed to discover that it had survived in several small villages near Nagasaki as a secret faith passed on from father to son, complete with Baroque images of the Crucifixion and the Virgin. See Boxer, *The Christian Century in Japan.*

[7] The reason for closing the country was not so much fear of contamination by foreign ideas as the possibility that an alliance between a foreign power and a feudal lord might plunge the country into renewed civil war. Whatever the reason, after the final victory of Ieyasu over his main rival in 1616, the exclusion laws were savagely enforced. In 1640 a ship arrived from Macao in the hope that the Shogun might have mellowed. All but thirteen on board were beheaded at Nagasaki and the vessel was burned. The thirteen survivors were sent back to Macao with the message: "The great Shogun has even caused the clothes of those executed to be burnt. Let the citizens of Macao and Europe do the same to us if they find occasion to do so. Let them think no more of us just as if we were no longer in this world." See R. Storry, *A History of Modern Japan* (London, 1960).

The members of the small Dutch trade mission in Nagasaki were in all but name prisoners,

In 1760, the year of Katsushika Hokusai's birth,[8] the shogunate had been in power for many generations; and Edo had become the world's most populous metropolis.[9] Its citizens lived under a tyranny, but a tyranny so entrenched that it seemed more part of the natural universe than a political system devised and imposed by men.[10] As in the natural universe, life on the surface continued to froth and bubble as individuals – most of them reasonably housed, fed and entertained – scurried around in daily pursuit of pleasure, success and even happiness. This was the Floating World – *ukiyo-e* – of Edo, the world of kimonos, cherry blossom, geisha houses and tea ceremonies which was to enchant the first European travellers a century later.[11] It would not, of course, survive their blundering intrusion; but, if reality was to disappear, something of it remains preserved in tens of thousands of drawings, paintings and prints. Above all, it survives in the art of Hokusai.

Hokusai was born in a working-class district of Edo, of poor and obscure parentage.[12] At eight he was a delivery boy for one of the city's numerous lending libraries, flourishing establishments which catered for a large and leisured upper class and a prosperous middle class.[13] They purveyed

forbidden to communicate with anyone except a few selected government officials. But the trade, though small in volume, was highly profitable to both sides by the end of the eighteenth century, and European illustrated books smuggled out of the mission circulated widely among the cognoscenti.

[8] Katsushika, meaning an old peasant, was one of at least fifty names used by the artist at different periods of his life, a new name often marking a new style or a new enterprise. He did not start to call himself Hokusai till his mid thirties.

[9] Its population at the time was probably about half a million.

[10] But not so entrenched as to be able to dispense with a vast network of secret police. The great feudal lords were seemingly absolute masters in their own domains and displayed all the trappings of power, but, apart from having to spend half of every year at the Shogun's court and having to leave their families there as permanent hostages, their every move was reported to the Shogun in Edo.

[11] The term *ukiyo-e*, meaning "images of the floating world", became synonymous in Europe with Japanese woodcuts towards the end of the nineteenth century. See J. Micherel, *The Floating World* (New York, 1954); G. Schack, *Aus der Fliessend-vergänglichen Welt*, exhibition catalogue (Baden-Baden, 1984); R. Neuer and S. Yoshida, *Ukiyo-e: 250 Years of Japanese Art* (London, 1990).

[12] There are now several excellent and authoritative monographs in English on Hokusai, including J. Hillier, *Hokusai: Paintings, Drawings and Woodcuts* (London, 1960); R. Lane, *Hokusai: Life and Work* (London, 1989); M. Forrer, *Prints and Drawings*, exhibition catalogue (London, 1992).

[13] Although there were other large urban centres in Japan, notably Osaka, the country's commercial capital, Edo was unique in being not only the seat of government but also the enforced second home of the country's aristocracy.

romances, poetry, children's literature, instructional manuals and erotica, most of the books being lavishly illustrated. The fact that Hokusai was allowed to carve his first set of wood-blocks at the age of fourteen, only a year after starting his apprenticeship, points to a precocious talent. By the age of eighteen he was a member of the workshop of Shunsho,[14] a successful print-maker; and, over the next twenty years, he drew, painted, copied and carved thousands of pictures and prints for the firm.

This was strictly commercial art, and Hokusai would remain a commercial artist for the rest of his life. Indeed, even if he often lamented the unremitting daily grind, the idea that art could exist independently of a pre-existing demand for no purpose other than itself probably never crossed his mind. Demand, of course, largely depended on the quality of the product; and from the start Hokusai's products were recognised as being among the best. But they were not yet in a class of their own. All that he created during these decades – his subjects, his formats, and the time allowed for each work – was strictly prescribed by the workshop; and even commercial artists need a measure of freedom to give of their best. But in Japan toward the end of eighteenth century to leave an established firm and strike out on one's own required courage bordering on the foolhardy. What eventually impelled him to do so is uncertain. Perhaps he was passed over for promotion. Perhaps he was sacked for moonlighting for rival firms. (He was by now responsible for a growing family and always short of money.)[15] More probably, he was touched by the political ferment of the 1790s.[16] Most likely his obsessive drive to expand and improve his repertory, to experiment and to spread his artistic wings, proved stronger than conformist pressures.

His timing was lucky in some respects, unlucky in others. His life was to remain a frantic struggle for the support of publishers, the benevolence of patrons and the fickle favour of the public. He would never know financial security, let alone the comforts of affluence. But he gained his freedom at a time when the Floating World (always a little bored) was prosperous and avid for excitement and novelty. New fashions, fads and crazes helped him

[14] Shunsho was fifty-two at the time and particularly famous for his theatrical prints.

[15] In 1794 his young wife died, leaving him with a son and a daughter. He remarried after a year and had another son and three daughters. One of his daughters by his second wife was the gifted painter O Ei.

[16] Coinciding with the last years of the Enlightenment and the French Revolution in Europe, the Kansei reforms were an attempt by the government to root out corruption and moral laxity by strict censorship. This attempt foundered largely on the resistance of the ladies of the Shogun's own court. These redoubtable women, many of them the extremely rich daughters of the feudal aristocracy, formed the backbone of the public for *ukiyo-e* prints, particularly those with theatrical or erotic subjects.

to prosper. One might seem quaint, even exotic to western readers if that same madness had not spread to Europe and America a century and a half later. Just as today one would have to be a monastic recluse to be born, start school, get a job, be sacked, marry, have children, go to prison, be promoted, be rejected, get divorced, break a leg, recover, retire, have anniversaries and of course die without being showered with pictorial messages conceived, composed and executed (but for a signature) by total strangers, so the art of the *surimono* or greeting card blossomed in Japan in the first decades of the nineteenth century.[17] It created an almost insatiable demand for prints, some representations of daily life, others appropriate commemorations of historical or legendary events, a few illustrating scenes from classical literature, some jocular and some rude. Hokusai was ready, single-handedly if need be, to satisfy the demand.[18]

At a higher artistic level the special appeal of the *kyoka* albums, privately printed anthologies of poetry, lay partly in their exemption from state censorship. The best were single or limited editions printed on hand-crafted paper, embellished with brilliantly coloured double-page illustrations. They were destined to be enjoyed and cherished by a few, like the illuminated Books of Hours of the European middle ages. But not quite. Unlike medieval monks, who would sometimes toil for weeks over a single capital letter, Hokusai produced his drawings in hours or, at the most, days. The printing took much longer. The evergreen appeal of Gothic novels also called for prints featuring the forerunners of *Ghostbusters* and other staples of today's children's literature.[19]

The 1790s were Hokusai's first golden decade, its artistic yield so varied

---

[17] Literally "printed item", it even anticipated the "pop-up" cards of today. The equivalent of the classical Christmas card was the New Year *surimono*. It was dispatched by the million. In addition to conveying a greeting, it also served to evade the government monopoly on calendars, indicating the long and short months of the coming lunar year in coded forms. See R. Lane, *Images of the Floating World: The Japanese Print with Illustrated Dictionary* (London, 1978); R. Keyes, *The Art of the Surimono*, 2 volumes (London, 1985).

[18] His pre-eminence in the field is shown by a print from a rival firm, showing a geisha picking up a card. "It must be by Hokusai", the geisha exclaims, lifting the *surimono* with her *samisen* and revealing some of her charms. Lane, *Images of the Floating World*, p. 48.

Among occasional purchasers were members of the Dutch House in Nagasaki: this was how the first examples of *surimono* art reached Europe. But the real revelation came decades later with the wrappings of Japanese pottery and porcelain imported to France, showing richly illustrated pages from books and even single prints.

[19] The literacy of Edo in Hokusai's day must have far surpassed that of any city in Europe. Hokusai's own output – and he had dozens of rivals – catered for every class of urban society. Edo was not of course the whole of Japan. The peasantry in most parts of the country subsisted in the same brutish conditions as those which prevailed in Europe.

and so rich that it is impossible to choose representative examples. A lively
scene from a mountain tea-house? A glimpse of street urchins on the banks
of a canal? A group of gallants and courtesans engaged in polite chit-chat?
A scene from a bath-house? A classical composition of cherry blossom against
the moon? Or an animated panorama of boatmen, travellers, pedlars, housewives and children caught in a summer squall? "There is nothing to compare
with these prints in European art of the past or the present", Edmond de
Goncourt enthused about them when – decades later – the first examples
reached Europe.[20] The rapture of the Impressionists and of atmospheric
painters like Whistler may seem surprising, since, on the face of it, their
diffuse pools of light and colour had little in common with the sharp sinuous
lines of Japanese art. But the immediacy with which Hokusai would capture
a passing moment was not far removed from the impulse behind much of
the best work of Monet and his iconoclastic troupe.

Fans, toys, screens, posters, calendars: nothing was outside Hokusai's
range. In his mid fifties he produced his best books of erotica. Tiptoeing
round the subject, early academic biographers have produced labyrinthine
explanations and even apologias. It is difficult to see the need for any
other than an appreciative market and the fact that, until the last quarter of
the nineteenth century, good sex was to Japanese as good food was to
Europeans;[21] and Hokusai's declared conviction that anything that Utamaro
and others masters of the past could do, he could do better. Better or not,
the virtuosity of these prints is almost as stunning as that of the performers.[22]
Huysmans, self-appointed high priest of *fin de siècle* depravity, declared *The
Diving Girl and the Octopi* the most exciting picture he had ever seen.[23]

Hokusai was constantly on the move. Since only samurai and the great
feudal lords could travel by palanquin or on horseback, this meant tramping

---

[20] Two important and surprisingly well-informed books were published in France within
a few years of the first study published in Japan (by Ijima Kyoshin): E. de Goncourt, *Hokusai*
(Paris, 1896) and M. Revon, *Etude sur Hok'sai* (Paris, 1897). There was also an important series
of articles by Siegfried Bing, "La vie et l'oeuvre d'Hok'sai", in the *Revue Blanche* in 1895–96.

[21] Even to the religious connotations of both. The lavishly illustrated albums of erotica were
titillating but no more shocking to the Edoite of Hokusai's day than cookery books and
magazines are to today's housewife. The converse may also be true. The art of *ukiyo-e*,
*surimono* and *kyota* embraces almost every aspect of daily life but hardly ever portrays food
and eating. The obsessive preoccupation of western art with men and women gorging themselves, or about to gorge themselves, or having their appetite whetted for gorging by images
of mountains of food (not to mention the acreage of print devoted to the subject today),
would have filled readers of Hokusai's erotica with amazement bordering on revulsion.

[22] See R. Lane, *Hokusai and Hiroshige*, 2 volumes (Tokyo, 1976); T. and M. Evans, *Shunga:
The Art of Love in Japan* (London, 1975).

[23] The girls were diving for pearls. Attack by sea monsters was a common theme.

across the country on foot with a heavy bundle on his back. Part of the reason was probably his insatiable curiosity; but business too played a part. Nagoya, a week's journey from Edo, became the centre of what amounted to a Hokusai cult. It was here, surrounded by friends and disciples, that he worked on his series of *manga* or instruction books. Painting was second only to versification as a popular hobby; and manuals for amateur artists were bestsellers. Nothing else, however, could compare with Hokusai's series of at least fifteen volumes, containing over four thousand plates and tens of thousands of sketched figures, for every grade of student; from toddlers just about to wield their first brush to semi-professionals. All show the depth of his concern with design, composition, balance and all the hidden technicalities of graphic art.

At seventy Hokusai could look back on an exceptionally productive life. Had he died at that age, he would still be remembered as one of the most accomplished *ukiyo-e* artists. But he went on to what he himself described as his second life, years of feverish activity in a virtually new genre.

He had, of course, experimented with landscape before. The European idea of perspective, trickling past the censorship which isolated as best it could the Dutch trade mission in Nagasaki, fascinated him.[24] But until the 1820s there was no demand for such prints, and publishers would not invest in what they regarded as an unsaleable commodity. What created the demand was another of the compulsions that gripped Japan a century or so ahead of western Europe and the Americas. Even the reasons were not dissimilar. Increasing prosperity fuelled the aspirations of ordinary people to travel, not on lordly educational grand tours or on business but for sheer pleasure. In Japan this had long been formally forbidden or at least restricted.[25] Now the prohibition suddenly became both irksome and difficult to enforce. The movement began with a wave of religious pilgrimages, one of the few kinds of travel tolerated by the government in Edo. Within a few years those travelling to distant shrines rose from a few thousand to over a million a year. Then the religious gloss began to wear off. The real attractions became the change, the excitements of the journey, the numerous inns, teahouses and pleasure quarters that sprang up along the main roads, the relaxation of inhibitions and usages imposed in the homes and, as usual, the fact that

---

[24] The *Thirty-Six Views of Mount Fuji*, though quintessentially Japanese, clearly show the influence of western ideas of perspective. The impact of these ideas was comparable to their impact on fifteenth-century Florentine artists.

[25] This was one reason why bridges were so few and why they were of such significance. Hundreds of Japanese prints show travellers fording rivers sitting on the backs of the ferrymen who substituted for bridges.

everybody else was travelling.[26] A side effect of this new-found freedom was a plethora of guide-books, travel brochures and souvenir albums, glossy and tempting. This was the origin of the *Thirty-Six Views of Mount Fuji*.[27]

Hokusai's choice of theme was not of course accidental. Since time immemorial the majestic volcano had been more than a geographical landmark. Surrounded by legend, it had become an object of veneration and even of worship. Almost every province had its own "Provincial Fuji", a local mountain vaguely resembling the sacred peak; and where no such geographical formation was available, mounds of earth or even artificial hills were erected to serve as centres of the Fuji cult. Hokusai liked to call himself "The Old Man Mad with Painting"; and, even if this contained an element of affectation, he could be so obsessed with a challenging new task that he probably did appear to be slightly demented. The way in which these masterpieces were created must also have demanded a degree of creative dementia. He probably had no more than a day or two to prepare each preliminary sketch. He would then check with the publishers that it did not resemble an earlier design too closely. He might spend another day or two preparing the final draft for the wood-block carver. This would then be pasted to the cherry-wood block and the outlines carved with the greatest possible speed. The proofs would be dispatched by courier to the publisher, who would hurriedly discuss the colour scheme with the artist. Deadlines were constantly looming to meet the needs of the season, fashion and finance.

Despite the pressures and the speed, not a single print in the series is just a passing impression. Every landscape, however traditional at a first glance, is dissected into basic shapes – squares, circles, triangles, empty spaces – and reassembled into something startling and new. Indeed, the avoidance of the obvious sometimes seems almost too strenuous. But Hokusai was consciously creating a new genre and he wanted to grip. Even the colouring is usually muted as if to express the artist's confidence in the perfection of his line and design.

In *South Wind: Clear Dawn*, known to every Japanese schoolchild as *The Red Fuji* (Plate 11), the eye is led gradually up the left slope of the mountain, past huge trees reduced to shrubs by the distance, past the tree line, past the brick-red peak and on to the autumnal summit capped by the first light snow of the coming winter. The dark masses are spaced far apart; the light areas adjoin like geological plates. The background is a plain caerulean blue with strata shaded from light to dark by cirrocumulus clouds, spaced like

[26] Lotteries were popular among the Edo proletariat and among the most coveted prizes were vouchers for travel.

[27] See J. Suzuki, *Katsushika Hokusai: Fugaku Hyakkei* (Hokusai's Hundred Views of Fuji) (Tokyo, 1986), in Japanese but superbly illustrated.

ice floes. The uppermost dark band fixes the composition. The whole is essentially only one line and three basic colours; but, as in all Japanese art, what is left unsaid is as important as what is explicitly stated.

In *The Great Wave*, as in several others prints in the series, the Sacred Mountain is only a distant spectator. The protagonist is the giant wave soaring up on the left. Its octopus fingers reach out for the sky and seem to hold the boat and the diminutive oarsmen clinging to their craft in their grasp. Undiminished by familiarity and countless inferior imitations, it remains a breathtaking conception. When it first crashed over Europe, forty years after Hokusai's death, it did literally that – take people's breath away. At least it did that of Rainer Maria Rilke who poured his sense of awe into *Der Berg*. Gide pronounced it "unsurpassable". Debussy was inspired by it to compose *La Mer*. The Hungarian Vajda wrote that it transformed everybody's perception of Man's relationship to Nature.[28]

Both *The Red Fuji* and *The Wave* are supreme simplicities; but Hokusai could also conjure up the intimate complexities of everyday life. *Sunset over Ryogoku Bridge* is a spacious orchestral tableau of the Floating World. Ferrymen, tradesmen, a bird-catcher, an itinerant pedlar, a masseur, a samurai, a man napping among the wayfarers, a woman doing her laundry from a houseboat, all pursue their tiny destinies against the solitary and permanent grandeur of Fuji. The picture has the haphazard intimacy of the snapshot; but it is anything but haphazard. The chain of circles leading from the laundry by way of the top of the pole and the parasol to the dancing rain-hats is carefully spaced along an imaginary curve with Fuji as its focal point. The arches of the bridge echo the shape of the wavelets. The vertical of the pole serves as a slashing line: it binds together the receding horizontal strata of shore, river and boat. There is in fact not a single print in the series which does not reflect Hokusai's lifelong preoccupation with design and a distillation of its basic principles.

In the west, and perhaps in Japan, the *Views of Fuji* are often represented as the culmination of Hokusai's life's work. But they were closely followed by other series, less well known but no less inspired. The scenes of the *Waterfalls* have the kind of staginess that would be intolerable if it were not wholly convincing. *The Bridges* include some of Hokusai's most haunting snowstorms. Moonlight, that most elusive of atmospheric phenomena, resonates in some of the *Rare Views of Famous Landscapes*. *Oceans of Wisdom* is a succession of scenes from the ordinary lives of peasants, fishermen and plodding humanity. Everything is transformed into visual poetry. Dating

[28] It is said that its impact is even greater on Japanese viewers who tend to "read" pictures from right to left.

from the same years, individual prints depict animals, flowers, sages, warriors, ghosts, courtesans and gods. Others were planned when the bottom
fell out of the print market.

Following a period of great prosperity, several years of crop failure in the
late 1830s led to soaring food prices and famine in parts of the country.
There were rice riots in Osaka and unrest in other major cities. The Tempo
reforms were the government's attempt to cope with the troubles – a barrage
of stringent regulations and sumptuary edicts designed to quell popular
aspirations, or at least any expression of them. But the austere fiscal measures
only deepened the crisis. There was also, for the first time since the institution
of the shogunate, a clear perception of danger from outside, as foreign ships
clamoured for admission into the country's ports.[29] But for Hokusai the
period remained one of intense activity. If prints would not sell in an
atmosphere of austerity, he would return to book illustration, recreating
both the now increasingly turbulent Floating World and the unchanging
beauties of Nature in cheaper formats.[30] But he was not striving for cheapness
alone.

Almost imperceptibly, for even Hokusai's earliest works seem to western
eyes models of economy, his last period reached a degree of simplification
which he had never achieved before. Leaves, flowers and birds were transformed into the very ideas of leaves, flowers and birds, and yet lost none of
their individuality or beauty. There was a total lack of pretentiousness about
these almost casual creations. Among his last projects was a multi-tome
instruction manual of how to paint like Hokusai. To Europeans, brought
up to reverence the mystique of artistic creation (or at least to pretend to),
it is mind-boggling to be told in kindergarten language how first to place
a dot on a blank sheet of paper, then step by step how to transform that
dot into a perfect and yet unique cherry blossom or an eagle, and then
how to create not one but a whole series of different Hokusai waves. Could
Michelangelo have compiled such a course for prospective decorators of
ceilings? Or Leonardo one on the art of painting enigmatic smiles? Was this
really, as Hokusai claimed, a quick and simple way of learning how to paint
like Hokusai? Whatever the answer to the first questions, the answer to the
last is a regretful but firm no.

---

[29] It was fourteen years after Hokusai's death, in August 1853, that Commodore Matthew
Parry of the United States Navy sailed with his squadron of Black Ships into the Bay of
Nagasaki and presented the shogunate government with what amounted to an ultimatum to
open trade negotiations. The visible end of isolation came four years later when United States
Consul-General Townsend Harris was ushered past members of the Shogun's great council
into the presence of Tokugawa Iesada, the thirteenth Shogun.
[30] J. Hiller, *The Art of the Japanese Book*, 2 volumes (London, 1987).

He was still continually on the move. By his own account he had fifty-six
lodgings in his late seventies – perhaps to escape creditors, perhaps because
he hated house cleaning and this could be avoided only by moving to new
quarters whenever the detritus of daily life threatened to engulf him. He was
plagued by periodic paralysis of the legs, a mysterious disorder impossible
to diagnose with any certainty across the time span of more than a century.
But he never ceased production. A famous print by his pupil, Tsuyuki Iitsu
II, shows him crouched on the floor covered with a quilt, presumably unable
to stand, but still assiduously painting. A large notice on the wall says: "No
more commissions accepted for albums or fan paintings." That was probably
more easily said than done. Times were hard: Hokusai at eighty, past his
novelty value, though not, in his own estimation, anywhere past his prime,
was probably glad to have any commission he could get. He illustrated five
volumes of T'ang poetry and ten volumes of a translated Chinese novel,
*Shinpen Suikogaden*.[31] Then came what might seem like a conscious farewell,
a return to the theme of what was still widely regarded as his master work.

*The Hundred Views of Mount Fuji* are as much a landmark in Japanese
book illustration as the *Thirty-Six Views* were in prints, the quality of the
small pictures for once matched by the standard of block-cutting and the
shading. Starting with pictures of the gods most closely associated with the
Sacred Mountain, there follows a *reprise* of the views of Fuji itself, stylised
in a seemingly inexhaustible variety of ways but instantly recognisable and
dominating. But if the last plates could serve as any great artist's epitaph,
this was not how the artist himself saw them. In a biographical postscript
to the first volume, he wrote:

> From the age of six I was in the habit of drawing all kinds of things. Although
> I had produced numerous designs by my fiftieth year, none of my work done
> before my seventieth is really worth counting. At the age of seventy-three I have
> come to understand the true forms of animals, insects and fish and the nature
> of plants and trees. Consequently, by the age of eighty-six I will have made more
> and more progress, and at ninety I will have got significantly closer to the essence
> of art. At the age of one hundred I will have reached a magnificent level and at
> one hundred and ten each dot and each line will be alive. I would like to ask
> you who outlive me to observe that I have not spoken without reason.[32]

But had he not reached that "magnificent level" already? Not, apparently,
in his own view – or indeed in the world's. In his mid eighties he was still
desperately poor, at times hawking his prints in the streets. What was the

---

[31] M. Forrer, *Hokusai: A Guide to the Serial Graphics* (London, 1974); P. Morse, *Hokusai:
One Hundred Poets* (London, 1989).

[32] Translated by Gakiorojin Manji and quoted by Forrer, *Prints and Drawings*, p. 89.

reason? Book illustration and print making was never a highly profitable profession, but others, including his younger rival, Hiroshige,[33] had made a living from it without having to scrounge and to scrape. His delinquent adopted son was a source of worry and perhaps a drain on his resources;[34] but other artists had troublesome families without being reduced to the brink of starvation. He was not, so far as is known, a gambler, and not extravagant except in his striving for perfection. His work was still popular; and as a person he was venerated. One can only guess that he was either monumentally improvident or totally indifferent to money, perhaps both. Whatever the reason, it was not a prescription for living to a hundred and ten.

His final illness struck him in the spring of 1849. He was looked after by a devoted daughter, O Ei (a good artist in her own right), and cheered or plagued by a stream of visitors. One of them recorded his last hours. "If Heaven will grant me but ten more years", he was heard sighing, "I promise to be a truly great artist." He paused for breath, but there was still something on his mind. The visitor moved closer. "I have only just learnt how to hold a brush properly. Even with five more years ..." Another friend recorded that the "denizens of the slum where he lived had never seen a funeral of one of their number attended by samurai and great lords in full regalia. They were beside themselves with wonderment and envy." [35]

---

[33] Hiroshige Utagawa was born in 1797 and died in 1858, aged sixty-one.
[34] Really his grandson, the son of a much-loved daughter who died young.
[35] Quoted by Lane, *Images of the Floating World*, pp. 465 and 668.

# 8

# *Renoir*

Cagnes-sur-Mer at the turn of the century was a thriving village of prosperous peasants. On the gently sloping hills around it olive and orange groves rose in tiers. The olive trees had been there since the time of François I; and for some reason they had never been trimmed as elsewhere in the south of France. They were – as they still are – huge and gnarled.[1] Their silvery leaves cast subtle shadows. The local produce was rich and varied. The orange blossoms were sold to perfumeries in Grasse. The wine was sharp but excellent, though it did not travel well. Every house had its own vegetable garden, chicken run and rabbits. At Les Collettes, Aline Renoir was to plant hundreds of tangerine trees. Their produce became famous among their friends. The little sardines which the wives of fishermen carried on flat baskets on their heads were delicious. And nothing could surpass the beauty of the valley of the small winding river with the Baou mountain just visible over the reeds. At least this is what Renoir thought. "It was a love story, deep and passionate, though, like all stories about Renoir, unsensational."[2] Yet, when

---

[1] Although difficult to harvest, aficionados maintain that their fruit is especially delectable.

[2] Jean Renoir, *Renoir, My Father,* translated by R. and D. Weaver (London, 1962), p. 82. Great artists often painted their children. Few of the children had the gift or the opportunity to repay their parent in kind. The film director Jean Renoir did so in his wonderfully affectionate and yet revealing memoir. Other evocative first-hand accounts of the artist include G. Rivière, *Renoir et ses amis* (Paris, 1921); *Lettres de Degas,* edited by M. Guérin (Paris, 1945); A. André, *Renoir* (Paris, 1928); A. Vollard, *Souvenirs d'un marchand de tableaux: en écoutant Cézanne, Degas, Renoir* (Paris, 1938); and J. Manet, *Journal* (Paris, 1979). The last was written by Manet's niece Julie, the daughter of Eugène Manet and Berthe Morisot, in the 1880s and 1890s; but it was not published till almost a century later. She vividly recorded many meetings and conversations with Renoir. Unfortunately, she stopped keeping a diary when she married Ernest Rouart, Degas' pupil. Letters to and from Renoir are included in L. Venturi, *Les archives de l'Impressionisme,* 2 volumes (Paris, 1939); R. Friedenthal, *Letters of the Great Artists* (London, 1963); and B. Denvir, editor, *The Impressionists at First Hand* (London, 1987). The first (and in some respects still the best) "history" of Impressionism was written by the critic, writer and friend of the artists, G. Geffroy, *Histoire de l'Impressionisme* (Paris, 1894). J. Rewald, *The History of Impressionism* (New York, 1946) remains a classic. Good monographs on Renoir include W. Gaunt, *Renoir* (London, 1952); B. E. White, *Renoir: His Art, Life and Letters* (New York, 1984); and P. H. Feist, *Auguste Pierre Renoir: un rêve d'harmonie* (Cologne, 1990).

the family moved there, he was already sixty and crippled by a painful and inexorably advancing illness.

He disliked extravagant phrases. When visitors described his struggle as "heroic", he punctured the adjective at once. Heroism implied a free choice. He had none. And, in any case, he did not think much of heroism if that meant pitting oneself against one's nature or destiny. That was always a mistake. Nor did he ever condemn what was often labelled cowardice. Everybody – and indeed everything – had a function in life, great or small. Some creatures seemed to fulfil their function better – or more easily – than others; but most of them tried. His own function was to paint. It also happened to be his joy. He was blessed.

It had been an unlikely career, and for most of his life a precarious one. He was four when the family moved from Limoges to Paris.[3] His father, a tailor, mother and five children lived in two rooms above the shop. The house was one of a row which separated the Louvre from the Tuilleries. It dated back to the Valois kings and had once been the quarters of the royal guards. Now, during the reign of Louis-Philippe, it was cramped and crumbling. The children played in the narrow streets and courtyards of the palace. Queen Amélie would sometimes lean out of the first-floor window and ask them politely to be a little less boisterous while she and her husband were entertaining foreign royalty or listening to the playing of famous musicians. The children would usually oblige and were rewarded with a few sous wrapped in scented tissue paper bearing the royal cipher.[4]

Such proximity to ordinary folk was of course intolerable to Napoleon *le Petit* when he took up residence in the Tuilleries in 1851. The houses were pulled down, a fate soon to befall most of old Paris. Renoir was not a sentimentalist. He liked Baron Haussmann's spacious new boulevards, but he detested the pompous architecture which rose on either side of them. It symbolised the world of bankers, speculators and entrepreneurs who seemed to be the mainstay of the Second Empire. "How do they get air into those rooms?", he asked his friend Bazille. "They have it delivered in expensive sealed bottles of course, like champagne", was the answer.[5]

By the time the family settled in their new home in the Marais in 1856, Auguste was fifteen and ready to start work. Soon he was decorating porcelain

[3] In 1845. Born in 1841, he was christened Pierre-Auguste but he was never Pierre. "Too many rs", said Mme Renoir.

[4] Opinions about King Louis-Philippe varied (as they still do) but everybody loved his Queen.

[5] G. Poulain, *Bazille et ses amis* (Paris, 1932), p. 129. This was only partly said in jest. "Health-giving" air bottled in various spas, the bottles to be opened in bedrooms at night, were widely sold before the First World War and hyped in much the same way as health-giving mineral waters are today.

plates in Monsieur Lévy's small pottery shop. He was extremely skilful. Starting with garlands of roses along the borders in the manner of Limoges, he quickly progressed to portraits of Queen Marie-Antoinette as a shepherdess after Mme Vigée Lebrun in the centre wells; or, for loyal supporters of the Bonaparte dynasty, Napoleon I in profile, surmounted by an eagle, after Isabey. He painted hundreds of those and he always maintained that he loved it. He was also fascinated by the firing process, a craft calling for dexterity and inspired timing. It was to become one of the attractions of modelling terracotta figurines, the unlikely passion of his old age. And all his life he poured scorn on the idea that "commercial art" was inherently inferior to the "fine arts", an expression he hated. The half-witted criticism that his bouquets of roses, bathing beauties and pierrots were "chocolate-box art", still occasionally heard, would have offended him not in the least. What was wrong with chocolate boxes? Only perhaps that the pictures on them were usually machine-reproduced and garishly printed instead of being hand-painted by a skilled craftsman like himself.

The cheap printing machine eventually put Monsieur Lévy's shop and hundreds of other small faïenceries out of business. By then young Renoir's skill was known in the *quartier* and, in the boom years of the early 1860s, he had no difficulty in finding another job. For another two years he painted scenic awnings – flying birds, rose-coloured clouds, distant landscapes, sometimes angels – on transparent paper, in great demand by the missionary Fathers as a substitute for stained-glass in French Indochina. Only the *patron*, Monsieur Jumeau, grumbled. He did not begrudge the young man his wages; but earning so much so young could lead to extravagant expectations. Perhaps he had a point. Renoir did buy little luxuries for others – a lace collar for his sister Liza, a gold-headed cane for his father. (He adored his mother but she would never accept such fripperies.) But he was abstemious himself, and by the age of twenty-two he had saved enough to buy an artist's palette, paints and brushes and to enrol in the painting atelier of Monsieur Gleyre.[6] The institution was discreetly promoted by the Ecole des Beaux-Arts and dedicated to the perpetuation of the precepts laid down by the great Monsieur Ingres for now and all eternity; it also promised to maintain a moral tone which could bring no blush to the cheeks of well-bred young ladies from the Faubourg St-Honoré. Painting in direct sunlight was shunned and the plaster models of Greek gods and goddesses were decorously draped before being mounted on the platform to be faithfully copied. It was in this

[6] In the historicising atmosphere of mid nineteenth-century France the ateliers pretended to be medieval workshops. Gleyre was not *professeur* or *maître* but *patron*, and the students were apprentices. See A. Boime, *The Académie and French Painting in the Nineteenth Century* (London, 1971).

elevated temple of the muses that Renoir first met Monet, Bazille, Sisley and Pissarro, and that Impressionism was born.

More precisely, it was born on outings from the Temple. Nobody could later recall what precisely made a few young men first set up their easels in the Forest of Fontainebleau, and later on the banks of the Seine and on the pavements of busy Paris boulevards, and begin to paint the sky, the river, boats, trees, people and houses not as they undoubtedly were but as they (also undoubtedly) appeared to be to the artists in fugitive moments of sunshine, rain, snow, dusk or dawn.[7] They called themselves *Les Intransigeants* and they had great fun. Bazille, a rich boulevardier and *doux chevalier*,[8] opened Renoir's eyes to the scintillating intellectual and artistic metropolis in which they lived but of which Renoir had been unaware. Sisley, half English, was a *vrai gentleman*, cool, charming and reserved.[9] Pissarro, the

[7] The *plein air* school of painting had been well-established in the Forest of Fontainebleau for some years by the time the Impressionists moved in; and Renoir always paid tribute to the forerunners – Théodore Rousseau, Paal, Daubigny and especially Diaz, "in whose paintings one can almost smell the dead leaves and the mushrooms". But he disliked Millet, whose peasants struck him as "bad actors dressed up as men of the soil". There were other painters too who liked to paint out of doors – Boudin in particular, who first introduced Monet to *plein air* painting in Normandy, and occasionally Corot. But none went as far as the Impressionists in their dedication to capturing the fugitive moment and leaving the impression unretouched. (Only Degas set his face firmly against the practice of "making painting into a sporting event".)

[8] Fréderic Bazille, one of the few rich members of the group, painted the best portrait of Renoir as a young man. Renoir reciprocated, perhaps a little less successfully. Bazille was killed by a stray bullet (probably French) while serving on the staff of General Barrail during the first week of the Franco-Prussian War. He was twenty-nine.

On the outbreak of the war Renoir was offered an easy posting by the art-loving Prince Bibesco: "Take your paints along, those German women will make excellent models." Though Renoir admitted to being terrified of gunfire, he did not want anyone else to take his place in the front line while he was painting pretty Fräuleins. In any case, he and Monet (who decamped to London) were among the few who took a less than sanguine view of the outcome of the war. "These Prussians have thrashed the Austrians and we're pretty much like the Austrians", Renoir said. Eventually, though he had never sat on horseback in his life, he was posted to a cavalry regiment in Bordeaux. (The General Staff felt that it was essential to boost the cavalry since horsemen would get to Berlin more quickly than the foot-sloggers.) When Renoir's total incapacity with horses became apparent, his commanding officer, who, like all good cavalry officers, did not mind losing his men so long as his horses were not maltreated, assigned him to giving painting lessons to his daughter. "She was a charming young woman", Renoir later recalled, "and not entirely without talent, but more interested in dogs."

After Sedan Renoir was demobilised and escaped, by the luck of the draw, the six-year military service compulsory for a third of all Frenchmen.

[9] Alfred Sisley came from a rich English family but was ruined financially by the Franco-Prussian War. Modest and shy, he was much loved by the other Impressionists. He died in Moret-sur-Loing in 1899, aged sixty. See A. Sharp, *Alfred Sisley* (London, 1966).

doyen of the group, was tense and exotic.[10] And, dazzling them all, there was Monet. Though apparently penniless, he wore shirts with Alençon lace at the cuffs, patronised the most expensive tailors in Paris, and insisted on cushioning the little wooden stool provided by Monsieur Gleyre for his students with a stuffed oriental saddle-bag. "You must forgive me, my dear", he told a woman fellow student who was (or possibly was not) making eyes at him, "but I only sleep with duchesses or prostitutes." Renoir was always attracted to people who were totally unlike him, provided they were genuine; and Monet delighted him.[11]

For many years the joy of having discovered an entirely new way of looking at the physical world and trying to reproduce that vision on canvas compensated for all material hardships. After leaving Monsieur Gleyre's Atelier – their funds had run out – Renoir and Monet shared a studio, models and a diet based on lentils alternating with beans. "It was a little hard on the stomach, but from time to time Monet would wangle a dinner from one of the tradesmen whose wife or daughter he or I had painted, and then we would gorge ourselves on turkey with truffles washed down with Chambertin." [12] Astonishingly, perhaps, they never contemplated giving up. Astonishingly, too, they met a few level-headed businessmen who not only professed to like their daubs but considered them acceptable speculative investments. Exclusive contracts were a new kind of art patronage to suit the new capitalist age, and many artists regarded them with grave misgivings. Renoir was not one of them. He had no ideological hang-ups: he would not adjust his style of life and painting to suit his dealers; but the dealers who accepted him as he was he treated as friends.[13] "Without old Durand we

[10] Born in St Thomas in the West Indies, the son of a Creole mother and a father of Portuguese-Jewish descent, he ran away from home and arrived in Paris in 1855. Of all the great Impressionists, he was the most consistent and uncompromising, as well as being an inspired teacher. But his life remained a struggle to the end against poverty and ill health. He went blind five years before he died in 1903, aged seventy-two. See L. R. Pissarro and L. Venturi, *Camille Pissarro: son art et son oeuvre*, 2 volumes (Paris, 1939).

[11] G. Geffroy, *Claude Monet: sa vie, son temps, son oeuvre* (Paris, 1922).

[12] J. Renoir, *Renoir, My Father*, p. 62.

[13] It was the great artist-collectors and dealers – Caillebotte, Chocquet, Vollard, the Bernheims, the Charpentiers, Javier – who were the new Medicis and saved the Impressionists. The greatest of them, Paul Durand-Ruel, was a friend as well as a dealer: his son, Georges, was Jean Renoir's godfather. The French state, by contrast, did not buy a Renoir till 1894; and, as late as 1900, the distinguished orientalist Paul Gerôme tried to bar the way of President Loubet when, at the opening of the Exposition Universelle in Paris, the head of state was about to enter a small room set aside for a few Impressionist paintings. "Stop, Monsieur le Président, this is France's shame!" Nor did the general public begin to buy Impressionists until just before the First World War.

would have starved", he later recalled. "Of course he was a reactionary; but we needed a reactionary to protect us." And they needed all the protection they could get.

For even more remarkable than the faith of a few businessmen was the venom of the art-critical establishment. "After the fire at the Opéra a new disaster has befallen the rue Pelletier", Albert Wolff wrote in the *Figaro*.

> An exhibition of what is described as painting has just opened at Durand-Ruel's. The innocent pedestrian, attracted by the flags outside, may go in for a look. But what a cruel spectacle will meet his eyes! Five or six lunatics – one of them a woman – make up a group of poor wretches who have succumbed to madness and ambition and dared to put on an exhibition of their work ... It is a horrible and pathetic spectacle, reminding me of the inmates of the Ville-Evrard Asylum.[14]

And column after column of such fulmination. Of course incomprehension and ridicule had often greeted new styles and unorthodox masterpieces in the past; but with Impressionism understanding flounders. Even allowing for the novelty of the technique, how could anybody fail to be ravished by the sheer sensuous beauty of Renoir's *La Loge* or the *joie de vivre* of his *La Grenouillère*? Yet unravished the critics remained or worse: most of them regarded the works as unworthy even of execration.

It went on for years, one flop after another. After each débâcle the commissions for portraits on which they depended dried up. Old friends were now earning respectable wages or salaries; many were married and settled in bourgeois comfort. Commercial and academic art beckoned. "But I had tasted the forbidden fruit; and I was not going to give up." Also, for some years at least, there was Monet to help boost morale. "Poor blind idiots", he raged, when a critic tried to explain to him that fog and smoke were not fit subjects for a picture: it only made him determined to find something even foggier. Of course. The Gare St-Lazare. A veritable dream world of fog! And, with Renoir in tow, introduced as his canvas carrier, he marched into the hallowed office of the stationmaster and congratulated him warmly. For long, Monet informed the bewildered official, he, Monsieur Monet, had hesitated between the Gare du Nord and the Gare St-Lazare. He was pleased to say that he had eventually decided in favour of the latter: it was richer in subtle atmospheric effects. There was no need to evacuate the platforms. All the artist required was to have the departure of the train to Rouen delayed by a few minutes. And the train was duly delayed as Monet had predicted it would be.

---

[14] Albert Wolff in the *Figaro*, 3 April 1876. He was wrong but a brilliant journalist. No art critic in a national newspaper would dare to write with such admirable venom today. He later partially changed his mind. Manet painted his portrait in 1877.

But such scrapes were more satisfying at twenty-five than at forty-five. Renoir was a man of simple tastes but neither a showman nor by nature a Bohemian. At fifty-two he met Aline Charigot. He was living on his own by then in a succession of dingy unfurnished rooms in Montmartre. It was a rough neighbourhood but cheap. He took his main, and often his only, meal of the day in a *crémerie* in the Rue St-Georges where he would eat the *plat du jour* next to the stove which warmed both customers and the *pot au feu*. The Widow Clément from Dijon, who ran the shop, usually kept a choice piece of cheese for him. "He was so well-bred but so thin that it wrung your heart." Of course she knew everybody in the neighbourhood who came from Burgundy (instantly recognisable by their richly resonant rs). Mme Charigot, who, deserted by her husband, was supporting herself and her daughter Aline by dressmaking, was one of her closest friends. "We must find Aline a husband or at least a protector, somebody rich and not too young." The Widow Clément had just the right customer, a middle-aged civil servant from the Ministère de la Marine. A meeting was duly arranged and the gentleman duly turned up. But the person who caught Aline's eye was the customer at the next table. He too was middle-aged, thirty years older than herself, but, despite his neat appearance, clearly not rich. Indeed, it soon turned out that he was penniless. But, for the rest of her life, for Aline there would be nobody else. As for Renoir, "I recognised at once not only the freshness, beauty and youth of your mother, but also the poise and dignity of my own mother", he would recount to his son, Jean, thirty years later. "The difference was that my mother was thin and your mother always liked good food. And it was a pleasure to see her eat." [15] It was to be a wonderfully happy marriage – but not yet.

The 1880s were in many ways Renoir's most difficult years. The difficulties were no longer financial or not mainly so. A few young artists had begun to rally round quite early. Soon after the first Impressionist exhibition a delegation called, announcing themselves as from the Ecole des Beaux-Arts. Renoir prepared himself for another burst of vituperation, perhaps even violence. But it was a class of final-year students who came to declare that they all wanted to paint like Monsieur Monet and Monsieur Renoir. As a token of their dedication, they had collected all the tubes and jars of black paint they could find at the school. Since Monsieur Renoir had declared that black did not exist in nature and that the "colour" should therefore never be used, they threw the lot into the Seine. Now some – still only a few – of their elders were beginning to see the light. Paul Durand-Ruel remained their main prop and financial support, showing their pictures in London,

---

[15] J. Renoir, *Renoir, My Father*, p. 136.

Boston, New York, Berlin and Antwerp. Most exhibitions were dismal and depressing failures; but in New York the Renoirs sold unexpectedly well.[16] Other dealers were beginning to take an interest – Petit, the Bernheims, Vollard – and an increasing number of rich private collectors. By solid bourgeois standards Renoir's finances remained precarious; but worries about next week's rent and the Sunday joint were receding.

Nor was his private life a source of anxiety. He did not marry Aline until 1890, five years after the birth of their first son, Pierre, but she filled his life with joy.[17] He painted her over and over again, alone or in company, nude or in finery, dancing, reading, and, unforgettably, holding baby Pierre to her breast. They acquired a wide circle of friends. The autumns they usually spent in Essoye, Aline's family home in Burgundy, the summers often in

---

[16] But Henry James, reviewing the second Impressionist exhibition in the *New York Tribune* of 13 May 1876, compared the exhibitors unfavourably to the Pre-Raphaelites and felt that the "Impressionist doctrines are ... incompatible with the existence of a first-rate mind".

[17] The fact that they had been living together for five years before they got married is oddly one of the few details of Renoir's life which Jean Renoir glosses over almost coyly. Yet the belief among artists, writers and the anti-bourgeois establishment that marriage had a disastrous effect on creative processes was a characteristic ingredient of the intellectual climate of the Second Empire. As early as 1846 Balzac gave a chilling illustration of this belief in *La Cousine Bette*, the story of a talented sculptor destroyed by conjugal indulgence; and two decades later the Goncourts painted a similarly devastating picture in *Manette Salomon*. Nor was this view confined to fiction. "A married man", Courbet pronounced, "is a reactionary in art." The mild-mannered and otherwise sane Corot expressed the opinion that marriage was "incompatible with landscape painting". The usually reserved Delacroix lost his temper when one of his pupils announced that he was getting married. "If you love her and she is pretty, it makes the situation that much worse. Your art is dead. An artist must have no passion except for his work and must sacrifice everything to it." Virtually all members of Renoir's circle lived by this creed, even if their later image became one of devoted family men.

Manet did not marry Suzanne Leenhof until 1863, by which time their son was eleven. Pissarro began an affair with his mother's maid, Julie Vellay, in 1858, had a son and then a daughter by her, but did not marry her until 1870 shortly before the birth of their third child, when they were in exile in London. Monet began his liaison with the model Camille Doncieux in 1865 and married her just before the outbreak of the Franco-Prussian War, when their eldest son was already three years old. Cézanne met a young Parisian bookbinder, Hortense Fiquet, in 1869, had his first son by her in 1872, but did not marry her till 1886. Rodin did not marry Rose Beuret until a few months before her and his death. The Sisleys were not yet in fact married when Renoir painted his wonderful double portrait of them, one of the rare and great celebrations of conjugal felicity in art. The long liaison between Renoir and Aline was therefore the norm and accepted as such by their friends and families. Such conventions do of course change every twenty or thirty years, as they have continued to change in the twentieth century. The generation of French artists who followed Renoir and the first Impressionists all married early.

Brittany, in Argenteuil or in Aix-en-Provence with the Cézannes. For the first time Renoir also travelled abroad, to Spain with Gallimard, to Algiers, to Italy, to London. In many ways life seemed to be rewarding him at last for his commitment and steadfast faith. But faith itself now threatened to desert him.

Renoir detested the ornate, lumpy, inherently fraudulent style still favoured by the art-political establishment, nor had he any use for the aridities of the Ecole des Beaux-Arts, but both by nature and by upbringing he was a traditionalist. He admired Ingres' draughtsmanship – though not his historic and religious confections – and the sheer technical competence of Raphael, Velasquez and Vermeer. Could the unrestrained exuberance of Impressionism ever match their achievement? Was it not too facile, too easily satisfied with superficial dazzle? Impressionism is often represented as the first of the modern styles, the beginning indeed of modern art, and in a sense so it was. Most artists who paint today – good, bad and indifferent – still work under the influence of the first Impressionist exhibition, held a hundred and thirty years ago. Reproductions of the Impressionists' work sell by the million, easily outstripping the products of any other school or group; and their actual paintings sell for millions. They are the almost automatic choice for hospital waiting rooms, being both contemporary and restful. Yet in one respect, and that perhaps the most fundamental, Impressionism was not the beginning of the modern but the end of the traditional: it was the last artistic movement which consciously searched for visual beauty and regarded it as its first priority. In his late fifties and early sixties, with material and personal success at last beckoning, that worried Renoir. He never pretended to be an intellectual like Manet or Cézanne (both of whose intellects he greatly admired),[18] but he was not an intuitive or primitive artist either. Was visual beauty enough? Especially when to him it came so easily. He was now painting charming society portraits and flower pieces for middle-class salons. Was he being seduced by the plaudits of *le Beau Monde*? The answer – or an answer of sorts – came in an unexpected way. One day, cycling home from a day's painting in the vineyards of Essoyes, he fell off his bicycle and injured his knee.

There is no evidence to suggest that severe, progressive rheumatoid arthritis is caused or even initiated by physical injury, but patients often date the

---

[18] Cézanne, a close and much-loved friend, gave himself no airs but was an intellectual in the sense that he pondered pictorial problems long and deeply. But Cézanne's theoretical preoccupations were lost on Renoir.

beginning of any chronic ailment to an accident.[19] It was so with Renoir. After 1890 his illness progressed by fits and starts for almost thirty years, with periods of remission and even apparent, though never long-lasting, improvements. The reason for those were – as they still are – entirely obscure, as difficult to explain as the painful reactivations. Seemingly out of the blue, though sometimes following a minor illness like a cold or by a gastrointestinal upset, he would be struck down with agonising acute joint pains and swellings, generally subsiding after a week or two but leaving behind crippling deformities. Bones, nerves and the skin would all gradually become involved; and for many years his eyesight too seemed threatened. Even during remissions and at rest pain was rarely entirely absent. Fortunately, he did not develop any of the systemic complications most feared today: he did not become severely anaemic and, so far as one can tell, his kidney function remained good. Perhaps the absence of such life-threatening complications was due to the primitive treatment available at the time. There were no steroids, no gold, no immunosuppressants and no powerful synthetic anti-inflammatory agents to give welcome symptomatic relief but also to introduce new risks.[20] Only salicylates in various forms offered respite,[21]

---

[19] Rheumatoid arthritis may have existed for centuries but in its clinically recognisable form it did not emerge till the middle of the nineteenth century. It then replaced gout, with which it was for many years confused, as one of the common chronic progressive joint diseases. (The third, osteoarthritis, the arthritis of "wear and tear" of the elderly, was not separated from the other two till Virchov's researches later in the century.)

The cause of rheumatoid arthritis is still unknown. It is essentially an inappropriately severe inflammatory response to – what? A virus? An immunological insult? A bacterial toxin? A food constituent? Nobody knows. The joints are always affected, most often those of small and medium size; but almost every organ and tissue in the body can become involved. Scar formation is a normal and usually beneficial sequel of inflammation; but, like the inflammatory response itself, it tends to be exaggerated in rheumatoid arthritis. This leads to the characteristic painful deformities. Even if the clinical history of Renoir's illness left any doubt, photographs of him taken late in life, especially those showing his hands, would be diagnostic.

[20] Suppressing the exaggerated inflammatory response by any means tends to improve rheumatoid arthritis; but the inflammatory response is one of the body's basic defence mechanisms, as well as a potential cause of illnesses, and therefore its suppression is never entirely without risk.

[21] The pain-relieving properties of extracts of willow bark may have been known to the ancient Greeks but were virtually forgotten till the nineteenth century. A bitter liquid called salicyn was then extracted from the bark by Jean Leroux and its fever-relieving action in "ague" (a name for any feverish illness, often malaria) was noted. Herman Kolbe first synthesised the active principle, salicylic acid, in 1873: this made its cheap and safe manufacture possible. A few years later it was introduced into the treatment of rheumatic fever, a dangerous acute illness of childhood which attacked the joints and the lining of the heart and which, despite its name, has nothing to do with rheumatoid arthritis. (It is now

unless patients in despair had recourse to opiates. Renoir never did; and even with salicylates he was sparing. He was always a light eater and drank only the occasional glass of wine; but he lost weight over the years until he weighed less than forty kilos. This made nursing easier in some ways; but loss of the cushioning effect of subcutaneous fat also made his skin over bony prominences more vulnerable. Despite devoted care by his family and nurses, in his last years he was to suffer from intensely painful and intractable pressure sores.

The illness was a calamity; yet its onset marked the end of his tormenting doubts, hesitations and self-questionings. Were the two events related? There can never be any certainty about such synchronicities; even worthwhile analogies are few. Physical suffering can ennoble but it can also destroy. Those with no personal experience of war or natural disaster find it incomprehensible that some of the survivors look back on its horrors with nostalgia. To many it was a time when their life was most fulfilled. For almost thirty years Renoir was effectively at war. It was a war he had to fight on his own and in the knowledge that he was bound to be the ultimate loser. It is futile to speculate whether or not he was happy. But there is no doubt that, despite being a physical burden, he engendered deep love in those around him – and what else is happiness? And there can also be no doubt that as an artist it was in those last decades that he most completely fulfilled himself. That is not to say that he painted better than before. Some will always prefer his boating parties, picnics, balls and café concerts. He did himself – sometimes – and he would never paint these again. But with great self-confidence and astonishingly simple means he now created a different world that was entirely his own and which to many remains an inexhaustible source of pleasure.

Although illness was never absent from Renoir's life after the late 1880s, his infirmities did not for some years severely restrict his own and his family's life. Jean Renoir was born in 1891; Claude, known to all as Coco, seven years after that. From Rembrandt to Picasso artists have painted some of their loveliest paintings of their own children; and Renoir was no exception. Coco in particular was a perennial source of delight and inspiration to him. Just before Jean's birth Aline Renoir imported from her native village Gabrielle, a second cousin, to help look after the boys. The young woman – she was

rare.) Combining salicylate with acetic acid produced aspirin, one of the triumphs of pharmacology, still unrivalled as a comparatively harmless pain-relieving and antifebrile drug. Proust, a notable hypochondriac as well as a notable writer, suggested that the first decade of the twentieth century should be called "the Aspirin Age". The drug was certainly the main standby in Renoir's illness: its comparatively rare harmful side-effects were not recognised until the 1950s. In addition to its still universal use as a painkiller, in small doses it is now also used to help prevent thrombosis.

fifteen when she joined the household – became the artist's favourite model.[22] He loved luscious female beauty; and to describe that love as "chaste" would be absurd. But if his models were to him objects of desire, they were never objects of conquest. His friend Rodin could not look at a woman – young, old or middle-aged – without wanting, needing even, to possess her; and he was firmly convinced that this was what all his prospective conquests expected. To Renoir his pretty models were gorgeous flowers to cherish and to paint. They were also, of course, flowers to be plucked – but not by him.[23] Nor did he seek any intellectual stimulus from them. He liked to listen to their chatter (as did Corot), so long as they did not expect any flashes of wisdom from him in return; and he loved to listen to their singing, especially when they sang slightly off-key.

For some years the family also travelled for holidays;[24] but walking was becoming increasingly painful and eventually impossible. The Bernheims were dealers, collectors and friends: they were also extremely rich. Distressed by the deterioration in the artist's physical state, they scoured Europe for a possible cure. Professor Rudolf Schade of the imperial city of Vienna had acquired the reputation of a medical miracle-worker. He had his own sanatorium in the Vienna Woods patronised by more than one Imperial and Serene Highness, as well as by the Rothschilds, cousins of the Bernheims.[25] But nothing could persuade Renoir to try another spa: he had already spent a few weeks in Vichy and Baden-Baden and vowed never to go near a *Kursaal* or bandstand again. But the Bernheims were undeterred and took their cue from the legend of the Prophet and the Mountain. The professor was summoned to Paris and, having examined Renoir from head to toe, expressed the opinion that he could make the artist walk within a fortnight. He charged a fee that was more than generations of Renoirs had earned in their combined lifetimes, but he was no charlatan. Installed in the Bernheims' palatial mansion in the Faubourg, he visited Renoir every day. He administered a range of mysterious homeopathic remedies. He radiated optimism. He never voiced a flicker of doubt. He designed and

[22] She remained part of the Renoir household till 1914 when she married an American painter, Conrad Slade, and went to live in the United States. She died in California in 1944.

[23] Renoir had had his share of sexual adventures as a young man and had lived with the model Lise Trehot from about 1865 to 1872. He also had an *affaire* with Suzanne Vallotton (who had not?). But Jean Renoir thought – almost certainly correctly – that he was never unfaithful to Aline after the birth of Pierre.

[24] Always third class, even after they could afford to travel first or second. Renoir liked train journeys but looking at the "always bored and boring" faces of first-class or second-class travellers "made him sick".

[25] G. Frankl, *Wunderdoktor* (Vienna, 1924). The professor died in a boating accident in 1897, aged sixty.

supervised every meal himself; but he professed to be won over by some of Aline's cherished homely remedies and dishes. (He made extensive notes of the recipes: would Mme Renoir permit him to pass them on to his chef in his sanatorium in Baden?) Contrary to the Bernheims' fears, the Renoirs loved him. How could they not? He never arrived without flowers for Aline and bon-bons for the boys. He was charmed by Gabrielle's new outfits and asked permission to present her with a small Viennese brooch to go with one of them. He admired on the walls not the Renoirs, Sisleys, Boudins, Corots and Monets but Mme Charigot's bird embroideries.[26]

Jean Renoir described the day when his father was due to rise from his wheelchair. And rise he did.

> The doctor lifted him out of his chair. "Now walk", he ordered. All of us watched transfixed as my father mustered all his energy and took a step. Then another. And another – even though lifting his foot off the ground was obviously agonisingly painful. He walked round his easel and back to his invalid chair.
> "Yes, I can do it", he sighed. "But it takes all my energy. I would have none left for painting. And if I have to choose, I would rather paint." [27]

He sat down on his wheelchair and never got up again. But from then on it was "fireworks to the end; as if his love of beauty and life which he could no longer enjoy physically were emanating from his brush".[28]

But to remain in Paris, even in the "mountain air" of their much-loved Château des Brouillards in Montmartre, would have been suicidal;[29] or that was the verdict of the omniscient Dr Gachet.[30] Their first home in Cagnes-sur-Mer was the post office, a real village shop. It clung to the side of the town where the main street began to mount steeply and merged into a sort of cobbled stairway. Renoir liked the constant coming and going. Their section of the building looked out on a quilt of orange groves against walled terraces descending as far as the road to Vence. The remains of ancient ramparts still hugged the sides of the village. The houses emerged from little gardens with

---

[26] They were in fact charming.

[27] J. Renoir, *Renoir, My Father*, p. 342.

[28] Ibid., p. 295.

[29] Nobody knows where the name of the row of tenements occupied in Renoir's day by workers from the Saint-Ouen industrial district came from: the place had nothing château-like about it, though *brouillards* (the Paris version of London's pea-soup smog) were common enough. The Renoirs lived in the top two floors of the last tenement in the rue Girardon. The Butte at the time had no stairs and was virtually unscalable for much of the year.

[30] Kindly Dr Gachet, the ubiquitous doctor, herbalist and amateur painter, seems to have looked after every Impressionist and Expressionist genius of his day without charging them anything. Van Gogh painted him most famously and he painted van Gogh on his death-bed. He awaits a worthy biographer.

their red-tiled roofs appearing as if piled up in layers. Above the roofs one could glimpse the old church with the bells hanging in their iron cage. When the weather was warm enough old Baptistin would hitch his horses to his victoria and drive Renoir into the countryside to paint. Otherwise he painted in the big drawing-room that had been converted into a studio.

Three years later they moved, a little apprehensively, into what was to be Renoir's last home. He had bought Les Collettes, an isolated farm outside the town, on impulse only to save it from being "developed". It was beautiful but remote, and remoteness was not to his liking. To ensure that he would not be starved of friendly bustle, the constant coming and going of people he liked, Aline had a small guest-house built opposite the main farm building. A stream of visitors, both local and from every part of France and indeed Europe, were accommodated there. Of course they were increasingly the younger generation.[31] Young Matisse came, Bonnard, Rippl-Ronai, Vuillard and other artists. Cézanne's son, Paul junior, was a frequent visitor and married a local girl, Renée Rivière. They settled not far from Les Collettes. Maillol, shy and a little gauche, sculpted in a single sitting a portrait bust of his host. Renoir and the family were profuse in their compliments. "But why does the master himself not try his hand at modelling?", Maillol asked. "He is a much greater artist than I will ever be." One can picture the look Renoir gave him. By then his hands were so painful and deformed that the brushes had to be "implanted" in his palms on small gauze cushions. He could manage to paint – just. But sculpture! The bearded Catalan was a charming fellow but he should not mock a cripple. But nothing, Maillol assured the older man, was further from his mind. And a few weeks later a pupil of Maillol's, Richard Guino, made his entry into the Renoir household, bringing with him a barrelful of clay from Banyuls, a present from his master. Renoir should dictate his sculptures to Guino. Guino would be his fingers. It was an unique and improbable collaboration, and it is impossible to envisage how it worked; but that it did work is not in doubt.[32] Not surprisingly, the terracottas became Jean's favourites among all his father's oeuvre. There was

---

[31] By the time of the Renoirs' move, most of his friends from his youth were either dead or disinclined to travel. Sisley had died in poverty in 1899, Pissarro in 1903 and Cézanne in 1906. Monet came once, in 1908, but did not like leaving Giverny after that.

[32] As the pair of hands of a genius, Guino, a Catalan like Maillol, was a near-genius himself, but he was no saint. Between sessions with the crippled master, he amused himself making sexually explicit "paraphrases" of Renoir paintings. (They were published eighty years later.) After his and Renoir's death, the two families became locked in lawsuit: Michel Guino, Richard's son and also a sculptor, claimed that the joint works should always be exhibited as Guino-Renoirs and that royalties and sales should recognise the joint authorship. He won his case.

also the magic of the changing seasons, so much more real than in a big city like Paris. In orange-blossom time young girls from nearby villages came to harvest the oranges. Later they came with long poles to harvest the olives. More than the style of most artists, Renoir's always reflected the place where he lived. Les Collettes became the perfect setting for his last (and to one admirer anyway) greatest period. The long summers were his favourite time of the year. "Under this sun you see bronze Venuses everywhere among the foliage", he told Maillol "Look! Is it not magic?" Despite the ordeal of his illness, one feels that he was for a few years idyllically happy – as was much of Europe before catastrophe put an end to all idylls. [33]

Both Pierre and Jean volunteered for the army in 1914 and both were wounded within a year. But the unexpected war casualty was Aline. She had developed diabetes which she kept a secret and neglected. When news came of Jean being wounded, she left Cagnes to nurse him. Jean thought later that she had saved his life. But it was a strain on her. The day after her return – a week after her fifty-sixth birthday – she died in her sleep. When, after the war, Jean came to look after his father, he found the house desolate, even sinister. The tangerine trees and the vineyard had gone wild. His father's suffering seemed intolerable. Yet the worse the suffering, the more he painted. And slowly the place flickered into life again. Friends in Nice found a new model, Andrée. She was sixteen, red-haired, plump and her skin "took the light wonderfully". Her joyous youth erupted on canvases among roses and the olive trees with their silvery reflection. Later she was to become Jean's wife.

Renoir's nights were becoming frightful. The slightest rubbing of the sheets would start a sore: in the morning it would have to be cleaned, powdered and dressed. He could hardly pick up anything any more. "It's like fire; like sitting on blazing coals." He would rage when his nose ran and had to be wiped for him. "Oh, I am a disgusting object!" But it was not true. He was clean as he had always been and as he wished to remain. He was washed and dressed while still half asleep; but he insisted on sitting up at table for breakfast. Then he would be transferred to his specially designed sedan chair and, according to the weather and light and depending on what he was working on, taken to the studio, a kind of glassed-in shed, or seated in the open in front of an ingenious construction which enabled him to roll and unroll the canvas.

[33] By the mid 1920s Cagnes was widely advertised in the American Press as "the Greenwich Village on the Mediterranean" and was mocked as the haunt of painters who could not paint and writers who could not write.

While Renoir is put in position the model takes her place on the flower-spangled grass. Somebody prepares his palette while he adjusts his stricken body to the hard seat. It is painful but it allows him to keep upright and a certain amount of movement. The piece of protective lint is folded into his palm and he points to a brush. "That one there ... no, the other one." It is given to him. Flies circle in a shaft of sunlight. "Ah, those flies", he exclaims in a rage, "they can smell a corpse." But then they stop bothering him and for a moment or two he seems somnolent, hypnotised by a butterfly or the distant sound of cicadas. "It is intoxicating." He stretches out his arm and dips his brush into the turpentine. But the movement is painful. He waits a few seconds as if asking himself: "Why not give up? Is it not too hard?" Then a glance at the scene in front of him restores his courage. He traces on the canvas a mark of madder red that only he understands. "Jean, please open that curtain a little more." Then, in a stronger voice: "Ah yes, it is divine." He smiles as he calls everybody to witness the conspiracy which had just been arranged between the grass, the olive trees, the model and himself. After a minute or so he starts humming. And a day of happiness begins for him, a day as wonderful as the one which had preceded it and the one which will follow.[34]

It was under these conditions that he painted the last *Bathers* (Plate 13). He considered it the culmination of his life's work; or, as he put it: "Rubens would have been satisfied with it." [35]

During the summer of 1919 the disease suddenly became quiescent and Jean and Pierre took their father to Paris to see some of his own work exhibited at the Luxembourg. It would be his last journey and he knew it. From the station they were driven to the palace to be received with all pomp and circumstance by the director. After their wartime exile the museum's treasures were being reinstalled and Renoir was wheeled and carried along galleries and corridors lined with scaffolding. News of his arrival spread within seconds. "I feel like the Pope", he said, but it was more like the progress of a tribal chief. His approach was signalled from afar by workers whistling, clapping and hitting their step-ladders with their hammers, and visitors and staff cheering as the procession passed. He looked at his recent nude next to a Veronese. "Not bad", he commented. "Which one, Maître?" "Le Veronese bien-sûr." That should have been enough. But after being lifted back into the car he expressed the wish to be driven to Chatou, to the inn of Le Père Fournaise. Pierre and Jean expostulated: it was late and it would be a long

---

[34] J. Renoir, *Renoir, My Father*, p. 365.

[35] But Monsieur Jallifet of the Louvre was not: he considered it too "loud" when the painting was offered to him by Jean and Pierre after their father's death. When the news leaked out, Barnes wired from Philadelphia to ask for it for his museum "at any price"; but by then Monsieur Jallifet had been overruled.

and tiring journey. But it was, their father insisted, the only reason why he had agreed to come. Pierre and Jean acquiesced. So they were driven to Chatou and then to very spot on the river bank where in 1881 he had painted the *Déjeuner des Canotiers*, the picture in which Aline Charigot, one of the young company on the deck, made her first appearance (on the left, holding a little dog). He did not want to get out of the car but, as silent tears began to roll down his cheeks, everybody else did. For a few minutes he was left alone with his memories.[36]

In November 1919 he developed pneumonia which kept him in his room, but on the morning of 2 December he seemed a little better. He asked for his paint box and brushes and started to paint the anemones which Nanette, his nurse, had gathered that morning. For almost an hour he painted, the pain in his chest and the breathlessness seemingly forgotten. Then he asked her to take the brush from him and whispered a few words about having discovered something. He dozed off and a few hours later he stopped breathing.

[36] It was the new railway line to St-Germain which in the 1860s had made the success of the place possible: the station at the Pont de Chatou was only twenty minutes' journey from Paris, and idyllic spots on the island, only a few minutes' walk from the station, were soon discovered by young lovers. An astute seller of lemonades, later to be known as Le Père Fournaise, enlarged his hut and turned it into a cheap but excellent restaurant and boating club. It quickly became the favourite haunt of Monet, Renoir and their friends, who painted it many times. The name "La Grenouillère" derived not from the thousands of frogs which populated (and still popluate) the river bank, or even from one of the delicacies on offer, but from a class of young women who were not exactly prostitutes but "good sorts", often witty and amusing as well as pretty, ready to satisfy every whim of poor struggling artists but moving with ease from garrets in the Batignolles to mansions on the Champs Elysées. They were the inspiration and belles of the *Belle Epoque*.

# 9

# *Maillol*

He was a late starter. Other long-lived artists who reached their creative peak late in life had made a start by forty. Aristide Maillol exhibited his first important sculpture when he was forty-one.[1] By then, for over twenty years, he had worked as a draughtsman, potter and weaver. He had made kitchen-ware for the weekly market at Perpignan and had helped to decorate the foyer of Paris's Moulin Rouge. What he had achieved was not negligible. But as a sculptor, had he given up at forty, he would barely rate a mention today.

He was born in Banyuls-sur-Mer, the last Mediterranean fishing port on the French side of the Pyrenees. The Maillols, like most of the villagers, were Catalans, descended from poor farmers, wine-growers, sailors and the most resourceful smugglers of the western Mediterranean.[2] French was their

[1] He was born in 1861. The "delay" tends to create a chronological dislocation. By age he was the contemporary (and friend) of the Post-Impressionist artists like Bonnard; but he began his career simultaneously with more modern figures like Brancusi, Arp and Duchamp-Villon.

Maillol's late start makes it the more remarkable that some of the most perceptive monographs about him and his work were published in his lifetime. Among them in French are O. Mirbeau, *Aristide Maillol* (Paris, 1925); M. Lafarge, *Aristide Maillol, sculpteur et litho-graphe* (Paris, 1925); P. Camo, *Aristide Maillol* (Paris, 1926); P. Sentenac, *Aristide Maillol* (Peyre, 1936) and J. Cladel, *Maillol: sa vie, son oeuvre, ses idées* (Paris, 1937); J. Romains, *Maillol* (Paris, 1940). In English see J. Rewald, *Maillol* (London, 1939) and J. Rewald, *The Woodcuts of Aristide Maillol* (New York, 1943); in German, H. Appel, *Das Meisterwerk Maillols* (Basle, 1940). Several books published after his death recount personal friendships and encounters. Among them are P. Camo, *Maillol, mon ami* (Lausanne, 1950), and H. Frère, *Conversations de Maillol* (Geneva, 1956). Other notable monographs include R. Linnekamp, *Aristide Maillol* (Hamburg, 1957); D. Chevalier, *Maillol* (Lugano, 1962); J. Masin, *Aristide Maillol* (Prague, 1963); G. Waldemar, *Aristide Maillol: l'âme de la sculpture* (Neuchâtel, 1964); W. George, *Aristide Maillol* (London, 1965); D. Vierny and B. Lorquin, *Autour de La Mediterranée* (Paris, 1986); and B. Lorquin, *Maillol* (Geneva, 1994).

[2] This ancient and gifted people, whose habitat straddles the Pyrenees, has produced a galaxy of notable artists over the last century – Dali and Mirò as well as Maillol and, in a supporting role, Mme Matisse. For historical reason Catalans on the French side of the frontier bore little animosity towards their state, unlike some of their cousins in Spain.

Maillol loved Banyuls but he was not a landscape painter. Fortunately, the Hungarian "Nabi", J. Rippl-Ronai (who died in 1940, aged sixty-four), was a friend, and painted beautifully evocative landscapes of the region while staying with the Maillols in 1899 and 1900 (now

second language: Aristide never learnt to speak it without an accent. One of
four children, he was farmed out as a boy to a maiden aunt. He became a
solitary child and his education was patchy. Some time in his teens he decided
to become a painter. Nothing is known about the reaction of his family; but
at twenty-one, with a token allowance from his aunt, he set out for Paris.[3]

There he knew nobody. He sat for the entrance examination of the Ecole
des Beaux-Arts and failed. He sat again and failed for a second time. After
gaining admission following his third attempt he found the teaching numbing.
The giants of modern art – Cézanne, Degas, Monet, Gauguin, Renoir, Rodin,
Toulouse-Lautrec among them – were all active in or around Paris at the time,
an explosion of talent comparable only to fifteenth-century Florence. Not a
tremor of this explosion penetrated the tenebrous classrooms in the rue
Bonaparte. Of course the Beaux-Arts had always been a bastion of tradition;
but never before had it sunk to such depths of dreariness. Young Maillol from
the furthermost corner of France was inexperienced and unsophisticated;
but the combination of arrogance and futility appalled even him.

For nearly fifteen years he lived in desperate poverty. Often for weeks he
slept rough. A near-starvation diet left him dangerously malnourished. He
spent several months in hospital with painful joint swellings, perhaps rheumatic fever.[4] The thought of ending it all in the Seine was rarely far from
his mind. A few artists from the south west of France, especially Bourdelle
and the kindly painter Lauge, gave him occasional shelter and food.[5] In
Catalan *maillol* means a young vine shoot. The growth of the Roussillon
grape had been known since Roman times to be tough. The artist survived
– but perhaps only just.

The last years of the nineteenth century saw the sudden revival of tapestry
as an art form. It was a revolt against the drab replicas of seventeenth- and
eighteenth-century wall-hangings churned out by the once-splendid
manufactories of Aubusson and Gobelin. It was also part of a wider reaction

mostly in the National Gallery of Hungarian Art, Budapest). Rippl-Ronai also painted the
best portrait of Maillol in his thirties (before the Catalan master became famous and his
beard turned white); it is now in the Musée d'Orsay in Paris.

[3] Twenty francs a month to be precise, just enough to prevent him from perishing within
a week. A *baguette* at the time cost four sous.

[4] This is how he referred to his illness in later life; and a history of painfully swollen and
knotted-up joints makes it a plausible diagnosis. But if it was rheumatic fever, he was lucky
to escape without permanent damage to his heart.

[5] Antoine Bourdelle came from Montauban and was Rodin's favourite pupil. He was
already a well-known sculptor but still poor when Maillol went to see him. He died in 1929,
aged sixty-eight. Henri Lauge came from Perpignan and never achieved fame. He died in
1915, aged fifty-two.

to the tidal wave of machine-made trash that was filling the ornate galleries of the new department stores and the houses of the prosperous bourgeoisie.[6] Maillol had always admired the unique collection of medieval weavings in the Musée de Cluny. The medium also seemed to suit the monumental style, popularised by Puvis de Chavannes, which Maillol admired.[7] But most importantly, he was a do-it-yourself enthusiast many years before that movement began to rival the great religions in popularity. He invented old wool techniques, preparing his own vegetable dyes from plants he had collected himself, and organised a small workshop first in Banyuls and then in Villeneuve-St-Georges. There was more than crankiness in this – or at least Maillol was more than a crank. He hated shoddiness, especially when it was overlaid, as it so often was and is, by fussy elaboration. And he accepted as a matter of course the setbacks and frustrations inseparable from perfectionism.

Maillol's tapestries have now lost their appeal of novelty, but, like the contemporary theatre posters of Toulouse-Lautrec, the book illustrations and stage designs of Bonnard and the glassware of Gallé, they still surpass in interest most so-called fine-art products of the period. And they did not remain unrecognised. Because of his uncompromising refusal to cut corners, he was never in danger of becoming rich; but his tapestries sold and he could make a living.[8] Even more important to him, his work was praised not only by a few well-heeled collectors and aesthetes but also by artists he respected.[9] On the strength of this he married one of his Banyuls assistants, the younger of the two Narcisse sisters, Clothilde. A son, Lucien, was born to them a year later.

Maillol was to look back on his years of tapestry-weaving as the happiest of his life. Its deliberate tempo suited his temperament and the apparent limitations of the medium favoured the essential simplicity of his vision. He would have happily continued but, almost certainly as a result of focusing on the loom for many hours not always in good light, his eyesight began to trouble him. Early in 1900 he was told by Professor de Launey, the eminent ophthalmologist, that he would be blind within five years or less if he did not abandon weaving.[10] He could have confined himself to designing and supervising, but that would have been a betrayal of his principles. Instead,

[6] The French equivalent of the Arts and Crafts movement in England.

[7] Pierre-Cecil Puvis de Chavannes was an aristocrat, mystic and "utterer of pallid harmonies" who bridged the gap between the academic establishment and the avant-garde without, it seems, making a single enemy. He died in 1898, aged seventy-four.

[8] His patrons included the Princesse Bibesco (who supplied Maillol with wool from her estates in Romania), Marie, Queen of Romania, and Maillol's countryman, Daniel de Monfried.

[9] Most importantly Paul Gauguin, the deepest influence on Maillol as a painter.

[10] Even eminent professors of ophthalmology make mistakes. Whatever Maillol's eye trouble was, it cleared up completely. Even in his eighties he did not wear glasses.

he returned to Banyuls and built a kiln. As if to clinch his change of direction, he discovered a fine bed of clay a few miles outside the village. He never thereafter bought the material commercially. Pottery was a craft he had already practised as a boy. Now, in addition to jugs and pitchers, he began to model small figurines, almost all female nudes. More or less generically he entitled them *Bathers*.

The second beginning was a little easier than the first. From his years as a weaver he had friends in the art world. One of them introduced him to Ambroise Vollard. Behind a mask of sleepy indolence, self-indulgence and boredom, the dealer was a genius in his own field.[11] He knew, he maintained, nothing about art except that some pictures and sculptures kept him awake at night whereas others made him yawn. Nor, of course, was he a businessman. His bankers would tell him when he was relatively flush and his accountants would rap his knuckles when he was on the brink of bankruptcy. If one believes his late-in-life autobiography,[12] he became the most successful art-dealer of his generation and a millionaire by pure accident and without intending to become either. He was also a collector but not a hoarder: at regular intervals he would sell the works he had amassed. By the turn of the century the mere fact that a piece had been in his collection sent the price rocketing. He told Maillol that he liked the *Bathers*, though small sculptures were not his cup of tea: he would show twenty or so in a little exhibition in a back room of his gallery and, if three or four sold, he might then finance something more substantial. When, on the day after the opening, the works disappeared, Maillol burst out in protest. Vollard listened to the Catalan politely, then informed him that, alas, all the works had been sold within an hour and the purchaser would not wait till the exhibition closed. It later transpired that the dealer had found the exhibits so *sympathique* that he had bought the lot himself "for stock".[13] The friendship endured and Maillol could now set to work on *La Mediterranée*.

It all seemed to happen within a short three- or four-year period, roughly between 1903 and 1906. In Paris, Picasso's *Demoiselles d'Avignon* and Braque's

[11] He was born of Creole parentage in 1868 on La Réunion, the French island colony in the Indian Ocean. He arrived in Paris ostensibly to study law in 1888 but started wheeling and dealing in *objets d'art* at once. His gallery in the Rue Lafitte always looked more like an Oriental souk than a picture gallery. No single person over the past hundred and fifty years has been painted by so many great artists, including Renoir, Cézanne, Picasso, Braque, Matisse and Bonnard. They all seemed to have liked him.

[12] Which one should not, though the book is an excellent read. A. Vollard, *Souvenirs d'un marchand de tableaux: en écoutant Cézanne, Degas, Renoir* (Paris, 1938).

[13] Unlike his other collector's pieces, Vollard kept the *Bathers*. He had one with him in the car at the time he was killed.

*Houses in L'Estaque* launched Cubism. At the Salon d'Automne, Matisse and *Les Fauves* made their first splash. In Berlin Munch exhibited *The Scream*. In Munich Kandinski showed his first abstracts. In Dresden four university students founded *Die Brücke* and invented German Expressionism.[14] And the first great female nude by Maillol, an artist twenty or more years older than the rest but no less revolutionary, established that "We need not fear. There will be sculpture even after Rodin".[15] André Gide was neither a lover of modern art nor a critic easily bowled over; but he celebrated the event in an almost breathless article. "Modern sculpture has emerged like Aphrodite from the waves. But also not like Aphrodite. *La Mediterranée* is beautiful not because the figure signifies beauty but because it signifies nothing." [16] Some of Maillol's friends resented this – was it not a typical Gide backhander? – but not Maillol himself. What Gide said was true. Maillol was a sculptor. In literary, ideological or art-political terms his work made no sense.[17]

In majestic succession other nudes followed. He hardly modelled anything else.[18] The titles did not matter; the faces were almost interchangeable. To

---

[14] They were Ernst Ludwig Kirchner, Erich Heckel, Karl Schmidt-Rottluff and Fritz Bleyl.

[15] The comment is Desiré de Bussier's and it reflects a widely held view of Rodin and of European sculpture in general. More than one art critic and art historian of the *fin de siècle* contrasted the relative decline of sculpture compared to painting over the previous three centuries. Even during the artistically dismal first three-quarters of the nineteenth century painting produced geniuses like Goya, David, Géricault, Delacroix, Ingres, Corot, Constable and Turner. The leading names in sculpture during the period were Canova, Thorwaldsen, Rude, Barye, Carpeaux, Falgière and Hildebrand, good artists all, but of the second rank. This was certainly not for lack of patronage. Whole mountains were hacked into statuary over that period to embellish some of the ugliest buildings ever built. Nobody can now say what started the decline and why it lasted for so long; but for once one can plausibly date the beginning of the recovery. Rodin did not reinvent sculpture; he was not even much of an innovator. Most protagonists of the sculptural renaissance of the twentieth century – from Maillol to Henry Moore and beyond – spent much of their time and energy running away from him. Brancusi's *The Kiss* was an open declaration of war. But there can be no reaction without action; and Rodin was the action. For the same reason many doubted for some time whether sculpture could "survive" Rodin without lapsing into imitative decline. It was such fears which were stilled by the emergence of Maillol.

[16] In the *Revue Blanche*, 28 (1905), p. 234. Many of the young artists who were the mainstay of the *Revue* – Bonnard, Vuillard, Sérusier, Maurice Denis – who called themselves the *Nabis* or Prophets, were among the most enthusiastic supporters of Maillol. Denis bought two of Maillol's early terracottas, as did the writers Octave Mirbeau and Alfred Jarry.

[17] Nor in truth did much of Gide's prose when he pontificated about art. He was a good writer but had no visual sense.

[18] But there were two notable exceptions. The *Boy with the Bicycle*, created soon after returning from Greece, is a lovely evocation of archaic Greek art; and on a visit to Renoir he modelled the best bust of the old master. He was often pressed to model a self-portrait but he always declined. See J. Rippl-Ronai, *Emlékezéseim* (Memoirs) (Budapest, 1911).

provide them with titles he often consulted literary friends "who understood such things". At their suggestion he would even add fussy embellishments – a shell to *Venus,* a cloth over the back of *Ile de France,* a garland of fruit for *Flora.* Fortunately, when it came to sculpture, his artistic common sense reasserted itself: after the first casting, most of the works were disembellished.

Until his last creations, all his nudes conformed to a certain physical type. They were healthy, muscular, broad-hipped and short-limbed: unmistakably natives of the Mediterranean littoral. They were also far from beautiful. And yet they were – and are – lovely. What is their appeal? Of all modern sculptures they are the most difficult to analyse. People are often captivated by a single glance but for different reasons. Some feel uplifted by their tranquillity. Some admire their monumental repose. Some are exhilarated by the vitality throbbing under the calm exterior. To Malraux they were unselfconsciously perfect "in the way clouds and hills are perfect". There is some truth in all these explanations, but, if pressed for a single reason, one might also point to a touch of awkwardness rather than to perfection, a faint hint of that golden moment when youth hesitates on the threshold of maturity.

As his fame grew, Maillol, like Rodin before him, began to be commissioned to commemorate famous Frenchmen. Nothing shows up the contrast between the two sculptors more clearly than these monuments. Rodin took liberties, but his *Victor Hugo* could never be mistaken for his *Balzac* or vice-versa. Maillol's memorials to Blanqui, the first and perhaps his best,[19] to Debussy and to Cézanne are three great nudes, but they bear no closer relationship to the individuals commemorated than *La Mediterranée* bears to her geographical namesake. Nor did Maillol pretend otherwise. He celebrated great men but he did not wish to portray them. Even less was he prepared to celebrate ideologies he did not understand or admire. As once again the Catholic Church became an enlightened and generous patron of modern art, agnostics like Matisse, Bonnard and Dufy, sceptics like Chagall, and even vocal Marxists like Lurçat and Léger, happily accepted lucrative

[19] Louis Blanqui (who died in 1881, aged seventy-five) was the archetypal nineteenth-century conspirator who plotted, always unsuccessfully, against every regime in France from the Bourbons to the Third Republic, and spent most of his life in prison. This would of course command nothing but admiration had he not used his few days of freedom to organise one of the most senseless massacres of the Paris Commune in 1871. Victor Hugo, who was not without sympathy for the oppressed, referred to him as "that baleful apparition in whom seemed incarnated all the hatreds born of every misery". Maillol nevertheless admired him. The statue is now better known as *L'Action Enchaînée.* It was in fact rejected by the commissioning body, the municipal council of Puget-Theniers, though for reasons of modesty rather than of history or politics. Mme Maillol was the muscular model: clearly not a woman to be trifled with.

ecclesiastical commissions. But not Maillol. It was not that he was anticatholic or even anticlerical. He simply felt that the main purpose of religious art was to expound the faith and to fortify the spirit of the faithful. It was an admirable aim, perhaps, but not his.[20]

Despite their differences, Rodin not only liked but also admired Maillol; and in 1905 he introduced the younger artist to Count Harry Kessler. Kessler was the civilised face of Europe's cosmopolitan upper crust. His mother, an Irish beauty, was the ageing Kaiser Wilhelm I's last mistress, and many believed that Count Harry was the Kaiser's son. (If so, he was incomparably the most intelligent of the Hohenzollerns.)[21] His banker father, created a count for services to the Reich, was financial adviser to several royal families and numerous archdukes, grand dukes and even ordinary dukes. Enriching them, he too became immensely rich. Count Harry's younger sister, Wilma, the Kaiser's godchild, married into the French aristocracy. Count Harry himself had been educated in Germany, France and England, and spoke all three languages like a native. His Italian, Spanish, Greek, Portuguese and Russian were, he bashfully admitted, a little less fluent; but to please his friend, Prince Paul Eszterházi, he had learnt several patriotic poems in Hungarian by heart. He was as much at home in the chancelleries of Europe as in the labyrinthine world of high finance, welcome in cultivated aristocratic salons and familiar with the hidden byways as well as the ways of the *Almanach de Gotha*. He also numbered scientists, writers and artists among his friends: Einstein, Gerhardt Hauptmann, Rilke, the Mann brothers, von Keyserling, Painlevé, Gide, Cocteau, Maeterlinck, Rodin, the Asquiths, Shaw, Gordon Craig, Diaghilev and Isadora Duncan all figure prominently in his memoirs.[22] His house in Weimar had been built by Henri van de Velde, apostle of Art Nouveau, and his garden was soon to be redesigned to display to best advantage some of Maillol's most successful nudes.

It was in some respects a highly improbable friendship: Maillol was a few years older than his patron, had received only the rudiments of a formal education, had no conversational skills, and never pretended to be anything but the scion of fishermen and peasants.[23] But in Count Harry's hothouse world and to Count Harry himself he became the incarnation of

---

[20] In this one respect at least there was a kinship between Maillol and Picasso. The latter too disapproved of artists who created works in honour of ideologies in which they did not believe. He was particularly cross with Matisse, "that old humbug", over the Vence chapel. Picasso too had Catalan blood in him.

[21] And the uncle of Wilhelm II, the Kaiser of the First World War.

[22] He was not a name-dropper but sadly not much of a writer either. His memoirs, *Memoirs of a Cosmopolitan* (London, 1937), written in France in exile, are disappointingly bland.

[23] He generally dressed like a peasant, too, often in home-made clothes.

the creative arts, nourished by nothing but native talent and preserved by a firm refusal to compromise in all matters artistic. With Hugo von Hofmann-sthal, Viennese-Jewish poet, aristocrat and librettist of *Der Rosenkavalier*, making up the third of an oddly assorted trio, Kessler took the sculptor on his first and only voyage around Greece and the Greek islands. Maillol loved the country and its archaic art (though not the Golden Age of Phidias or the Hellenistic period). On his return he set to work on *La Nuit*, a better work according to many than *La Mediterranée*. But the first phase of the Kessler-Maillol friendship almost ended in disaster. A few days before the outbreak of the First World War, Kessler (always in the know) sent a despairing telegram to Maillol: "Bury your statues and your art stop all is finished stop war is here stop Kessler". The message caught the attention of the ever-vigilant French Counter-Intelligence (passing through one of its bouts of malignant spy fever) and only Clemenceau's intervention saved the artist from the fate of Mata Hari.[24]

Maillol and his art survived the war, as did Count Harry Kessler and his villa in Weimar. Kessler had always voiced vaguely republican sentiments and became the young Weimar Republic's first ambassador to Poland and then to the League of Nations. More importantly, he continued his career as an international patron and impresario. He founded the Cranach Press, the printers of some of the finest books of the interwar years, and persuaded Maillol to illustrate them. Characteristically, Maillol insisted on manufac-turing his own paper, to be the most expensive in Europe and probably the finest since the parchments of the late middle ages.[25] Once satisfied, he created several series of woodcuts, illustrating Longus's *Daphnis and Chloe*, Ovid's *The Art of Love*, Virgil's *Georgics* and *Eclogues* and Horace's *Odes* among other classical texts: in their small scale and economy of line they are as much part of Maillol's oeuvre as his sculpture. Count Harry also arranged triumphal tours for his protégé in Germany, Eastern Europe and Scandinavia; and Maillol's fame in these countries soared.[26] The seventieth birthday of "Europe's Greatest Sculptor in the Twentieth Century" was

[24] "I shall personally put a bullet through the head of any idiot (*chameau*) who arrests Maillol." Perhaps the danger facing Maillol was later exaggerated.

[25] Maillol had been experimenting with paper-making for some years. Matisse later described a day he spent with the Maillols in the 1920s when "the legendary pillage of the linen cupboard" took place. In the evening Maillol extracted a grey mass from his mouth, a piece of linen which, much to Matisse's distress (did his host suffer from toothache to explain his grimaces?), he had been chewing all day. He pounded it with his hand and then stretched it out on the table. "There is my paper", he announced. But not all the paper for the Cranach Press was manufactured in Maillol's mouth. The manufactory of Monval in Marly-le-Roi used mainly Norwegian sail-cloth with no added chemicals. The firm still makes fine artist's paper.

celebrated in Berlin and fittingly commemorated with a photograph: it shows Maillol, a tall bearded prophet flanked by Europe's intellectual elite, with Einstein on one side and Max Liebermann, president at the time of the Berlin Academy of Fine Arts, on the other. (A few years later most of those gathered for the celebration would be in exile, in concentration camps, or dead.) In the 1930s he occasionally grumbled that he was more appreciated abroad than in his not-quite-native France. This was a little unfair. Some of his projects, like his memorial to Zola, were rejected, but his admirers included most of the country's literary sages as well as leading artists. The first issue of *Verve*, probably the most important avant-garde artistic publication of the interwar years, carried an appreciation of his work by Judith Cladel.[27] In 1938 he shared the honour of the unveiling Rodin's *Balzac* with Despiau. He was also the most sought after sculptor for war memorials; and for the towns and villages of his native region – Banyuls, of course, but also Ceret, Pont-Vendres, Elne and Perpignan – he obliged. Apart from his costs, always modest, he accepted no payment for these works: not perhaps his best but, in their carefully chosen settings, among his most memorable.

Maillol was seventy-three when, in the spring of 1934, Dondel, an architect friend,[28] mentioned a young woman to him. She was fifteen, the daughter of a pianist and composer of Russian extraction. Dondel had been enchanted by her "untamed and yet well-bred beauty, her intelligence and her zest". Since her manifold interests apparently included sculpture, Maillol invited her to visit him and his family in their house at Marly-le-Roi. Dina Vierny had not seen any of Maillol's work before; but, encouraged by her parents who moved in artistic and literary circles, she boarded the suburban train to St-Germain-en-Laye, then the station for Marly. There, on a fine summer Sunday afternoon, she was warmly received by Maillol and his wife, their son Lucien, now a painter himself, and their guests. Though she mistook Van Dongen's even bushier white beard for the Master's and thanked the painter warmly for the invitation, the gaffe was overlooked, and, with his

[26] Almost every continental Modern Artists' Association elected him an honorary member.

[27] The magazine had been, prepared with immense care in the studio of Fernand Mourlot and had a stunning cover by Matisse – a horse in motion placed against cubes of different colours. It also contained articles by Maurice Heine ("The Blood of the Martyrs") and John Dos Passos ("Fire"), as well as Judith Cladel's on Maillol. The photographs were by Man Ray and Henri Cartier-Bresson. The publisher was the art lover Efstratios Eleftheriades, better known as Tériade: his American backers placed an order for 15,000 copies. The publication survived for two and a half years.

[28] Later the designer of the Musée de l'Art Moderne in Paris.

countryman's slow courtesy, the Master showed her round the self-built shed where he worked. He explained his technique in simple terms, asked for her first impressions (though of course it takes months to get to know a sculpture) and urged her to come again if she wanted to see how the pieces progressed. She was, as she later wrote, entranced but also devastated. She was entranced by Maillol's unselfconscious and unpatronising interest, so different from the self-centred eccentricity of the "stars" who patronised her parents' salon. But she was also convinced that she had hopelessly irritated her elderly host with her ignorant chatter ("except that I never thought of him as elderly"). In fact, he knew at once that late in life – too late, surely – he had found the embodiment of his ideal female beauty, and perhaps of the ideal female.

Maillol's relations with his models were not as platonic as Renoir's, but none before had become important in his life. Now Dina came again after her first visit and then again. The following summer she spent a holiday in the small Hôtel de Commerce in Marly near Maillol's house. In 1938 she went to Banyuls for the first time. Her image and her personality began to dominate his life – and his began to dominate hers. For the first two years of their friendship he drew and sculpted only her face. Then she modelled for him in the nude for the first time. Mme Maillol had always been a possessive and a slightly ill-tempered wife, but she had no choice but to accept the relationship. Lucien and Dina became friends.

The shadow of the Second World War already hung over them. When it came, Maillol shut up the house in Marly. He did not expect to return. He had recently lost two of his oldest friends. Harry Kessler had died in 1937, a refugee from Hitler, his world shattered. A year later Vollard died in a car accident. In the summer of 1939 Dina enrolled as a student of chemistry at the University of Montpellier, and promised to write a postcard from time to time. She had blossomed into a young woman of great beauty and many accomplishments, but Maillol did not expect to see her again.

In Banyuls he moved out of the family home to a farmhouse he had bought a few years earlier. It stood – as it still stands – on the northern slopes of the Roume valley, opposite the old family farm which had gone to his sisters. It is a coarse stone structure, simple but spacious, with a steeply sloping roof of rounded red tiles. A curtain of trees shields the terrace at the back: Dina was later to call it her "posing room". From the front one can look down towards the river, its banks verdant with fig trees, myrtle and cork oak; or up towards the majestic range of the southern Pyrenees. It is a life-enhancing view; but few families today, poring over holiday brochures, would consider it for their summer cottage. The nearest shop was more than three miles away, the only link a steep footpath, slippery after rain and sometimes impassable in winter. Horace Brenson, an American admirer who was taken to the house in 1939, departed in despair: surely this was no place for a man of eighty, however hardy. But Maillol assured his guest that he could manage admirably: he was used to doing his own cleaning and cooking.[29] He also had a few books and even a gramophone with a few records of Catalan music. He intended to visit his son and wife every Saturday and lay in provisions for a week. He would enjoy the little walk, especially the return journey. A slight physical exertion, he claimed, always cleared and refreshed his mind. Anyway, he had no plans for continuing with his sculpture while the war lasted. Visitors, of course, might find the approach a little daunting; but he did not expect any.

In this last expectation he was proved wrong. Dina came, first for a day or two, then for longer. First she stayed in Banyuls, but then she moved up to the farm. She posed for him, she read to him,[30] she talked to him, she sang to him, she filled his existence. He began to draw and paint again; he tried his hand at fresco. Then it was back to clay. His last and greatest creations were taking shape.

But the outside world could not be ignored. Maillol listened to the news and grieved over the fall of France, but he had no wish to get personally involved.[31] By tradition and upbringing, he had always been a moderate conservative and had nothing against the Germans as such. Wars of every kind were follies. Was one not enough in a man's lifetime? Like his colleagues and friends scattered in the south of France – Bonnard, Matisse, Dufy among them – he was probably hoping to sit it out in unostentatious withdrawal. He was never given the option. Dina hated the Nazis and after 1941 she identified with the sufferings of Russia. Nor was she satisfied, as were so many others, with wringing her hands, deploring the carnage and cultivating the black market. She and Maillol were ideally placed to help fugitives and escaped prisoners of war find their way to neutral Spain across the mountains. Maillol's abandoned studio in Puig del Mas became a recognised staging post. Heinrich and Golo Mann[32] and Franz Werfel[33] were among the

---

[29] Maillol was abstemious in his habits but cooking was one of his hobbies, as it was that of his fellow-sculptor Brancusi.

[30] On his own he tended to read old favourites like Victor Hugo and Anatole France. But Dina read to him poetry – Valéry, Mallarmé and *Les Fleurs du Mal* – philosophy, history and religion, everything in which she was interested. She introduced him to Freud, Heidegger and Sartre.

[31] Lucien had fought in the First World War and Maillol had vivid memories of the earlier years of anxiety.

[32] Thomas Mann's brother and nephew.

[33] Author of the *Song of Bernadette* and many other fine novels.

celebrities whom she helped to escape. There were hundreds of others less celebrated. Her activities could not be kept a secret for long. She was put under house arrest, escaped to Paris and was arrested again. This time she was sent to the notorious prison at Fresnes.

Maillol was in despair. Then he remembered – or rather, a news item on the radio reminded him of – Arno Breker. Breker had come from Germany to sit at the master's feet in the palmy days of the early 1930s. Maillol never regarded him as a promising pupil but appreciated his boundless enthusiasm and impeccable manners. Since then the young German had risen to dizzy heights. His gift for monumental banality was first discovered by Speer, Hitler's architect and aesthete in chief, and later by the Führer himself. Now he was the Führer's favourite sculptor and ambassador-at-large of Aryan culture to decadent Europe. An exhibition of his indomitably heroic youths and fecund Teutonic maidens was soon to open in the Orangerie in Paris.[34] Maillol wrote to his erstwhile pupil offering to write a laudatory introduction to the catalogue. At the same time he pleaded for Dina's release. Breker was a worthless artist, but there was nobody in France whom he venerated more than Maillol; and he understood the coded message. At some risk – or at least inconvenience – to himself, he intervened with General von Stolpe, the deputy military governor of Paris. Maillol wrote his nauseating appreciation. Dina was set free.

Though Dina could not return to Banyuls (she was still under police surveillance and was reluctant to endanger Maillol),[35] Maillol resumed his work with his peace of mind restored. Inspired by her, he had already created two of his greatest nudes, *Air* and *Spring*. Now he was finishing, stage by stage, what was to be the last – *Harmony* (Plate 19). None of the six extant versions are in fact completely finished. But they all represent, especially the last, the peak of Maillol's art. After contemplating it for many a silent minute and uncharacteristically overcome by the experience, six months after

[34] This was one of those deeply shameful occasions which were too well-documented and accompanied by too much publicity to be conveniently forgotten after the war. No French art lover could honestly pretend that Breker's work was anything but terrible; yet the exhibition, sponsored jointly by the German occupying power and the Collaborationist French establishment, mustered among its patrons the cream of French intellectual life. Among those swooning over Breker's Aryan youths were not only lickers of any boot going, like Kees van Dongen, but also poets and writers like Cocteau and Sacha Guitry, actors and actresses like Arletty and Bonival, and artists of established reputation like Despiau, Vlaminck, Dunoyer de Segonzac, Friesz, Belmondo and Derain. Despiau wrote a booklet to accompany the catalogue in which he traced not only the development of "Breker's genius" but most other "encouraging recent developments in the fine arts" to the "fructifying effect of Hitler's lofty ideas". In Julien Benda's famous phrase, it was truly *la trahison des clercs*.

[35] She was in Paris when General Leclerc's Free French entered the city.

Maillol's death, Matisse pronounced it the "Great Summation". The pronouncement has often been quoted; but it expressed only part of the truth. The sculpture was as much a beginning as a summing up, what Picasso once described as a "threshold work".

Maillol had often in the past been labelled a highly physical sculptor. One reason why professional critics (as distinct from the uninformed public) found it so difficult to describe his creations – or so many maintained – was that they were never conceived in terms of ideas. In exasperation Jean Bonnet suggested that his women were all body and no soul. When Maillol was interviewed and asked about the criticism he surprised the newspaper reporter by not disagreeing. "A sculptor", he was quoted as saying, "was limited by his material, like any artist. In stone or bronze one could try to create or recreate physical characteristics but not, by the very nature of the material, characteristics of the spirit." [36] However clumsily expressed – like many great artists he tended to lapse into the platitudinous in print – it was a belief which he had firmly held all his life. Then, at eighty and in *Harmony*, he resoundingly disproved himself, creating the most spiritual as well as arguably the most beautiful nude of the century. Like all such achievements in the visual arts, it was the product of a combination of circumstances: the character of his muse – serenity, courage, and beauty – and his own long experience. Both were aided and abetted by that greatest and most elusive of creative gifts – love.

To speculate what an elderly Mozart or Raphael might have achieved in their seventies is to lament two untimely deaths. One does not usually lament the passing of an eighty-three-year-old artist as "untimely". But Maillol was a late starter; and in his last sculptures he seemed to be poised on the threshold of a new and exciting phase. It was not to be. The bells of Liberation were ringing out over France.[37] Hope and promise (mingled with less worthy sentiments) were in the air.[38] On 20 September, elated by the news that the last German troops had left French soil, Maillol walked to Banyuls in his mountain espadrilles, wearing his customary large red beret and carrying a folder of drawings. He was to be given a lift by his doctor, Dr Nicoleau, to visit his old friend Raoul Dufy. But, turning a sharp corner on the winding mountain road, the driver braked suddenly and his passenger was thrown against the windscreen. He injured his jaw, not at first sight severely. He was

[36] J. Bujard, "Maillol", *Esprit*, 2 (1931), p. 33.

[37] Banyuls itself had been liberated without a fight early in August.

[38] Some of Maillol's prewar colleagues and friends – Derain and Kees van Dongen among them – were under a cloud, in Germany with the Vichy crew, or being investigated for collaboration.

taken to hospital in Perpignan unable to speak, conveying his wishes in a school copybook. They were simple but peremptory. Under no circumstances would he agree to his beard being shaved off; and he wanted to be sent home. There seemed to be no compelling reason to keep him in hospital; but at home he died quietly in his sleep two days later.[39]

[39] Dina was already at the centre of the reviving art world in Paris. Françoise Gilot met her for the first time in Picasso's studio in the rue des Grands-Augustins. "I will always vividly remember the impact of her arrival ... She was the very image of victory, the perfect Nike of the ancient Greeks. Perfectly poised and intelligent, she was in the full bloom of youth ... Her bearing was regal; she was more than a muse, she was the priestess of art. She was the exact symbol of life, a rock of affirmation and certainty. Picasso already knew her, and, far from being ironic or sarcastic, as he often was with other guests, he was pleasant, even subdued, perhaps because it was her first visit to his studio since Maillol's death in 1944 ... Because of his tribulations with his first wife, Olga, Pablo was always in awe but also wary of Russian women. He was deferential, even attentive – a most unusual attitude indeed – as if beguiled by her charm and modesty ... Instead of being flirtatious, he treated Dina like a queen, perhaps thinking that not only Maillol but Ambroise Vollard, Maillol's great friend, or even Phidias himself, would rise from the grave to protect their goddess from his sacrilegious thoughts." See F. Gilot, *Matisse and Picasso: A Friendship in Art*, translated by Nan A. Talese (London, 1990), p. 10.

With the help and support of Matisse, Dufy, Bonnard and the architect Auguste Perret, Mme Vierny (as Dina became) established one of the most successful private art galleries in the rue Jacob in Paris, sponsoring many leading figures of the avant-garde as well as championing the posthumous fame of Maillol. She donated her collection of works by Maillol, Matisse, Picasso and other artists to the French state. The collection is now housed in the Musée Maillol in the rue de Grenelle, opened by President François Mitterrand in 1985. Over it Mme Vierny still gracefully and energetically presides.

# 10

# *Munch*

Many watched with foreboding the lights going out in Europe in August 1914.[1] Many more thronged the squares in front of parliaments and royal residences in an ecstasy of joy, hoarse with cheering. Of course outbreaks of war, promising escape from years of frustration or sheer boredom, have often been greeted with jubilation in the past. But to Europe's bourgeoisie the years before 1914 had been extraordinarily kind, and it was they who led the cheering. Their outburst stunned the politicians whose bumbling had precipitated what many had declared to be an unthinkable disaster. "They have gone out of their little minds", Count Berchtold giggled, watching students and professors of Vienna University singing under the windows of the Ballhausplatz.[2] He was clearly not a reader of Dostoievski, a Baudelaire fan or a devotee of Mahler.

Writers, poets, painters and musicians are often better guides to the prevailing mood of an age than statistics on population growth and per capita income, miles of railway line, tons of pig-iron, rates of illegitimacy, levels of literacy or infant mortality. And never did Europe's creative riff-raff sound more tormented than during the last sunlit years of the Long Peace.[3] The sound was not, as often in the past, the wailing of helpless creatures trampled by horsemen of the Apocalypse. Nor was it the babble of a future generation contemplating the extinction of the species. It was the articulate despair of intelligent individuals suffocating in a morass of plenty. It inspired poems, novels, plays and philosophical works which are among the most pessimistic in European literature. It throbbed in the tormented music of the late Romantics. It writhed in the frozen arabesques of Art Nouveau. And it pierced the cosy world of bourgeois *Gemütlichkeit* with Edvard Munch's *The Scream*.

"Disease, insanity and death attended my cradle and have followed me

---

[1] The phrase attributed to Sir Edward Grey, Foreign Secretary in Asquith's Liberal Cabinet.

[2] Austria-Hungary's Foreign Minister, framer of the fatal ultimatum to Serbia and one of history's great gigglers.

[3] There had been no general European conflagration since the Napoleonic Wars and no conflict between Great European Powers since the Franco-Prussian War of 1870–71.

through life", Munch recounted in middle age.[4] Few would have noticed the gathering at his birth.[5] The Munchs of Hedmark in Norway were a respected family of professional men, scholars, pastors and public servants. Edvard's father was an army doctor and later a district physician in Oslo.[6] Peter Andreas Munch, the revered historian of the Norwegian people, was a great-uncle.[7] They belonged to a class which a hundred years earlier had been hardly more than a political figment and which now effectively ruled Europe and very nearly the world.[8] His mother, one of twenty children, came from a more humble stock of sailors and fishermen. But Edvard was only five when his mother died, and his father never recovered from the loss.

> When anxiety did not possess him, he would joke and play with us ... but when he was angry and punished us he could be almost insane with violence. But worse than physical punishment was the terrible threat of Hell that hung over our heads.[9]

Of his mother's death Edvard retained only a dim memory. But he was eighteen when his sister, Sophie, two years younger than himself, died after a long lingering illness. That memory was never to leave him.

Edvard's wish to become a professional artist inevitably met with strong paternal opposition. This was not unreasonable. The doctor was not rich, and financially a career in the arts was insecure – to say the least. Even more seriously, the path of an artist was beset with grave moral temptations.

[4] Recalled by Dr K. E. Schreiner, Munch's physician, in 1946 and quoted by J. P. Hodin in *Edvard Munch* (London, 1972).

  Two important monographs on the artist were published in his lifetime: J. Thiis, *Edvard Munch* (Berlin, 1934); and Pola Gauguin, *Munch* (Oslo 1933). J. P. Hodin's *Edvard Munch, Genius des Nordens* (Stockholm, 1948), already contained an extensive bibliography. Other useful monographs, some containing personal reminiscences, are H. E. Gerlach, *Edvard Munch: sein Leben und sein Werk* (Hamburg, 1955); A. Moen, *Edvard Munch: Graphic Art and Paintings*, 3 volumes (Oslo, 1956–58); S. T. Madsen, *Edvard Munch* (London, 1960); J. H. Langaard and R. Revold, *A Year by Year Record of Edvard Munch's Life* (Oslo, 1961); and the work by J. P. Hodin mentioned above. Two useful exhibition catalogues were published in England: *Dreams of a Summer Night*, Arts Council of Great Britain Exhibition in the Hayward Gallery (London, 1986); and *Edvard Munch*, Royal Academy of Arts (London, 1993).

[5] He was born in Oslo, then still called Christiania, in 1863. Norway was still linked to Denmark by the crown: it did not become an independent kingdom (for the first time since 1319) until 1905. But nationalist feeling was strong for at least a hundred years before independence.

[6] He did much to extirpate cholera from the city.

[7] He died in Rome in the year of Edvard's birth. Another paternal great-uncle was a bishop.

[8] Only the United States and Japan were truly independent powers outside Europe; and in Europe (outside Russia) effective power was passing into the hands of the middle classes.

[9] Hodin, *Edvard Munch*, p. 48.

1. Giovanni Bellini (1430–1516), *Lady at her Toilet* (detail). Probably Bellini's last painting: a shaft of light into the future. (*Kunsthistorisches Museum, Vienna*)

2.  Titian (Tiziano Vecellio) (1487–1576), *Self-Portrait, c.* 1560 (detail). Old and a little tired looking, but still at work. (*Prado, Madrid*)

3. Tintoretto (Jacopo Robusti) (1518–1594), *Deposition*. Tintoretto's last painting. He is the bearded mourner kneeling next to Christ. (*San Giorgio Maggiore, Venice/Bridgeman Art Library*)

4. Gianlorenzo Bernini (1598–1680), *Gabriele Fonseca*. Bernini's last sepulchral monument. (*Fonseca Chapel, San Lorenzo in Lucina, Rome/Bridgeman Art Library*)

5. Claude Lorrain (Claude Gelée) (1600–1682), *Landscape with Aeneas and the Cumaean Sybil*. One of Claude's last drawings in his *Liber veritatis*. (*British Museum*)

6. Jean-Baptiste-Siméon Chardin (1699–1779), *Self-Portrait with Bésicles*. The unvarnished truth: Chardin's last self-portrait. (*Louvre, Paris*)

7. Francisco José de Goya y Lucientes (1746–1828), *Saturn, c.*
1821–23. One of the Black Paintings for the Quinta del Sordo
(*Prado, Madrid*)

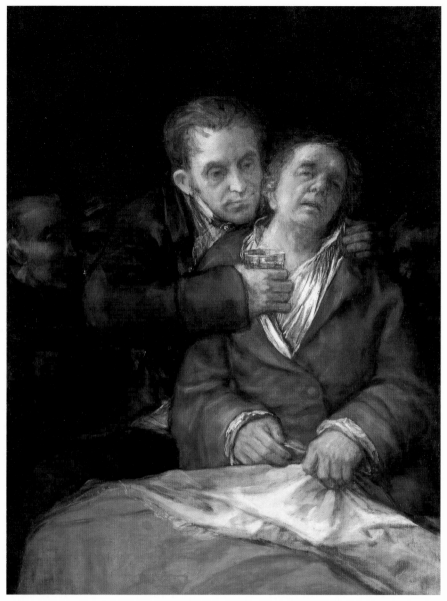

8. Francisco José de Goya y Lucientes (1746–1828), *Self-Portrait with Dr Arietta*, 1820. An attack of cardiac asthma: one of the greatest medical documentaries ever painted. (*The Minneapolis Institute of Art, Minneapolis, Minnesota*)

9.  Jacques-Louis David (1748–1825), *The Princesses Charlotte and Zenaïde Bonaparte*, 1821. One of David's last portraits: unconvincing anatomy but brilliant characterisation. (*Paul Getty Museum, Malibu, California*)

10. Jean-Auguste-Dominique Ingres (1780–1867), *The Princesse de Broglie*, 1853. The last society portrait of a doomed princess. (*Metropolitan Museum of Art, New York*)

11. Katsushika Hokusai (1760–1849), *The Red Fuji*. The ultimate perfection of design.

12. Joseph Mallord William Turner (1775–1851), *The Grand Canal, Looking towards Santa Maria della Salute, c.* 1840, one of Turner's late water-colours of Venice. Venice at its loveliest and Turner at his best. (*Tate Britain, London*)

13. Pierre-Auguste Renoir (1841–1919), *Bathers*, 1919. The last of the *Bathers*. A crippled old man's vision of beauty. (*Musée d'Orsée, Paris/Bridgeman Art Library*)

14. Renoir in his wheelchair, with Andrée Heuschling (Dédée), 1915.

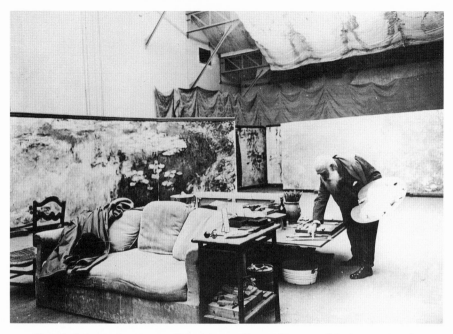

15. Claude Monet (1840–1926) in his studio at Giverny. "Only a pair of eyes — but what a pair!", said Cézanne; but by now Monet was almost blind. (*Private Collection/Roger-Viollet, Paris/Bridgeman Art Library*)

16. Auguste Rodin (1840–1917) and sculpture. The former builder's mate, by now the most famous Frenchman in Europe. (*Collection Kharbine-Tapabor, Paris/Bridgeman Art Library*)

17. Pierre Bonnard (1867–1947) painting. His obituarist was to describe him as "a discreet genius". (*Private Collection/Roger-Viollet, Paris/Bridgeman Art Library*)

18. Vasili Kandinski (1866–1944), painting in December 1936. The great wanderer at the beginning of his last exile in Paris. (*Private Collection/Roger-Viollet, Paris/Bridgeman Art Library*)

19. Aristide Maillol (1861–1944), in his studio at Banyuls-sur-Mer in 1940, sculpting *Harmony*. Matisse was to describe *Harmony* as the great summing up; but it was more an unfulfilled beginning. (*Mme Dina Vierny/ADAGP*)

20.  Edvard Munch (1863–1944), *Self-Portrait: Between Bed and Clock*, 1940–43, oil on canvas. Munch confronting his last ghost: old age. (*Munch Museum, Oslo/Munch-Ellingsen Group/DACS 2000*)

But the boy was sickly and it seemed doubtful if he could complete the rigorous course in engineering for which his father had enrolled him. Several knowledgeable friends also spoke highly of his gift at drawing.[10] The doctor eventually gave his blessing and the young man entered the Oslo School of Design. This was mainly a school of industrial draughtsmanship; but it did have a course in the fine arts and some practitioners on its staff.[11] Edvard impressed them: he was, as he would always remain, reserved but respectful, a polite listener in the company of compulsive talkers. Despite his apparently frail health, he was also a hard worker. But Oslo was an artistic backwater, "my Siberia" as he would refer to it later.[12] Ambitious local artists, especially those with a rebellious streak, had traditionally migrated to Copenhagen or Düsseldorf or, more recently, to Munich, Rome and Paris. The scene was changing, but slowly. Established modes of expression in the Romantic-Naturalist style were taken for granted if for no other reason than because no other style was known. Nothing in this setting can account for the *The Sick Child*. Munch was twenty-two when he painted his masterpiece, not just portraying the illness and death from tuberculosis of a beloved sister, but documenting one of the nightmares of the age.

By the end of the nineteenth century the European middle classes lived longer and in greater comfort (as distinct from great but uncomfortable luxury) than any ruling class had lived before them.[13] Yet no ruling class had ever been so obsessed with disease or had lived in such dread of it.[14] The fear was part of the middle-class ethos. Illness is an intensely personal experience; and reverence for individuals rather than for lineages, clans or tribes was a middle-class invention. What had mattered to the dynasties who had lorded it over Europe for centuries was the dynasty. What shattered the Munch family of Oslo was the death of Sophie.

[10] Notably Dr Munch's friend, the lighthouse keeper and amateur draughtsman C. F. Diriks.

[11] Among them were Christian Krogh, Fritz Thaulow and Eric Werenskiold, all three good painters in the Naturalistic tradition, and Munch's generous champions.

[12] But it is possible to exaggerate the country's artistic isolation. (Some of Munch's biographers may have taken their cue from the artist himself.) Many Norwegian artists working abroad maintained close links with their homeland; and a lively and gifted artistic colony was established in Fleksum in 1884. An international art exhibition in 1879, which Munch visited more than once, showed several contemporary French works, including paintings by Courbet. In 1882 Krogh, Thaulow and Werenskiold inaugurated an annual autumn exhibition of Norwegian artists.

[13] Compared to a prosperous middle-class home in 1914, living (let alone dying) in Versailles, Schönbrunn or even the seats of the Whig grandees in England in the eighteenth century must have been far from comfortable.

[14] The great epidemics of the past were not illnesses in the nineteenth-century sense. People did not live with the plague any more than they lived with earthquakes: they were ways of dying or of surviving.

There were other reasons too. Private wealth and public virtue were not only the ideals but also the invincible defences of the bourgeois. Not quite invincible though. Many of the pestilences of the past had been conquered or at least banished to the new industrial suburbs. Some continued to mock material, moral and scientific progress. Pillars of middle-class probity lived in dread of the insanity of tertiary and congenital syphilis.[15] The effects of alcoholism could destroy whole families. But the undisputed leader of the pack and the disease which killed Sophie Munch was tuberculosis.[16] It cut across social barriers and picked out young people in their prime. Its natural history was unique. Pain, the most cruel destroyer of character, was usually absent; and the love of friends and family was never therefore put to the test. Nor did physical suffering blunt the patient's yearning to live. Hope was kindled when, often for no obvious reason, the disease underwent extraordinary remissions. Yet even during remissions spikes of low-grade fever often continued. They consumed the patient's strength but also acted as a drug, heightening awareness and perhaps stimulating creativity. And in the end victory usually went to the disease – but often only by a heart-breaking hair's breadth. The clinical course remains enshrined in thousands of old medical tomes, as well as in a few great works of literature, but none convey what the young Norwegian artist conveyed with astonishing economy by a few strokes of the brush and a few thin pools of colour.

The Sick Girl had a mixed reception. Critics unanimously condemned the "incoherent daubs"; but some of Munch's fellow artists, even those puzzled by the strange young man and his even stranger art, sensed genius in the making. "He is so reticent, even secretive, that it is hard to know what he thinks", Christian Krogh wrote, "but I do not think that he is deliberately trying to shock us." [17] Krogh was right, but his faith was soon to be even more severely tested. If The Sick Child disturbed the public by its style, Puberty seemed an outrage against common decency.[18] Only a year earlier, at the opening of the new Christiania Museum of Sculpture, a strange

[15] It was the subject of Ibsen's Ghosts and a subsidiary theme of several other of his plays (including The Doll's House). Munch painted congenital syphilis too, a little-known and not very good picture of a syphilitic mother cradling an infant with the stigmata of the disease, entitled Inheritance. It is in the Munch Museum in Oslo.

[16] See T. Dormandy, The White Death: A History of Tuberculosis (London, 1999).

[17] Quoted by J. Thiis, Edvard Munch, p. 124.

[18] At a time when pregnancy was never mentioned by name in polite society, even the title was a provocation. Had he called the picture Awakening, as other artists did (notably the Finn Magnus Enckel), it might have been acceptable – just. But even Frank Wedekind's sensitive and poetic play about adolescent sexuality, Frühlingserwachen (Spring Awakening) created a furore when it was first produced in 1890 and was banned in most countries until after the First World War.

ceremony had taken place. A Bible was handed to the director, a man in holy orders. "I attest before God", he intoned, "that the viewing of nudes can be pure and elevating. No Christian need feel ashamed or sinful in deriving pleasure from them." But there are nudes and nudes. Puberty was not a cool classical goddess whose naked beauty transcended any hint of carnality. Nor was she a coy Victorian maiden titillatingly hiding her charms behind artfully arranged drapes or foliage. She was not even a brazen creature of sexual commerce whose portrayal might be condoned for pointing a moral. She was a naked girl on the threshold of womanhood, her arms crossed in a shiver in front of her budding breasts, her thighs convulsively pressed together. There is fear in her eyes, the sense of menace magnified by her unnatural (or badly painted) shadow on the wall. She has just glimpsed Munch's fourth ghost. Sex had caught up with disease, insanity and death.

The shrillness of the public outcry no longer worried the artist. At twenty-six he was about to leave his native land. He was also embarking on a more momentous journey, not measurable in miles. He was plunging from the cocoon of middle-class security into the dark and turbulent waters of Bohemia.

The word "Bohemian" is still widely used,[19] but real Bohemia exists no longer. It has disappeared, together with the bourgeois world whose mockery and destruction was its *raison d'être*, both consumed by two world wars. The true history of its last decades, Munch was to say in old age, would never be written: by then most of its erstwhile inhabitants were dead and nobody who had not dwelt in it could recapture its unique atmosphere. For reality had moved a long way from the charming and tearful world of Murger and Puccini.[20] The Bohemia of Munch's generation was squalid, sick, degrading, cruel and self-destructive; but it was also, for a few decades, the main repository of the European spirit at its most creative. The country had no fixed geographical frontiers and its outposts had acquired distinctive local characteristics to colour shared ideals and sustaining hatreds. The Bohemia of Oslo where Munch took the plunge was small, grim and literary. It clustered around the Zolaesque figure of Hans Jaeger, whose powerful though excessively long novels about prostitution provided the focal and obligatory scandal.[21] It was

[19] It has been since the eighteenth century when it was widely believed that vagrants and gipsies came from the Habsburg land of Bohemia. Thackeray described Becky Sharp's parents as having a "Bohemian" lifestyle.

[20] See below, Chapter 14, pp. 210–11.

[21] Munch painted an excellent portrait of him, now in the Oslo National Gallery. He died in 1902, aged fifty-three.

inspired by Ibsen [22] and spell-bound by Nietzsche,[23] Dostoievski,[24] and the recently rediscovered works of Søren Kierkegaard.[25] Munch was to read and reread their books all his life.

After intense but provincial Oslo, Paris's Bohemia was the Mother Country, the largest and oldest of all the Bohemias. It had jealously guarded territorial enclaves on the Left Bank and in Montmartre – cafés, artists' studios, brothels and a few aristocratic mansions. It was Paris which had launched the drink, drug and international emblem of Bohemia, absinthe, and it was the *Parisien* Zola who described its unique effects.[26] Oslo's Bohemia had been rich in talent, but Paris was awash with genius. In the 1890s, when it engulfed Munch, it was under the spell of the Symbolists – self-consciously depraved, and captivated by mysticism and the bizarre workings of the human mind. Munch attended Dr Charcot's public lectures on madness,[27] listened to Mallarmé's poetry, shuddered over Huysmans' erotic fantasies,[28] and inevitably succumbed to the Green Fairy. But even Paris was only a stop-over: it was Berlin's Bohemia which for more than a decade became his home.

Berlin's Bohemia gloried in the negative reflection of the respectable world around it. The capital of Wilhelmine Germany was brash, materialistic, rich, hypocritical and arrogant. Its Bohemia was therefore anarchic, subversive, dissolute and ostentatiously preoccupied with sex. Munch's closest companions were Stanislaw Przybyszevski, an occasionally brilliant but more frequently hallucinating Polish-German poet, and his angelically beautiful and amoral mistress Ducha;[29] but it was a crowded and cosmopolitan scene. There was August Strindberg from Sweden, patently a genius but no less

[22] He treated many of the subjects dear to Bohemia in his revolutionary plays, but in private life he was never a Bohemian. He died in 1906, aged seventy-eight.

[23] He died insane from tertiary syphilis in 1900, aged fifty-six.

[24] Dostoievski died in 1881, aged fifty-nine, but most of his works were not translated into German (and then into the Scandinavian languages) until ten years after his death.

[25] He had died in 1855, aged forty-two, never recognised as a thinker and a prophet in his lifetime.

[26] See below, Chapter 14, p. 211 n. 51.

[27] Charcot was one of the great clinical teachers of the age; but his clinical fame was eclipsed by his weekly public lectures at the Hôpital Salpêtrière, where he demonstrated the effects of hypnosis on hysteria. Munch and his friends who attended might have glimpsed young Dr Freud from Vienna among the medical visitors.

[28] Always written in Indian ink because it was "so beautifully black". Munch's contact with the Impressionists or other painters was surprisingly slight. He met Theo van Gogh but was not impressed by Vincent's work. He visited the Louvre only once.

[29] Many of the characters who appear in Munch's paintings are recognisable as his friends in Berlin's Bohemia. Przybyszevski is the bearded face in *Jealousy*. After Ducha left Berlin she got involved with a young musician in Odessa who, in a fit of jealousy, shot her and then himself.

obviously mad, intermittently convinced that Munch was poisoning him and conducting dangerous chemical experiments in his hotel room.[30] Axel Gallen-Kallela from Finland, the future illustrator of the *Kalevala,* was slipping in and out of depressive crises, half-living in a mythical world of trolls, fairies and magicians.[31] Gustav Vigeland of Norway was already wrestling with heroic sexual kitsch.[32] Richard Dehmel from the Rhineland was preaching anarchism (when sober).[33] Julius Meier-Graefe, the future historian of modern art, was still plotting to set the city's art galleries on fire.[34] They were a diversity of talent, or talent *manqué,* but united in their loathing of bourgeois complacency, materialism and repression. They would meet at the Schwarzer Ferkel, once the haunt of Heine and E. T. A. Hoffmann, in the Café Bauer, or at the flat of the Przybyszevskis, where Ducha would dispense tumblers of absinthe and consume it herself with apparent immunity. They would drink, talk and argue through the night; they would recite poetry; they would play and listen to music; and they would admire – and occasionally destroy – each other's paintings. They would discuss sex in all its wonderful and sordid ramifications and rage against outmoded romantic conventions.[35] Then they would romantically fall in love, attempt suicide, recover (usually), and argue and fall romantically in love again.

If Munch was deeply inside Bohemia, he was never quite *of* it. In between heroic drinking bouts and monumental hangovers, he painted. Bohemia was a literary milieu and all his paintings of that period have literary resonances; but, unlike many other artists in his circle, he never quite succumbed to themes which were irredeemably non-visual. *Jealousy, Despair, The Lonely Ones, Ashes, The Morning After, The Wake of the Vampires* and of course *The Scream* are spine-tingling evocations of poetic subjects, but they are all conceived as paintings and succeed as such. Nor did he ever entirely lose his

[30] August Strindberg, thirteen years older than Munch, was a powerful painter (and a perceptive writer on art) as well as a great dramatist, but he turned to painting only for short periods and in times of crisis, as after his first traumatic divorce in the 1890s. He died in 1912, aged sixty-three.

[31] He died in 1931, aged sixty-six.

[32] He is held in high esteem by many of his countrymen and has a public park in Oslo devoted to his sculpture. Munch did not regard him highly as an artist but liked him as a man. He died in 1943, aged seventy-eight.

[33] He was an excellent poet and in *Zwei Menschen* wrote at least one great novel. He died in 1920, aged fifty-three.

[34] He introduced Impressionism to Germany and later edited the influential magazine *Pan.* He died in 1938, aged sixty-seven.

[35] They would also discuss Marx and Kropotkin, but Bohemia was, on the whole, non-political or at least studiedly indifferent to money and economics.

Nordic calm; and his professionalism was oddly unbohemian. He exhibited widely, delivering his pictures on time and in the format stipulated. His talent was disconcertingly recognised by a few pillars of the bourgeois world as well as by his fellow Bohemians.

Walter Rathenau, one of the most powerful industrial barons of the Empire,[36] became a patron and introduced him to influential dealers and art lovers.[37] Could his mad pictures conceivably be sound financial investments? One could not be sure. They were certainly "powerful" and power was something every good German understood. Max Reinhardt commissioned him to design the sets and costumes for Ibsen's *Ghosts*.[38] The play and production scandalised Berlin and reverberated throughout Europe; and much of the notoriety rubbed off on Munch. Yet, unlike so many of the so-called avant-garde, he was not socially impossible. Indeed, Herr Munch was always eminently *salonfähig*, a little stiff perhaps, especially after his first bottle of cognac, but impeccably groomed and mannered. The cultivated home of Dr Max Linde, a fashionable physician in the old Hanseatic city of Lübeck, provided him with an occasional haven from the stresses of Berlin. Although Linde politely declined to install Munch's *Frieze of Life* in the nursery – the boys would love it, Frau Linde declared, but it would send prospective governesses screaming from the house – the family portraits were appreciated.

Yet Munch was still relentlessly pursued by his four ghosts – disease and death and their two outriders, sex and insanity. At least two weighty monographs, one of the Freudian and one of the Jungian persuasion, have been devoted to Munch's psyche, and especially to his obsession with women. To non-specialists they add little to the eloquent testimony of his

[36] He was seven years younger than Munch but already the heir to the presidency of the Allgemeine Elektrizitätsgesellschaft, one of Germany's industrial cartels. Unfettered capitalism was still being worshipped as one of the eternal verities and the heads of these cartels and trusts were powerful as well as rich. They were also, on the whole, a dismal lot: most became Hitler's ardent backers and toadies. Though ruthless in business, Rathenau was an exception: an excellent engineer as well as a poet, he was also an enlightened patron of the arts. Munch painted one of his best portraits of him. In 1922 he accepted the thankless post of Foreign Minister and negotiated the Rapallo Treaty, the first breach in Communist Russia's international isolation. A few months later he was assassinated.

[37] Among them was Albert Kollmann, a rich and eccentric collector, whom Munch later described as his "Mephistopheles"; and Paul Cassirer, the influential art dealer and secretary of the Berlin "Sezession", the rebellious group of young Berlin artists (including Munch) who "seceded" from the more respectable Verein Berliner Künstler.

[38] Together with *Hedda Gabler*, it was one of the famous director's and theatrical innovator's first productions. In 1933 he was forced to leave Germany. He died in the United States in 1947, aged seventy.

pictures.[39] He saw women as objects of desire, victims, vampires or possessive mothers; and it was his good or bad fortune that, tall, spare and ascetic, he was and would remain attractive to them. One night early in his passage through Bohemia he was roused from sleep by friends. A young woman he had apparently loved but abandoned was on the point of death and wanted to speak to him for a last time. Munch in distress accompanied the troupe to the woman's house. She was lying on a bed, with her arms folded, between two lighted candles. But she was not dead. There were guffaws from the friends as Munch approached her in horror. It had all been a hoax. Then, as he withdrew, she sat up and pointed a revolver at her breast. She would shoot herself if he left her. Munch tried to wrench the weapon from her. A shot rang out and a bullet shattered Munch's right middle finger. Perhaps the episode marked him for life. More likely, he did not need much marking.[40] He had several transient love affairs but backed away as soon as they threatened to become more than transient. He painted a few brothel scenes, none of them very good. "Copulating", he wrote, "is to me like mating with death." It was drink rather than sex which precipitated his breakdown. In November 1908 he arrived in Copenhagen for an exhibition. Two weeks later he was admitted to Dr Daniel Jacobsen's clinic, trembling violently and muttering incoherences, unable or unwilling to eat or drink, ghostlike in appearance. The diagnosis was "extreme nervous prostration", a coded definition of delirium tremens.[41] His collapse put an end to twenty years of rootless wandering and his most abundant period as an artist. He was forty-eight.

Psychotropic drug therapy was in its vigorous infancy and Munch seems to have had every form of treatment, including electrical convulsions.[42] He himself never doubted that Jacobsen saved his life. The *Self-Portrait* he

[39] Like other such retrospective delvings into the psyches of dead celebrities (to which doctors are astonishingly prone), they add little if anything to the testimony of Munch's paintings. It was not just Munch but the whole of the literary-artistic *fin de siècle* which was choking on suppressed sexuality. Munch stands out only because of his genius in expressing it in painting, just as Freud stands out because of his gift for coining striking new expressions (like the Oedipus Complex) for ancient ideas and for basing on them an elaborate analytical system.

[40] A passion for elaborate practical jokes is probably as good a measure as any of the sheer boredom of a society or a social class; and it was one of the few shared addictions of Bohemia and High Society. The fact that it reached its greatest popularity in the decade before the First World War may help to explain why the outbreak of the war was greeted with such an ecstasy of joy. Boredom can be a very dangerous (and an underestimated) motive force in history.

[41] Seen nowadays more often after the withdrawal of addictive drugs.

[42] This was galvanic "stimulation", not yet Electro-Convulsive Therapy (ECT).

painted after nine months' therapy shows him a changed man. He looks relaxed, rubicund, almost chubby. He would never touch alcohol again, though he remained an occasional smoker. But most important was a complete change of lifestyle. After renting a succession of country estates on the coast of Norway, he bought a rambling farmhouse with extensive grounds at Ekely near Oslo. It was to remain his home for the rest of his life. He lived frugally though he had become wealthy. In Europe among the cognoscenti he was already famous. Now it was the turn of his native country. Jens Thiis, an old friend from Bohemia, had become the director of Oslo's new National Gallery. He bought eight canvases from Munch, the beginning of an extensive collection. A rich collector, Olof Schou, added others. Exhibitions were arranged and opened by royalty. Most resoundingly, to mark the centenary of Oslo University, he was to be invited to paint the murals of the new Aula. That at least was Thiis's plan. The project soon became a battleground.

Munch had many friends and admirers on the university senate, but the silent majority were as happily hidebound as the silent majorities of such bodies usually are. Silent and happy, that is, until roused. Twenty-five artists had submitted projects. Jens Thiis hand-picked the expert jury. The university senate packed the building committee. Amid a crescendo of bickering, the twenty-five submissions were whittled down to six. Tactlessly the building committee made its "unalterable choice" clear before the expert jury had had time to pronounce its recommendation. The expert jury dug their heels in (instead of gracefully resigning) and recommended Munch. The building committee rejected the recommendation and shuffled the jury about. The new jury again recommended Munch. The building committee again rejected their recommendation and again shuffled the jury. The jury again recommended Munch. The building committee wavered. Then an eminent organic chemist invited them to adjourn and view some of Munch's past work in the National Gallery. *Puberty, Madonna* (with a foetus in one corner) and a particularly bloodcurdling version of *The Vampire* had just been added to the collection. Was this the kind of imagery with which the university wished celebrate its anniversary? With stiffened resolve the building committee not only rejected Munch "once and for all" but cancelled the murals. With pleasing fitness the money collected for the project was reallocated to build a new museum of fossils. But this played into Thiis's hands. The money had been collected for the murals. The building committee had no power to reallocate it. In any case, if money was the obstacle, he could raise the sum by private subscription. He did so in a matter of weeks and for the specific purpose of commissioning Munch. The paintings were to be executed on board rather than directly on the wall, and were to be offered as a gift to the university from the people of Oslo. With the bad grace characteristic of cornered academic bodies, the senate capitulated.

The university murals were Munch's first major work after his breakdown and recovery. They are still one of Oslo's cultural prides. "To enter the Aula", the official guidebook instructs the visitor, "is like entering a cathedral ... In glowing colours you will be confronted with the very spirits of History, Scientific Discovery, Research and with the symbolic figure of the Alma Mater." There is no arguing with such perceptions; but, to anyone who has been gripped by Munch's earlier work, the murals will probably seem a little tame, even trite. Symbols are a treacherous device in any setting whose very nature transforms the ordinary into a symbol. Munch was of course an experienced artist with a keen eye for striking effects; and there are many details to admire. But there always will be visitors who feel that the university building committee in their obtuseness may have been right for the wrong reasons.

Much of what Munch painted over the next thirty years evokes a similar, faintly guilty response. The guilt is for wishing him tormented and haunted by ghosts when at last he was clearly at peace with himself. It is not that madness guarantees greatness in art any more than does sickness or poverty.[43] But Munch needed ghosts to inspire him to create masterpieces. Of course his work during the interwar years was not without merit. He painted some colourful landscapes; and his depictions of rural life showed flashes of his old power. In paintings like *The Duel* or the *Split Personality* (of the *Mephistopheles* series) he was also dipping into deep psychological waters; but the works were the comments of an onlooker, not of a participant. He probably knew this himself. As if for reassurance, he returned again and again to images of the past, reworking them in new formats and new media.

In terms of esteem and success the quality of his more recent output hardly mattered. Among lovers and buyers of contemporary art, the battle of Expressionism had been won during the first decade of the century; but the movement remained a minority cult. Then, as Europe emerged from the First World War and contemplated the slaughter and its legacy, Expressionism became the natural language of revulsion. Munch was now a recognised as a forerunner, an "historically important figure" in art-historical jargon, bracketed with Van Gogh and Gauguin. His paintings were shown at grand retrospective exhibitions in Germany, Switzerland, France, Italy, the United States and Scotland.[44] Up until 1936 he himself attended some of these functions, showing new works with the old. They were politely

---

[43] As brilliantly discussed by A. Mezey in *Muse in Torment* (London, 1997).
[44] But not in England, where he was hardly known until the 1950s.

received; but sometimes his living presence seemed to surprise the public and even the organisers. In 1933, to mark his seventieth birthday, Jens Thiis and Pola Gauguin published the first monograph on his life and work. France had already honoured him with the Legion of Honour: now he was made Commander of the Norwegian Order of St Olav. Recognition of a different kind descended on him a few months later. On Hitler's orders, eighty-two of his paintings in museums and private collections in Germany were declared "degenerate" and ordered to be removed from view.[45]

Of the two events which shaped Munch's old age the first was public and can be accurately dated. On 10 April 1940 German troops occupied Norway. They were to remain in occupation for four years, until a few months after the artist's death. The second event was gradual and private but no less momentous. Some time in his early seventies Munch began to be haunted by a new ghost. It was the ghost not of illness or of dying but of growing old.

Munch's response to the first event was "the silence of the sea".[46] In Nazi ideology Norwegians were the backward kinsmen of the *Herrenvolk* and were therefore to be treated as distant relations. The policy never worked: while the occupiers cultivated the relationship, the occupied cultivated the distance. Two Norwegians in particular were in Dr Goebbels's sight as likely recruits to the New Order, both in their dotage but both enjoying great prestige at home and abroad. Knut Hamsun, the Nobel Prize-winning author of *Hunger* and a dozen other great novels, proved an easy target.[47] Edvard Munch, his past degeneracy forgotten, was courted even more assiduously but remained stolidly unresponsive. To persecute him openly would have drawn attention to the failure; after a few months he was simply but malignly ignored. With food and fuel becoming increasingly scarce, and even good-quality oil-paint in short supply, being *persona non grata* in German-occupied Norway was no laughing matter.

Colonel Otto von Ferbach, a professional soldier, was well aware of this. He came from an old Hamburg family and his father, a city councillor in

[45] Most of them were fortunately sold at auction in Zurich to raise foreign currency for the party, rather than destroyed, as was Hitler's intention.

[46] The title of Vercors's (Jean Bruller's) once-famous book on the silent resistance in France.

[47] Until the German occupation there were parallels between the careers of Munch and Knut Hamsun; and they were often linked by critics. Munch himself thought highly of the writer: Hamsun's most poetic (as well as shortest) novel, *Pan*, was one of his favourites. But Hamsun was a friend of the Nazi puppet, Quisling, and he himself became in his eighties an ardent collaborator. After the war he was considered too old to stand trial. He died in disgrace in 1947, aged ninety.

the 1920s and a friend of Thomas Mann, had been a collector of modern art. Defying Hitler's directives, a Munch landscape still hung in the dining-room of the family home on the Alster. Both father and son detested the Nazis. Soon after being posted to Oslo in October 1942, the colonel wrote to Munch requesting a date when he could pay his respects. The letter remained unanswered. Von Ferbach wrote again and then again. There was no reply. Since Munch's telephone had been cut off, von Ferbach eventually set out on an unannounced visit. His car was loaded with army rations and he carried an album of family photographs. He found his way to the old farmhouse with some difficulty – by 1943 road signs had been removed on the coast of *Festung Europa* – and the door was opened to him only after prolonged ringing and knocking. The colonel recognised Munch at once from his self-portraits. The artist looked gaunt and his threadbare clothes hung on him loosely; but he held himself erect, a stiff soldierly figure. The colonel (in uniform) introduced himself and referred to previous letters. There was no response. The colonel explained that he had come not to harass the master but to pay his respects and convey greetings from his father. Silence. He had taken the liberty to bring a few trifling presents, tokens of his esteem. Nothing. Could the colonel come in and take up a few minutes of the master's time? Fifteen years later the colonel was to remember the glacial look and the ice in the voice. "Es ist nicht angenehm",[48] Munch said and shut the door.[49]

Resistance hardened and reprisals became more savage. Outside German propaganda films, cultural life ground to a halt. It seemed doubtful if it would ever revive. But, for the first time since his breakdown and recovery thirty years earlier, Munch was again painting masterpieces. They were mainly self-portraits but self-portraits of a special kind: not just images of a lonely old man but documents of the loneliness of old age. Painting his ghosts had always been his way of coping with them.

Chronic insomnia in the elderly is one of those terrible afflictions which are dismissed as trivial even by the sufferers. The silent agony is difficult to recreate in daylight and lacks the heroic dimension of pain or nightmares. Medical textbooks list a hundred causes: in other words the cause is un-known. Apart from a few memorable bars of music,[50] and perhaps a line or two of poetry, the experience had never been portrayed in art; nor, on the face of it, can it be. But Munch at his greatest was always reaching for

[48] Roughly, "It is not convenient".

[49] Based on a personal account given to the writer in 1958.

[50] Most poignantly perhaps in the introductory music to King Philip's monologue in Verdi's *Don Carlo*. Insomnia is not of course the same as having nightmares, which have been hauntingly portrayed by many, including Goya.

the impossible. In *The Night Wanderer* he caught the despair of the solitary wakeful moments before dawn. He himself subtitled the picture *Peer Gynt*. Perhaps he identified with Ibsen's wayward anti-hero, seeking rest after a lifetime's wanderings. But Ibsen is a cataract of words; Munch is congealed silence.

The first impression of *The Cod Dinner* is that of an elderly gourmet tucking into a half-forgotten delicacy. But after a second or two one is assailed by the similarity between the fish and the fish-eater and by the glint of bare teeth in the fish's skull. The man himself seems suddenly frozen with knife and fork in mid-air. It is the well-bred formality of the setting as much as the central character which generates the pathos. The artist has combed his hair and donned his tie and jacket in tribute to the fish, a present from a friend, as if he were presiding over a company of fellow gourmets assembled to partake in a rare treat. But his look is unfocused: he is not looking at anyone because there is no one to look at.

Most memorably, however, he painted himself standing upright in an open door between his bedroom and his studio (Plate 20). As in the ghost-ridden images of his youth, there is an abundance of literary props. The figure is hemmed in by a grandfather clock – has it just struck? – and a brass bedstead. The picture of a young female nude hangs near the margin of the wall. But their contribution is subliminal. The picture is simply that of an old man. He is not a grotesque like Rembrandt in his last self-portrait, nor a fierce patriarch or a benign grandfather. Both the character and the scene is totally devoid of self-pity. The setting is cheerful, even garish. The man is neither ill nor destitute. Of course his clothes do not quite fit; but even that has to be qualified. As in adolescent boys, it is not the clothes which do not fit the body but the body which no longer fits the clothes. And only a tiny feature, the slight outward bowing of the thighs, allowing a glimpse of light between the trouser legs, is an instant marker of old age. One has seen the cleft a thousand times in old people, but has it ever been painted? "Remote, unfriended, melancholy and slow",[51] the picture is indeed that of a traveller nearing the end of a long journey. It is not a happy prospect, especially when the mind is still fresh, and in so many respects youthful and ambitious, and much of the body is still responsive. But to depart life is part of the human condition and perhaps better than an indefinitely continuing slow decay. Anyway, hemmed in between bed and clock, there is no choice.

A few days before Christmas 1943, the day after Munch's eightieth birthday, the Resistance blew up the Fliupstad Quay in Oslo. The blast shattered the windows at Ekely. The weather had turned bitterly cold. In his last painting

---

[51] Oliver Goldsmith, 'The Traveller', line 1.

Munch shows himself behatted with coat-collar turned up, wandering in the wintry desolation of his garden. The picture is barely more than a diary jotting but executed with all the boldness of the artist's youth. He caught a chill. Kindly neighbours called, made him bowls of soup, and pressed him to summon Dr Karger, the local doctor. A German army ambulance would take him to the hospital. He declined. On the morning of 23 January he was found dead, lying on his bed, dressed and shaved as always. Dostoievski's *The Idiot* lay open on his bedside table.[52]

[52] Based on an account by Dr E. Ovren.

# 11

# Kandinski

Many places in Europe during the winter months of 1943/44 were infinitely more desolate and frightening than Paris, but for sheer drabness the former City of Light would have been hard to beat. Its buildings were black with grime, its grand boulevards potholed and dirty, its formal parks bleak and unkempt. Except for military vehicles and a few heavily curtained official limousines, its streets were deserted. Nobody lingered out of doors except in queues and then, more often than not, in vain. A few places of entertainments, cafés and restaurants, were still open, mainly for soldiers of the Wehrmacht on leave, but in most the lights and the heating had been permanently turned off. In the Métro the smell of unwashed bodies was overwhelming: soap was one of the shortages and the maintenance of the ventilation shafts not a priority. Huddled into threadbare overcoats and whatever other garments could keep out the cold, people walked in a hurry, reluctant to stop and not looking around. When they did, fear was stamped on many faces.

Whatever constitutes the artistic life of a big city, it was to all appearances extinct. The museums were closed, their collections dispersed. Even the German-sponsored exhibitions, a ritual during the early years of the Occupation, had ground to a halt. Paint and canvas, like almost everything else, were still obtainable on the black market; but who, apart from a few millionaires and favoured collaborators, could afford them? Yet somehow many did. In their unheated studios painters painted, sculptors sculpted and potters potted. Picasso had stopped expecting to be arrested any day and was experimenting with new ways of painting faces.[1] Braque was quietly refining his cubes and triangles. And in total isolation but unperturbed in his flat in Neuilly, Vasili Kandinski, degenerate artist par excellence, was creating his most extraordinary paintings.

Even during the last years of the uneasy peace, between his arrival from Nazi Germany in 1933 and the fall of the city in 1940, Kandinski had never

---

[1] He was expecting it after being photographed attending the funeral of his Russian-Jewish friend, Chaim Soutine, in 1942. (Soutine had been in hiding when his duodenal ulcer burst. By the time he arrived in hospital, he was dying.) Picasso was the only artist of note present: Derain, Vlaminck, Van Dongen and other old *copains* studiously kept away.

been part of the froth and bubble that had made Paris for a last glorious
fling the artistic capital of the world.[2] Of course he was famous; and some
commentators suggested that his reputation would outlast that of many
glitzier names. And of course one knew that he was about, even if Neuilly
was at the end of a long and tedious Métro line. But Paris was still in all
but geographical fact a Mediterranean city, where artistic life was lived
scandalously and excitingly in cafés, in bistros, on the benches of the Luxembourg, on the *quais* and in cheap but cheeky or ostentatiously opulent
galleries, and where it was recounted daily in the gossip columns as well as
in the weighty ruminations of an outrageously free press. From all these
venues Vasili Kandinski was usually absent.

His isolation was in part – though only in part – self-imposed. He liked
France and became a French citizen just before the war, a gesture of courtesy
to his hosts as much as a safeguard against yet another expulsion.[3] He spoke
French in the fluent staccato of the educated classes of Tolstoy's Russia. He
had devoured Jules Verne as a boy, had warmed to Anatole France in his
youth, and had made (in Nina Kandinski's words) several attempts to read
Proust. Above all, he liked the view of the roofs of Paris from his window,
even the much-maligned silhouette of the Eiffel Tower. But he had always
disliked public eating places; he did not stop to gossip in the tobacconist's
shop on the corner; he did not require the services of the local doctor and
dentist; and he was barely on nodding terms with his neighbours
in the block. Nor, on the wider stage, did he cultivate the friendship or ire
of the intellectual oracles of the day, and he hated the crush and chatter of
private views.[4]

To those who sought him out – and there were still plenty of celebrity
hunters who did – he was often a disappointment. He did not *look* like the
most revolutionary painter of the century – or any kind of a painter. More
like a retired colonial governor, an American college president or a bishop.

---

[2] Born in Moscow 1866, he was sixty-seven when he and his wife arrived in Paris in 1933
for their final exile.

   The large Kandinski literature now includes M. Bild, editor, *Wassily Kandinski* (Paris,
1951); W. Grohmann, *Wassily Kandinski: Life and Work* (London, 1959); Nina Kandinski,
*Kandinski und Ich* (Munich, 1976); V. Barnett, *Kandinski's Water Colours* (New York, 1980);
R.-C. Long, *Kandinski: The Development of an Abstract Style* (Oxford, 1980); K. Lindsay and
P. Vergo, editors, *Kandinski: Complete Writings on Art* (Boston, 1982); H. K. Roethel and
J. Benjamin, editors, *Kandinski: Catalogue Raisonné of the Oil Paintings*, 2 volumes (Ithaca,
New York, 1982); R. Tio Bellido, *Kandinski: The Masterworks* (London, 1987); J.-P. Bouillon,
P. Vaisse, F. Thurlemann, K. Flinker and A. Perez, *Kandinski* (Paris, 1991); P. Weiss, *Kandinski:
The Artist as Ethnographer and Shaman* (London, 1995).

[3] He had become a German citizen in 1928, while on the staff of the Bauhaus.

[4] See C. Derouet, *Kandinski in Paris, 1934–1944*, translated by E. Levieux (New York, 1985).

Even in striped pyjamas he seemed well-dressed, and no unexpected visitor ever caught him with paint under his finger-nails. His manner could be positively grand-ducal – or so people who had hob-nobbed with grand dukes attested. In less extravagant parlance, he was affable, polite, puzzled and remote. He was also extremely short-sighted; and, as he peered with intense concentration at his visitors' faces, many felt disconcerted. "I swear that he was seeing me as a pink blot on a green triangle", the lovely Suzanne Patou confided to a friend in *Vogue* (and to a million *Vogue* readers), "and you know, I don't think he thought that I was a very interesting pink blot." His sense of humour was a matter of dispute. Klee, his dearest and oldest friend, once described it as "ein bischen hermetisch". He laughed often and heartily but almost always at his own jokes. Often nobody else did. He was easy to make fun of; but, at the end of a leg-pull, it was not always clear who was having on whom. At a loss for the right cliché to describe him, western journalists tended to sum him up a little lamely as "thoroughly Russian". Whatever that meant, it was at least true – or almost true.

Although he described himself a Russian, spoke Russian as his native tongue, loved Russian art, history and literature, had a Russian icon hanging over his bed and clearly thought of himself as a Russian, he used the term in a widely embracing sense. His mother's family were Baltic Germans and it was German fairy tales in German that were read to him as a child by his maternal grandmother. His father's family had been exiled to Siberia in the reign of Alexander I and it was only Vasili's father who was allowed to return to Moscow. "My great-grandmother", Vasili was to tell Jean Arp during his Parisian exile, "had arrived in Russia from the mountains in the north, trotting on one of those miniature chargers of the Steppe with little bells." She bequeathed to her great-grandson not only his Mongolian eyes and prominent cheekbones but also his reserve and dignity. The further in time and space providence removed him from his Siberian roots, the more they would haunt and inspire him.

By the time Vasili was born in 1866 his father was a prosperous tea-merchant and the family lived in solid middle-class comfort.[5] Though his parents later separated, he had, by his own account, a happy and secure childhood. At the University of Moscow he studied law, and at the age of thirty wrote an authoritative treatise on legal precedents governing employment. This led to the offer of a chair in Dorpat in Estonia.[6] But two seemingly unrelated experiences, Vologda and a painting by Monet, combined to abort

---

[5] There was a strong bond between the son and the father, "a man of learning and a deeply loving soul". They visited each other in Germany and Russia every year until the father's death in 1926.

[6] Now Tartu. The Baltic states were then part of Russia.

his blossoming academic career. He had developed an interest in ethno-graphy, then a fashionable subject among the Moscow intelligentsia,[7] and in 1896 he was offered a bursary by the Moscow Ethnographical Society to explore the Vologda region on the edge of north-western Siberia. It was one of the most remote and isolated provinces of the empire, and it had aroused the curiosity of ethnographers, despite (or because of ) its desperate poverty. Its inhabitants, the Zyrians, Ostyaks, Voguls and Yarmuts, had for centuries resisted Russification. They were not even Slavs or Mongols but Finno-Ugrians in origin, remotely related to the Finns, Lapps and Magyars.[8] More than their westernised cousins, they had retained much of their ancient language and folk art. Their religion was a unique mixture of medieval Orthodox Christianity and even older shamanic beliefs and rites.[9] Kandin-ski's journey lasted six months and covered no great distances; but the physical experience was dwarfed by its psychological impact: the legends and traditions of the people, their painted villages and magnificent onion-domed churches set on the banks of huge slow-moving rivers and sometimes in the middle of dark forests, fantastically rich despite the abject poverty of those who had built them, left a never-to-be erased impression on him. Yet he rarely spoke or wrote about his memories; and in his art it would take a lifetime before the submerged images unfolded in their full riches.

The second and better-known experience had a more immediate sequel. A few months before his planned departure from Moscow, he visited an exhibition of contemporary French painting. There, in front of one of Monet's *Haystacks*, he was granted one of life's sudden illuminations. Perhaps his poor eyesight had as much to do with it as Monet's sorcery; perhaps it was the different shapes of French and Russian haystacks which grabbed his attention. Whatever it was, after staring at the picture for some minutes, he decided that he had no idea what it represented; but, at the same time, he was in no doubt that it was the best work in the exhibition. There was only

[7] Almost every year the empire was acquiring vast stretches of sparsely inhabited and hitherto unexplored regions beyond the Urals. The "primitive people" who lived there exercised a continuing fascination on the minds of Russian academics and artists.

[8] They were left behind in Asia when other tribes migrated westwards. Kandinski later recognised many links between these people and the heroes and legends of the Finnish epic, *Kalevala*. They were – and are – also of abiding interest to Magyar historians and ethnographers.

[9] They were inextricable at every level. Every peasant house or hut, however poor, had its home altar with an icon; behind every icon were a few sheaves of rye (the only staple to survive in the region) to ward off evil spirits.

For an exhaustive academic compendium on traditional and surviving shamanism, see V. Dioszegi and M. Hoppál, editors, *Shamanism in Siberia* (Budapest, 1978).

one way to resolve such a conundrum. He abandoned his legal career and took off for Munich to study painting instead.

Munich in the 1890s offered budding artists from eastern Europe almost everything an ardent young soul could desire.[10] What it did not offer was an avant-garde.[11] Few missed it; Kandinski certainly did not. Before settling in Munich he had already spent several months in Paris, getting to know the works of Cézanne, Gauguin and Van Gogh. They threw him into a state of mental agitation from which he took some time to recover;[12] but he could not personally relate to any of them. He also saw many more Monet haystacks and other Impressionist paintings, and liked what he saw; but even then he knew that Impressionism was "too pretty" to become his personal pictorial language. But neither did he find his own mode of expression for some years. Back in Munich he continued to paint charming Biedermeyer scenes – skating parties, crinoline groups and knightly processions – as well as illustrations of old Russian fairy tales. Not surprisingly, Gertrude Stein thought him backward.[13]

The eruption of Jugendstil into this pleasant torpor has sometimes been compared to the beginnings of other artistic movements – the first Impressionist exhibition, the first stirrings of Cubism, the first Salon d'Automne. Such comparisons are a little misleading. Jugendstil, the German sibling but not the identical twin of Art Nouveau (in England), Floreale (in Italy) and

[10] See below, Chapter 22, pp. 309–10. The ruling Wittelsbachs provided a particularly cherishable succession. Ludwig I, a great patron of the arts (and of the Spanish dancer, Lola Montez), was forced to abdicate in 1848. His grandson, Ludwig II, Wagner's patron and the builder of Bavaria's fairy-tale castles, was also forced to abdicate in 1864 and shortly after committed suicide or was murdered. His brother Otto proved equally artistic and insane. Ludwig II's son, Luitpold, much loved and merely eccentric, ruled as regent for him. Ludwig III succeeded his father in 1913 and reigned until the proclamation of the republic in 1918. In 1871 Bavaria had become part of the German Reich, dominated by the parvenu Prussian Hohenzollerns, but in internal affairs and courtly pomp it retained much of its operetta independence.

[11] The city had never hosted a French Impressionist exhibition: even the German variety, led by Slevogt, Liebermann and Corinth, was suspect. The most "modern" trend, hesitantly admitted to the yearly Salon, were the *Stimmungslandschaften* or "atmospheric landscapes" by Holzl, Dill and their followers, vaguely reminiscent of the French Barbizon school of fifty years earlier.

[12] His apparent calm and reserve, even coldness, hid a highly-strung nature, especially when confronted with artistic problems. After his visit to Paris he developed symptoms suggestive of a nervous breakdown and had to spend several weeks recovering in the Swiss spa of Reichenhall.

[13] The American poetess ("a rose is a rose is a rose") and patroness of Matisse, Picasso and other members of the avant-garde. She died in 1946, aged seventy-two.

Style Liberty (in France), was both more and less.[14] It was less because it was not a style which could be developed or even sustained.[15] But it was also more because it irreversibly changed the perception of artists east of the Rhine both of themselves and of their place and mission in society.

When Kandinski first arrived in Munich no artist outside the lunatic fringe would have questioned that the fine arts served a practical if elevated purpose. They existed to decorate the ceilings of opera houses, to embellish the walls of churches and council chambers, to commemorate the great and the good, to bring cheer and comfort to middle-class homes, and to perform countless other useful and uplifting tasks. This meant that, above all else, a work of art deserving of the name had to *fit*. No bank could be expected to mount an allegorical sculpture in its marble vestibule which did not extol the blessings of honest usury. No private citizen could be expected to purchase a painting for the family dining-room which might adversely affect the unimpeded flow of the gastric juices. No prince or princeling could be blamed for rejecting a portrait of his wife, daughter or mistress which did less than justice to their charms (or at least virtue). In short, painters were expected to paint pictures for which there was a wall on which to hang them.

To all those ancient and seemingly unassailable assumptions Jugendstil said a ringing no. Art, the movement proclaimed, did not exist to save opera-goers from dying of boredom, or to induce pious thoughts in religious congregations. It was under no obligation to encourage drinking or to commemorate anything or anybody. It did not have to entertain, educate, titillate, divert or edify. It existed because it was – or could be – the sublime expression of man's eternal striving for things higher and infinitely more important than wealth, comfort, success, power or even (or most of all) conventional morality. This was not Art for Art's Sake, an earlier and more feeble notion. It was Art for the Sake of Man's Soul. And to thousands of artists, poets, musicians, architects, potters and fashion designers – some good, some bad, most, as always, somewhere in between – it meant exactly what the flagship of the movement, Vienna's new periodical, proclaimed in its title: *Ver Sacrum* or *Sacred Awakening*.[16]

---

[14] There were affinities between the chairs of Charles Rennie Mackintosh of Glasgow, the writhing metal fronds of the Paris Métro (dreamed up by Hector Guimard), the electric gardenias of Tiffany, the mauve and lilac glass of Gallé, the architectural stalactites of Gaudi and the products of the Wiener Werkstätte; but they differed in the intensity of their spiritual message. In passion and exuberance (and the hostility it provoked) Jugendstil surpassed all others.

[15] Which is not to say that while it lasted it did not inspire some excellent artists (including Klimt and Schiele) and some good as well as much bad craftwork.

[16] Sacred Awakening is a somewhat inadequate translation. The periodical lasted only a few years but its influence was immense.

The decade between the explosion of Jugendstil and that of the First World War became Kandinski's new beginning and delayed but heroic youth – as it was for Braque, Einstein, Picasso, Freud, Gropius, Maillol, Le Corbusier, Schönberg, Bartók, Stravinski, Brancusi, Ehrlich, Matisse and Lenin. It was to be a fight to the finish between the old and the new, the outmoded and the revolutionary, the irrelevant and the irresistible. Only a few years earlier, Munich had been a byword for beery bonhomie; now it was becoming a battleground. For it was not to be expected that the backward majority would retire without a fight: they fired warning shots and issued anathemas. But so did the children of the *Sacred Awakening*. They formed brotherhoods, opened galleries in disused basements, launched short-lived but tempestuous periodicals, printed incendiary pamphlets and revelled in the huffing and puffing of the dinosaurs. Most disturbingly to the old guard, they also at times presented themselves not just as a new wave but also as the old masters of the future; and there were always a few deluded collectors and dealers who were prepared to give that absurd claim the benefit of the doubt. Kandinski and his companion, Gabriele Munter, a gifted artist who came as a student and stayed as a mistress, were at the centre of the effervescence.[17] He in particular became not only a member but also intermittently the secretary or president of the new clubs – the Phalanx, the Neue Künstlerverein, the Blaue Blätter and, last and best, the Blaue Reiter.[18] There could be no artistic movement without a manifesto and nobody could write more rousing (if also mistier) manifestos than the Russian expatriate. But he was not just a rebel and a visionary. Older than most of his comrades, there was about him an almost priggish air of rectitude which encouraged hard-headed businessmen to talk to him, and, even more remarkable, warring rebels to listen with respect to his adjudications. Sixty years later, still mourning their romance, Gabriele Munter was to describe him as a "Holy Man".

In the midst of these upheavals he wrote a book, *The Spiritual in Art*, one of history's most unlikely bestsellers. The first edition had to be financed privately by Bernard Kohler, the indulgent father-in-law of one of the new wave of artists, August Macke. During the first month after publication it

---

[17] She was fifteen when she arrived in Munich hoping to study at the Academy of Fine Arts but, as a woman, was not admitted. Kandinski as a young lawyer in Moscow had married his cousin, Anna Chinyakin; but, though they remained on friendly terms, they were divorced in 1911. He never married Gabriele. See J. Eichner, *Kandinski und Gabriele Munter: von Ursprüngen der Modernen Kunst* (Munich, 1957).

[18] Kandinski, Munter, Alexei von Jawlenski, August Macke and Franz Marc were the core group. The association lasted three years, an ideal period for any avant-garde artist's association, from 1911 to 1913. See V. Kandinski and Franz Marc, editors, *Der Blaue Reiter*, facsimile edition of No. 30 of 1912 (Munich, 1979); R. Gollek, *Der Blaue Reiter* (Munich, 1982).

sold eight copies. Then the highly respected *Münchener Zeitung* mentioned it in a distressed editorial, deploring that such a book should have been published in Bavaria's once so respectable and "luminous" capital. Thereupon the book took off, went into edition after edition (many pirated but even so multiplying Bernard Kohler's already considerable fortune), being translated into ten languages, including Japanese. It has never been out of print since.[19] It also made Munich one of the bastions of the international avant-garde and Kandinski one of its stalwarts. To the chagrin of the respectable press, the city now played host to the works ("if so the ravings of foreign lunatics and confidence tricksters can be described") of Braque, Picasso, Rouault, Derain, Vlaminck, Van Dongen, Barliuk, Malevitch, Arp, Delauney and Larionov. But even more deplorable was the disgrace brought on the city by local residents like Macke, Marc, Klee, Jawlenski and his mistress, Marianne von Werefkind, and of course Kandinski and Munter.[20] In return Kandinski was

[19] As a document of the period it remains fascinating reading, especially the first part which deals with the spiritual foundations of art. It glows with faith in the onset of a new era in which the spirit will move mountains, and art will overcome any remnants of materialism by actually demonstrating the primacy of spiritual values and by appealing directly to what is good in man. In some sections the tone becomes apocalyptic with terms like "the spirit", "soul", "life", "world", "universe" and "mankind" appearing in every sentence, with frequent references to both the Old and New Testaments. There are also intense passages about images like the "spiritual triangle", the lower segment of which is occupied by atheists ("Heaven has become uninhabited, God is dead") and the loftier segments by positivists, naturalists, men of science and art students. "They are dominated by fear because the inexplicable has entered the realms of possibility." But confusion seems greatest at the top where "the abandoned churchyard quakes, the forgotten graves yawn open ... and all the artificially contrived suns explode into so many specks of dust ..." There are references to Maeterlinck, Schumann, Wagner, Böcklin, Rossetti and Segantini, all charismatic names in the 1900s, but also to Cézanne, Picasso and Matisse. It is hard to believe from reading the book that in everyday life Kandinski was not a raving visionary. But all contemporary evidence points to his practical good sense. Often reprinted, the first edition of *Über das Geistige in der Kunst* (Munich, 1912) is now a collector's piece.

[20] August Macke came from a well-to-do family and retained in his bold and interesting paintings a pleasing touch of gentility. He was twenty-seven when he was killed during the German advance to the Marne in 1914. Franz Marc, perhaps the most gifted of the Blaue Reiter group, combined Expressionism with the lyrical touch of the German Romantic tradition. He was killed at Verdun in 1916, aged thirty-two. Paul Klee was born in Berne in Switzerland and was thirty-one when he moved to Munich. Except for some black-and-white work, he had earned his living until then as an orchestral violinist. He was soft-spoken and undogmatic, temperamentally almost the opposite of Kandinski; but their friendship endured. Alexei von Jawlenski, like Kandinski, was in his early thirties when he threw up a promising (if stormy) career in the Russian Imperial Guard to become a painter in Germany. His art became increasingly Byzantine in inspiration. After the war he became crippled with arthritis and died in Wiesbaden in 1941, aged seventy-seven.

now dispatching his own paintings to Dresden, Berlin, Paris, Moscow, Odessa, Rome, Brussels, London and even – who would have believed it only a few years ago? – New York.[21]

He was overflowing with energy as if he had forced himself to hold back for years – as perhaps he had. To catch his breath between battles, he and Gabriele bought a house in Murnau, a pretty village in the Bavarian Alps between Staffelsee and Moos. For eight years the countryside around it became his Mont St-Victoire, his Argenteuil, his pipe, his bottle, his spectacles, his odalisques, his balconies and his cypresses. But the decisive moment came sometime in 1910 as another of life's sudden illuminations. He realised that recognisable objects like mountains, trees, nudes and flowers could be a hindrance to expressing the spiritual in art. Such illuminations must be acted on at once. He painted his first abstract water-colour.

Of course Kandinski did not invent abstract art any more than Einstein invented relativity or Freud invented the subconscious (all at about the same time). Indeed, unlike Einstein and Freud, both of whom contributed liberally to modern man's treasury of clichés, Kandinski was not a wordsmith. He disliked the term "abstract" and never described his own abstracts as anything but "pure" or "concrete". Perhaps this was a little more than semantics. While Kandinski was exploring what he perceived as the spiritual core of art, influential aesthetes like Worringer and philosophers like Bergson emphasised intuition as a guiding light in a rather murky universe. Others preached reliance on serendipity. Kandinski had no truck with such imprecision. He professed and would always profess an unshakable belief in a hidden but rigorous cosmic order to which artists had to respond in their own language but with comparable rigour. He certainly never regarded abstract (or "pure" or "concrete") art as an excuse for relying on chance or a licence for anarchy. Nor would he ever reject the term "representational". Only the thoughts, feelings, urges, conflicts and hopes he wished to represent required a language other than the traditional visual images of western art. And the reverse was also true. Disconcerting some of his more doctrinaire followers, he was prepared to use "devices of abstraction" – blotches, lines, geometrical shapes – to convey the feel of autumn in the Bavarian mountains, the freshness after a spring shower or the intimacy of an Alpine village.

In the summer of 1914 he was part of a lively cosmopolitan scene, with many of his closest friends Germans. But he had never lost touch with Russia,

---

[21] There was one Kandinski painting in the epoch-making Armoury Show organised in the training hall of the 69th Regiment of the New York National Guard ("The Fighting Irish") in 1913; effectively America's introduction to modern European art. But, despite being widely discussed, Kandinski sold comparatively little. He was never destitute but often not very far from it.

or regarded himself as anything but Russian;[22] and a few weeks after the outbreak of the war he returned to Moscow.[23]

Though Kandinski always jealously guarded his privacy, in Munich before the war and in Weimar, Dessau and Paris between the wars, he could never escape the importunities of budding art historians, journalists and academic nosey parkers. They left behind a mountain of documentation about his doings, sayings and "innermost thoughts". No such documentation exists about his years in Russia. Indeed, until comparatively recently, the whole Russian artistic experiment between 1905 and 1925, one of the most exciting in modern art history, has been smothered in Stalinist secrecy and terror.[24] Yet, even before the First World War, the Moscow avant-garde rivalled that of Paris in boldness and brilliance;[25] and, almost to his consternation, Kandinski on arrival found himself hailed as a "forerunner", very nearly "a

[22] He had revisited Moscow regularly during his sojourn in Munich.

[23] In part his decision was fuelled by one of the recurrent crises in his relationship with Gabriele Munter. In a nutshell, she wanted marriage and he did not.

[24] In 1919, on the wave of the Revolution, a new Museum of Artistic Culture was set up in St Petersburg (then Petrograd) dedicated to the avant-garde. In less than seven years, mainly under the directorship of Kazimir Malevitch, it amassed over five hundred works of contemporary artists, illustrating all the revolutionary movements since 1905: Cubism, Futurism, "Cézanneism", Suprematism, Constructivism and others. By 1924 the movements and their protagonists were running into difficulties, and under Stalin and his artistic supremos the entire collection was banished from sight. Virtually nothing was known about it in the west until the 1980s when the collection emerged from the cellars and a selection of works began to go on tour. To many it was a revelation. See C. Gray, *The Russian Experiment in Art, 1863–1922*, revised and enlarged by M. Burleigh-Motley (London, 1986), a pioneering book when originally published in 1962; and *New Art for a New Era: Malevitch's Vision of the Russian Avant-Garde*, exhibition catalogue, Barbican Art Centre (London, 1999). See also A. Bird, *A History of Russian Painting* (Oxford, 1987); J. Bowlt, editor, *Russian Art of the Avant-Garde: Theory and Criticism* (New York, 1988); C. Cooke, *Russian and Soviet Avant-Garde, 1915–1932* (New York, 1992); T. Messer, *Kandinski* (London, 1997).

[25] Like most modern movements in the west, the Russian avant-garde emerged between 1905 and 1910, an extraordinary diversity of talents and schools, competing but also inspiring each other. Closest to Kandinski as a person was Kasimir Severinovitch Malevitch, who started to experiment with abstract painting in 1905 still as an art student – he was born in 1878 – and began to create works as prophetic, revolutionary and brilliant as anything created by Kandinski, Matisse and Mondrian at the time. By 1914 several avant-garde groups were flourishing in Moscow and in Petrograd under such picturesque banners as "Jack of Diamonds" and "The Donkey's Tail" as well as, more conventionally, Futurists and Suprematists. Until the collapse of Communism in Russia in the 1980s Malevitch was known in the west only by some thirty paintings shown in a retrospective exhibition in Berlin in 1927 and acquired (against fierce opposition) by the Stedelijk Museum of Amsterdam. He was prominent in the Revolution as a teacher and administrator, a charismatic figure, branching out, like Kandinski, into ceramics. Like most of the avant-garde, he fell into disgrace under Stalin and painted

grand old man". At the same time, to many of the younger artists buzzing around him he was no longer particularly relevant. It was a traumatic experience; and, for the best part of two years, he painted almost nothing. In 1916 he travelled to Stockholm, ostensibly to help Gabriele Munter organise an exhibition of her works, but more to see if he could repair the rift between them and even recover his own creative impulse. The trip was a failure; after two months, he returned to Russia for good.[26] Or even for better. Visiting a picture gallery he met and fell in love with Nina de Andreevski, the eighteen-year-old daughter of a general. They married; and she was to remain his adoring and irrepressible wife for the rest of his life. But their romance was played out against a background of turmoil and bloodshed. They returned from their honeymoon in Finland to a Tsarless Russia, a country of breadlines, riots and administrative chaos. A little boy was born to them in September 1918.

Both before the Revolution and in later life Kandinski expressed no interest in politics or political ideology; but there is no doubt that he was part of the artistic and literary fireworks that greeted the fall of the discredited

only conventional portraits and landscapes after 1927. He died in 1935, disillusioned and ignored by officialdom.

Throughout his career Malevitch was locked in rivalry with Vladimir Tatlin, who ran away from his comfortable middle-class home at the age of twelve. After a few adventurous years at sea, he joined a Russian peasant dance group, impersonating a blind accordionist. In this role he was so successful that in Berlin the Kaiser, moved by the tragedy of the unfortunate youth, presented him with a gold watch. Tatlin promptly sold it and went to Paris on the proceeds, hanging around in Picasso's studio until his money ran out. Returning to Moscow, he painted some of his best pictures and became Kandinski's friend. In 1918 he was appointed head of the Moscow section of Narcompos, the department of fine arts of the Commissariat for the People's Education where, for a few months, he shared a room with Kandinski. After the Stalinist freeze, he largely confined himself to theatre design. He died in 1953, aged sixty-eight.

According to Kandinski, the brightest of the revolutionary galaxy (and there were at least two dozen whose works have survived forty years in museum vaults and now dazzle spectators in the West) were Olga Rosanova, who died aged thirty-two in 1918, and Alexander Mikhail-ovitch Rodchenko. The latter divided his talents between photography, painting and politics. He too survived Stalin, even experimenting in the 1940s with "drip painting", reminiscent of Jackson Pollock's work a few years later. (The two artists could not have known about each other.) He died in 1956, aged fifty six.

The young Chagall quarrelled with Malevitch and, like Kandinski, left for the west in 1922.

[26] He wrote an introduction to the catalogue, praising Munter as an artist; but he did not want to commit himself to her as a person. They never saw each other again; but Munter continued to love and revere him. She was eighty-eight when she died. See Eichner, *Kandinski and Gabriele Munter*; W. Gregg, "Gabriele Munter in Sweden: Interlude and Separation", *Arts Magazine*, 55 (1981), p. 116.

old regime. Even in the midst of military defeat, who could doubt that it was the great leap forward for which most of Russia's best artists, writers, poets and thinkers had been waiting (and in some cases praying, suffering and dying) for a century, a vindication of the memory of the martyrs of 1825 and 1905? Many leaders of the new wave in the arts – Malevitch, Rodchenko, Tatlin, Goncharova, Larionov, Chagall, an astonishing explosion of talent – were Kandinski's personal friends.[27] He readily accepted public appointments, first from Kerenski's government and then from Lunacharski, Commissar for Enlightenment under the Soviets; but he never became part of the revolutionary inner circle. There was something faintly utopian even in his titles and assignments. In a devastated country in the grip of civil war, he was charged with the reorganisation of regional museums and with the revised syllabus of art teaching in primary schools. He was also painting, but paradoxically in a more traditional style than he had done for many years or would ever do again. Nor were his pictures particularly good: some later became popular Christmas cards. On the public stage he was never important enough to become the target of a hate campaign after his move to the west; and he himself never wrote books in the lucrative "I Chose Freedom" or the even more fatuous "I Saw the Future and it Works" vein. To his and Nina's grief, never to be assuaged, at the age of two years and nine months their little boy Volodya died. A few weeks later Vasili accepted a nebulous commission to go to Germany and study new developments in art teaching. On Christmas Eve of 1922 the couple arrived in Berlin. His "crisis of success" was over.

Germany had been Kandinski's home for twenty years; but this was not an auspicious homecoming. His precious official allowance of German marks just covered the cost of the tram tickets from Berlin's Ostbahnhof to their hotel. Inflation was spiralling into the stratosphere. To pay for their food and accommodation Nina had to sell small segments of her gold necklace, snipped off and weighed each morning. The nest egg Vasili had left behind

[27] Many of the Russian avant-garde had travelled to Paris; but even those who did not knew some of the best works of Van Gogh, Gauguin, Matisse, Picasso, the Fauves and other French pioneers from the collections amassed by the Moscow merchants Sergey Shchukin and Ivan Morozov. (These too were kept out of sight under Stalin.) Among the many groupings, subgroupings and regroupings of Russian revolutionary artists the most significant was the division between "Westernisers" like Malevitch (whose Suprematism anticipated Rothko and the Abstract Expressionism of the post-Second World War decades) and those, like Larionov, Goncharova, Lentulov, Falk, Rodchenko and Tatlin, who claimed Russian icons and folk art as their main source of inspiration. Kandinski's paintings at the time might have placed him into the second group; but he kept out of the fray. See also P. Wood, *Great Utopia: Russia and Soviet Avant-Garde, 1915–1932* (New York, 1994).

in 1914 was not worth the postage necessary to claim it. There were unexpected difficulties in recovering the paintings stored in Munich with Gabriele Munter. His friends from prewar days were, with one exception, scattered or dead. The exception was Paul Klee. No better off than the Kandinskis, he had accepted an appointment on the teaching staff of a financially tottering school of art and design in Weimar. The institution, founded on a wave of optimism in the early years of the century, had a history of going bankrupt, losing directors and closing for lack of students. The building itself, a gem of Art Nouveau, was in a dangerous state of disrepair. The city of Weimar had been the seat of one of Germany's Pumpernickel Courts before the war,[28] and was more heavily encrusted with etiquette and *Kultur* than most; but it was stolidly conservative and provincial. Indeed, it had hardly changed since Goethe presided benignly over its affairs a hundred and fifty years earlier. In the postwar economic collapse the municipality had no funds to maintain essential services, let alone subsidise avant-garde schools of art and design; and the regional government of Thuringia was and remained actively hostile.[29] Not surprisingly, the institution had more unfilled vacancies than staff; and its new director, the well-known architect and former officer of the 17th Uhlans, Walter Gropius, was in no hurry to leave his Berlin offices and take charge of the ruins.[30] But Klee rang the Kandinskis on Gropius's behalf to ask if Vasili might be interested in the chair (or team-leadership as professoriates were to be designated) of mural painting. Mural painting was one of the few branches of the visual arts which Kandinski had never practised and about which he professed to know nothing; but Klee assured him that as newly-appointed team-leader of textile design – "sag mir, Vasilii, was ist das eigentlich Textilkunst?" – he was in the same boat. The prospect was irresistible; Kandinski accepted.[31]

Despite a large and factually informative literature,[32] the meteoric success of the Bauhaus has never been satisfactorily explained. A country still reeling

[28] William Gerhardie's phrase.

[29] B. E. Lewis, *Art and Politics in the Weimar Republic* (Madison, Wisconsin, 1971).

[30] Gropius was already famous as a pioneering architect and designer of the Fagus Shoe Factory in Alfeld-an-der-Leine in 1914 and the Model Factory for the Werkbund Exhibition in Cologne. For good or ill, he was also, for a short time, one of the post-Mahler (but pre-Kokoschka and pre-Werfel) husbands of Alma Schindler.

[31] See J. Muraközi, *Mein Freund Klee* (Munich, 1959) p. 158. See also P. Klee, *Diaries* (London, 1965).

[32] One of the best is F. Whitford, *Bauhaus* (London, 1984). First-hand accounts include O. Barna, *Bauhausi Emlékek* (Budapest, 1939); O. Schlemmer, *Briefe und Tagebücher*, edited by T. Schlemmer (Munich, 1958); H. Bayer, W. Gropius and I. Gropius, editors, *Bauhaus*, originally published in 1938 (New York, 1959).

from the physical and psychological trauma of a lost war, in a state of
economic collapse and moral shock, may provide the appropriate backdrop
for a few rogue rebels; but a school, aspiring to publish syllabuses, devise
courses, fill classrooms, hold examinations, collect tuition fees and pay staff,
usually needs a little more than creative chaos. Yet, on any heat-sensitive
map of Europe showing the concentration of genius in the late 1920s, the
spot marking the Bauhaus would have gone up in flames;[33] and seventy years
later its doctrines still influence the way ordinary people live, eat, drink,
shop, sit, sleep, cook, work and relax.

The school did in fact have one asset which was not immediately obvious.
Gropius had no equal in eloquently propounding popular doctrines about
the potential contribution of modern art and design to the happiness of the
masses, about the fructifying links between industry and the creative arts,
and about a host of similar perennially nebulous topics, only to jettison his
messages the moment they threatened what in truth was the sole guiding
principle of the institution: the nurturing of individual talent. Less obvious
but no less important were the school's negative advantages. Today, when
hecatombs are offered in daily sacrifice by academic institutions to the holy
trinity of administration, management and public relations, it is hard to
believe (but nevertheless true) that the most creative art college of the
century had not a single administrator, manager or public relations officer
on its staff. Nor was it constrained by job descriptions and management
reports. Founded on the idea of uniting all the arts and crafts in the service
of building and architecture, the Bauhaus had departments of pottery,
textiles, metalwork, typography, glass, window display, drama and many
others – but no department of either building or architecture. Committed
to social engineering and to serving working communities rather than rich
elites, the school shunned sociology (a "nonsense science" according to
Gropius) and banned all discussions of politics. Music, by contrast, which
Gropius loved, was deemed essential for future town-planners and furniture
designers; and no Bauhaus course was complete without a visit from Bartók,
Busoni, Stravinski or Schönberg. Not only was Kandinski in charge of mural
painting and Klee in charge of textiles, but the foundation course was
entrusted to that universal genius Laszlo Moholy-Nagy, whose German was
incomprehensible except (allegedly) to a fellow Hungarian from Hodmezö-
vásárhely. When in Paris Kandinski was asked by an interviewer to explain

---

[33] The school reached its peak in 1926, after its enforced move from Weimar to the industrial
city of Dessau. The new building there, designed by Gropius, became a flagship of modern
architecture. The next few years coincided with the brief period of international confidence
and economic recovery generated by the Locarno Treaty.

the secret of the famous school, it was Nina who answered for him: "But how could it *not* be successful when it was such fun?" [34]

Yet, although undoubtedly fun, work at the Bauhaus, especially after its move to Dessau, was also serious.[35] It was during the Bauhaus years that Kandinski's style became most abstract or "pure".[36] It also became most "metaphorical" – at least to those who resonated with his spiritual preoccupations. To them the central triangle in *Contact 14* became the expression of spiritual enlightenment, a "pyramid of humanity"; and the whole complex configuration could be interpreted as a "parable of Genesis ... the event represented by the contact of the circles with the life-giving triangle, the perfect balance on its tip ... demonstrating spiritual equilibrium". In *Soft Hard 27* the initiated could see a "parable of creativity ... in which the infinite

[34] In Dessau, she went on to relate, they and the Klees shared a house specially designed for them by Gropius. "It was lovely, except for the glass wall which gave everybody in the street a chance to see everything, and I mean everything, that was happening inside. So Vasili painted our half of the glass screen blue and Paul [Klee] painted his side red. Walter [Gropius] thought that was simply marvellous. Marcel Breuer produced some nice rectangular furniture for our dining room but Vasili was going through a circular phase, so all the straight tubes had to be bent ... making the chairs pretty but very uncomfortable. Every evening the Klees played piano duets or string quartets with friends while Vasili was getting addicted to jazz and played jazz records on our gramophone. What a din! But the Bauhaus band was getting quite famous and was asked to play at parties at the nearby Junkers aircraft factory. To say thank you one of the Junkers aeroplanes dropped a bouquet and a parcel of presents on Vasili's birthday; but it hit the Klees' flat roof which collapsed into their bedroom. What a hoot." F. Barna, *Csalfa Emlékek* (Paris, 1966), pp. 248–49.

[35] The theoretical programme of the school was set out in a series of brilliantly written publications. These had tremendous influence worldwide and came to enshrine the Bauhaus ideal of functional simplicity. But Gropius never made any effort to straitjacket the wayward geniuses on his staff and it needs mental acrobatics to fit the ideas of Kandinski, Klee, Feininger, Muche, Schlemmer, Marcks, Anders, Breuer and Moholy-Nagy into a single Bauhaus concept. Nor was this concept static. Initially there was comparatively little emphasis on machines or the relationship between art and industrial society and more on the "spiritual content" of art. The emphasis gradually shifted as architecture became the "unifying" discipline. "We want to create a clear organic architecture", Gropius declared, "whose inner logic will be radiant and naked, unencumbered by lying facades and trickeries. It will be an architecture adapted to our world of machines, radios and fast motor cars." And it was in architecture and interior design that the Bauhaus exercised its most profound influence, though Marcel Breuer's tubular steel chairs also became classics, as did ceramics and metalwork developed under the guidence of Marcks, Moholy-Nagy, Schlemmer and others. Moholy-Nagy and Tschichold revolutionised photographic display and typography. But much of what was to become known as Bauhaus standard units – stacking chairs, stools, dinner ware, lighting fixtures and furnishing textiles – were designed by "classes" rather than by individuals (or so the Bauhaus pamphlets emphasised). Several of Kandinski's paintings of the period are in fact signed "W. K.'s Klasse".

[36] See P. Hahn, *Kandinski: russische Zeit und Bauhausjahren*, exhibition catalogue (Berlin, 1984).

empty space of blue symbolises Creation in its topographical and cosmogenic aspects". The artist here

> was not unaware that the world has been made flesh [but] his logic also told him that only transmutation brought about through feeling is capable of reconciling the human with the divine or discipline with freedom: it alone is rooted in spiritual harmony that makes no distinction between divine nature and nature as a speculative on-going force.[37]

"Abstract" certainly did not mean that his paintings did not have a declared theme and often a lesson to teach: they were planned as meticulously as any laboratory experiment. *Upward Tension 24* demonstrated the "three factors which determine the Absolute Sonority of Forms ... first, the sonority of straight lines; secondly, the sonority of inclinations in relation to the tensions created by greater or lesser forces; and, thirdly, the sonority of a tendency towards a dominance, more or less total, of the plane". What, if anything, did this verbiage mean?

Recent research has revealed astonishing parallels between Kandinski's paintings and the shamanic cult and language of "primitive" people.[38] In the light of these revelations it is possible to detect "transfigured" motifs of serpents, eggs, knightly riders on horseback, stars, arrows, lances, floating shamanic robes and other ancient symbols, almost all derived from Finno-Ugrian mythologies. These pagan images are further complicated (and enriched) by the Christian overlay, the dragon-slaying St George (often hinted at by a lance) being a recurrent and powerful motif. But why did Kandinski, a man of integrity as well as the most explanatory of great artists, never explain this himself? Was he deliberately secretive about his sources (not unlike the original shamans)? Did he feel that his "transmutations" of shamanic images would be interpreted in too facile a manner? Or was he actually fighting such a "literary" content which might weaken or discredit his cosmological messages? To many his own lengthy exegeses add little to his work. He was an intellectual with an unusual grasp of complicated philosophical concepts; but he was not a great thinker or cosmologist. He was also a deeply moral person with a true understanding of spiritual values; but he was not a great mystic.[39] He felt, like many sophisticated modern artists, an intuitive affinity with the art of "primitive" people, but he was

---

[37] The quotations are from R. Tio Bellido, *Kandinski*, translated by Jane Benton (London, 1988).

[38] Weiss, *Kandinski and Old Russia: The Artist as Ethnographer and Shaman*. This is one of the comparatively few ground-breaking contributions to modern art history.

[39] Vasili was never a regular churchgoer but Nina was devout; every Easter they travelled to Dresden for the Easter Service in the Russian Orthodox cathedral there.

not an ethnographic scholar. What he was was both simpler and infinitely more complicated: a great artist. And that was not to come to full bloom until his last years.

Almost everything he painted at the Bauhaus succeeds today (or occasionally does not) in terms of colours, shapes and other more or less conventional visual values. His paintings, in other words, *look good*: indeed, with the passage of every year they look better. As a cocky young Muscovite intellectual he wrote angrily about a critic who praised the work of another artist for its "ethnographic and psychological interest". "Psychology, ethnography, archaeology! What has all this to do with art? ... The content of painting is painting. Nothing has to be deciphered."[40] By the time he arrived at the Bauhaus he would have admitted that they all had something to do with each other: that the past, the present, the future, creativity, experience, knowledge, speculation and a dozen other "separate compartments" could never be wholly separated. But nor was it easy to define their relationship. At times he himself became a little exasperated with theorising. "Ask yourself", he told a too persistent student, "whether a work of art has carried you to a world unknown to you before. If it has, what more do you want?" But for his final illumination and advance to his own personal summit he himself needed yet another uprooting and the liberating effect of old age.

On 11 April, 1933, the first day of what was scheduled as the summer term, police and a detachment of the SS arrived in lorries at the gates of the Bauhaus. By then it had moved from Dessau to Berlin and one did not have to be politically astute to realise that its days were numbered.[41] Its last director, Mies van der Rohe, did his abject best to ingratiate himself with Hitler; but, to Mies's later good fortune, the Führer hated the Bauhaus and all its works.[42] The few people inside the building were told to leave unless they wanted to accompany the uniformed thugs to party headquarters and lodge an official protest. None did. Then documents, files and other movables

[40] Quoted by Weiss, *Kandinski and Old Russia*, p. xiii.

[41] Gropius left Germany in 1933, moving first to London and then, in 1938, to Cambridge, Massachusetts, to become head of the School of Architecture at Harvard. He died in Boston in 1969, aged eighty-six.

[42] This forced Mies to emigrate to the United States, where he became extremely successful and influential. He died an American hero in Chicago in the same year as Gropius, aged eighty-three. Moholy-Nagy moved first to London and then to Chicago, where he founded the New Bauhaus. He died there in 1946, aged fifty-one. Klee moved from the Bauhaus to Düsseldorf but had hardly time to take up his appointment when he was dismissed by the Nazis (sadly proving his pianist wife Lily right about Nazi intentions and methods). They moved back to Switzerland.

were loaded onto the lorries, the main gate was padlocked and a notice was affixed to it: "Geschlossen".[43]

After an inglorious departure from Berlin, the Kandinskis' reception in Paris was even less triumphant. Among well-known artists only Joan Miró and the Surrealist doctor-painter André Breton hastened to welcome them. Jeanne Bucher assured them that her gallery would be at his disposal for the sale of works. The ever-reliable clown of the avant-garde, Maurice Duchamp, found a flat for them in Neuilly.[44] But, to the unforgiving disgust of Nina, the charismatic figures of the Left Bank stayed away. It was not that Picasso, Braque or Matisse did not recognise Kandinski's eminence. They just did not speak the same language. A picture of black and purple rings and blue triangles they could accept. But the philosophical text which accompanied it – "the great Nothing before all beginnings ... thus perhaps did the Earth resonate in the Glacial era ..." – left them with nothing to say; and to reduce a Parisian artist of the voluble 1930s to speechlessness was an unforgivable sin.

Nor did the Paris art world of the day respond to the idea that art served a lofty metaphysical purpose beyond day-to-day politics, intrigues and ideologies. How could such metaphysical speculations be applied to the Civil War raging in Spain, to the problems facing the Front Populaire, to the nefarious intrigues of Mme des Portes at the Matignon or the mysterious sex-appeal of Greta Garbo? Kandinski, on his part, seemed to show little interest in Spain and none whatever in Mme des Portes' (or anybody else's) political intrigues. He did not participate in the famously outrageous Surrealist exhibition of 1938, nor was he asked to decorate a pavilion or even a wall in the Exposition Universelle in the same year. His last trip abroad was to visit his dying friend, Paul Klee, in Switzerland. Klee was by then recognised as a great artist by other artists, but this only added to the apparent zeal of the Berne bureaucrats to hasten his demise.[45] Kandinski was depressed

---

[43] The word was becoming very familiar in Germany in the 1930s.

[44] Joan Miró, a Catalan by birth, was forty at the time and was attracting attention. André Breton, psychiatrist-turned-painter, was forty-one and the author of the Surrealist Manifesto. Jeanne Bucher presided over a small avant-garde gallery and organised Kandinski's last one man show (during his lifetime) there in 1942. Only two pictures sold, both to a German army surgeon from Dresden, Oberst Wolf König. Both were destroyed later in the war. Marcel Duchamp, forty-seven at the time, was one of the original Dadaists, his *Nude Descending a Staircase* becoming one of the sensations of the Armoury show in New York.

[45] He had been suffering from recurrent bronchitis and heart-trouble since his arrival from Germany. The condition was eventually diagnosed as scleroderma, a progressive, painful and at the time wholly untreatable drying up of the mucosal linings of the body. He was badly off financially and his sufferings were aggravated by the news of the wholesale destruction of his works in Germany and the hostility shown to him by Swiss artists and the bureaucrats

by the physical decline of his friend; but he maintained an outward appearance of hearty optimism. When he left, Klee was asked whether the visit did not tire him. "Not at all", he replied. "It is good to see somebody who does not believe in dying."

Yet, remote though Kandinski often seemed from mundane practical matters, he saw, unlike his more worldly-wise colleagues who talked about the war incessantly but never expected it to happen, that the conflict was inevitable; and he was at least mentally better prepared for it than many.

Kandinski had left Germany under a cloud – the very name Bauhaus induced apoplectic fury in Göring – and France's sudden collapse and German occupation in the summer of 1940 put him in a position of real danger. Fortunately, though unbeknown to him, he was classified in French police files (eagerly opened for perusal by the Gestapo) as an "antibolshevik refugee from Russia",[46] not as a "degenerate painter and fugitive from Nazism". His many admirers in the United States, some of them former colleagues from the Bauhaus, intervened on his behalf in Washington; and he and Nina were offered immediate visas to the United States.[47] He was touched by the gesture but declined: he was seventy-four and, even for a twentieth-century artist, he had had more than his fair share of uprootings and migrations. Nor did the shortages of the later war years distress him unduly. He had been brought up in solid bourgeois comfort and liked the small luxuries of life; but he could do without green chartreuse and Russian caviar. Indeed, as happened to more than one artist trapped by the war, even to those facing personal danger, an almost frivolous mood of *joie de vivre* crept into his work. *Bleu de Ciel*, which he painted immediately after the fall of Paris, may or may

in Berne. The latter, anxious under no circumstances to offend Switzerland's mighty neighbour to the north by helping refugees from Nazism, surpassed themselves in pedantry and obstruction, delaying confirmation of his Swiss citizenship to which he was clearly entitled. But Braque came to see him in 1937 to express his admiration, and Picasso (whom Klee regarded as the greatest contemporary painter) came twice and was enthusiastic about Klee's last works. But when Kandinski arrived a few weeks later, he was grief-stricken to see his friend a shadow of his former self, barely able to move or speak. Kandinski had no faith in orthodox medicine and had earlier tried to persuade Klee in several letters to come to Paris and consult the famous acupuncturist Dr Soulié. He now realised that it was too late. Klee went on working almost to the end, his titles – *Early Suffering, Explosion of Fear, Death and Fire* – speaking for themselves. He died in 1940, aged sixty, a few weeks after the collapse of France. A letter arrived from Berne the day after his death, confirming his Swiss citizenship.

[46] At one time he was even approached by the "Romanov Court" in exile, functioning under the patronage of the Germans. He would have nothing to do with them.

[47] Until 1942 the United States maintained friendly relations with Vichy France and had a mission in occupied Paris.

not be replete with shamanic messages, but it is a bubbling delight. He had always been (to adopt his phraseology without, of course, trying to emulate his philosophical profundities) a blue artist. In Munich there was the Blaue Reiter. From the Murnau days it is the rich ultramarine skies that linger longest in the memory. Even his yellow-dominated and at times slightly arid Bauhaus pictures are often enlivened by an impudent blue dot. But never before had he given such free rein to his blueness. The extraordinary creatures which seem to have suddenly emerged from some forgotten recess of his imagination and which populate the canvas – are they microbes or birds or turtles or mythical shamanic creatures? Does it matter? – wallow in it. But they also enhance its unsullied calm, depth and sweep.

He was reproached at the time, and has often been since, that his last period was one of escapism, understandable under the grim circumstances of the Occupation but a trifle disappointing nevertheless. His late pictures are also sometimes described as "biomorphic" in contrast to "pure" or "abstract". None of these omnibus terms explain what was clearly a last blinding illumination. Recognisable shapes and objects *could* undoubtedly be a hindrance to the expression of the spiritual in art; but the converse was also true: a strict prohibition on anything remotely lifelike was equally limiting. And so *Composition X* is not only celebratory in tone but also has a narrative content of sorts. It shows an almost recognisable face with a querulous comma which seems to be gazing at an air-balloon attached to a gondola; white sheets of paper are blown around in the wind; and hieroglyphics hint at some magical incantation. There is certainly magic about the finished product, the colours glowing against the dark background.

If the mood of the first wartime pictures was joyous, the exhilaration did not last. Nervous tension and physical menace were becoming more intense. Visits from friends ceased; correspondences fizzled out. Were the friends still about? Were they still alive? Often there was no way of finding out. In 1942, at the age of seventy-six, the painter also began to suffer from headaches and he had several attacks of giddiness.[48] But he was still painting; and there is nothing in his last works to suggest a tired or ailing mind. The reverse is true: the late wartime pictures became his apotheosis as a great artist. It was not simply a question of being more "representational". It was the end of a long journey of happiness, grief, wars, crises, revolutions, triumphs and defeats which had begun fifty years earlier. Even in the twentieth century, no great European artist had experienced such constant turmoil. None was more ready for the final unfolding.

For many years Kandinski seems to have been haunted by the prospect

---

[48] Perhaps minor strokes.

of being labelled an "ethnographer", an illustrator of the picturesque tales of exotic people, a kind of Chagall of the remote Finno-Ugrian tribes of Siberia. It is possible with hindsight to detect elements of Vologda lore even in his most abstract creations; but he himself, in his voluminous writings, sedulously avoided referring to them. What he wrote about (sometimes confusingly though never boringly) was the universe, life, the great nothing, creation, conflict and such abstract concepts, not the various incarnations of the shaman (which included St George), evil spirits, horses and riders, magic caftans and other bizarre but concrete images of a colourful mythology. Now, as war and old age isolated him from disciples, students, critics and other artists, no longer part of a group or a school, no longer feeling under an obligation to proclaim universal principles of art and life, the fears and inhibitions suddenly melted away, and the world and imagery of his youthful experiences in the wilds of Siberia emerged in their full mysterious panoply. His last works, probably his greatest, are replete with transformed but clearly recognisable images of the shaman and his magic gear, his Christian *alter ego*, St George on horseback, fighting the serpent and evil spirits, golden all-seeing eyes, flying caftans, mythic birds, evil creatures, angels of death, arrows, amulets and a host of other symbols. To go unashamedly "native" was not of course an automatic prescription for success. The works are his most successful because he now felt free to shamanise without having to pay lip-service to universal doctrines of abstraction or "purity" or "concreteness", and without fear of being labelled a mere "illustrator".

*Around the Circle*, dating from 1941, is almost a summation of shamanic lore; but it is not necessary to decipher it to be overwhelmed by its riches. The language may be foreign but it is made eloquent by art in the same way as a text in a foreign tongue can be made moving when set to great music. Of course "understanding" the symbols does add an extra dimension. In *The Arrow*, painted in 1943, the shaman in a trance and flight is joined with the figure of the dancing shaman, the emphatic magic arrow challenging the serpent. In *Brown Elan*, St George, the archetypal ikon and Christian incarnation of the shaman, the image with which the artist most closely identified, has undergone an astonishing transformation: from invincible rider he has metamorphosed into a vulnerable though still undefeated hero. Skeletonised and wearing his regenerative ribbed breastplate and visored helmet, he straddles his horse with its checked and tasselled saddle-blanket, arching its neck and rearing gamely above the upended serpent. But the rider leans back, recoiling from the fatal confrontation: his lance is broken on a wayward triangle. Towards the upper left, in the "celestial quadrant", rises a figure which may represent the soul of the saint. Between the horse's neck and the saint looms a shamanic mask. On the right, as if tossed aside, the magic drum with its attached pendants strikes a note of hope and healing.

In April 1943, one of the darkest months of the war, he returned in *The Circle and the Square* to other submerged memories: the painting presents two shamanic couples both separated and linked by the figure of destiny and death, recognisable by its chequerboard mask, skeletal body and scythe-like arms. In *Red Accent* St George's horse has become finally bereft of its rider: only the lance and the empty halo remain. The tumbled knight lies a step below, his coat slipped off, his fall emphasised by a cascading arc. Late in 1943, and in the first months of 1944, the paintings took an even more sombre turn. In *The Green Bond* he painted an almost representational image of himself assuming the shaman's sacrificial role for his last journey. Ascending the triplicate trunk of the world tree on the right, he wears his distinctive breast-plate, a motley caftan, a feathered head-dress and leggings with articulated joints, his drum floating near his head and his mallet just below. Nothing in this complex picture is there just for the sake of colour or pictorial balance, no dot or arrow is just an amusing "feature" as such motifs so often became in the works of other "folklorist" artists who had drifted far from their roots. It is indeed this purposeful feel, whether under-stood or not, which gives these works their gripping power. In *Tempered Elan,* the last painting to be entered into the artist's studio catalogue and probably painted in preparation for what he may have felt would be his last St George's Day, he presents himself in all his three incarnations: as eques-trian knight; as the biomorphic shaman St George; and as the magic caftan. What did he mean (if anything) by the title? Perhaps it is a hint that, at the end of a long quest, it was time to "temper" his *élan* which had carried him to the limits of geometrical abstraction. But perhaps not. Together with the last water-colours, the painting resonates with sombre premonitions and yet it is more quietly optimistic than the works of a year before. The "six-months" journey begun fifty years earlier was drawing to a close; and, as with some other great artists far removed from Kandinski in style and content, the intervening years seem to have been nothing but a preparation for the leave-taking.

By the summer of 1944 there was at last something to celebrate. After a few tense days of sporadic gun fire and confusion, Paris was liberated in September; and, for wanderers like the Kandinskis, another war seemed to be over. Old friends suddenly reappeared and there was a rush of new ones. Art-loving members of the Allied Forces, who laid siege to Picasso, Braque and other surviving prewar icons, were kept at bay by Nina; but he welcomed letters and news from colleagues in the United States. The idea of a projected ballet to be choreographed by Thomas von Hartmann and the prospect of a film about his paintings excited him. Close friends gathered to celebrate his seventy-eighth birthday on 4 December. It was a happier occasion than it had been for many years: champagne flowed (courtesy of Major Kovacevic, US Army) and there were Havana cigars (courtesy of Colonel Bounine of the Free French) and chocolates (courtesy of General Sir Bernard Montgomery of the British Army).[49] Hosts and guests discussed future exhibitions and who would be the first to travel to Moscow. (Nina had already applied for a visa: she longed to visit Volodya's grave which had been looked after by her sister during the war.)[50] They sang Russian songs. Vasili recited a favourite poem by Pushkin. Perhaps so much exuberance was a little unwise. Next morning he felt tired; but he had not consulted doctors since leaving Russia and saw no reason to do so now. He died in his sleep a few days later, as private a departure as had been all his comings and goings in this restless world.

[49] Montgomery's taste in the visual arts, and his admiration for Kandinski, was as unpredictable as most of his extra-professional likes and dislikes.
[50] Nobody in Paris knew at the time (or for many years) about the little boy.

PART TWO

The Art of Old Age

Francisco José de Goya y Lucientes (1746–1828), *Aun Aprendo* (I'm Still Learning), 1824–26. A sarcastic echo of Michelangelo. Black chalk (*Prado, Madrid*)

# 12

# An Elixir of the Gods

All the case histories point in one direction – the extraordinary flowering of artistic genius in old age. But, if their message is clear, it is also a puzzle. Olympic athletes are past their prime at thirty-five and Wimbledon champions at forty. Memory freaks last longer but rarely into their eighties. Of course painters and sculptors do not have to jump, run, swim, carry torches, swing a racquet or contort themselves on the parallel bar. Nor are they asked to memorise telephone directories. "At my age", Shaw told a visiting journalist on his ninety-fourth birthday, "one is either well or dead."[1] But, to create a great work of art, a little more is needed than being well in this rather restricted sense. And at a time of life when many, or most, physical skills and mental faculties begin to decline, one might expect a complex function like artistic creativity to decline too.[2] Yet it did not happen: at least it did not happen to the artists in this study. What is the explanation? And, no less important, what is not?

In answer to the second question, one false explanation is so beguiling that it has to be promptly eliminated. Theoretically artistic creation could act as a preservative, an elixir of the gods, retarding the decline of muscle strength, coordination, sight, nervous control and other physical and mental endowments. It is an immensely attractive notion. Not only would it explain the late flowering of artistic creativity, it would also point to a revolutionary new approach to geriatrics. Even if no amount of retraining at sixty-five could transform everyman into a Titian or Monet, the concept of an elixir would be a therapeutic pointer. Unfortunately (like so many revolutionary new approaches to geriatrics), it is contradicted by the facts.[3]

Neither physically, nor mentally did the great artists whose artistry blossomed in old age differ from their less spectacularly gifted contemporaries. It is true that Vasari's hero-worshipping eyes detected a spark of *giovinezza*

---

[1] Quoted in B. N. Arnot, *Wit and Wisdom* (London, 1962), p. 89.

[2] See above, Chapter 1.

[3] This must not be taken to imply that art therapy is useless in old age: the evidence to the contrary is overwhelming. But its objective must be to enrich old age rather than to overcome or retard it.

in the eighty-nine-year-old Michelengelo, still hammering away at his blocks of marble; and sycophants at the Ecole des Beaux-Arts liked to address Ingres at eighty as "our young master". But Vasari was still a young man when he visited Michelangelo; and, then as now, the young probably regarded creativity, like sexual vigour, as a preserve and manifestation of youth.[4] The old man himself knew better. His artistic vision was undimmed, but he resented being congratulated on his physical fitness. To ward off such impertinences, he had half a dozen ailments up his sleeve. He was racked by renal colic,[5] tormented by headaches, suffered from shortness of breath, and was subject to incapacitating spells of giddiness. Physically he felt every day of his age. Why then did he go on working? Ah, but sculpting a *Pietà* was not work, any more than was expressing his hopes and fears in a sonnet. They were his forms of prayer.[6] And even Ingres protested (or pretended to) against "the malicious insinuations of youth". "I dye my hair to please my wife.[7] But I beg you not to compare me at eighty with the cretin I was at eighteen."[8]

Physically there was nothing abnormally young about the other aged masters either. There is still no certainty why, on the threshold of what in the Florence of his day must have been reckoned as old age, Donatello turned from marble and bronze to painted wood; but he or his patrons may have been influenced by his failing physical strength. Such carvings did of course have a glorious tradition in Florence, as in many parts of Europe; but they were no longer in fashion. And the artist was almost certainly partially paralysed, perhaps following a series of minor strokes, when, with the help of several assistants, he created his supreme masterpieces, the bronze reliefs on the San Lorenzo pulpits. In his affectionate portrait of the seventy-year-old Bellini, Dürer noted the old artist's forgetfulness as well as his surpassing excellence in painting. The observation is independently supported by

[4] Michelangelo was working on his last sculpture, the unfinished *Rondanini Pietà*, when "Master Giorgio" visited him.

[5] He had "gravel" in his urine for many years for which he had more than one irrigation of the bladder. This must have involved the passing of a metal catheter.

[6] In contrast to Donatello, Uccello, Bellini and other masters of the early Renaissance, much biographical detail is available about Michelangelo. Apart from two biographies by near-contemporaries, who knew him personally, and a wealth of official documents relating to his work, he left behind more than 300 personal letters as well as his imperishable sonnets. See A. Condivi, *Vita di Michelangelo Buonarroti*, originally published in 1552, edited by E. Spina Barelli (Milan, 1964); G. Creighton, *Complete Poems and Selected Letters of Michelangelo, with Foreword and Notes* (Princeton, 1980).

[7] He did so even in his last self-portrait, in which he repainted his hair a rather unlikely ginger.

[8] Quoted on uncertain authority in J. Alazard, *Ingres et l'Ingrinisme* (Paris, 1950), p. 232.

nineteen surviving letters of increasing exasperation from Isabelle d'Este, Marchioness of Mantua, concerning a painting promised and paid for but never delivered.[9] At the time when Titian painted his last great works for Philip II of Spain, Niccolò Stoppio wrote that the artist "was virtually blind and all his new works are done by a German assistant".[10] If Stoppio was one of those unsavoury characters who in every age slither about in the undergrowth of the art world and try to ingratiate themselves by denigrating rivals, the Spanish ambassador, Don Guzman de Silva, was not; and his comments were no less sombre. "Unfortunately he is unsteady and subject to extremes of mood ... and sometimes he seems surprised at what he himself has just said or falls asleep ... His temper, usually benign, has also become uncertain, and he can be terrible when roused."[11] Yet, at about the same time, Titian was dispatching a huge altarpiece, *The Martyrdom of St Lawrence*, to Spain for the new monastic church of the Escorial. It was a difficult nocturnal scene, handled with almost ostentatious virtuosity.[12] A letter accompanied the painting, assuring Philip that every brushstroke was authentically the master's. The statement was hardly necessary: the spiritual resonance that had developed between the King and the artist had by then reached a stage when the former could instantly distinguish between a new autograph work and a studio copy.[13] But that was not all. Did His Majesty, Titian's letter

[9] The picture was probably the one known today as *The Feast of the Gods*. Bellini offered to repay the advance but the offer was declined and the painting was eventually delivered. See R. Palluchini, *Giovanni Bellini* (Venice, 1949).

[10] Probably an artist by the name of Amberger who worked in Titian's workshop. See C. Hope, *Titian* (London, 1980), p. 152.

[11] See R. Palucchini, *Tiziano*, 2 volumes (Florence, 1969), ii, p. 342.

[12] When the order arrived Titian was in Brescia, and his assistant and pupil of thirty years' standing, Girolamo Dante, offered to supply a copy of an older altar-piece. But on his return Titian rejected this and decided to send a new one. Unfortunately the picture proved too big for the new church (dedicated to St Lawrence) and had to be placed in the old chapel. There it still is, almost invisible in the dark.

[13] It was a remarkable artist-patron relationship. Philip II was an obsessive bureaucrat and a Catholic of the most unbending kind. Immured in El Escorial, the gloomiest of royal residences, "Yo el Rey" was the most powerful but also perhaps the most joyless of Christian rulers. He worked like a slave for the success of his policies but almost knowingly courted disaster. When it struck, he rose above it. It was magnificent but not a prescription for either success or happiness.

Titian was forty years older and in almost every respect the King's opposite. He was the patriarchal head of a close and gifted, if at times wayward, family. Beyond the family he had always had a wide circle of friends, both reputable and disreputable. With the shockingly amoral but exceedingly clever Aretino and the smooth and ambitious Sansovino he had once been one of the city's "Unholy Trinity": their escapades in youth were still fondly remembered. And he was still a man of the world, at ease in it and charming when he made the effort.

went on, wish to order a series of ten paintings of a similar size, showing earlier scenes from the martyr's life? [14]

Such contradictions are inescapable when trying to assess the physical health of long-dead men and women, even kings, queens and popes, let alone individuals of no social importance like painters. About the time Hals was commissioned to paint *The Regents and Regentesses of the Men's and Women's Almshouses, Haarlem*, a recent portrait of his of Herman Langelius, a celebrated Amsterdam preacher, prompted the versifier Frederik Waterloos to mock the artist:

> Old Hals, why do you try to paint Langelius?
> Your eyes are too weak for his learned rays
> To express the superhuman peerless
> Mind of this man and teacher.
> Although Haarlem boasts of your art and early masterpieces
> Our Amsterdam will now witness with me that
> You did not understand the essence of his light by half.[15]

Yet, even if Hals's last two group portraits did not prove the contrary, Cornelis de Bie wrote at the same time in his *Golden Cabinet of the Fine Arts*: "Hals is still active in Haarlem and miraculously excellent at painting portraits and counterfeits which are very rough and bold, nimbly touched and well ordered. They are pleasing and ingenious and, seen from afar, they seem to be alive and lack nothing." [16] One can take one's pick. But even those who praised the surviving artistry of old masters did not suggest that their general health had remained preternaturally blooming.

Though medicine limped ahead, the picture hardly changed over the next centuries. While people in their late seventies, eighties and nineties in the

His religion was probably sincere but inclusive and uncomplicated: his biblical narratives were applauded even if he often got a canonical detail wrong. Yet, though they never met after Philip succeeded to the Spanish throne, a true understanding developed between the King and the artist. The widely acclaimed bravura pieces of Titian's youth had left Philip cold: the portrait the artist painted of him in Augsburg was "a little slapdash". But the passionate, sombre and cruel late creations, though far less finished, moved the King deeply. Perhaps the suffering almost invariably portrayed in them exposed in him – but also perhaps assuaged – a hidden inner need. To Titian too, hundreds of miles away, the King's patronage came to mean more than financial security. The link developed at a time when the world around him was changing and he may have felt more and more alienated from it.

[14] He may have been trying to promote the career of his elder son, Orazio, who, he suggested, might act as his assistant.

[15] A. F. Waterloos, *De Hollantsche Parnas* (Amsterdam, 1660), quoted by S. Slive, *Frans Hals*, exhibition catalogue (London, 1989), p. 352.

[16] Cornelis de Bie, *Het Gulden Cabinet* (Antwerp, 1661), quoted by Slive, *Frans Hals*, p. 356.

seventeenth, eighteenth and nineteenth centuries were probably fitter than their coevals are today, they were not immune to the afflictions of old age. Bernini's right hand was paralysed by a stroke some time before his death, a loss he bore with characteristic fortitude. "It is right that God should put my right hand to rest first: of all my bodily parts it has worked hardest." [17] Claude at eighty was a magician with the brush but he had to struggle to remain uncompromising in his commitment to faultless craftsmanship. Several slightly incoherent letters from Henrico von Ottenheim, a cleric acting as the agent for Count Johann Friederich von Waldstein in Rome,[18] retell the progress of two comparatively modest biblical paintings ordered by the Count. "Even after varnishing the master keeps retouching [them] to bring them to an even greater degree of perfection. But he is still infirm with the accursed gout and ... needs to bathe his fingers in hot wax and exercise them for hours every morning when otherwise the light would be most propitious." [19] And a few days later: "Patience, Herr Graf, and more patience! ... One of the paintings is almost finished ... but every movement seems to cause the master great pain." [20]

Chardin's debility, which forced him to change from oils to pastels, has been described, as has Goya's and what is known of Hokusai's health in old age. David remained in comparatively good physical health till shortly before his death.[21] Turner at seventy-three described himself as a "toothless ruin", though he remained a cheerful toothless ruin to the end. Corot shunned society in his last years because of his "liver": his appearance at the Salon in 1874 surprised many of his friends. "Fancy Old Corot is still about", Countess Juliette Pálffy wrote home about the time when the artist was painting his masterpiece, *The Lady in Blue*. But "we were distressed to see

[17] See H. Hibbard, *Bernini* (London, 1965), p. 203.

[18] A discerning patron of the arts and kinsman of Wallenstein, the Duke of Friedland, he later became Archbishop of Prague. He was an ancestor of Beethoven's friend and the dedicatee of the piano sonata in C, Op. 53.

[19] Gout, a specific biochemical disorder of uric acid metabolism, may have been more common in the seventeenth and eighteenth centuries than it is today – many of the Medicis almost certainly suffered from it – but the term was also used to describe many other forms of painful and crippling arthritis. The fact that Claude had to wait for his joints to "loosen up" in the morning suggests that he may have suffered from osteoarthritis, a disease not clearly recognised and separated from gout and rheumatoid arthritis until the researches of Rudolf Virchow in the 1860s.

[20] M. Hutterbach, *Die künstlerische Waldsteins* (Vienna, 1924); see also H. Langdon, *Claude Lorrain* (London, 1989).

[21] His last illness began with a street accident in August 1825 when he was knocked down by a carriage as he was leaving a theatre. This was followed by a series of minor strokes. He died after the last on 29 December.

him so frail. His complexion is sallow and he walks with a stick. Still, he is a tough old bird. And he deserves to live to a hundred." [22] Perhaps he did deserve to; but six months later he was dead from carcinoma of the stomach.[23] Ingres lost little of his combative malice in his eighties. "Contradicted", Théophile Silvestre (who counted himself among the artist's friends) wrote, "he sulks, shakes his fist, stamps his feet, storms and finally offers himself as a sacrifice. Always on horseback in his sentiments, he carries on his disputes unflaggingly until he ends up in the right by the sheer force of being in the wrong." [24] Ingres' enemies – and they were numerous despite the adulation heaped on him by the Establishment – expressed themselves less charitably.

Degas must have suffered agonies in his seventies and eighties as his vision deteriorated, though he never complained.[25] After their quarrel and estrangement over the Dreyfus affair,[26] Monet was touched when his erstwhile friend turned up at Giverny for the funeral of Alice Monet;[27] but, as he watched the blind man walk with a white stick, he was full of foreboding. Was this the fate that awaited him too? [28] Rodin, the insatiable lover, could no longer at seventy-two take up the offered challenge of making love to the beautiful Mlle de Cheminard in the snow. "My doctors won't let me", he mumbled.[29]

Matisse created his greatest cut-outs in bed or in a wheelchair, nursing

---

[22] Quoted in J. Pálffy, *Parisi Emlékek*, edited by M. Pálffy-Brionne (Budapest, 1932), p. 238.

[23] He is the first among the long-lived great artists about whose terminal illness there is a detailed and reliable medical account. Corot's physician, Jean-Pierre Morel, a pupil of the great clinician Trousseau, diagnosed the artist's illness from an enlarged lymph-node in the neck six months before the artist's death. A post-mortem was carried out and confirmed the diagnosis.

[24] T. Silvestre, *L'apothéose de M. Ingres* (Paris, 1868) (author's translation), p. 38.

[25] The disease was some form of progressive retinal degeneration, the cause of which is impossible to diagnose in retrospect. Degas attributed its onset to the privations suffered during the Siege of Paris in 1871.

[26] Alone among the Impressionists, Degas was an ardent anti-Dreyfusard (as, to start with, were most Frenchmen). He had a mystical vision of France and an undeservedly high opinion of the corrupt French officer corps. His antisemitism has been exaggerated: the Halévys, a prominent, rich and artistic Jewish family, were among his best friends. But, like most intelligent people (and, next to Manet, Degas was the most intelligent of the Impressionists), Degas could be very silly. See D. Halévy, *My Friend Degas*, translated and edited by M. Curtiss (Middletown, Connecticut, 1964).

[27] In 1911. See C. Joyes, *Monet at Giverny* (London, 1975).

[28] His cataract was already troubling him though not yet enough to persuade him to seek medical advice.

[29] The story, recounted by Baron B. Hatvany (who knew Rodin), is apocryphal but not implausible.

with some devotion his several chronic ailments.[30] Some artists – Nolde, Kandinski and Bonnard among them – never moaned, or, if they did, their moans were not recorded; but there is nothing to suggest that they were uniquely free of some at least of the common infirmities of old age – creaking joints, failing eyesight, frequency of micturition, impaired hearing, tinnitus, breathlessness on exertion, attacks of vertigo, muscle cramps and the occasional inability to remember the names of their nearest and dearest.

[30] They dated back to 1942 when a comparatively minor abdominal operation was followed by a pulmonary embolism which nearly killed him. He continued to suffer from poor circulation in the legs.

# 13

## *Travelling Hopefully*

If high artistic creativity did not keep physical illnesses at bay, nor did it keep mental processes abnormally nimble. A general slackening of pace, a disinclination to master new skills, or a lack of interest in recent fashions are of course difficult to document in long-dead individuals; but travel to foreign parts puts many youthful mental attributes to the test – or did before the emergence of the tourist industry – and the travelling habits of a number of celebrated artists are on record. Some, of course, were intelligent enough to deplore the very idea of unnecessary physical displacement from childhood onwards. Even in the fifteenth century northerners flocked to Venice, but good Venetians (not unnaturally) hated to cross to *Terra Firma*. Titian travelled but always for some compelling practical reason, not to broaden his mind, let alone to see new places. His lengthy sojourn in Rome at the invitation of Paul III Farnese was probably prompted by his hope of wangling a lucrative ecclesiastical living for his much-loved but good for nothing younger son, Pomponio. To achieve this he was prepared to paint "not only every accursed Farnese but even their cats". (He failed in his purpose: Pomponio had to wait a little longer.) His journey to Augsburg was to paint his great equestrian portrait of the Emperor Charles V, then at the height of his power: the commission could not be refused by a Knight of the Golden Spur.[1] Hals regarded a summons to Amsterdam, only a few hours' journey even in the seventeenth century, as a terrible imposition and protested vigorously though in vain. Claude in Rome kept in close touch with his family in Lorraine and remained surrounded by Lorrainers; but he did not embark on a journey home after the age of thirty. To Bernini the mere thought of abandoning his sacred trust, supervising the rebuilding and beautification of St Peter's, was abomination; nor would his friend and patron, Urban VIII Barberini, countenance such a desertion.[2] If crowned heads or powerful

---

[1] He put it off for the best part of a year.

[2] His appointment to the post of chief architect to St Peter's Basilica at the age of twenty-five was one of the first acts of his friend and patron, Maffeo Barberini, on being elected to the papacy as Urban VIII in 1623. Bernini remained in this post until his death, an unprecedented and unsurpassed fifty-seven years.

prelates wanted their likenesses carved in marble by Europe's greatest sculptor, they had to have their court painters paint triple portraits – left profile, full frontal, right profile – and dispatch the artefact to Rome to "sit" for the master.[3] Lesser mortals had to make the pilgrimage in person. When, in his sixties, political pressure from the young Louis XIV, one of the church's new-style protectors, forced Bernini to undertake the arduous journey to Paris, it was to him a terrible sign of the times.[4] Chardin was never subjected to this kind of pressure and he never expressed the slightest desire to explore the wilderness that reputedly lay beyond Fontainebleau.

Most long-lived artists were, nevertheless, enthusiastic travellers in their youth and middle age, and travel to distant places often powerfully affected their development. Nolde's tour to the Far East and Pacific islands with their so-called primitive culture was a formative influence on him.[5] Memories of

---

[3] The origin of Van Dyck's superb triple portrait of Charles I and of Philip de Champaigne's no less striking Cardinal Richelieu.

[4] The journey is generally described as a success; but Bernini, though a model of courtesy, did little to endear himself to his hosts. When asked by the King what he thought of the Tuilleries, he answered that it seemed to him "a huge little thing … like a great squadron of tiny tots". The new dome of the Val-de-Grâce made him think of "a little cap on a big head". Colbert's new palace prompted him to observe that "it is not money but taste and brains which makes great houses". The much-vaunted panorama of Paris from Meudon reminded him of a carding comb. François Mansart, France's leading architect, "could have become a great architect had he been sent to Rome to study in his youth". And he assured courtiers that "his" King – the bust he carved of Louis XIV and still by far the best piece of sculpture in Versailles – would long outlast "their" King. Yet Bernini scholars still profess to be at a loss to explain why the Sun King took such an unreasonable dislike to him. When Bernini's equestrian statue of the King arrived in Versailles after the sculptor's death, it was banished to a distant corner of the park and entrusted to a court hack to "improve" it. Bernini's plans for the Louvre were also rejected, ostensibly on the grounds of cost. The only person who may be said to have benefited from the visit was a young Oxford professor of astronomy on a short visit to Paris, who attended Bernini's oration to the Académie Royale and made good use of Bernini's teaching when designing the new St Paul's Cathedral in London twenty years later. The other indirect benefit was the splendid day to day diary kept by Paul Fréart, Sieur de Chantelou, who had been assigned to accompany the King's guest in France. Chantelou was charmed by Bernini's slightly acid wit and left an affectionate pen portrait of him. (This should have done something to redress the balance of hostile biographies, concentrating on Bernini's alleged ill temper, but it has not.) Chantelou's diary was not discovered until the 1880s by L. Lalanne, who edited and published it under the title *Journal du voyage du Cavalier Bernin en France* (Paris, 1885). It is the source of the above quotations.

[5] It is still not known why, in 1913, he was invited by the German Colonial Office to join a "fact-finding expedition" to the German Pacific Islands (in fact an expedition designed to irritate the British Government and the Kaiser's much-loved cousin, George V). It took him and his wife, Ada, to large tracts of virtually unexplored Oceania, as well as to India, China and Korea. He was fascinated by native art, but resented it being described by his naval officer

an ethnographical journey to the remote Vologda region of Russia by the young Vasili Kandinski, still a promising lawyer at the time and without a thought of becoming a painter, continued to resonate in his mind throughout his later wanderings.[6] Most French Impressionists found the pea soup smog of London a visual feast, the deadlier the better. Monet's impressions of the Thames in London are medico-social documents as well as lovely paintings. Pissarro and Sisley among others left charming impressions of London's blossoming suburbia. Both Renoir and Monet succumbed to the magic of Venice, though neither added greatly to the city's incomparable iconography.[7] Corot loved travelling, especially to Italy: he was to look back on his first sojourn there as the happiest time of his life. Ingres hated Rome but, though he would have hotly denied it, the thousands of portrait drawings he pencilled there are among his enduring masterpieces. Hokusai was inspired by his arduous journeyings in shogunate Japan.[8] After being introduced to London by Robert Louis Stevenson and W. E. Henley, the city became Rodin's longest-lasting love affair.[9] Munch almost became a Berliner in his thirties. Matisse liked travelling to the United States and did his stint in the Pacific, following in Gauguin's footsteps. On his first and only Mediterranean cruise the remains of archaic Greece enchanted Maillol, though the monuments of the golden age of Phidias left him unmoved. But the greatest artist traveller – his travels and art inextricable – was Turner; and it is his peregrinations that provide a test case of youthful resilience.

The son of a Covent Garden barber and wig-maker, Turner started to go on his sketching tours when he was thirteen; and for ten years he spent three or four months every year on his "rambles". Later in the century the term might conjure up an image of picnic baskets, butterfly-nets and herbaria; but the young cockney planned his journeys as purposefully as would any commercial traveller. Carrying no more than a change of linen, his flute and

---

hosts as "primitive". He was also saddened to "live in an age in which the white man is bringing the whole world into his servitude ... It will end in disaster." Quoted in W. Haftmann, *Nolde* (Cologne, 1958), p. 234. The news of the outbreak of the First World War reached the expedition in Cairo, on their way home.

[6] As revealed by the researches of P. Weiss, *Kandinski and Old Russia* (London, 1995).

[7] Did anybody after Turner? Perhaps Parkes-Bonington and John Singer Sargent came nearest to achieving the nearly-impossible. The Impressionists tried too hard to impose their technique on what was already an Impressionist dream.

[8] See above, Chapter 7, pp. 100–2.

[9] It was fully reciprocated. Uniquely, perhaps, he was equally fêted by leaders of Edwardian society and by young artists from the Slade. Oxford (lagging only two years behind Glasgow) bestowed on him an honorary doctorate.

the tools of his trade,[10] he would often cover twenty miles a day by foot. A ruined abbey, a desolate farmhouse, an old mill, an ancient bridge, a brook, a lake, everything that suggested an image both recognisable and picturesque was marked on his map. It was "fixed" in his sketchbook with a few strokes of a pencil on site. Sometimes patches of colour would be added in the evening in the inn where he spent the night. The aide-memoires would eventually be turned into thousands of topographical prints, the foundation of his fame and fortune.

The pattern changed in 1802. After years of hostilities with Revolutionary France, the Treaty of Amiens once again opened the door to Englishmen wishing to travel on the Continent.[11] Thousands jumped at the chance. Among the academicians were the President of the Royal Academy, Benjamin West, a future President, Michael Archer Shee, Fuseli, Smirke and the youngest full member, twenty-seven-year-old Turner. It meant leaving behind his mistress, Sarah Danby, and their new baby daughter, but that could not be helped. Fifty years earlier Smollett had described the road to Dover as the worst in England and it had not improved since. In a "fast" coach the journey to the coast took the best part of a day. The port itself was "a den of thieves" who made their living by piracy in war and by fleecing travellers in peace. The chamber in the inn where Turner stayed, reputedly the best in town, was cold and comfortless, the bed paltry, the cooking execrable, the wine poisonous, the attendance bad, the publican insolent and the bill extortionate.[12] Turner cursed but did not mind. The actual crossing could take as much as fourteen hours, passengers wishing to be "out of the elements" crowding into a single cabin below deck, the majority suffering all too obviously from terrible *mal de mer*. But Turner was a good sailor and adored the sea in all weathers. Deluges of spray kept his sketchbook closed in the small boat that ferried travellers ashore; but no sooner had he set foot on the Continent of Europe than he recorded the scene on the first page, "Landing in Calais in France for the first time – nearly swamped".[13]

After the always memorable first occasion, with another break during the Napoleonic Wars, there would be another fifty such landings in Turner's life. There was one momentous change though. A barely visible wisp of smoke rising from a boat in an otherwise unremarkable water-colour sketch

[10] Water colours in solid form and later in tubes were among the unsung but momentous achievements of the Industrial Revolution. See also A. Wilton, *Turner in his Time* (London, 1987); and A. Bailey, *Standing in the Sun: A Life of J. M. W. Turner* (London, 1997).

[11] Neither Bonaparte (still First Consul) nor the British Government had any intention of observing the provisions of the treaty, and the peace lasted less than two years.

[12] Quoted in Bailey, *Standing in the Sun*, p. 124.

[13] Ibid., p. 135.

of the Seine near Le Havre, dated 1823, signalled a revolution. Steam travel had arrived and Turner was there to welcome its fantastic visual effects as well as its conveniences. He made his first crossing on the steam packet *Rob Roy* from Dover to Calais in two hours in the same year. Two years later he painted the beribboned paddle steamers, *Lord Melville* and *Talbot*, which could be boarded at the Tower of London and which crossed to France in six hours or even less. On the French side too one could now take a *bateau à vapeur* as far as Rouen. But even in this brave new age travelling in Europe still meant treating little local wars, revolutions, brigandage and outbreaks of cholera as no more than minor contretemps. Indeed, compared to other more endemic discomforts and inconveniences, they were hardly more than that.

Of course there was travel and travel. Accompanied by an army of servants, guides, tutors, with a pile of personal introductions to private houses and a virtually bottomless purse, the grand tours of a century earlier could still be re-enacted. But no continental luxury hotels would ever be called Turners to commemorate his voyages, as they would commemorate the semi-royal progressions of Frederick Augustus Hervey, Earl of Bristol, Bishop of Derry, and his vast entourage. Turner liked to travel on his own,[14] made sure that his every penny was well spent (if it had to be spent at all), and explored the countryside on foot. On his last tour of Alps, at the age of sixty-eight, his tough new walking boots had to be resoled half way through the journey. By then he had explored all the major and many of the minor waterways of western and central Europe, a fabulous record of vaporous beauty in a medium which would soon be known on the Continent as the English Art. He had crossed many of the most dangerous passes of the Alps, painting them in all their awesome majesty. He had visited and painted lakes, castles, waterfalls in rain, snow, sunshine and mist. He had climbed thousands of feet only to be able to look down and paint the nestling valleys below. Following in his hero Claude's footsteps, he had tramped the mosquito- and brigand-infested countryside of central Italy. Above all, he became the greatest visual chronicler of Venice at a unique moment in the city's history.

In every respect save one, the Venice which Turner first visited in 1820 was at the nadir of her fortunes. After two hundred years of melancholy decline, in response to a contemptuous ultimatum from General Bonaparte, the Republic had voted itself out of existence in 1799. The last Doge, Ludovico Manin, meekly abdicated. Nobody, it seems, shed a tear. The French introduced some overdue social reforms and French military engineers,

---

[14] He had no real interest in foreigners (except beddable "Switzer" girls and Italian *ragazze*), though he taught himself a few useful phrases in French, German and Italian.

Bonaparte's pride, surpassed themselves in dismantling everything movable, including the bronze horses of San Marco, and sending the loot back to Paris.[15] Fifteen years later the city emerged from the Congress of Vienna as a Habsburg province. Since Austria's Italian possessions largely paid for her elephantine bureaucracy, Austrian rule was rarely gratuitously malign; but the once great port and Arsenal shrivelled in the shadow of the cosseted imperial city of Trieste. The famous industries of luxury goods (except for Murano glass), potential competition to the Austrian homelands, were taxed out of existence. The city's population declined from about 130,000 in 1793 to about 110,000 in 1824; but, because neglect had made whole districts uninhabitable, the crumbling palaces on the Grand Canal were spilling over with squatters. The French had dissolved the *scuole*; and many of the churches, which had once resounded to the antiphonies of the Gabrielis, stood dark, echoing and empty. An Austrian military band played *Platzmusik* in the Piazza but there were few tourists to listen to Herr Strauss's polkas and gallops. The British still revered Palladio as they did no other architect; but his domestic work could be better admired on the Brenta; and about the rest of the city, cultivated opinion tended to agree with Edward Gibbon that "while Venice, by virtue of its situation, can afford a few hours' distraction, [its] centre is disfigured by a large empty space decorated with the most barbarous architecture one is likely to see in Italy".[16]

Yet, to the elect with eyes to see and a mind to respond, Venice must have been more entrancingly beautiful than it had ever been before or would ever be again. At the height of its prosperity, its buildings continuously being pulled down and rebuilt, its churches and palaces hidden behind scaffolding, ostentation rampant, it was probably as repellent as any booming megalopolis is today. A few years after Turner's last visit it would start to sink under the feet of a million tourists, the honeymoon capital of Mitteleuropa, the city to which writers, poets and composers from both sides of the Atlantic would flock to dream and to die. But in 1818 Byron still saw "From out the waves her structures rise, As from a stroke of the enchanters wand",[17] and he was intoxicated by its beauty. And Turner, whose coarseness of speech at the dinner table could reduce well-bred young ladies to tears, copied a stanza from *Childe Harold* as soon as it was published into his sketchbook:

> In Venice Tasso's echoes are no more,
> And silent rows the songless gondolier;
> Her palaces are crumbling on the shore,

---

[15] The second Treaty of Paris in 1815 obliged France to return some of it.

[16] J. E. Norton, editor, *The Letters of Edward Gibbon* (London, 1956), i, p. 248.

[17] Lord Byron, *Childe Harold*, canto iv, stanza 1.

> And music meets not always now the ear;
> Those days are gone – but Beauty still is here.[18]

It was indeed; and the comical elderly Englishman, with his stove-pipe hat, furled umbrella and pockets bulging with bottles, scraps of paper and other artist's paraphernalia, still bears witness to the truth of Byron's vision.[19]

Yet passionate and indefatigable a continental traveller as Turner was, even he stopped his grand tours at sixty-nine. He last crossed the Channel to visit Le Tréport and Eu on the Picardy coast in 1845, the only occasion when he was entertained by royalty.[20] After that he and Mrs Booth, now resident in Davis Place in the quiet riverside village of Chelsea, still went on boat trips to the Kentish coast and liked to visit Margate, their favourite seaside resort.[21] Once or twice a week he would also set out by foot along the King's Road to walk to Queen Anne Street;[22] but he was no longer prepared to venture further afield. He loved Venice, but, advancing in his seventies, there was now "too much aggravation on the way".[23]

What was true of the greatest travelling artist was also true of other, less dedicated travellers. Ingres at seventy-one pleaded multiple infirmities when invited to attend the unveiling of his self-portrait in the Uffizi, not an occasion he would have missed twenty years earlier. Corot last visited Italy at sixty-two; even then everything seemed to have changed. "But perhaps it is only me who has changed",[24] he wrote to Gaston Destruel. Monet did not like to leave Giverny (except for occasional trips to visit Bonnard in nearby

---

[18] Ibid., canto iv, stanza 3.

[19] See A. J. Finberg, *In Venice with Turner* (London, 1930), p. 65; and L. Stainton, *Turner's Venice* (London, 1985).

[20] French, needless to say, not English. (Medals, knighthoods and invitations to Windsor were showered on artists, most of them mediocre, some unspeakably bad, by the young Queen Victoria and her Consort; but no signal of royal favour or recognition ever came the way of the disreputable Turner.) His arrival in Eu, where he stayed in a fisherman's cottage, was reported to King Louis-Philippe, holidaying at the nearby château of the Orléans family. A dinner invitation followed which Turner tried to decline, pleading lack of suitable attire. He was overruled. Mme Demeran, the fisherman's wife, sacrificed one of her treasured white linen sheets to fashion a suitable neck-cloth for him; and Turner (as he later reported) spent one of his jolliest evenings with his old Twickenham crony. (He and the King had met in the 1820s when Turner had a villa on the Thames and the future King of the French was in exile in England not far from there.)

[21] Where, in the boarding house kept by Mrs Booth, they first met.

[22] Where he had his private gallery. It became more and more derelict as he spent less and less time there. The house no longer exists.

[23] Finberg, *In Venice with Turner*, p. 65.

[24] M. Delaroche-Vernet, *Corot* (Paris, 1938), p. 135.

Veronnet) after Alice Monet's death. Renoir travelled once after his sixty-fifth birthday and then only for a day-trip to Paris.[25] Munch did not leave Ekely after the age of sixty-four. Nolde stayed in Seebüll after the war. Kandinski, the great wanderer, did not move from Paris after 1937,[26] not even to escape to physical safety in the United States. When, two years before his death, Rodin tried to repeat his earlier triumph in Rome,[27] the sojourn was a failure and he returned to Paris deeply discouraged. David at seventy could not be persuaded to travel to the United States and accompany the triumphal tour of his vast *Coronation of Napoleon*,[28] let alone take up a permanent appointment in Berlin. He had no wish even to return to Paris from his comfortable exile in Brussels.[29] Fleeing from the advancing Germans with a United States visa in his pocket in 1940, Matisse turned back at the Spanish frontier. Admiring biographers have spun heroic yarns around this episode; but, great painter as he was, Matisse was not in the least heroic.[30] He simply decided that at seventy-one the journey would be too much for him and that he would rather sit out the war in Nice. Bonnard was a passionate traveller in three continents between the wars (so far as his wife Marthe would let him); but he turned down all invitations for celebratory occasions outside the south of France after the Second World War. "I still love travelling", he told Henri Cartier-Bresson who came to photograph him in Le Bosquet in 1946, "provided I can come home for *le déjeuner*".[31] Even Hokusai reluctantly settled in Edo at seventy-four. Goya is the exception to the rule as usual,

---

[25] See above, Chapter 8, pp. 122–23.

[26] Except once, to visit his dying friend, Paul Klee, in Switzerland.

[27] When a few years earlier he went with his mistress, the Duchesse de Choiseul, she had the Capitol illuminated in his honour and the couple were fêted by the Monde and the Demi-monde. The ostensible reason for his last journey, accompanied by his long-time common-law wife, Rose Beuret, was to model a portrait bust of Pope Benedict XV; in fact it was to escape from the hysterical atmosphere of wartime Paris. But Rome was no better and Benedict proved a "fidgety sitter". (The poor man had much to fidget about, his devoutly Catholic flock on both sides of the trenches claiming God's undivided patronage.)

[28] A copy of the painting now in Versailles. It established itself as one of the obligatory illustrations in history books.

[29] Though David was a regicide (having voted for the death of Louis XVI in the Convention) as well as a Bonapartist, Louis XVIII bore him no personal ill will and an amnesty would have been readily granted had he petitioned for it. Characteristically, David maintained that he could not bear to "humble" himself to the Bourbons. This was nonsense. He had no objection to selling his paintings to them: he was simply happy in his comfortable house in Brussels, with his son and his former pupil, Baron Gros, looking after his business interests in Paris.

[30] He deplored the "unnecessary" involvement of Mme Matisse and his daughter in the Resistance.

[31] Bonnard's friend Jean Bernier's recollection.

going into voluntary exile for no very clear reason at eighty, and then on to Paris for a mysterious three months' visit. After that, even he settled in Bordeaux.[32]

If artistic creativity neither stops the body from growing old, nor preserves the mental agility and adventurous spirit necessary for travel, the explanation for the soaring artistry of great artists in old age must be sought elsewhere. And indeed, to many artists, old age did bring new benefits as well as new burdens and restrictions. The former were of two kinds.

First, changes in external circumstances were often benign. Wealth, security, fame and freedom from distractions, often lacking in youth and middle age, came to many artists in their last years. There was also the inevitable consequence of longevity, the chance to experience and to learn more. The impact of these "external" gains will be examined in the next three chapters.

The second kind of benefit was less tangible. Old age tends to bring about a slow and mysterious but extraordinarily powerful shift in the inner forces which impel men and women to create. No single term adequately describes these forces; but, for convenience, let them be called the "mainsprings of creation". Because they are not always easy to trace and are impossible to quantify, they tend to be neglected, even ignored. Yet, in the life of most long-lived artists, they have been more important than all the external circumstances put together. After the effects of those circumstances have been examined, it is this momentous inner shift which will need to be explored.

[32] See above, Chapter 5, pp. 73–76.

# 14

## *A Roof Over One's Head*

One cannot reasonably maintain that a measure of comfort and security or, to put it more modestly, a sufficiency of food, drink, tobacco and a roof over one's head, is not a help rather than a hindrance in artistic creation; and, searching for external circumstances which may have changed for the better in old age, improved finances is an obvious one to investigate. The change would have been the more welcome since none of the artists who flourished in old age was born to riches, and the youth and middle age of many was a struggle for survival.

Little is known about the family background of Donatello, but he was apprenticed at fourteen to the workshop of Ghiberti to earn his living. Michelangelo was proud of the ancient lineage of the Buonarrotis;[1] but lineage carried with it no wealth, and he too started as an apprentice in his teens.[2] Of the succession of long-lived Venetian painters, Bellini was the son of a painter, Titian the son of a notary and Tintoretto the son of a dyer: none belonged to the city's financial elite. Hals's parents seem to have been no more than modestly prosperous.[3] Bernini's father, a competent sculptor,[4] gave his son a good grounding in his craft but left him no fortune. Claude arrived in Rome from Chamagne, his native village in Lorraine, as an apprentice pastry cook;[5] and his introduction to the fine arts was to be

---

[1] They were magistrates in the small Florentine commune of Caprese.

[2] In Ghirlandaio's workshop, engaged at the time on a fresco cycle in the church of Santa Maria Novella.

[3] See above, Chapter 3, p. 33 and n. 12.

[4] He was highly regarded in Rome (whence he moved from Naples), and some of his surviving work is excellent, but he was inevitably overshadowed by his son.

[5] This was fitting. Nobody could ever decide where the duchy of Lorraine began or ended and politically it never had any clout; but, situated at the cross-roads of Europe, Lorrainers were recognised – as they still are – as the heirs to the best in the cuisines of the north, the south, the west and the east. The melting macaroons of Nancy, the celestial bergamots of Barre-le-Duc, the little fluted cakes named madeleines (after a pretty maid in the duke's household) and immortalised by Proust, the featherweight doughnuts wickedly known as *pets de nonne*, the rum-babas invented by a Duke of Lorraine (who liked to dip his Kugelhof in rum), the Arcadian *bouchées de reine* (sent to Louis XV's Queen during her first pregnancy), and of course an endless variety of *quiches lorraines*, were already celebrated in Claude's day and made cooks from Lorraine eagerly sought after in civilised households everywhere in Europe.

promoted to general dogsbody in the studio of the fashionable painter (and central character in one of Rome's more bloodcurdling scandals) Agostino Tassi.[6] Monsieur Chardin senior was a respected cabinet-maker, but he was also the feeder of many hungry mouths; and his numerous offspring had to start earning their living at an early age.[7] Contrary to his occasional romancing, David's family was never really hard up; but a life of leisure was nonetheless never open to him.[8]

Poverty, more or less abject, was the natural state of the vast majority of the population of Europe until the Industrial Revolution (as it still is in the Developing World); and for a great artist to be born into the aristocracy or nobility or to inherit some of their wealth was statistically against the odds.[9] In many countries even the self-styled nobility was poor. Goya's family belonged to the impoverished Aragonese aristocracy; but his parents could not have paid for the education he received free from the Pious Fathers of Saragossa.[10]

The distribution of wealth gradually changed during the nineteenth century and so did the background of artists. Monsieur Louis-Jacques Corot was a hard-working draper from Burgundy. Mme Corot, née Oberson, came from the orderly Swiss city of Fribourg. She ran a fashionable milliner's shop on the ground floor of the family house on the corner of the Quai Voltaire and the rue de Bac.[11] The convulsive political events of the Revolution, Consulate

[6] The ingredients were murder, rape, adultery and incest; and the female protagonist, Tassi's lover and victim, was Artemisia Gentileschi, wife of the painter Orazio Gentileschi and herself the most gifted woman artist of the age. Tassi's misdemeanours eventually earned him a period of five years banishment from Rome; but he was back in time to resume his career and engage the services of Claude, who thought highly of him. See A. Lapierre, *Artemisia: The Story of a Battle for Greatness* (London, 2000).

[7] See above, Chapter 5.

[8] His father was killed in a duel – the circumstances are obscure – when he was five. It was on his mother's side that he was related to François Boucher, master of Rococo arcadias, who helped him to be admitted to the Académie school but whose artistry David continued to despise and, when safe to do so, denounce.

[9] The same was true of musicians though not, oddly, of poets.

[10] A man of infinite contradictions, Goya savagely attacked the clergy in many of his etchings and drawings, yet throughout his career venerated the saintly founder of the Order, St Joseph of Calasance (who died in 1648, aged ninety-two, after a life of much suffering and great achievements). See above, Chapter 5, p. 72 n. 10.

[11] The house has now disappeared, but from first-floor level, the view over the Seine and to the Tuilleries Garden cannot have changed much (except for the disappearance of the burned-down Tuilleries) and, on an autumn evening with the petrol fumes rising in thick clouds from the *quai* to reproduce Corot's mist, it could have been painted by him. (It very nearly was; but the painting in the Musée Carnevalet is from a point slightly further east.)

[12] Camille was born on the last day of Messidor in Year IV of the new Revolutionary

and First Empire affected them little;[12] and in 1812 they could afford to buy a modest country property in Ville d'Avray, not far from Paris.[13] Camille, their only son, loved it, and it was to remain his spiritual home for the rest of his life;[14] but the couple were horrified to learn of his plans to become a professional painter. Only when their elder daughter died on the eve of her wedding did they, grief-stricken, convert her dowry into an allowance for the boy. It was a modest sum but his needs too were modest and, living at home and helping with the household,[15] he managed to pursue his chosen career. It was twenty years, though, before he could support himself and another ten before the demand for gracious living by the new-rich bourgeoisie of the Second Empire catapulted him to fame and affluence.[16] Both his parents were dead by then. Ingres entertained warm memories of his parents, as he did of his birthplace, the attractive market town of Montauban in the south west of France;[17] but his father was a feckless provincial artist who deserted his wife and never contributed to the cost of his children's upbringing. While studying to become a painter, the young Ingres made ends meet by playing the fiddle in the operatic band in Toulouse.[18]

Calendar. The Revolution had only recently culminated in the indiscriminate slaughter of the Terror, followed by a spasm of Counter-Terror; and the Directory, soon to be swept away by Bonaparte, was still at war with half of Europe.

[13] The village of Ville d'Avray (between Sèvres and St-Cloud) has now been engulfed by Paris but some of the garden, with the artist's *cabane*, survives. There is a surprising and rarely reproduced altar-piece by Corot in the local church of St-Nicolas: it deserves but does not get a star from Michelin.

[14] He painted hundreds of pictures of the garden with its old trees and lake and the house in the distance. Forgers painted thousands of the same.

[15] He was a dutiful rather than an inspired uncle and later great-uncle: he lacked the spark of subversion and subvention which can make the relationship so memorable. He never married.

[16] The class was crass, but, like London's Edwardian rich, it tried to disguise its coarseness with the trappings of Rococo elegance. Corot's silvery landscapes, the fruit of his uncanny gift to recreate eighteenth-century elegance a hundred years after Fragonard, admirably filled the bill and became the rage. "You have not seen my Corots yet in the music room", Sir Robert Chiltern small-talks to Mrs Cheveley in Wilde's *Ideal Husband.* "Corots go so well with music, don't you think?" By music he surely meant the Mozart of the Salzburg serenades, early Haydn and the painter's own favourite, Gluck.

[17] A Musée Ingres there, housing his rich artistic bequest (not all of it on public view), is now one of the added attractions.

[18] It is here that he developed his obsessive interest in the story of Stratonice, the wife of King Seleuceus, whose son, Antiochus, developed a guilty love for her. The story, originally one of Plutarch's popular *Lives,* inspired one of Racine's great tragedies; but Ingres' acquaintance with it probably derived from the popular operatic adaptation by Mehul, the artist's favourite composer.

All Mr William Turner's thrift and pride in his son's artistic genius did not allow him to contribute more to his son's career than his devoted service as a business manager and housekeeper; "Dad never praised me for anything but saving halfpennies", was how the artist fondly remembered him.[19] Hokusai emerged from Edo's teeming proletariat and went to work at thirteen. The grinding poverty of many of the French Impressionists is sometimes represented as one of the trials of youth. It was not. Renoir, the son of a tailor from Limoges, was in his early fifties and had a wife and child to support when he confessed to Paul Durand-Ruel that, in breach of their agreement, he had sold a number of canvases direct to a rich collector.[20] "The pictures I have sold to the Abbé would have been thought horrible by you", he wrote in embarrassed self-defence (he was as bad at inventing spurious excuses as he was at all forms of deception), "and horrible is what they were. But if I sold only good pictures, my family and I would die of hunger."[21] While fashionable charlatans exhibiting at the Salon raked in unheard of fortunes, Monet at forty-four still had to wait for Durand-Ruel to send him the train fare before he could move his family from Pontoise to Giverny; and he could not begin to think of buying the famous house and garden for another ten years. Jean-Baptiste Rodin, Auguste's father, migrated to Paris during the early years of the French Industrial Revolution, when tens of thousands of impoverished families swarmed to the big cities from

[19] "Dad" was the one exception to Turner's legendary parsimony. They were chips off the same block: both were short, long-armed, bandy-legged, beak-nosed, pop-eyed and incoherent in speech. Turner senior happily performed all the menial chores in his son's studio. Billy fretted and fussed over his father's health and diet. (Turner's mother died insane in a lunatic asylum when he was twelve.)

[20] Paul Durand-Ruel followed in the footsteps of his father, who, as an art dealer, championed Delacroix in the 1840s and 1850s. There can be little doubt that Impressionism would have foundered without his support and patronage; and he very nearly went bankrupt in the process. The exhibition organised by him in New York in 1886 was a turning point. "We owe it to the Americans that we did not die of hunger", Renoir was to say later in life when anybody suggested that American collectors were looting the treasures of the Old World. See J. Renoir, *Renoir, My Father*, translated by R. and D. Weaver (London, 1962), p. 248. But the exhibition at the Georges Petit Gallery in Paris was still a failure. The going was even tougher in London, the richest and most philistine of European capitals, where Durand-Ruel tried to make up for the failures in Paris. A photographic record of the exhibition he organised at the Grafton Galleries in 1905 shows some of the greatest treasures of Impressionist painting covering the walls, including eight fabulous Renoirs (among them the *Boating Party*) and twelve Monets. The prices were laughable. Not one of the paintings sold.

Durand-Ruel and his family remained close friends of the Impressionists. He died in 1922, aged ninety-one, a rich man as well as a great one.

[21] I. Venturi, *Les archives de l'Impressionisme*, i, p. 122.

declining market towns.[22] He became a low-grade functionary in the police and counted himself lucky not to lose his job during the slump of the 1830s.[23] But working the normal ten hours a day for six days a week, he never earned more than 1800 francs a year, just enough to raise his family into the ranks of the respectable *petite bourgeoisie*. As a non-paying pupil, his son acquired from the Christian Fathers of the Val-de-Grâce impeccable manners and a grave courtesy which he never lost; but he remained a slow reader and a little hesitant about his tables.[24] But at least Paris was his home where he knew every street corner and cheap *brasserie*. Maillol's struggles in a strange metropolis speaking an alien language were probably more painful.[25]

After such a start, and often after the continuing hardships of middle age, many artists found themselves comfortably off for the first time in old age. Bernini died in a palazzo and left his heirs a fortune.[26] Even in exile, David remained one of the highest-paid portraitists in Europe. Ingres and Corot were men of substance in their last years (though not by the standards of the aristocrats and entrepreneurs who were their principal patrons). Rodin was immensely wealthy in his last decades and had to be watched by his self-appointed well-wishers lest his natural open-handedness led him into insane acts of generosity.[27] Pissarro died poor as well as blind, but Monet and Renoir were, without quite realising it themselves, millionaires in their last years. Maillol always lived simply, but he could afford to buy a farmhouse in Banyuls to which he could withdraw. After the Second World War, Matisse could command almost any price for his most casual doodle.

[22] Yvetot in Normandy, where the Rodins came from, is now once again flourishing.

[23] In addition to their conventional duties, the Paris police, Fouché's creation, supervised gutters, drains, market stalls, the conduct of pedlars, porters and hackney drivers, and the unloading of boats on the Seine; they tested weights and measures, fixed the price of bread and tasted wine before it could be put on sale; they inspected schools, hotels and hospitals for general orderliness; licensed and supervised brothels and prostitutes (estimated to number about 50,000 in a city of one million); and, most importantly, kept a beady eye on impecunious and therefore suspect foreigners, ranging from Italian stonemasons and Belgian labourers to English art students like Thackeray, Polish piano teachers like Chopin and German journalists like Heine.

[24] But, as happens to many late starters, he became an avid reader of the classics. He was never without a cheap edition of Dante, "the greatest literary sculptor" (the highest praise in Rodin's book), and he loved Michelet, Lamartine and Balzac.

[25] See above, Chapter 9, p. 126.

[26] 400,000 scudi. The annual income of a tradesman in Rome was at the time of the order of 500–1000 scudi. The exiled Queen Christina of Sweden let it be known that she considered it a paltry sum for a genius like Bernini; but that was probably only to annoy her enemy, Innocent XI Odescalchi. In this she was entirely successful as usual.

[27] Eventually (ostensibly to safeguard the future establishment of a Musée Rodin), he was persuaded to transfer all his property to the French state.

To all these artists financial security, even luxury, in old age must have been a change for the better; but, as the chief reason for the late flowering of their art, it is unconvincing. First, by no means all long-lived artists died wealthy. Donatello in his last years was dependent on municipal charity. Hals did not perish in the gutter but he was not rich. Hokusai died a pauper. Rembrandt, who earlier in his career had earned and spent several fortunes, was famous but destitute in the last years of his life.

Success can also work in all kinds of ways. Generally speaking, as Renoir's finances became more secure and there was no longer any need for him to churn out painted canvas by the yard, his art benefited. But the reverse can also happen. Even geniuses can produce rubbish – some produced a great deal – and when every absent-minded finger exercise is snatched up, placed under glass and put on the market with all the razzmatazz of a long-lost masterpiece, financial success ceases to be the guarantee of quality. This has always been recognised by artists themselves. Picasso is said to have sent a too persistent collector packing when the latter tried to have a drawing authenticated with the master's signature: "It's a fake even if you saw me draw it with your own eyes. I often draw fakes."

At no time perhaps was the lack of financial motivation of great artists more obvious than in German-occupied Europe during the Second World War. By then the works of Kandinski, Munch and Nolde were fetching high prices in North America; and all three had more than one chance to escape. And of course they did escape, only not in the geographical sense. The wartime trials of Munch and Kandinski have already been described.[28] Emil Nolde's choices were perhaps the hardest.

In the summer of 1938 he was convalescing after an abdominal operation in Switzerland.[29] Recent events in Germany had already driven him to the edge of a nervous breakdown, as well as undermining his formerly robust physical health. More than most who mouthed slogans about *Blut und Erde*, Nolde was a son of the German soil. His parents were Friesian farmers – or peasants as they still called themselves in his youth – who had been working the same small plot of land for generations.[30] They were Protestant

[28] See above, Chapter 10, pp. 150–53; Chapter 11, pp. 173–77.

[29] He had a perforation of his stomach diagnosed at the time as being caused by cancer. With hindsight it was probably a non-malignant ulcer.

[30] His real name was Hansen. Because of its Danish ring, he changed it to Nolde when he became a full-time artist. Nolde is the name of the town of his birth, not far from the German-Danish frontier. This had been a disputed and an ethnically mixed region for centuries. After the First World War the town was attached to Denmark and the artist became and technically remained a Danish citizen.

and steeped in religion: Luther's majestic translation of the Bible was their daily reading. As a younger son, Emil himself had been apprenticed to a carpenter in Flensburg and had largely taught himself to paint. After the First World War, horrified, as were many of his background, by the moral degradation that seemed to accompany the humiliation of defeat and economic collapse, he had been among the first ten thousand to join Hitler's Nationalist Socialist Party. It offered hope, moral regeneration and, above all, Germanness. The last was an attribute which had no equivalent in other western European countries. Many in France hated the work of Matisse, but nobody hated it because it was un-French. Many in Britain admired Augustus John, but nobody praised the Welshness of his draughtsmanship. But to Nolde, as to many German artists, Germanness was a burning issue. "Glory be to our strong, healthy German art", he wrote in his book of reminiscences, *The Years of Struggle*. "We may respect the art of the Latins; but German art has our undying love. The southern sun, tempting us, the Nordic people, since time immemorial, stealing what is most our own, our strength, our reticence, our inmost tenderness ...",[31] and pages more of such drivel. But how "Nordic" was Nolde's *Maria Aegyptica*? Or any other of his large-scale works? Oddly, perhaps, nobody in the "morally degraded" 1920s questioned it. Indeed, for the first time, the Expressionist avant-garde in Germany, ridiculed and execrated before the war by the Wilhelmine establishment, was receiving official recognition. Formerly reviled figures or figures of fun – Dix, Kirchner, Schmidt-Rottluff, Kokoschka – were lecturing to respectful classes of students in universities, designing banknotes or sitting in prestigious curatorial offices. Nolde's sixtieth birthday in 1927 was celebrated with exhibitions of his work in Dresden, Berlin and Cologne, the last opened by the President of the Republic. A year later he was elected honorary member of the Prussian Academy of Art.

But if he expected that this would continue, with a few extra fanfares and the fluttering of Nazi flags, after Hitler's rise to power, he was to be disappointed. In 1933, the year of Hitler's appointment to the Chancellorship, he was still offered the presidency of the State Academy of Arts; and a year later he signed a round robin in the *Völkischer Beobachter* urging Hitler to assume the powers of the Presidency as well as those of the Chancellorship. But odd rumours were beginning to circulate. Hitler, it was said, had berated Goebbels after Speer had told the Führer that the Reichspropagandaminister had two Nolde water-colours hanging in his office. They were to be (and were) promptly removed. A year later Nolde was devastated to learn that

---

[31] E. Nolde, *Jahre der Kämpfe, 1902–1914* (Berlin, 1920), p. 128. The 6th edition (Cologne, 1991) is slightly expurgated.

the Führer regarded not only a few water-colours but the artist's entire oeuvre (as well as those of many of his closest friends) as *schweinerisch, entartet* and, worst of all, *Jüdisch*. While the painter was convalescing in Switzerland, he was informed by friends in Germany (whose number seemed to be plummeting) that museums and private collectors were instructed, first privately but then officially, to remove his work from view. It was also rumoured that in the forthcoming official exhibition of *Entartete Kunst* (degenerate art), to be organised in Munich under the Führer's personal auspices, he would figure prominently as an exhibitor. Indeed, with no less than thirteen exhibits, including his great religious cycle, *The Life of Christ*, he was to be one of the star attractions of this first ever feast of non-art.[32] By chance, some of his sojourn in Switzerland was spent in the company of Paul Klee, who had already been expelled from his teaching post in Düsseldorf and had left Germany. However different in background and personality, the two were old friends; and Nolde had faith in Klee's judgement. Klee tried to explain to him that to be disliked by Hitler was a very different proposition from being ridiculed by a harmless clown like the Kaiser. Indeed Klee had no doubt that if Nolde returned to Germany he faced, at best, official ostracism as an artist, and, at worst, prison and death in a concentration camp. To reinforce Klee's plea, a generous contract was offered to Nolde by the Zurich-based Munte Gallery if he stayed in Switzerland. From the United States Walter Schattner, a former art teacher in Berlin, wrote. Schattner also, as he admitted, had entertained hopes of the Nazi

---

[32] If the number and quality of exhibits and the number of paying visitors can be accepted as the chief criteria of the success of an exhibition – and it is difficult to think of better ones – then Hitler, Goebbels and the unspeakable Professor Adolf Ziegler can be credited with staging the most successful art exhibition ever. A staggering two million people visited the Ausstellung der Entartete Kunst (roughly Exhibition of Degenerate Art), which opened in Munich on 19 July 1937, the average daily attendance being 29,252. The figures are the more remarkable since, far from being housed in splendour, with enticing drinks and food laid on to take the pain out of *Kunst*, the exhibits were housed in deliberately unattractive surroundings and required a long climb up rickety stairs and the exclusion from consciousness of a pervasive smell of stale cabbage. But the 1200-odd exhibits represented artists – or "so-called artists" as the catalogue put it – who had been household names in Germany for a generation and whose downfall and ridicule therefore commanded lively *Schadenfreude*. Among the unconsulted exhibitors were a sprinkling of Jews like Liebermann and Kirchner, and a few grotesque foreigners like Gauguin, Chagall, Mondrian and Munch; but the majority – including Beckmann, Marc, Kandinski, Kirchner, Dix, Grosz, Schmidt-Rottluf, Heckel, Schlemmer and Barlach – could be loosely described as German Expressionists. And, as befitted a leading figure in this movement, seventy-year-old Emil Nolde was one of the chief attractions. Among those who congratulated Herr Goebbels on the "timely exposure of artistic rubbish" were several eminent British art historians, including Dr J. B. C. Grundy of Oxford.

take over.[33] Like so many others (but not nearly enough), he had recognised the barbarity of the regime before it was too late. But he assured Nolde that an artist of Nolde's stature would be welcome and honoured in America. From inside Germany, Barlach, an artist Nolde loved,[34] urged him not to return under any circumstances. "But I can only paint in Germany", Nolde expostulated. "It is the only country where soon you will *not* be able to paint", Klee replied.[35] Klee was right and Nolde almost certainly knew it. But a week later he returned to the *Vaterland.* Whatever his reasons, it was not for material gain.

A more interesting external circumstance than money is acclaim. Nowadays the two tend to go hand in hand; but this was not always so. And the chronology of the event – the time of life when great artists could expect to become famous – has changed dramatically.

For the first thirty years of his career Donatello was widely acclaimed not only as Italy's greatest but also as its most innovative sculptor. No age was more besotted with innovation, and he never disappointed. His memorial to the *condottiere* Gattamelata[36] in Padua was the first equestrian statue to dominate a public square since Antiquity.[37] His bronze David was the first life-sized male nude for a thousand years – and to many it is still the most beautiful and homoerotic.[38] There can be few old parish churches in Europe whose funerary art does not echo the tomb he designed for the Antipope

---

[33] As did several other sophisticates like Gropius. There was initially a certain affinity between the younger generation of Expressionists and the early Nazis. Both movements babbled about a brave new world – Expressionist manifestos used terms like the Third Reich as freely as did the Nazis – and both flavoured their talk with a mystical element; both bandied the term "purity" about as some kind of a Holy Grail (meaning of course different things) and both were inherently violent. Although Hitler, alone among twentieth-century monsters, regarded the visual arts as important, his taste was firmly for pornokitsch. Adolf Ziegler, "Master of the Pubic Hair", was his favourite painter.

[34] Ernst Barlach, a man of great moral stature as well as probably the greatest sculptor of his generation, was already gravely ill. (He died in 1938, aged sixty-eight.) His illness saved him from a concentration camp but not from having many of his works destroyed.

[35] R. Huertli, *Eine Freundschaft* (Basel, 1957), p. 87.

[36] It is not known why the baker's son, Erasmo de Narni, earned his nickname (meaning "honeyed cat"). He served as a successful mercenary general first Florence, then the papacy and finally Venice, which paid for the monument. Padua was his birth-place. It is uncertain whether or not Donatello met the *condottiere* in life – he could have done – but the face is full of character.

[37] It is still arguably the best. The equestrian Marcus Aurelius on the Capitol in Rome and the bronze horses of San Marco in Venice were ancestors but not direct models.

[38] All the great Renaissance and Baroque sculptors created a David (or in Cellini's case the substitute figure of Perseus). They are inevitably overshadowed by Michelangelo's; but Donatello can hold his own.

John XXIII.[39] He probably invented the *relievo schiacciato*, the flat relief carving that could place figures into space. It struck contemporaries as near-miraculous – as indeed it was.[40] Even more astonishing was his ability to breathe new life into old forms. The saints and prophets he carved for Brunelleschi's Duomo, the Orsanmichele,[41] and the high altar in Padua, were no longer mere tokens of virtues, carriers of saintly attributes: they were heroic fighters and thinkers. Only the heroic in Donatello's art always remained mansized or womansized. "Speak, speak!", he is said to have exclaimed as he stepped back from the finished *Habakkuk*;[42] and his exclamation expressed more than his confidence in his mastery at creating real characters. One feels that if his heroes could utter sounds, they would not be the grunts, wails or blood-curdling ululations of Superman but the clear if slightly harsh accents of intelligent Tuscan speech.

In his late fifties he was still acknowledged as a trend-setter. He presided over a flourishing workshop and formed partnerships with other masters in order to fulfil a steady stream of commissions.[43] He was also part – though

[39] Happily, antipopes are an extinct species. John XXIII was the Neapolitan Baldassare Cossa elected during the Great Schism to replace the two popes already disputing St Peter's throne. In the event he proved to be the third and least worthy. In a celebrated passage Gibbon relates that at the Council of Constance (convened to end the Schism) "the more scandalous charges against him were suppressed and the Vicar of Christ was accused only of piracy, murder, rape, sodomy and incest". See E. Gibbon *The History of the Decline and Fall of the Roman Empire* (Folio Society edn, London, 1997), viii, chapter 7, p. 319. This was par for the course in Renaissance polemics and he was imprisoned by the Emperor, Sigismund of Luxembourg, not for his misdemeanours but to extort a colossal ransom from the ex-antipope's friends. Fortunately for Cossa, Cosimo de' Medici was among them. The ex-antipope ended his life as cardinal archbishop of Tusculum and Cosimo's honoured guest in Florence.

[40] But nothing he ever did was for effect only. In *The Assumption of the Virgin* on the tomb of Cardinal Brancaccio in Naples only the Virgin has real depth, and only her praying hands are truly three-dimensional. The angels who float in and out of the clouds are the products of the barest declivities or mere scratches. There could be no better way of conveying the spiritual as well as the historical singularity of the event.

[41] This was the communal religious shrine of the Florentine guilds which commissioned Donatello to commemorate their numerous patron saints. It also served, when not in use as a shrine, as a grain exchange and warehouse; an example of Tuscan practical common sense.

[42] Or Zuccone. The anecdote comes (like most good if not wholly trustworthy anecdotes) from Vasari and the full quotation is "Speak, speak, or may you die from dysentery". See G. Vasari, *Le vite de' più eccellenti pittori, scultori ed architettori*, edited by G. Milanesi, 9 volumes (Florence, 1906), iii, p. 348. Perhaps it was significant to an age more conversant with the greater and lesser prophets than the present that Habakkuk was the most thunderously outspoken critic of graven images. "Woe unto him that saith to the wood Awake, or to the dumb stone Arise ..." (Habakkuk, 3, 12) and much more in the same disapproving vein about molten images and teachers of lies. Donatello may have been stung.

[43] R. Lightbown, *Donatello and Michelozzo*, 2 volumes (London, 1980).

probably never the focal point – of a sparkling coterie of historians, anti-quaries and men of letters whose chatter was transforming people's perception of themselves and of the world they lived in. Perhaps, like every-body else, he collected newly discovered antique masterpieces: his opinion about new finds was certainly sought.

Then the data about his doings and achievements become scanty. That in itself may be significant. Renaissance chroniclers wallowed in blood and gore, and loved nothing more than tales of poisoning of the most fiendish kind, but they shunned the less dramatic decrepitude of old age. In his sixties and seventies, even during his somewhat mysterious self-imposed exile in Siena, he was still revered, and younger Florentines like Andrea della Robbia were looking forward to being one of his pall-bearers when the sad but inevitable event occurred. His funeral would be the occasion for an exciting line-up of new talent. But alive he was no longer a man of consequence, at least not someone important enough to gossip about.

Modern biographers of old masters sometimes relate that their subjects' exceptional gifts were recognised early by established practitioners or prospective patrons; and that it was this recognition which fuelled the ambition of the gifted youths to embark on a career in art. This was certainly true of Donatello. Michelangelo's talent, too, was recognised at the court of Lorenzo de' Medici and news of it preceded his arrival in Rome.[44] Claude's mastery of landscape was spotted by emissaries of Philip IV of Spain, on the look out for works of art to embellish the latest of their master's follies.[45] A portrait bust carved by the eleven-year-old Gianlorenzo Bernini in his father's workshop won such acclaim that the Pope, Paul V Borghese, expressed the wish to see him. In the pontifical presence the youth sketched a head of St Paul "with free, bold strokes in a few minutes to the keen delight of the Pontiff".[46] As a reward he was given the run of the Villa Borghese, crammed with priceless works of art as well as exotic junk, and his future education was entrusted to Cardinal Barberini, "already a great

[44] It was this which probably prompted Cardinal de la Groslaie, representative of the King of France at the Curia, to entrust the young man with his first *Pietà* (now in St Peter's behind bullet-proof glass), which the aged prelate wanted erected over his tomb.

[45] The King (Philip II's grandson) was an enthusiastic patron of the arts – Velasquez who immortalised his bizarre court apparently liked him – while he left affairs of state to his favourite, the Count-Duke of Olivarez. Buen Retiro, which eventually housed numerous Claudes, started as a quiet country villa for assorted royal mistresses, but, bit by bit, it acquired a theatre, a menagerie of wild beasts, a hippodrome for equestrian events, an enormous park dotted with "hermitages" as well as a picture gallery.

[46] F. Baldinucci, *Vita de Bernini* (Florence, 1682), translated and edited by C. Enggass (Phil-adelphia, 1966), p. 122.

patron of the noblest arts".[47] Young Chardin was "discovered" by two
academicians in the Place Dauphine.[48] And one can think of many such
more or less well-documented examples of auspicious beginnings.

The second part of the statement, by contrast, about recognition fuelling
young would-be artists' private ambitions, would have struck older masters
as gibberish. Private ambition did not come into it – or hardly. Without the
approval, even the command, of established masters or princely patrons, it
would never have occurred to young men, however gifted, to harbour ambitions about, let alone embark on, a career as a professional artist. Tintoretto
would no doubt have followed in his father's footsteps and become a respected master dyer, and Claude would have become one of the five hundred
chefs from Lorraine employed by the nobility of Rome. Two centuries later,
young Turner of Covent Garden decided to become a professional artist
because his sketches found favour with the customers of his father's barber's
shop, not because he was besotted with the skies of Claude.

Conversely, the idea that young men or women might rely on nothing
more than their own judgement and the approval of their friends, and sometimes actually defy the advice of established authorities, would have struck
Tintoretto's family – as it would have struck those of Donatello, Bernini,
Claude and Turner – as preposterous. Society's acceptance of such self-
assessment as reasonable (if not necessarily wise) is quite recent; indeed its
beginning can be accurately placed and dated. Since it was probably one of
the most momentous changes in the social history of western art, including the
role and place of old artists, it deserves to be described in a little more detail.

Bohemia was born on the Left Bank of the Seine in the Paris of the late
1820s. The France of the Bourbon Restoration had been bled white by the
Revolutionary and Napoleonic Wars; and it was the flower of the country's
youth that had perished. By the time the next generation reached manhood,
they faced a stark choice. They could conform and accept the precepts of
the timorous but vengeful survivors of the slaughter, or they would be treated
as outlaws.

The young Bohemians whom Henri Murger would soon portray with
such charm were not of course criminals.[49] They were poor, laughter-loving,

[47] Ibid., p. 165.

[48] See above, Chapter 4, p. 48 and n. 10.

[49] As a student Murger himself was one of the Bohemians. His charming sketches, *Scènes
de la vie de Bohème*, remained popular in France for most of the nineteenth century, but they
would hardly be remembered in the English-speaking world today had Puccini not based his
opera on one of them fifty years later. (Murger also wrote a successful but not very good
play entitled *La vie de Bohème*.) Yet the opera, simply entitled *La Bohème*, for all its magic,

irreverent, at times heroic, more often merely silly, always disorderly, sentimental, careless of the law, inconsiderate of landlords and contemptuous
of the stultifying virtues of their elders. They were also, to Murger's generation, essentially transient and almost by definition ineffectual, the noisy
but ephemeral products of a post-cataclysmal decade, like the Flappers would
be in the 1920s or the Teddy Boys in the 1950s. Colline, the philosopher
who sells his much-loved old overcoat to buy medicine for Mimi, has one
of the best arias in *La Bohème*; but one doubts whether his philosophical
musings will transform men's notions of the universe. Nor can one believe
that the kindly Schaunard's great symphony, *The Influence of Blue on the
Arts*, will ever resound in the concert halls of Europe; or pin excessive hopes
on Marcel's canvas, *The Crossing of the Red Sea*. Even Rodolphe casts his
poetic masterpiece into the fire, in search of a little heat, without a catch
in his voice.

Yet Murger and his generation were wrong. Paris's infant Bohemia soon
lost its innocence but it did not die. By the time Munch plunged into it in
the 1880s, first in Paris and then in Berlin,[50] it was soaked in absinthe,[51]
weakened by malnutrition, and riddled with tuberculosis and syphilis. The life
expectancy of its guerrilla forces was desperately short; but during their spasm
of life they remained brilliantly creative. The convulsions of two world wars
destroyed the pattern: more precisely, they destroyed the faith of the bourgeoisie in their role as the pace-setters of mankind along the path of slow
but uninterrupted progress; and collapse of bourgeois faith extinguished the
fires of rebellion of Bohemia. Without a target there could be no sniping,
just as there can never be an avant-garde without a garde.[52] But by then the
chronology of artistic fame and acclaim had irreversibly changed.

The common recognition of youthful talent before the emergence of

---

is far removed from the light-hearted tone of the book in which Mimi and Musette are only
two of the many midinettes who flit in and out of the lives and beds of the Bohemians.
Murger himself died of tuberculosis, like Mimi, in 1861 at the age of thirty-nine.

[50] See above, Chapter 10, pp. 143–47.

[51] The drink, drug and emblem of Bohemia in its last thirty years, it had an alcohol content
three times as high as ordinary brandy and owed its green sheen and bitter flavour to
wormwood (*Artemisia absinthum*). Its Swiss inventor, Dr Ordinaire, sold the recipe to Monsieur Pernod; but imitations were widely distilled. Zola described its unique effects in
*L'Assommoir*: the wandering glazed look, the cold, clammy skin, and the extraordinarily vivid
hallucinations, by turns maniacal, lachrymose and stupid. But drinkers often did not appear
drunk until they suddenly became delirious, began to throw fits or collapsed and died. Verlaine,
Baudelaire, Rimbaud, Strindberg and the Hungarian Ady were among the poets who celebrated
*la Fée Verte*; Degas, Manet and Munch painted her lovers; and Toulouse-Lautrec among many
others laid down his life on her altar.

[52] Sir Hugh Casson's phrase.

Bohemia often had a more sombre sequel. During the centuries when artists gained fame and acclaim before reaching middle age (or what was in their day regarded as middle age), their hour of glory rarely lasted long. Like Donatello, many continued to be venerated – but no more. Titian in his eighth and ninth decades was reverently called upon by every important state visitor to Venice – at eighty he chatted amiably in French with Henri III of France on the occasion of the most sumptuous and last display of Venetian power – and copies of many of his early works continued to sell in every corner of Europe. But nobody except the royal recluse of El Escorial waited impatiently for his latest autograph works. Rome and Florence would fight over Michelangelo's earthly remains as a matter of prestige, but nobody was particularly keen to lay their hands on his last unfinished work. The pattern did not significantly change in the autumnal years of the Age of Reason. The Comte d'Angiviller, Superintendent of the King's Buildings, did not hesitate to put the seventy-five-year-old Chardin firmly in his place. "I have read your request [for an improved pension] with some dismay", wrote the Count after toning down a more acerbic draft by Jean-Baptiste Pierre, the King's First Painter, "and it seems to me ill-founded ..."

> Whilst your work testifies to your just renown in one genre ... you must admit that that genre cannot be regarded as the highest and noblest; and your paintings have never entailed as much expense or required as much time and diligent historical research as those of some of your younger colleagues who are now assiduously cultivating higher genres. I hope that in future you will spare me the distasteful task of having to refuse you.[53]

The Count's hopes were only partly fulfilled, for soon it was Mme Chardin who was petitioning him; but she too was turned down.

It was the generation of David in France, Goya in Spain and Turner in England which marked the end of the old chronology. David was recognised as a great artist in his thirties, long before the Revolution.[54] Goya's bumptious talent carried all before him by the time he was thirty; and one of Ferdinand VII's few redeeming caprices kept him in modest comfort in old age;[55] but, outside his closest family and a small circle of friends, his death passed almost unnoticed; and nobody in Spain clamoured for the return of his headless corpse.[56] Turner too reached his peak of popularity and financial success in

---

[53] Quoted by M. Roland Michel, *Chardin* (New York, 1996), p. 98. See above, Chapter 4, p. 53, for another passage from the same correspondence.

[54] See above, Chapter 6, pp. 81–83.

[55] See above, Chapter 5, pp. 69, 73, 75.

[56] This was a fittingly Goyaesque postscript to the artist's life. In 1888 the Quai d'Orsay, anxious to establish friendly relations with Spain, but also to help to save the municipality

his thirties, mostly with prints of meticulously topographical landscapes. Forty years later *Punch*, with inimitable wit, proposed an all-purpose title for a Turner painting: "A Typhoon Bursting in a Simoon over a Whirlpool of a Maelstrom in Norway with a Ship on Fire, an Eclipse and the Effect of a Lunar Rainbow".[57] More succinctly, Thackeray professed to be reminded by Turner's sun of "a huge, slimy poached egg"; and, with the solicitude already characteristic of English royalty, Prince Albert wondered if an operation on his eyes might correct the old man's deranged vision. Turner had been around for too long.

The generation of Ingres and Delacroix straddled the divide. Both were ignored or reviled in their youth, but recognition came to them before they reached forty. The next generation – Corot and Ingres among them – had to wait longer. But they were lucky compared to the one following them, the generation of the Impressionists. And at the turn of the millennium in a society which expects its star performers in other fields to have made their first million by their mid twenties, late recognition of the best artists is still the norm.

As if to make up for the incomprehension, ridicule and hostility shown to the young, the late nineteenth century also invented and the twentieth century brought to perfection a new role for aged artists. The surprise of masters like Tintoretto at seeing young men and women embarking on artistic careers because of their often exaggerated view of their own talent, even, almost incredibly, against the advice of their elders, would be as nothing compared to their consternation on seeing the godlike status accorded to some of the delinquent young once they had reached old age.[58] The explanation is not of course aesthetic; nor is it an expression of society's wish to make amends for past mistakes. It is the emergence of art as an investment.

---

of Bordeaux the expense of reburial when the Cemetery of the Grande Chartreuse where Goya had been interred was scheduled for redevelopment, offered to repatriate the body. No snags were anticipated, although it was known that the artist had been buried in the same grave as his friend, Juan Martin Goichoechea. But when the remains were examined in the presence of the Spanish consul, the bones of the two skeletons were found to have been mixed up and Goya's skull was missing. Who took it, why and when? – the mystery has never been cleared up. But gestures of international goodwill could not be imperilled by such pedantries; and in reply to the consul's panicky message, "Goya's skeleton headless", the prompt answer from Madrid was, "Dispatch Goya with or without head".

[57] Quoted by J. Walker, *Turner* (New York, 1976), p. 65.

[58] Many of course never did. Van Gogh would have been fifty-five at the time of the first Expressionist exhibition which began to establish his fame: by then he had been dead for eighteen years. Modigliani, dead at thirty-six (in 1920), and Schiele, dead at twenty-eight (in 1919), would have had to wait about twenty years to become acknowledged masters and sound speculative investments. Other examples are too numerous for comfort.

Nothing comparable has been seen in the western world since holy relics became the first international currency in the middle ages. Just as the nails, hairs, skulls and toes of the meek and the martyred became, in the twelfth and thirteenth centuries, gilt-edged securities or tempting speculative ventures, so in the professedly rational twenty-first century the most trivial works of a few once-derided young but now aged or safely dead artists have become the bedrock of many a successful businessman's investment portfolio. Not all of these works have artistic merit, just as not all miracle-working relics of the middle ages worked miracles; but that does not matter. They are reassuring and inflation-proof declarations of wealth, and transportable in an emergency.

Does this belated adulation and attendant wealth help explain the creativity of old age? Or, to look at the mirror-image question, does the hostility from which many artists when young now suffer stifle their creativity? One is tempted to parrot received wisdom and suggest that no young artist was ever prevented from creating masterpieces by material hardship or lack of recognition. But this is only one of those dubious generalisations from which elderly and by and large well-fed members of the bourgeoisie have always drawn comfort. Nobody can say how many potential old masters, as great perhaps as Michelangelo, were deflected in youth from a career in the arts by indifference, ignorance and meanness, just as nobody can say how many budding Turners were slaughtered on the battlefield of Waterloo or infant Hokusais incinerated in Hiroshima. In answer to the first question, however, all the evidence suggests that new-found wealth in old age has never been a decisive factor in the late flowering of great art. Even after the 1820s and during the decades of unabashed capitalism, when earning capacity became the touchstone and measure of success in most fields, it never became the chief motive force of the best artists. What all of them wanted was enough to live on, a roof over their heads.

On his first visit to London, Rodin was taken by W. E. Henley to see Sir Frederick Leighton, then President of the Royal Academy.[59] The Frenchman, who understood English but refused to speak it, listened politely as the President explained to him how to get on and make a fortune in London Society. When Sir Frederick finished, Rodin turned to Henley. "Que ce que c'est *getting on*?" When the meaning of the expression was explained to him – Henley suggested that it was akin to *se debrouiller* – the artist again turned to the interpreter. "Dites au sir que je ne veux pas '*get on*'. Je ne désire que

---

[59] The poet of muscular Christianity was, with Robert Louis Stevenson, among the first in England to recognise Rodin's genius. As editor of the *Magazine of Art* he was influential in promoting the sculptor among potential English patrons.

mes gages honnêtes." [60] And his honest wages were (by London standards) far from exorbitant.

This is not to say that among the long-lived great artists some were not grasping and greedy. Rightly or wrongly, the reputation of being mercenary still clings to Titian; and, dealing with the rich, the titled, the crowned and the tiaraed, perhaps not significantly different in his day from what they are today, he needed to be.[61] Chardin, well matched by the second Mme Chardin, may have been something of a miser. Goya immortalised the heroic struggle of his people against their French oppressors; but that was after the event. Turner's ferocious tussles with his engravers, he always wanting both the best and the cheapest, were legendary: Sir Walter Scott was probably accurate describing "his palms as itchy as his fingers are ingenious ... he will do nothing without cash and anything for it".[62] But neither the best nor the worst of the works of Titian, Chardin, Goya or Turner were the outcome of financial inducement or the lack of it; and affluence in old age was no spur to Monet, Renoir, Bonnard or Matisse to paint more and better poppy fields, nudes, breakfast tables or odalisques.

What was true of wealth was also true of acclaim. Toward the end of long lives some great artists experienced extravagant praise, others near total neglect. Their responses were not always rational, but neither treatment significantly affected the quality of their work. The only person Hokusai wanted to satisfy toward the end of his life was himself. In his youth and at the height of his popularity Turner would splutter if he felt that his "transcendent genius" was insufficiently appreciated.[63] In his late fifties, his star already waning, all he worried about was "idiot praise". Ingres, a vain and easily offended artist in his years of struggle, pointedly ignored the request of admiring visitors to view his paintings, and treated them to long concerts on his violin instead.[64] They mostly suffered in silence; but "he is a good violinist for a painter" was the Duchesse d'Iéna's verdict.

[60] L. Hatvany, *Rodin* (Budapest, 1928). The anecdote is based on hearsay but sounds plausible.

[61] Neither the Emperor, Charles V, nor that great patron of the arts, Paul III Farnese, ever paid him except with praise, medals and titles. (Of course their patronage was valuable publicity.) Philip II was an honourable exception, settling his father's debts as well as his own.

[62] Quoted in A. Wilton, *Turner in His Time* (London, 1987), p. 138. It has to be remembered, though, that Turner had emerged from a background where poverty meant loss of independence, and loss of independence often led to total degradation. In matters financial he was as much the child of the Industrial Revolution as any self-made iron-master or mill-owner. However tight-fisted he often was, he never prostituted his art as did so many of his more gentlemanly successors in' the Victorian dawn of cultivated refinement.

[63] "Transcendent genius" was Ruskin's phrase, but not one with which Turner would have disagreed.

[64] The term *"violon d'Ingres"* became a conversational cliché in French.

A healthy disrespect for received opinion is often regarded as a characteristic of youth; and as a form of rebellion perhaps it is. But disrespect for
shibboleths, publicity, consensus, fashion and the encyclicals of academe has
always been the attribute of old age. Only Renoir in his seventies could have
described Leonardo, the holiest of sacred cows of western art, as boring: "he
ought to have stuck to his aeroplanes". Bonnard at seventy-eight was given
a one-man conducted tour of the first few rooms of the Louvre to reopen
after the Second World War.[58] He flitted from bay to bay, gazing out at the
Left Bank where he had spent much of his youth. "What I have always liked
about this place", he told his escort in his precise schoolmasterly voice, "are
the windows." Only Sickert in his late seventies could have summed up
Ingres' much acclaimed *Turkish Bath* as a bowl of spaghetti. If old masters
felt free to be disrespectful about art-historical icons, they felt even less
respect for the adulation – or the opposite – of their contemporaries.

---

[65] In 1946. It was a wonderful jumble, no effort having yet been made to sort out the
pictures by style, period, artist or any other system.

# 15

## *The Fleeting Moment*

Affluence and acclaim are not the only circumstances which change in old age. There is also time – the minutes, hours and days that are available for an artist to create. Even more critically, the meaning of time changes. Old artists often have more of it but also less: in television jargon, their hours of transmission get longer but their prime time shrinks. There is also a growing consciousness that it is not an inexhaustible commodity. To the young *Memento Mori* is never more than a boring cliché. To the old the approach of death can add new urgency to thought, action and prayer. In many ways, some obvious and some less so, changed perceptions are reflected in their creations. Their responses to the pressures of the fleeting moment change. One often senses in their work a new understanding of the value and limitations of spontaneity. Whether or not of necessity, there may be a new striving for economy, a will and sometimes the capacity to achieve the desired effect by extraordinarily simple means. As physical skills decline, they may acquire a mysterious new capacity of exploiting accidents. Could these trends account for their mastery?

Spontaneity is highly prized today. Fledgeling artists are continually urged not to belabour their works. "If it's not quite right, discard it and start again", they are told, the habit of many Pre-Raphaelites endlessly to repaint their canvases being held up as a terrible warning and contrasted to the lightning sketches of Monet and his fellow Impressionists. There is a grain of good sense in this, as there is in most well-intentioned advice; but the paintings reputedly ruined by the Pre-Raphaelites by endless retouching were probably even more deplorable in their pristine freshness; and, contrary to legend, Monet in old age often added a brushstroke or two – or even many – to his ostensibly finished pictures. He would probably want to do the same today if he were conducted around the Orangerie in Paris, as Renoir wanted to retouch his paintings on his last ceremonial visit to the Luxembourg. Would he be allowed to? In response to Renoir's entreaty, his escort tactfully pretended to be deaf.

Neither Monet nor Renoir were given to artistic theorising; but Bonnard had a gift for expounding general principles. "Take all the time you need for seeing the picture with your mind's eye on the blank canvas. Then paint

it before it disappears. But, once painted, leave it alone." But the advice was
the fruit of youthful confidence, not of the wisdom of old age. During the
Second World War the Bernier family cherished Bonnard's occasional visits
for Sunday lunch, but they also dreaded them. Their house was full of his
paintings, which they loved:

> but, unless we spent some of our Sunday mornings unhooking and hiding our
> favourites, a faraway look would soon come into [his] eyes as he contemplated
> them; and within a few minutes he would ask our permission to take them home
> for minor improvements. Of course in the fullness of time we would always have
> them returned and none of us could ever detect the slightest difference; but he
> would assure us that he was able to effect important reparations.[1]

The golden rule, as always in artistic creation, is that there is no golden
rule. No artist ever combined such laser-sharp precision with complete spontaneity as Ingres did in the portrait drawings of his youth, yet laboured for
so long and seemingly so stolidly at his last portraits in oils. For the former
he never used an eraser or a ruler and, with his models often waiting impatiently for the finished product, the first versions always had to be the last;
but any one of thousands of sheets could serve as an instruction manual of
higher draughtsmanship.[2] The same artist would agonise for years over every
detail of his last portraits; and even the most bigoted champions of spontaneity
cannot withhold a nod of approval when confronting the melancholy
opulence of the finished image of the Princesse de Broglie (Plate 10).[3]

[1] Jean de Bernier's recollection.

[2] Picking one almost at random: behold his *Paganini.* Check with a ruler the precise
convergence of the shoulder of Paganini's coat, the line of his pocket, the line where the
cravat meets the lapel, the line of the reverse of the collar and the right side of the coat-line
above the left hand on the pupil of the leading left eye, none of which could of course have
happened in real life but which give the image its commanding unity. Add such virtuoso
refinements as the imaginary extension of the last line just touching the tip of the violinist's
bow. One could go on and subject hundreds of other sketches to a similar and more thorough
technical dissection. These *tours de force* probably took the young draughtsman less than an
hour. Other even more deceptively simple sketches were completed in less time than it would
take a modern paparazzo to focus his multiple lenses.

[3] Born Eleonore-Marie-Pauline de Gallard de Brassac de Béarn, the Princesse, soon to be
Duchesse, was twenty-eight when Ingres finished his portrait of her and was already known
to be delicate. Five years later she was dead from tuberculosis, a disease which at the time
permeated all classes of society. One remains haunted by the veiled tragedy, framed in ice-cold
regal splendour, long after one has dissected Ingres's countless compositional devices and
felicities. (But to do the old conjurer justice just one: behold the nearly perfect oval of the
face sharply crowned by the jewel-encrusted pin and black velvet toque and then softened
by the undulant crescents of the hair and ostrich plumes; and, inverted, the same pattern
supporting the chin, the plunging double pearl necklace joining the sinuous contours of
the fingers. The tight cluster of strands echoes – more nervously – the tassel of the cushion.)

In so far as there *is* a golden rule, it is that a rigid time scale imposed by circumstances – whether by the need to feed hungry mouths or by the lure of an irresistibly lavish offer for an unworthy effort – is usually bad. Good painting, like good walking, good eating and good love-making, has its own natural and individual rhythm. A calendar month in terms of creative time, the only kind of time that really matters to an artist, may be no more than a fleeting second, just as a fleeting chronological second may be enough to bring forth a revelation, a timeless vision of beauty.

Rodin's appreciation of "real" or creative time, like that of many other artists, stemmed from a youth spent under the tyranny of clock and calendar. Many of his early years, conventionally labelled "the best", were spent on building sites and in masonry yards, slaving away as sculptor's mate, pointer, carver, hewer, polisher, cleaner, gilder or whatever job was going in the trade. He never complained. Perhaps unconsciously he realised that, without the insatiable appetite of Second Empire Paris, transforming itself under the wand of Baron Haussmann, for stone caryatids, nymphs, grotesques, titans, cornucopias, graces and ornamental figures of no clear ancestry or function, he could never have trained himself as a sculptor.[4] But the pressure to hurry and to finish on time never let up. At the time he met Rose Beuret he was carving yards and yards of garlands of roses and myrtles on the ceiling of the new Théâtre des Gobelins.[5] She was a fresh-faced country girl of nineteen from Joinville on the Marne, who worked twelve hours a day, six days a week, in the dress shop next door. Their romance nevertheless blossomed and soon they were pooling their resources and setting up house together. During the fantastic building boom of the late 1850s and early 1860s Auguste became an assistant to Ernest Carrier-Belleuse, the most flamboyant of artistic entrepreneurs in an age of entrepreneurial flamboyance.[6] He had a finger in every architectural pie. To Charles Garnier's colossal confection, the Opéra, he and his *équippe*, Rodin included, contributed the pair of

The Ducs de Broglie traced their title and descent from a famous marshal under Louis XIV. The untitled de Gallard de Brassacs did not bother to trace their lineage beyond Charlemagne. Such matters never failed to inspire Ingres.

[4] The Baron was appointed Prefect of the Département of the Seine in 1853, with the brief from Napoleon III to make Paris safe from insurrections and barricades. The city's wide boulevards and wonderful vistas were largely his achievement: only in their professed objectives did they fail. He was forced to resign in 1870, a year before a slightly wider set of barricades toppled his master. He died in 1881, aged eighty-two.

[5] The garlands remained in place till 1958 when they were destroyed as part of a redecoration scheme. *Le Monde* protested but too late.

[6] Rodin later described him as a "paltry artist but a good craftsman, a businessman second to none and not a bad fellow really".

caryatids – *La Comédie* (with mask) and *La Danse* (with tambourine) – which still adorn the east chimney of the Grand Foyer, and the torch-bearing nymphs (if nymphs they are) who illuminate the Grande Escalier. (All are in "galvanoplastic", a sadly indestructible electrochemical substitute for bronze.) Erecting another famous Second Empire landmark, the Hôtel Pavia (now the Travellers' Club in the Champs Elysées), Rodin probably fashioned one of the two bronze ladies who still support the malachite panel in what was once the Marquise de Pavia's much-frequented bedroom. At the same time, he and his fellow wage-slaves were churning out statuettes, vases, epergnes, inkstands, candelabras, clock-cases and ornamental statuettes in endless profusion, a staggering variety of busts ranging from Vercingetorix the Gaul to George Sand, and from celebrated courtesans like Mlle de Varenne to the Emperor himself.[7] No allowance was ever made for any sickness of the body or soul, let alone the whimsical inspiration of the muse. When the outbreak of the Franco-Prussian War dried up business in Paris, Carrier-Belleuse and his troupe decamped to Brussels where he was immediately commissioned to redecorate the Bourse. Rodin had no choice but to follow, leaving Rose, their young child and his aged parents behind.[8] But in Brussels at long last he succeeded in emancipating himself;[9] and, once he was his own master, however precarious his independence, he would never be pressurised again. He was to the end of his life a model of financial rectitude; but, to the despair of his patrons and commissioning committees, contractual dates of completion remained to him verbal flourishes, legal curlicues, at best expressions of pious hope, of no practical significance whatever.

The Balzac memorial was a watershed. Partly through Zola's influence he received the prestigious commission of the Societé des Gens de Lettres to carve the long-planned monument to the great writer. He immersed himself in the colossal oeuvre with enthusiasm, travelling to the Touraine to follow in the novelist's footsteps. He had warned the society that to represent a literary titan would take much thought and some time. But how much was

[7] A variable distance.

[8] Unlike his friend Monet, Rodin was conventionally patriotic and volunteered for the army as soon as war had been declared. Perhaps it sheds some light on France's unexpected but massive defeat that he was rejected on the grounds of poor eyesight.

[9] His first major independent work to be publicly exhibited was the magnificent *The Age of Bronze* (originally *The Vanquished*) modelled during his stay in Brussels. Like almost all his creations, it unleashed a storm of protest, fuelled on this occasion by the idiotic accusation that it had been "cast from life".

The charge had to be dropped when Rodin's model, a Belgian soldier, threatened to travel to Paris, strip in front of the Salon jury and insist on their comparing his measurements with those of the statue; but Rodin thereafter never modelled a life-sized statue.

much and how some was some? After three years the society was becoming restive and appointed a working party to investigate and report on progress. Rodin received them with his customary courtesy and showed them a few maquettes. After the scandal of the Victor Hugo monument, which showed the great novelist naked, flanked by two scantily dressed muses ("just imagine Lord Tennyson sitting naked with a top hat in Hyde Park", Arnold Bennett reported back to London), the working party may have been relieved to see that Balzac was at least draped; but the shapeless dressing-gown (which the artist insisted on calling a Dominican habit) was in some ways even more offensive. After an acrimonious exchange of letters, the society expressed themselves gravely dissatisfied and threatened legal action. Rodin unwisely sent a preliminary model to the Salon to test public response, if any. His doubts were hopelessly naive. Only the Dreyfus affair unleashed such passions. Conservative newspapers fulminated. The Archbishop of Lyon suggested that the work had been inspired by Satan. The Comte de Laune, an elderly Senator, tabled a motion prohibiting the public exhibition of the shameful object. The commissioning society formally forbade casting the work in bronze. Threatening crowds hurled abuse at it. But there were two sides to the conflict. Students of the Sorbonne mounted guard when the police refused to do so. The municipality of Brussels begged the artist to let them erect the monument in their city. Eventually, in his polite way, Rodin sent everybody packing. The work was withdrawn from the Salon. The advance of the society was repaid with interest. Zola never spoke to Rodin again. But the principle of the artist's freedom from dates and deadlines had been upheld.[10]

Yet outside pressure was not always bad. In old age, as in childhood, there is often a journalistic deadline element in artistic creation, as there is in poetry, music, philosophy and scientific research. Many famous artists of the past complained bitterly that they were being bullied by their patrons. Michelangelo's tempestuous relations with Julius II della Rovere make a popular chapter in art history.[11] Much as David hero-worshipped Napoleon,

[10] For decades *Balzac* could be glimpsed in the garden of Rodin's villa in Meudon and many of those who saw it there were stunned. "Solitary and mysterious", Alphonse Daudet wrote, "it is a menhir with a human face. But it is also the essential Balzac, the Balzac of self-abandonment and the ailing heart, the dying visionary of the *Comédie Humaine*, who had at last emerged from literary servitude." Revived agitation to have the work erected in a public place was cut short by the outbreak of the First World War. The campaign was relaunched in the 1920s; but the solemn unveiling (by Maillol and Despiau) in the Boulevard Raspail was not performed till 28 July 1939. By then Rodin had been dead for twenty-two years and another war with Germany was only six weeks off.

[11] The anecdote of Michelangelo espying the Pope dressed as a cleaner trying to snatch a glimpse of the unfinished ceiling of the Sistine Chapel originates with Vasari but has been extensively embroidered since.

he resented being told that his battle-scenes should take no longer to paint than the battles took to fight.[12] To Hokusai the pressure from publishers for eye-catching novelties never let up. Such artists probably felt relieved when, late in life, they were no longer exposed to such tantrums and castigations; and the art of some may have improved as a result. But not of all. For who can doubt that some of the summits would never have been reached without pressure, even bullying. This was certainly true of Monet's last *Water Lilies* and of Clemenceau's role in their flowering.

Monet's vision began to trouble him during his last visit to Venice in 1906; and his final twenty years were a continuous struggle to overcome the effects of cataracts and to cope with the aftermath of operations. In the spring of 1925 he had reached the age of eighty-four and his cup of suffering overflowed. He wrote a carefully composed letter to the President of the Republic. In it he gave formal notice that, regrettably, he would not be able to fulfil his contract for the twelve large canvases of *Water Lilies* which he had promised five years earlier. He recounted that for the past few weeks he had toyed with the idea of destroying all he had so far achieved and starting again. Then

> I realised that I simply have to abandon the project. I am eighty-four and almost completely blind. Or worse. My eyes continually deceive me. When a singer loses his voice, he retires. When a painter has to undergo operations for cataract, he should renounce painting. That is what I should have done ... but have been incapable of doing! But now at last I have come to a decision. It is irrevocable.[13]

A copy of the letter was sent to Georges Clemenceau in Jard-sur-Mer in the Vendée, where, out of office and disgruntled, he was working on a slow-moving volume of memoirs.[14]

Monet and Clemenceau had been friends for more than fifty years.[15] Neither

[12] David's battles of Antiquity looked like closing scenes from a ballet. He also had a penchant for painting heroic but lost battles like Thermopylae, and who wanted those? Not, certainly, the First Consul and later Emperor.

[13] R. Friedenthal, editor, *Letters of the Great Artists* (London, 1963), p. 131.

[14] He had been acclaimed "Père de la Victoire" by a jubilant Chamber of Deputies in Paris on Armistice Day, 11 November 1918; but when, in 1920, at the peak of his wartime fame, he stood for the largely ceremonial office of President of the Republic, he was heavily defeated (not unlike Winston Churchill in 1945). His worthy but colourless opponent, Paul Deschanel, had a mental breakdown six months later, but Clemenceau never re-entered politics. He wrote books, including a touching and perceptive critique of Monet's last *Water Lilies* and a not very good novel.

[15] Clemenceau was born in Mouilleron-en-Parèds in the Vendée ten months after Monet.

could recall the exact circumstances of their first meeting, but it was at a time when Clemenceau was still a general practitioner in Montmartre,[16] and Monet was about to liberate himself and his friends from the dreary atelier of Monsieur Gleyre. Thereafter they remained close, despite their numerous, apocalyptic but highly enjoyable disagreements.[17] They had more in common than either perhaps realised. They were both staunch republicans who did not think that there was much scope for improving on the ideas, as distinct from the methods, of Robespierre and Saint-Just. They were fiercely anti-clerical (though not atheist), convinced egalitarians (as between all men but definitely not between men and women),[18] and firm believers in personal honour and the supremacy of the individual conscience.[19] They were also French patriots of the non-mystical variety, who, in the 1890s, found the idea of sacrificing the charmless but plainly innocent Captain Dreyfus for some nebulous concept of *La Patrie* intolerable.[20] And they were both, like Robespierre, provincial townsmen to whom Paris was worth a Revolution (but not a Mass) and to whom France's deeply conservative Catholic peasantry had no appeal.[21] In art they began as uncompromising rebels against *ces*

[16] When the two men met it was still a working-class village. An almost invisible plaque in the steep and narrow rue des Trois-Frères, winding its way between the Boulevard Roche-chouart and the top of Montmartre, now marks the place of Clemenceau's surgery. Although he later abandoned medicine for politics – he was mayor of Montmartre during the Siege of Paris and the Commune in 1871 – medicine was in his blood: his father, an uncle and at least one great-uncle were doctors.

[17] Both were gourmets and excellent cooks. The relative merits of the cheeses of Normandy and the Véndee were recurrent topics in their disputations.

[18] Clemenceau's affairs of the heart were no less celebrated than his affairs of honour; but they did not stop him from divorcing and hounding his much-provoked American-born wife after her first timid attempt at infidelity.

[19] In Clemenceau's case it made him one of France's most redoubtable duellists. Monet thought that duelling was a *bêtise* but he was scrupulously honest in his financial dealings.

[20] Zola published his famous and courageous open letter to the President of the Republic demanding Dreyfus's rehabilitation, *J'Accuse*, in Clemenceau's newspaper, *L'Aurore*. Monet, who had earlier quarrelled with Zola over the latter's unpleasant book, *L'Oeuvre*, wrote to the author at once expressing his support.

[21] The mistrust was fully reciprocated. During most of Monet's life the peasantry of Giverny (whose offspring today make a handsome living from the Monet industry) regarded the painter and his family with deep suspicion and at times outright and sullen hostility. They did not consider painting a proper occupation for a man, and his aloof manner did not help. Also, he dressed like a peasant in sabot and beret, but his finely pleated cambric shirt with cuffs projecting over his slender hands and his jabot instead of a tie were the accoutrements of a dandy. The children, especially the girls in their bright check dresses and vividly coloured parasols, did not fit into the category either of poor but decent countryfolk or of visiting and well-heeled urban gentry. Only Mme Hoschedé, later Mme Monet, always an impressive figure in sober print foulards, was respected. The villagers also claimed compensation for

*pompiers*,[22] Clemenceau in sympathies,[23] Monet in action, and ended baffled by the Cubists and the Fauves.[24] But they remained convinced that anything new in art was worth trying and almost anything new was worth supporting.

Both men had several spectacular ups and downs in their careers. In his sixties, after years of grinding poverty, Monet was beginning to be recognised as one of the masters, an ornament of French culture.[25] After his marriage to Alice Hoschedé he also became, in name as well as in fact, the undisputed head of a crazily but happily mixed-up household.[26] About the same time Clemenceau, though still recognised as a formidable duellist,

damage done to their crops by the family, and when Monet was painting his series of *Haystacks* took delight in demolishing them before he could finish the picture. Monet's idea slightly to divert the Ru and construct a lily pond met with outrage and stubborn resistance: the village women maintained that they would be deprived of the best water for washing their clothes, and several farmers testified that the strange new plants imported by the painter were already poisoning the river as drinking water for their cattle. Ironically, the anticlerical Monet's only local friend was the curé, a learned naturalist, the Abbé Toussaint.

Not surprisingly, apart from the house and garden which they loved, Monet and the Monet family disliked Giverny with the same intensity with which Mozart hated Salzburg, Kafka hated Prague and James Joyce hated Dublin.

[22] Monet's favourite expression in youth to describe the hidebound and mostly terrible painters of the Salon. There is still some uncertainty why Paris's gallant fire brigade should have had their designation hijacked to describe this unpleasant artistic species; but it may have been the frequent use of subjects culled from classical antiquity by Salon painters (as in David's *Rape of the Sabine Women*) and the resemblance of Greek and Roman helmets to the protective headgear of the firefighters.

[23] He was painted by Manet as a rising young politician and sculpted by Rodin late in life.

[24] But they admired the "Post-Impressionists" like Bonnard, Monet's last close friend, as well as Vuillard and Roussel.

[25] He was already acclaimed as such at the Exposition Universelle in Paris in 1900; but he never became a member of any official body.

[26] Alice Hoschedé's first husband was the rich and charming businessman and collector, Ernest Hoschedé. The family lived in some style, spending the summers at the Château de Rottenbourg in Normandy. Here Monet became a special guest: Ernest admired his paintings and Alice and the five (later six) children adored him as a person. In the summer of 1877 Hoschedé was summoned to Paris: his business had collapsed under mountainous debts. He could not face his family and, after toying with the idea of suicide, escaped to Brussels. The Hoschedés' every possession, including their paintings, had to be sold. Alice was left destitute except for a pittance from her family earmarked for the education of the children. She tried to make ends meet by dressmaking for friends. In 1878 the Monets and Hoschedés (now without Ernest) decided to spend the summer together in Vetheuil and stayed there for three years. It was cheaper to live in the country than in Paris and much of their meagre possessions, including one smart dress between the two ladies for going to Paris, could be shared. But in 1880, shortly after giving birth to her second son, Camille Monet died of tuberculosis. Dazed and distracted, Monet left the care of the children to Alice; and with extraordinary resources of strength and practical wisdom she began to rebuild a family from two shattered homes on the flimsiest of financial foundations. In 1889 Hoschedé's personal

polemicist, journalist and *tombeur des gouvernements*, was generally dismissed as a man of yesterday, an unfulfilled promise. His own first government had been notably ineffective and nobody expected him to be given a second chance.

Then, in his early seventies, Monet's slowly but inexorably encroaching blindness became punctuated with personal tragedies. In 1911 Alice Monet slipped away after a short illness, an irreplaceable loss. Two years later his son by his first wife Camille, Jean Monet, died from a lingering and exhausting neurological ailment. His passing devastated Jean's wife, Blanche, who was also Alice Monet's daughter from her first marriage.[27] When the war came, the German advance almost reached Giverny. For some months at night the cannonade could be clearly heard from the direction of Beauvais. Then came the seemingly endless stream of ambulance carts trundling along the Chemin du Roy, bringing the wounded from the front. Monet would not hear of moving or even of sending his collection of paintings away. Alone in the big house with Blanche, they waited anxiously for news about Michel Monet, Jean-Pierre and Albert Saleron,[28] Pierre and Jean Renoir, Michel Clemenceau and their friends. Like countless other households in war-torn Europe, they followed the movements of armies on a huge map pinned to the dining-room wall. After a time there was not much movement, only a seemingly unending list of the dead. Amidst the slaughter of the young, the passing of old friends – of Degas, Rodin, Debussy, Mirbeau and Aline Renoir – went almost unnoticed by the world at large but not by Monet.[29] Only his oldest and still his closest friend remained very much in evidence both on the world stage and in Giverny. After decades in opposition, Clemenceau at the age of seventy-three was called back to office and invested

honour was vindicated and Christmas and birthday cards were exchanged until he died not quite two years later. His funeral took place in Giverny. Monet was now undisputed head of the family; but a slight awkwardness remained. Alice was religious herself and had braved her Catholic family's disapproval when she had gone to live with a man she could not marry. Monet was irreligious but nevertheless (as he was getting on in years) an upholder of social conventions. When Alice's daughter, Suzanne Hoschedé, was due to marry a young American, Theodore Butler, Monet wanted to give her away in church. So in a quiet ceremony Alice and Monet were married four days before the sumptuous village wedding of Suzanne and Theodore. A few years later Michel Monet married Blanche Hoschedé; and when Suzanne died tragically after the birth of her daughter, Lily, Theodore married her sister, Marthe.

[27] A gifted painter herself, she remained Monet's faithful housekeeper and nurse until he died.

[28] The sons of Germaine Hoschedé and Albert Saleron.

[29] It was the loss of Aline Renoir which distressed Monet most. He loved her as did everyone who had met her.

with near-dictatorial powers.[30] In his country's darkest hour his brief was simple: to win the war. The one-time radical relished the task, but it did not stop him from assuming a second and more personal role as well. His oldest friend had become, in reality if not in name, his patient. The patient's will to work had to be rekindled. To achieve this, the patient had to be persuaded to have an operation. Clemenceau set about achieving his two objectives with the same steely resolve.

The Peace Conference of 1919 was still in progress when it was officially announced that Monsieur Monet had offered to paint and to donate to the state twelve large canvases of *Water Lilies* to be housed in a specially designed building in Paris. It was a project Monet had often contemplated but which, for many years now, had seemed like a distant dream.[31] But Clemenceau at his most tigerish was not an easy person to deflect; and by the spring of 1919 a third big studio with a huge skylight and a complicated system of swings and pulleys was rising in the grounds of Giverny (Plate 15). At first Monet was reluctant even to inspect it. He had often protested against "the atrocities" committed against the countryside by greed and selfishness. Now he was having this hideous structure erected himself. And for what purpose? His vision would surely not stand up to the vast project.

In the summer of 1922, in response to Clemenceau's unremitting bullying, he at last consulted Dr Charles Coutela, Clemenceau's choice from among leading Parisian ophthalmologists. Coutela confirmed the earlier diagnosis of bilateral, involutional cataracts.[32] He urged the patient to have an operation,[33]

---

[30] In 1917, after widespread mutinies in the French army, the President, Raymond Poincaré, was faced with a stark choice between entrusting the government to his friend, Caillaux, an amiable but weak and defeatist politician, or to Clemenceau, who had been his political opponent and whom he personally detested. To his own ill-concealed disgust but also to his credit, he chose Clemenceau.

[31] He had by then been painting his lily pond for many years and the paintings were well-known to his friends.

[32] Cataracts are opacities of the lens due to the fragmentation of the large protein molecules whose precise alignment and cross-linking accounts for the crystalline translucency of the organ. There is a long list of precipitating causes, ranging from maternal infection before birth to injury; but the cause of the commonest form, "senile" cataract, is unknown. The process is irreversible and incurable except symptomatically by surgery.

[33] The simplest operation, so-called "couching", was invented in India at least three thousand years ago and in remote rural districts is still practised there. A needle is passed into the eye at the border of the iris, and the bands (or "ligaments") which normally suspend the lens and keep it in position behind the pupil are severed with a quick flick of the wrist. The cataractous lens then falls to the bottom of the eye and a measure of blurred vision is restored. The main risk is infection, which can spread from one eye to the other and cause total blindness. Although experienced couchers kept their infection rate remarkably low, it was

but he also prescribed mydriatic eye-drops.[34] For a few weeks their effect seemed miraculous: "I have not seen so well for a long time ... the drops have permitted me to paint a few good things at long last." But, as expected, the effect was transient. In November Monet wrote to Clemenceau, spilling out his apprehensions. He recalled not only the unsuccessful cataract operation on Daumier, but also the more recent case of their dear friend, Mary Cassatt. She too ended up blind.[35] Better to cancel surgery.

Clemenceau was unmoved. He travelled to Giverny and raged. Monet had made a solemn promise to complete the *Water Lilies*, a gift to France. The promise must be kept. The only hope lay in having an operation. He must have it. Monet gave in; and in early December Coutela performed an extracapsular extraction of the right cataract under local anaesthesia.[36] Even though, as a special concession, the patient was allowed to continue to chain-smoke during convalescence,[37] the ten days of absolute postoperative immobilisation in the dark were a nightmare.[38] In some respects the subsequent few months were even more discouraging. The posterior lens capsule (which was normally left behind until the Second World War) became

probably this complication which destroyed Daumier's sight in 1877. It was one of the reasons why Monet so strenuously and for so long resisted the idea of surgery.

[34] Mydriatic drops dilate the pupil and are based on the action of belladonna (the parent substance of atropine) on the autonomic nerves supplying the eye. They are an ancient remedy, as well as an ancient aid to seduction. Large pupils may cause some blurring of near vision, but, as the *belle donne* of Venice discovered centuries ago, the beauty of lustrous black eyes could make up for the slight handicap of not seeing their conquests too clearly.

[35] See J. G. Ravin, "Mary Cassatt's Cataract", *Ophthalmic Forum*, 1 (1982), p. 71.

[36] This operation, a great advance on couching, was pioneered by Jacques Daviel, Louis XV's famous eye surgeon. Daviel claimed to have performed 434 operations with only fifty failures; but 150 years later the accepted failure rate was considerably higher. With the natural lens replaced by spectacles with a powerful glass lens, vision could be good, though with a much-enlarged image brought unnaturally close. (Modern cataract surgery is a child of high-technology medicine and consists essentially of replacing the removed cataractous lens with a suitable lens implant. The result is usually excellent.)

[37] With slightly fraudulent statistics (as are often generated by antismoking campaigners), one could easily "establish" a *positive* correlation between longevity, genius and smoking. Of the artists in the present study born after 1780, Rodin, Monet and Kandinski virtually chain-smoked cheap *Caporals* all through their long lives. Corot, Turner and Ingres were heavy cigar smokers. Bonnard was a heavy cigarette smoker until his last years. Maillol in his poverty-stricken youth would rather go without bread than without a smoke. Matisse smoked twenty to thirty cigarettes a day until he died. Braque was lost without his famous pipe and Nolde was a heavy smoker till he was sixty. To say, as did an eminent Monet scholar recently, that smoking grievously contributed to the artist's final illness (at eighty-six after a lifetime of robust health and prodigious creativity) is not unlike praising Hitler for being a rabid anti-smoker.

[38] This was regarded as essential at the time.

opaque; and the patient's vision not only rapidly deteriorated again but also became disturbed by intrusive floaters. "Now I cannot see anything with my right eye, with or without glasses", Monet wrote to Coutela. "I am finished. I regret having had this fatal operation." But the complication was not unexpected. It could be put right by a second operation. "Never!", Monet wrote to Clemenceau. Clemenceau came and threatened to stay in Giverny until Monet changed his mind. Blanche protested. Georges was a dear friend but a day or two of him as resident guest was enough. After a few days Monet once again acquiesced, provided the operation could be performed at home. Now it was Coutela's turn to be bullied by Clemenceau. He too surrendered with surprisingly good grace.[39]

Not for the first or last time, doctor and patient differed in assessing the result of the second operation. In the summer of 1921 Coutela wrote to Clemenceau that "Monsieur Monet's near vision can be considered nearly perfect after correction ... For distant vision the result is slightly less extraordinary. He has a 3/10 or 4/10 vision which is not bad but will require a little bit of retraining. In brief, I am satisfied." About the same time Monet wrote to the surgeon: "I am absolutely desolate. I feel that every time I try to take a step I will fall. For near and far everything is deformed and often doubled. It is intolerable. Your treatment has been a disaster."[40] A few months later his visual balance improved but his colour sense remained a cause of torment. "I am destroying all that I have done", he wrote to Clemenceau in the summer of 1923. "I hide my despair as much as possible but life is hell."

In 1922 a friend and fellow artist, André Barbier, saw a newspaper advertisement of the Zeiss Optical Company for a new kind of a lens which offered a wider visual field and better correction than the standard cataract lenses. The Zeiss representative in Paris directed him to a young research ophthalmologist, Dr Jacques Mawas.[41] Barbier consulted Mawas without mentioning

[39] Several detailed accounts of Monet's cataracts exist in the medical literature, notably P. G. Moreau, "La cataracte de Claude Monet", in *Ophthalmologie des origines à nos jours*, 3 (1981), p. 141; J. G. Ravin, "Monet's Cataracts", *Journal of the American Medical Association*, 254 (1985), p. 3. Monet's letters to Coutela have also been deposited with the French Ophthalmological Society. The translated quotations are by kind permission of the President and Council.

[40] Coutela never took offence. Perhaps, being a French rather than a British or American surgeon, he was used to having long and frank exchanges with his patients about the merits of his ministrations.

[41] Recounted by J.-P. Hoschedé, *Claude Monet, ce mal-connu* (Geneva, 1960), p. 83. Much to his credit, Mawas could never be persuaded to publish details of his treatment of Monet; but he occasionally gave informal and delightful talks about his illustrious patient. He died in 1958, aged sixty-eight, in Paris, mourned by his patients and indeed by all who knew him.

the patient's name or telling Monet; and Mawas, wonderfully confident at twenty-eight, was in no doubt that he could help. When he heard that the patient was a well-known artist, he offered his services free. "I would do it free for any artist", he assured Barbier; but in fact he had guessed the patient's identity and there was nobody for whom he had greater admiration. (This contrasted with his vociferous lack of admiration for Dr Coutela and most other established figures in his profession, the equivalents, he would later explain to Monet, of the artistic *pompiers* of Monet's youth.) After a good deal of toing and froing to square his visit with medical etiquette – he would just happen to drop in at Giverny, a distant relative of Alice Monet, and, surprise, surprise, take an interest in his host's visual troubles – he was invited to stay for lunch. Clemenceau watched him like a hawk, but Monet at once took to the irreverent young man and was charming. "I see blue but not red and yellow", he explained, "and this is terrible. I know that these colours exist and that they are on my palette; and I can even recall in my mind what sort of a colour they used to give me." Mawas understood perfectly: it was a simple matter of correction which might take a few weeks, perhaps a month or so. And, putting on an American accent: "No problem!" (Both he and Monet – though not Clemenceau – believed that the Americans were the last word in technical advances: anything invented by them simply had to work.) He provided Monet with his first pair of tinted lenses which, for a time and perhaps by their sheer novelty, lifted the artist from his trough of depression. Over the next few years Mawas became a regular and frequent visitor, experimenting with a succession of new lenses (sometimes going back to lenses he had already tried but which had been rejected). Whatever his optical skills, he was a brilliant psychologist. His difficult patient was actually prepared to listen to him. Eventually the patient came to rely mostly on the vision in his right eye while wearing glasses to correct the left. (The left lens in his last pair of glasses was in fact an occluder.) [42] It was too good to last.

Before he wrote his final letter to the President of the Republic, Monet wrote to his young oculist: "You tried your best and I am deeply grateful; but it is hopeless. I have just burnt six canvases in the garden with the dead leaves of the autumn. I am gripped by anxiety as soon as I open the studio door. I know I am finished. A blind man cannot paint. *Fini.*" [43] Clemenceau got the copy of Monet's letter to the President four days later. He could be tender and solicitous when he wanted to be, but he could still be roused to terrifying fury. "I have received a shocking letter from Monet", he wrote to

[42] Preserved in the Musée Marmottan in Paris.
[43] Quoted by J. G. Ravin, "Monet's Cataracts".

Blanche, "and I will not stand for it. By the same post he will get my answer. You may find it a little harsh; but I absolutely mean every word of it. If he does not alter his decision and finish the *Water Lilies*, he is a coward and a cheat and I shall never speak to him again." [44] It was pure schoolboy bullying, mild compared to the abuse Monet had suffered with lofty equanimity from critics as a young man. But this one came from his oldest friend, who clearly meant what he said. So Monet meekly reversed his irreversible decision and set to work again. And after six months the miracle of the last *Water Lilies* had been accomplished.[45]

What worked for some artists did not work for others. In many ways the pressure of the fleeting moment did impress itself on the style, the technique and the content of the art of old age; and all of these need to be examined. But the effect on sheer inspiration was too unpredictable to be a credible explanation for the astonishing late-in-life achievement of the masters.

[44] All their lives they remained on formal terms of address. See Hoschedé, *Claude Monet*, p. 121.

[45] Once accomplished, Clemenceau sensed that his friend was reluctant to part with the paintings. It was also obvious that the artist was nearing the end. Clemenceau did not press the matter and the *Water Lilies* were not installed in the Orangerie in Paris till after their creator's death.

*Le Tigre* made one more characteristic appearance in Monet's life or rather death. On 5 December 1926, he was one of the pall-bearers at Monet's funeral in Giverny. (The others were Bonnard, Roussel and Vuillard.) As the coffin was about to be draped in the customary black cloth, he rasped: "Pas de noir pour Monet". He produced some gaudily coloured material and covered the coffin with it. Nobody dared to contradict him and the coffin was duly bedecked with an exuberance of yellow and purple chrysanthemums.

# 16

# *Still I'm Learning*

Not quite an external circumstance but a side-effect of a long life is the opportunity to learn and experience more than those who die young. "Ancora imparo", "Still I'm learning" was the aged Michelangelo's favourite maxim; and who can doubt that he lived by his splendid precept till the day of his death. Neither would one want to question the dying Renoir's whispered confidence to his nurse, Nanette: "I have just discovered something interesting"; nor smile over Corot's promise to his friend Robaut on his death-bed that in future he would try to paint better skies;[1] nor dismiss David's claim in his last letter to his son that he was beginning to understand Rubens.[2] The never-ending process of learning may be no more than a fragment of the explanation of the late flowering of genius, but it is not a fragment to be ignored.

Of course learning in Michelangelo's or in Corot's sense had little to do with erudition. A few great artists were erudite; and some, like Poussin, allowed their erudition to percolate into and enrich their art. But others, like Poussin's fellow expatriate and drinking companion in Rome, Claude, did just as well without the enrichment. Technically, painting and sculpture are neither more nor less difficult than cooking or brain surgery: either of these skills, without the frills and the chat, could be acquired by a group of industrious apprentices in a crash course of a few months. At the end of it the level of proficiency in the class would vary; but the variations would reflect differences in inborn aptitude; and further vocational training would not significantly affect the results. Turner was not so dismal a figure painter as is sometimes suggested;[3] but nothing could have transformed him into

---

[1] His reputed last words on his death-bed, "I hope there is painting in heaven", are almost too good to be true; but (except for the un-Corot-like confidence in his destination) not entirely uncharacteristic.

[2] In David's youth, among his friends, Rubens stood for everything that high-minded classicists despised. His "grossness and vulgarity" were often contrasted with the "sublime purity" of Poussin.

[3] John Ruskin, second to none in his admiration of Turner's landscapes, spoke almost with pity about his "roly-poly bag of potatoes of people"; and Kenneth Clark thought that they looked like "current buns, sausages and poached eggs". But, when he set out to draw figures,

another Ingres. Ingres in turn was as good a draughtsman at twenty as he was ever going to be – that is brilliant – but no amount of further learning could have turned him into a more than passable history painter. But this was clearly not what Michelangelo and other artists meant by *imparo*. Learning in Michelangelo's sense, the gathering of new experiences, new impressions and, most important, new insights into the long familiar, is continuous; and if it is in childhood that fresh material is absorbed most quickly, it may be in old age that it is assimilated most creatively.

But absorption and assimilation suggest a passive process, a kind of soaking up of new information. In fact, the learning of old artists was more often a highly targeted, even obsessive, search for what might prove useful to them in their craft. The disinclination of old people to explore unfamiliar territory, much repeated in textbooks of geriatrics, must at least be qualified. It is true that no artist in his or her sixties, seventies or eighties sought new experiences for the sake of novelty, thrill or self-knowledge; but their search for new and better ways of expressing themselves remained intense. Picasso is said to have deflated a fulsome interviewer who congratulated him on his never-ceasing "Promethean search" for new techniques: "I don't search. I find." It was a clever put-down but in artistic terms the two, the seeking and the finding, are the same. Only the circumstances vary.

New techniques or genres were sometimes forced on old artists by circumstances beyond their control. Illness or general infirmity was inevitably the commonest. Physical weakness may have been one reason why in his sixties Donatello turned from marble and bronze to wood carving. A crippling allergy impelled Chardin, the least adventurous of artists, to try his hand at pastels for the first time in his late sixties. Neither treated the new medium as *Ersatz*. One can think of no contemporary work, not even his own *St John the Baptist* in the Frari in Venice, to compare with Donatello's transcendent masterpiece of the *Penitent Magdelen*. The figure has been described as the first exploration in European art of extreme ugliness; and at a first glance the lady is certainly ugly. But she is also beautiful. The beauty is not, of course, of the glossy magazine variety (though one need not look at the ravaged features for long to recognise the remains of great sexual allure); but her tragic spiritual beauty is overwhelming.[4] And Chardin in old age became

Turner could be as good as any figure artist: see his brilliant sketch of the nude Sara Danby or occasional drawings of his fellow travellers. Like his idol, Claude, he was probably not very interested in people on canvas or perhaps even off it.

[4] Until the 1970s the two wooden statues were widely regarded as Donatello's last works and they are certainly the creations of his old age; but the cleaning of the *St John* in Venice revealed the date of 1438 and the *Magdalen* is unlikely to be much later. The rich polychromy

France's second greatest pastellist.[5] A hundred years later Degas, too, took up pastels as his eyesight continued to deteriorate; and when he realised that even pastels (or a bizarre combination of pastels and photography) were beyond him, he started modelling. It was to him "the art of the blind", and perhaps he never took it too seriously. When his friends heard about the venture, they were sceptical. They knew and on the whole admired him as a very painterly painter. He was also, like Chardin, conservative, even reactionary in his habits as well as in his politics. But Renoir, already disabled himself, memorably described his first encounter with a Degas figurine.[6] "I was wheeled into this room full of paintings to see how my own pictures had been hung. And all I could see was a little dancer by Degas, ludicrously dolled up with tulle and ribbons, tucked away in a corner, yet shining forth like a fragment of the Parthenon."[7] Considering that it is usually impossible in a mixed exhibition to distract an exhibiting artist's attention from his own works, this was a rare compliment. And Renoir continued to maintain, rightly perhaps, that it was his exasperating friend rather than Rodin who was the greatest French sculptor since Houdon.

As Degas turned to modelling, Rodin in his seventies moved in the opposite direction and embarked on his "one-minute drawings". Drawing had been his introduction to art: as a dim-witted schoolboy, a "big head with a carrot-coloured mop of hair swaying perilously on his spindly body",[8] it was the only subject at which he was any good. But once he had discovered clay – "it was like ascending to heaven" – he had for many years no use for anything else.[9] Instead of sketching, he would knead lumps of clay into hundreds of eloquent shapes as he watched naked models, sometimes as many as ten or twelve, milling around his

---

of the latter was not discovered until the statue's restoration after the disastrous flooding of the Arno in 1960.

The writer is not alone in this somewhat breathless response. Charles VIII of France, Florence's first modern foreign conqueror, offered the city an enormous sum for the statue, the only work of art, apart from Giotto's fortunately immovable bell-tower, which he coveted.

[5] See above, Chapter 4, pp. 54–57.

[6] It is sometimes said that Degas's wax figurines were never exhibited or written about in his lifetime. This is not entirely true. They were well known to his circle of friends and a few made fleeting appearances in public. But the great majority were discovered in a parlous state in the artist's studio after his death. They were then cast into bronze (destroying much of their charm) and soon sold to museums and collectors for exorbitant sums.

[7] J. Renoir, *Renoir, My Father*, translated by R. and D. Weaver (London, 1958), p. 102.

[8] Judith Cladel's flight of fancy in *Rodin: l'oeuvre et l'homme* (Brussels, 1913), p. 8.

[9] Quoted by F. V. Grunfeld, *Rodin* (London, 1987), p. 342.

studio.[10] But at seventy he could no longer handle the material with the same ease; or perhaps he discovered – or rediscovered – the magic of the drawn line. Whatever the reason, he would now sit for hours gazing at his models of all ages as they undressed, moved about, embraced, sat down, stretched, yawned, crouched, collapsed with fatigue, picked themselves up, danced and kissed; and jotted it down on sheets of paper. He had no need to take his eyes off the moving figures; his pencil followed the commands of his subcortical brain unerringly. His knowledge of the living female anatomy was total. With a tiny inflexion of a straight line but with the utmost precision he would indicate the last half-inch of the *Tibilais Anterior* muscle tensed with effort. With a minute but perfectly placed dip, marking the insertion of the *Supraspinatus*, he would transform an uninteresting curve into the outline of a shoulder. Each drawing consisted of barely a dozen lines but each captured "une allure, une constellation, ou une lassitude". "Sometimes", he confided in Jean-Marie Charpentier, "I like them more than I do my sculptures." [11] And sometimes one almost does.

From drawings to cut-outs was but a step, but (to paraphrase Cézanne about Monet's eyes) what a step! In 1942 the seventy-three-year-old Matisse was recovering in a hospital bed in Lyon from a routine abdominal operation which nearly killed him.[12] Frustrated by the enforced idleness, he asked his nurse, the future Soeur Jacques-Marie, to paint sheets of paper with bright primary colours. Matisse in a wheedling mode was hard to resist, and, though artistic eccentricities were even less encouraged in hospital wards in the 1940s than they are today, his wish was granted. Then he took a large pair of scissors to the painted sheets and began to carve his first "sculptures in pure colour". Probably even he did not realise that the venture would lead to such works as *Mimosa, Snake* and the last *Blue Nude*, and transform the world's perception of primary colours; his medical and nursing attendants certainly did not. Dr Maurice Jacquemart, who cherished an earlier *Odalisque* in oils given to him by the patient, ruefully recalled many years later that, presented with a "sheaf of wrapping paper ornamented with random

[10] P. Gsell, *Auguste Rodin par lui-meme.* (Paris, 1946), p. 89. He also rolled and kneaded pellets of bread at table and modelled them into human shapes when he had gobbled up his food and was bored with the conversation – which was often.

[11] Quoted by G. Lecomte, *Rodin, tel que je l'ai vu* (Paris, 1958), p. 109.

[12] The illness began with recurrent attacks of sub-acute intestinal obstruction (the cause of which was never established but may have been a small internal hernia). After the operation Matisse developed a deep-vein thrombosis in the leg and this led to a pulmonary embolus. He was fortunate that one of the pioneers of vascular surgery, René Leriche, was on the staff of the hospital. It is not clear from various memoirs what operation Leriche performed but it seems to have saved Matisse's life.

coloured shapes", he lost no time in consigning the package to the hospital incinerator.

Not illness but political pressure, more ruthless than anything experienced by European artists before the twentieth century, forced Nolde in his "Bunker" in Seebüll to start experimenting with a new technique in his late seventies. He withdrew to the house with his ailing wife, Ada, after being declared "degenerate" by Hitler and being formally prohibited from painting. Rising from the bleak North German Plain the building is, even today, a somewhat forbidding structure,[13] but during the war years its commanding view of the countryside and of approaching unwelcome visitors endowed it with an unplanned amenity. It might be thought that, during the years of Stalingrad, the Allied landings in France and the destruction of German cities from the air, the Hamburg police would have had more pressing business to transact than to check on the activities of a discredited old man living alone with his sick wife; but an order from the Reichspropagandaminister endorsed by the Reichsführer SS could not be ignored. At irregular intervals a posse of police descended on the house to check that the delinquent Nolde, erstwhile painter, was in fact refraining from any such noxious activity. It might also be thought that, despite such commendable vigilance, painting was not a difficult activity to disguise. But the smell of turpentine is powerful and lingering;[14] and policemen, who did not hesitate to examine the suspect's fingernails for encrusted pigment, would never have missed the presence of a freshly painted canvas. If he wanted to paint – and work was to him, as to most painters, more addictive than any drug – he had to use scraps of paper or whatever was available and could be hidden, and odourless crayons and water-colours which could be smuggled into the house.[15] Yet his *Ungemalte Bilder* were not just the doodles of a compulsive personality. With the obstinacy of his Friesian peasant forebears he created a new technique – or non-technique. "In der Beschränkung zeigt sich erst der Meister" – "It is in constraint that mastery reveals itself" – Goethe said; and, though only a mediocre artist himself, he understood and loved art.[16]

If new explorations were often forced on old artists by ill-health or political tyranny, they were not the only reasons. Many embarked on experiments

[13] He designed it himself in the, for him, prosperous 1920s.

[14] Acrylics were not available in wartime Europe.

[15] Let at least one of the smugglers be remembered by name. He was Alois Wegeber who delivered coal to Seebüll. He died in 1960, aged seventy-two.

[16] "I have lived among painters and have learnt to look at objects with the eye of an artist", he wrote. He founded two art periodicals, and for several years, as minister in Weimar, ran an annual art competition. Some of his art criticism is inspired.

impelled by no more than artistic curiosity – or because a new technique or a new genre promised better to express new experiences. Goya, in his late sixties, discovered the extraordinary expressive potential of still lives and painted a superb series of them;[17] and he started to experiment with lithography at eighty. Even more astonishing perhaps was the adoption of clay modelling by the crippled Renoir, or rather the adoption of "dictating" sculpture to a skilful amaneuensis.[18]

Of course such late-in-life experiments were not always successful. Corot in his sixties became fascinated with a method of engraving on photographic ground-glass plates, known as *cliché-verre*, and spent much time perfecting the technique. It never caught on and he never became a notable engraver. Braque, a naturally conservative artist who recoiled from Picasso's ceaseless experimentation, was persuaded at seventy-eight by the flamboyant lapidary, Baron Heger de Loewenfeld, to collaborate in the design of jewellery. It was to be the ultimate metamorphosis of Braque's two-dimensional shapes into three-dimensional objects, the realisation perhaps of his ambition to excel (like the terrible Pablo) as a sculptor as well as a painter. He was by then one of his country's cultural totems; and the financial and critical success of the venture was a foregone conclusion. The exhibition of "the first hundred pieces" (also the last) in the Pavillon Marsan was visited by 50,000 people. The state, in the munificent incarnation of De Gaulle's minister of culture, André Malraux, purchased eleven pieces; and examples which come up at auction from time to time still fetch high prices. But the ruby birds and diamond clouds are pure kitsch.

The omnivoraciousness of youth was also gone. No master in his eighth or ninth decade would travel long distances and spend days immured in galleries, churches and museums, trying to winkle out the secrets of his predecessors. Indeed, many resolutely shut themselves off from clamorous but to them irrelevant influences. Turner in his seventies painted a lustrous water-colour of the Accademia in Venice; but there is no record that he ever set foot inside the gallery:[19] nor, so far as is known, did he look at the Tintorettos in San Rocco's or visit the church of the Frari to gaze at Titian's *Assumption*.[20] And Kandinski politely but firmly declined an invitation to the opening of the Poussin exhibition of 1938: "I have been trying to unlearn what Poussin has taught me for the past thirty years."

Nor were the aged masters necessarily receptive to the latest movements

---

[17] See below, Chapter 21, pp. 293–94.

[18] See above, Chapter 7, p. 120.

[19] It had been opened as a public art gallery by the Austrians in 1815.

[20] Nor was Turner's hero, Lord Byron, much of a gallery-goer.

– or crazes – in art. Renoir admitted to being bewildered by the young Matisse's unabashed use of black. "I don't understand", he would say in genuine puzzlement, "why you use a colour that does not exist in nature. It simply makes a hole in the canvas." But he had the grace to add: "And yet it does not make a hole in your pictures. So, I suppose, you must be a good painter after all." [21] A generation later it was Matisse's turn to confess himself *effrayé* by the catalogues of Abstract-Expressionist exhibitions sent to him by his art-dealer son, Pierre, from New York. "I don't know what they are trying to say," he wrote back, "and I am not sure if I want to know." [22]

But even such apparent lack of interest was not a terminal curling up and turning to the wall. Time and effort are precious commodities to the old: they must not be frittered away on frivolities. But no effort was too great when the old artists felt that they were in pursuit of experience which might be genuinely useful. Strictly confined to bed by his doctors during his last illness, David gave his nurses the slip. Contrary to the rhetoric he had practised on the soap-box and in the Convention – "Let the citizens see the masterpieces of the past: the masterpieces belong to them!" – he had always hated museums.[23] When, before the Revolution, he was given rooms in the Louvre, he approached them by a back staircase to avoid confronting the royal collection. And when, many years later, news was brought to him that the second Treaty of Paris would oblige France to return its looted art treasures to their rightful – or at least previous – owners, his only comment was "the sooner the better". But now, fighting his terminal illness, he laboriously made his way to the Musée des Beaux-Arts, knowing that the exertion might precipitate his final collapse, as indeed it probably did. "But", he wrote to his son, "I had to refresh my memory … of the way Rubens used his reds. What an artist!" [24] He had obviously forgotten – or wanted to forget – that the Flemish master had for many years been the target of his vitriolic execration. And almost completely blind, with no realistic hope of ever regaining his sight, Degas continued to haunt the salerooms to buy old and contemporary prints. "It is not greed", he explained to friends, "but an investment. They set me off. I shall need them when I start painting again." [25]

---

[21] Recounted by Françoise Gilot in *Matisse and Picasso: A Friendship in Art*, translated by N. A. Talese (London, 1990), p. 182.

[22] H. Matisse, quoted in J. Flam, *Matisse* (New York, 1988), p. 342.

[23] E. J. Delécluse, *Louis David: son école et son temps* (Paris, 1955), p. 78.

[24] M. Barbel, *David à Bruxelles* (Brussels, 1937), p. 87. It was only by chance that Rubens' monumental series of canvases commemorating the betrothal and marriage of Henri IV and Marie de' Medici survived David's spell as artistic dictator during the Revolution.

[25] M. Guérin, editor, *Lettres de Degas* (Paris 1945), p. 348.

Sometimes it was only in old age that formerly struggling artists had the means, the leisure or the self-confidence to fulfil a life-long ambition and venture off their own beaten track. It was rarely a popular decision with their admirers: indeed, the more ardent had been the admirers' admiration for an artist's earlier work (and for their own perspicacity in spotting his genius ahead of the multitude), the more the decision was received with misgivings. Occasionally new departures provoked a full-dress art-political scandal.

When, in his late sixties, Rodin decided to help save France's architectural heritage, he was probably unaware that he was blundering into a minefield.[26] Yet anybody less naive could have warned him. Unlike his friend, Monet, he did not court controversy: he was, by and large, respectful of authority, hated blasphemy and disliked coarse language. But caution and circumspection were not among his principal virtues. Academics do not welcome enthusiastic amateurs barging in on their disputes even when their field of expertise is as dead as a lunar landscape. But few topics were so poisonously alive in the France of the 1890s as the restoration of its historic buildings. By the time Rodin entered the fray, serried ranks of born-again saints were lining the great portals of Reims, newly-hatched gargoyles were sprouting from every drain-pipe in Paris's Notre-Dame, re-erected battlements battled with the elements in Amiens, and formerly sedate buttresses flew in Orléans. Rodin hated everything spurious, and he was convinced that the insights vouchsafed a practising artist like himself would be received with tears of gratitude by well-intentioned but sadly misguided "antiquaries".

The uproar over his book, *The Cathedrals of France*, was not unworthy of the wrath generated thirty years earlier by the Balzac memorial.[27] From the text Professor Rouvière of Lille had no difficulty in picking out a few howlers. "The terrible replacements of the windows in Reims which hurt my eye" (Rodin) turned out to be unretouched fourteenth century; and "the gloriously inspired medieval workmanship suffused with the faith of archangels" (Rodin) in Laon reflected credit on Mme Frère, the wife of a local dentist. Rodin's literary style gave even more offence, not because of his squirmingly purple prose – he was, like Turner, a plain and often incoherent speaker but a Baroque writer – but because it showed that "even at his advanced age the

[26] But he had already provoked controversy by saving part of the façade of the Château d'Issy threatened with demolition by developers. He paid an exorbitant sum to have it transported to Meudon and re-erected in the garden.

An excellent account of the controversy over the cathedrals is given in F. V. Grunfeld, *Rodin* (London, 1987).

[27] A. Rodin, *Les cathédrales de France* (Paris, 1914).

author was susceptible to quite unworthy urges".[28] "To understand those lines so tenderly modelled, traced and caressed, one has to be lucky enough to be in love", he had written about a carving which Jean-Paul Viarège, a leading expert in medieval restorations and a Commander, no less, of the Legion of Honour, considered a late Romanesque ornament of no art-historical significance whatever. Even more shockingly, in a little church in Beaugency,[29] Rodin had

> espied a young girl, a little lily of a French valley, sitting in a pew in a new gown ... The lines of her adolescent body still innocent of passion. What modesty! What grace! She could have recognised her own portrait among the saints in the portal ... for she was the embodiment of our style, our art, our native land ...[30]

("And clearly as unlike our dear Duchesse as can be", the malicious Mme Loubet is said to have commented.)[31] The art critic of *Le Matin* objected to the passage: "There is in this alcove a luminous mist in which light slumbers evenly as though in a little valley ... but only people who have visited the

[28] The phrase of an anonymous reviewer, quoted in Grunfeld, *Rodin*, p. 356.

[29] Much of the book, ostensibly about cathedrals, is about small and insignificant country churches. He often visited them at the crack of dawn and sometimes spent hours inside them "inhaling their atmosphere". He had no formal religion but a deep reverence for a "Being Who Created Sculpture".

[30] Grunfeld, *Rodin*, p. 128,

[31] The Duchesse de Choiseul was at the time Rodin's *grande amour* (as distinct from his innumerable *cinque-à-septs*. She was an American heiress, one of five daughters of the socially prominent New York lawyer Charles Coudert, and had married a penniless but titled fortune hunter, the Marquis de Choiseul (later self-promoted to Duc). Approaching forty and childless, she set her heart on becoming the muse and lover of France's greatest artist. Rodin's friends and later biographers are so unanimous in describing her as vulgar, grasping, bossy, snobbish, uncultured, vain, stupid, domineering and near-alcoholic that she must have had a great deal going for her. No woman without a deep intuitive understanding of men could have wormed her way into the heart of an artist who had once been the lover of Camille Claudel and Gwen John. (The latter, alas, was more one of his *cinque-à-septs*: he liked her and she adored him, but he never appreciated her as the great artist she was.) For about seven years – while he was writing his book on the cathedrals – the Duchesse became the centre of his existence. Even her enemies conceded that she had wit, intelligence and a certain raucous gaiety. She also brought his chaotic finances under control, even if the control was hers rather than his. She championed his work among her rich American friends and had the Capitol illuminated in his honour on their visit to Rome. (The Duc was more than happy to bask in her reflected glory.) Above all, she had the supreme gift of making Rodin feel, as he advanced through his sixties and early seventies, not just a giant among men but also a wonderfully youthful giant. (One only has to glance at Rodin's portrait bust of her to get an inkling of what he saw in her.) Their rupture was largely engineered by some of Rodin's admiring but entirely self-appointed well-wishers, who hailed it as a triumph. Rodin's personal life was downhill all the way after that.

church at dawn and have breathed the scented air can appreciate its beauty." "This", the expert commented acidly, "was art criticism by inhalation." And why ever not?

Perhaps surprisingly, most opprobrium clung to the illustrations. The "so-called architectural draughtsman" had clearly disdained the use of a ruler and a compass and had failed to grasp the elementary rules of projection and elevation. Urging the prohibition of the purchase of the book by any publicly funded library, Professor Lampou stated that "the so-called architectural sketches" – some of the loveliest ever to grace a printed book – "would bring a blush to the face of the most mediocre student in any of our municipal schools of design". This attack particularly perplexed Rodin. He had never, he maintained, intended to write a textbook for students. "Why, I am still a student myself!" And indeed, like the aged Michelangelo, he too was still learning.

"Learning" in old age did not always mean a dramatic new departure, the adoption of a new technique or interest in a new genre. In some cases old artists simply and unobtrusively continued to develop in new directions in response to the changing world around them. Hals never ceased to advance and deepen his understanding of the human physiognomy;[32] but he never changed his basic approach. It is Claude, "the most witless of artists" – certainly one of the most unsophisticated and unpretentious – who still provides the best example of such a late learning process.[33]

Following the fireworks of the Counter-Reformation and its side-effect, an economic boom, Rome's fortunes suddenly began to decline – and decline precipitously – after the religious settlement of 1648.[34] It did not at first

[32] See above, Chapter 3, pp. 37–38.

[33] The epithet is Roger Fry's and in old age he repented. What needled Fry was Claude's assertion that the jottings in the Liber veritatis, now one of the treasures of the British Museum, were simply safeguards against fakers and plagiarists. "What was he trying to safeguard?", Fry asked. "His trees, skies, coves and rocks were there for everybody to see. Even his mannerisms were easy to copy." Why, then, did others not paint Claudes? Claude himself attributed it – or so he said – simply to his rivals' lack of patience and application.

The popular myth of the genius-simpleton is an attractive one but a myth it is. A simpleton could never have painted Claude's late landscapes any more than a simpleton could ever have composed Schubert's String Quintet in C major.

[34] This was probably the most sudden, unexpected and least understood watershed in European history until the similarly sudden and unexpected collapse of Communism in the 1980s. For over a hundred years the torches and stakes of warring Christianity had illuminated and nearly consumed Europe. To generations they seemed inextinguishable. Tens of thousands of heretics and witches were judicially tortured and burnt. Then, quite suddenly, as the Thirty Years War drew to a close – it officially ended in 1648 with the Treaty of Westphalia – the

bring any significant change in the demand for Claudes. Many of his commissions came from abroad or from foreigners resident in the city;[35] and
their expectations probably chimed in with his personal taste. What his
northern patrons wanted were landscapes and seascapes, mementos of the
malarial beauty of the Roman Campagna or the fairy-tale prospect of a
southern port. They admired his skies, his trees, his classical ruins, the
magically receding masts and sails of his ships, his sense of space and
distance, the lustre of his water and the transparency of his air. They accepted
the convention of a story line indicated by diminutive figures dotted around;
but whether their comings and goings represented the departure of a saint
or the revels of a pagan queen, and whether these activities were a matter
for rejoicing or lamentation, exercised them not at all. As a northerner
himself, Claude probably accepted these priorities for most of his life. But
his more discerning local patrons had always wanted more. Of course they
admired his renderings of nature – who would not? – but they also wanted
the scenes to commemorate recognisable events. Indeed, they wanted the
events and the landscape to resonate in some subtle way. Perhaps it was
their gentle prodding as much as his natural inclination which was to propel
Claude to his personal summit.[36] And beside the prodding, there was his
gradual immersion in the nostalgic golden-age world of Virgil.

flames turned into wisps of smoke. With the fires disappeared the sublime Augustinian vision
of *Civitas Dei*, the kingdom of indivisible and triumphant Christianity. (It had been the last
time in history when millions of ordinary people seriously believed that not only Christianity
but also their particular brand and no other would soon be the faith of all mankind.) For no
obvious reason the Second Age of Martyrs was over. Few seemed to mind. The good old
mixture of a little virtue and a little vice – what came naturally to most men and women –
once again seemed not only natural but also desirable. "Cuius regio, eius religio", that faith
was to be a matter for local rulers, whether the Holy Roman Emperor or a little princeling
on the periphery of the Continent, to settle for their subjects, probably the most cynical
compact of the "haves" in European history, was greeted not with outrage but with almost
universal relief. It left Europe more or less fairly divided between Protestants and Catholics.
In Protestant lands the secular rulers had long held sway over their local churches. Now
Catholic rulers too reasserted their powers. It was the end of Rome and of the papacy as the
centre of Catholic Christianity. It also spelt the sudden end of the city's prosperity.

[35] Philip IV of Spain was one of his first patrons. He painted many of his loveliest middle-
period canvases for the saintly (and rich) Sieur de Bourlemont, France's long-time ambassador
in Rome. Other French buyers were Philippe de Béthune, the Comte de Selles, the Duc de
Bouillon, the Comte de Brienne and the Marquis de Fontenay-Mareuil. Many other commissions came from Antwerp, Vienna and England.

[36] Unlike his almost exact contemporary and near-neighbour in Rome, Bernini (and many
lesser artists associated with the Counter-Reformation), Claude's reputation did not suffer
an eclipse after his death; but it was mostly outside Italy and only as a landscape painter that
his fame lived on. Horace Walpole called him the Raphael of Landscape and Goethe waxed

Gentle Virgil had always occupied a special place among Latin poets. Long before the Renaissance reawakened interest in the works of Greece and Rome, monkish scholars interpreted the cryptic prophecy uttered in Eclogue IV as a divinely inspired prediction of the coming of Christ.[37] "Saint" Virgil never acquired canonical status, but he was generally accepted as being at least on a par with the lesser of the Old Testament prophets. Dante inevitably chose him as his kindly guide on his journey through Hell. Epic poets, commemorating Christian deeds of valour not only in Italy but in countries as far afield as Hungary and Portugal, took his pagan masterpiece as their model. But nowhere did he hold such sway over the minds of men as he did over those of the beleaguered aristocracy of late seventeenth-century Rome.

To outside observers the slow crumbling of the fortunes of that aristocracy has always held a melancholy charm. English grand tourists, in particular, found the combination of graceful decay and art treasures at bargain prices deeply moving. But to Goethe and the Romantics too the physical decline of the city provided the right backdrop to inspired brooding over the fickleness of fortune and the proper setting for moralising over the vanity of worldly fame. To the participants it was less appealing. Perhaps a more provident breed could have foreseen the lean years and might have prepared for it. But the Colonnas and Borghese were not provident. Their crazily opulent life style and their patronage of beauty (both on canvas and in the flesh) had always been based on the ancient and to them unalterable economic doctrine of windfalls. The election of a benevolent and slightly senile second cousin to the papal throne could restore the fortune of an extended kinship.[38] Entering into, or judiciously keeping out of, little local wars could prove unexpectedly lucrative as well as occasionally ruinous. But ultimately these happy occurrences depended on the pious wish of the faithful around the globe (if it really was a globe rather than a dish) to see the indivisible Catholic Church's transcendent glory reflected in the temporal magnificence of Rome.

Romans, it has to be said, have always been good at playing their part.

---

lyrical about his "paradisiacal prospects of beauty". To Turner he was God: "pure as Italian air, calm, beautiful and serene spring forward the works and with them the name of Claude". To Hazlitt his landscapes were "more perfect than any that have been or ever will be painted". Constable wrote to his wife: "it is scarcely surprising that you are jealous of Claude; if anything could come between our love, it is him".

[37] Virgil was the master of veiled prophecies after the event; but the celebrated passage forecasting the coming of the Messiah probably refers to the coming of the poet's patron, Augustus.

[38] Even the most devoutly corrupt were staggered by the titles, cardinalates, benefices and lucrative offices showered on the Barberini clan by the newly-elected (and in his personal habits almost ascetic) Urban VIII Barberini. The Barberini bees still buzz all over Baroque Rome.

Their churches, ceremonies and display of holy remains never disappointed the millions who flocked to see them. Now the divine Bernini's lofty new colonnades, which replaced the warren of mean streets and dangerous alleyways around St Peter's shrine, opened their welcoming arms to the world. Even their scandals were on a magnificent scale. Some of the city's unique collection of holy relics, both ancient and modern, were cherished in palaces and humble cottages in four continents. But, though Rome was still good at the act, by the end of the 1640s the act was no longer wanted. Kings and prince archbishops did not stop fleecing their flocks, but in a more secular age they now tended to keep the proceeds themselves. In any case, the devout peasantry of the Ukraine, Mexico and Ireland had little left to contribute. But without such contributions how were the grandees of the pontifical city to maintain themselves in the state which was (they firmly believed) expected of them, even by God? Nobody knew the answer. Where in the past Romans had sold trinkets and indulgences, they were now reduced to selling genuine heirlooms and antiquities. Of course there was still much accumulated wealth. The Altieri and the Borghese were not exactly beggars; but they all felt the chill wind of the future, and the prospect of genteel penury, however relative, filled them with despondency, even alarm. Fortunately, there was one possession which would always remain theirs and which was now more precious than ever. They could boast – and did – of an incomparable lineage. Their genealogy was not the kind of vulgar conceit that made crowned rustics in Germany, France and England claim descent from Abraham, Solomon or Julius Caesar. Every vista and every stone around Rome proclaimed the glorious past, and every line in Virgil bore witness to its continuity with the present.

Claude was not a classical scholar, nor, one imagines, an avid reader of poetry. Even less was he a learned antiquarian. Architecture interested him as a feature of the landscape, but he could never have held forth (as Poussin could and did) about the mystical significance of the Doric Order. Least of all was he a member of the class which now turned to Virgil for solace and reassurance. After working in Rome for more than thirty years, he had come to value some of his patrons as friends. He appreciated the self-effacing erudition and mourned the death of Cardinal Massimi.[39] He had a soft spot for Clement IX Rospigliosi. But most of the Roman grandees who bought his pictures lived a life which he neither understood nor admired. In the wake and on the fringes of the Thirty Years War, his family had known real

---

[39] Camillo Massimi was himself a gifted painter and the discoverer of the antique Roman paintings in the Thermae of Titus, among the few paintings to survive from Antiquity.

poverty in Lorraine.[40] Despite their lamentations, his Roman patrons in their professed destitution remained paragons of extravagance. It is even harder to believe that he took their dynastic pretensions seriously. If the Altieri wanted their family flag with their ridiculous coat of arms to flutter from the masthead of Aeneas's ship, he was ready to oblige. If the Colonnas wanted to remind the world of their unbroken descent from that pious windbag, King Numa Pompilius, there was no harm in that either. But such airs and graces were not his style. And yet, as he grew older, he came to understand the uniquely Virgilian mood as no artist had done before him. It linked the past, the present and the future, and it sought and found in nature the continuity between brief individual destinies. Virgil expressed that continuity in a stately outflow of hexameters and pentameters. Claude was to express it in painting.

The distant past of the Virgilian hero, the Augustan age of the poet and the seventeenth-century present of the painter, a time-span of over two thousand years, merge in the masterpieces of Claude's late seventies. *Evander, King of the Arcadians, Invites Aeneas and his Troops* was commissioned by Don Gasparo Altieri, nephew of the reigning pope, Gonfaloniere of the Church, and linear descendent (of course) of the Trojan leader. It is loaded with contemporary signs and symbols. But it is the landscape under the wide Roman sky – what Turner two hundred years later would describe as "Claude's rich, harmonious, amber-coloured ether" – which establishes the continuity in time. As Evander leads Aeneas and his followers to his feast, the sites of future (in the painter's day already ancient but still recognisable) are all around them. There is the Capitol, "now marble and gold but once wild and ragged", the citadel on the Janiculum, Mount Aventine crowned with the Pantheon and, above all, the Tiber flowing majestically towards the sea.

There was yet another direction in which Claude advanced in his last decades. Whether or not he ever actually said that he charged his patrons for the landscape, the figures he gave away free – and it sounds a little too clever – he did for the best part of forty years consider himself exclusively a landscape painter. He lavished more care on his grazing cows than on his heroes and heroines, perhaps because, unlike posturing humans, grazing cows never threatened to disrupt nature's subtle harmonies. But as he slowly penetrated Virgil's world and began to absorb its moods, humans began to be part of

---

[40] The great etcher and chronicler of the horrors of the Thirty Years War, Jean Caillot, a Lorrainer like Claude, was a personal friend. During the war the Dukes of Lorraine displayed an almost supernatural gift of turning their coats at the wrong moment. The consequences for their dukedom were dire.

the message. This did not mean that they became more naturalistic: the very reverse. What he began to represent were not ordinary mortals or even Olympian gods, but Virgil's heroes – stiff, weird, often doomed, but also immortal in a sense more real than the dubious immortality of the Olympians. Virgil himself used external characteristics as a code for character. Latinus, the aged king, hears that "tall strangers have arrived"; and King Evander recalls Anchises as "he walked towering over the rest". In the same vein the painter made elongation of the body a code for leadership, much as El Greco in his last apocalyptic visions had made it an expression of ecstasy.[41] But often a conventionally proportioned shepherd sits in the foreground, representing a different century or even millennium and yet part of the same picture.

In Claude's last Virgilian panorama Ascanius is two heads taller than his companions, and he aims his bow at the strangely elongated neck of Sylvia's sacred stag. The brushwork is of ethereal delicacy, and the landscape at a first glance is one of the most harmonious he had ever composed. But in the midst of Arcadia there is also menace. A storm is rising in the distance. A shaft of light catches a gloomy castle on the craggy hillside. The tops of the trees – has anybody ever rendered the feathery patterning of trembling leaves so convincingly? – are beginning to stir. A taut imaginary horizontal links the bow of Ascanius, "his hands guided by some deity" to the stag, "its horns decorated with garlands". The animal gazes back frozen with fear. Clearly this is more than an episode from a hunt. The killing portends terrible events. The great slabs of masonry and fallen columns lying half-buried in the grass are – or will be – part of them. They are the remains of the city which will rise a thousand years after the hunt and will be admired by Virgil in its Augustan splendour. And sixteen hundred years after that they will be the gracefully decaying ruins of Claude's present. To visitors four hundred years after Claude the image is still full of the whisperings mysteries of time.

"Ancora imparo" then, whether the seeking or the finding of new things to express, and new ways of expressing them, deepens rather then explains the mystery. Claude's artistry rose to new peaks in old age because he was inspired by Virgil's world. The same sequence was true of other artists. They remained inspired not because they continued to explore new territories; they continued to explore new territories because they were inspired. Without a satisfactory "external" explanation, it is time to turn to those more powerful inner forces which impel men and women to create.

[41] El Greco, born Doménikos Theotokopoulos in Candia in Crete, was fifty-one years older than Claude. He died in Toledo in Spain in 1614, aged seventy-four.

# 17

## The Mainsprings of Creation

All creative artists want to express themselves and to communicate. Though these two urges, dubbed in an earlier chapter the mainsprings of creation, are difficult to measure, they are not hard to identify. There is in fact nothing specifically artistic or creative about either. Without perhaps realising it, the same two motive forces prompt many of our most humdrum actions and utterances. One passes an acquaintance in the street and says "Good morning". This is an abbreviated form of a wish, and wishes are among the commonest forms of self-expression. But in addition to wishing the person a good morning, the greeting may also aim at conveying to that person a measure of good will on our part. To that extent the greeting is not just self-expression but also communication.[1] But the two motive forces are not always linked. The drunk utters an obscenity as he collides with a lamp-post. He is not trying to communicate with anyone, not even the deity. His utterance is pure self-expression. By contrast, a doctor instructs his patient about a diet. Unless he is a sadist or a saint, both fortunately rare, he is not giving vent to secret urges. His words are – or should be – an attempt at pure communication.

The Swan of Avon and the Sage of Dulwich are, as always, inexhaustible sources of less pedestrian examples. Disregarding the fact that Hamlet may be ruminating in front of a rapt audience of thousands, his question on the stage whether to be or not to be is not addressed to anyone in particular. Like millions of less famous ditherers who talk animatedly to themselves, he is merely expressing his private anxieties. The question is a form of self-expression. Anthony's breast-beating expressions of private grief over Caesar's body are, by contrast, a sham; his lamentation is a successful exercise in communication. Similarly, Bingo Little's "stricken woofle, like a bulldog who has been refused a sweet" must be classified as self-expression, whereas Jeeves's "one soft, low, gentle cough, like a sheep with a blade of grass stuck in his throat" is a fine example of communication.

An artist is always impelled by a mixture of the two impulses; but their

---

[1] From wish to prayer is but a small step, Taine said. If so, the wish of an atheist might be described as self-expression, the wish of a believer as communication.

relative contribution varies. It varies from artist to artist and from work to work; but, most importantly, the balance shifts with age. To understand the achievement of new heights of creativity late in life, it is the chronology of that shift which has to be traced.

The art of small children is pure self-expression. The toddler will look askance though usually forgiving when an adult appends an explanatory caption to his or her creation: "This is our house" or "Jenny on the swing". Why the exegesis? The artist has made a statement: he or she has expressed himself or herself. Whether or not that statement is understood matters to him or her not at all. It is this blessed absence of any urge to inform or to instruct, the bane of adult intercourse, which gives the creations of childhood their ineffable freshness. It also accounts for the fact that by and large they do not wear well. They are not of course meant to. At first glance the abstract of a two-year-old may be as good as a middle-period Kandinski, but on the sitting-room or office wall, and to all but the most doting parent, it may pall after a few months. Fortunately, there is always a supply of new masterworks in the pipeline.

As the years pass the balance of motive forces begins to shift. The picture of a five-year-old still aims mostly at expressing an inner vision; but the need to convey that vision is now beginning to matter. "No, of course it's not a boat, you silly. Can't you see? It's a mountain." And the shift will continue: the wish to communicate will be more important at ten and may assume overriding importance at twenty, thirty and forty. There are many reasons for this.

The belief that skill in communication is the supreme mark of civilisation (as well as, incidentally, the surest way to success) permeates teaching both at school and in the home. There is a fine but critical gradation in importance between what one thinks and what one says one thinks, and an equally fine but no less critical difference between what one says and what one is understood to have said. Quite early in life children are taught to observe this hierarchy. What they think of Uncle Bill matters, but it matters less than what they say about Uncle Bill. And what they say about Uncle Bill matters, but it matters less than what Uncle Bill has understood that they have said. By persuasion, and even more by example, parents and teachers drill the overwhelming importance of communication into a child just as it has been drilled into them by their own parents and teachers. The drilling is underpinned by numerous examples of a good cause being ruined by poor communication, and by even the least deserving cause being improved by skilful packaging. Faced with such evidence in fields as diverse as business, politics, the law, religion, crime, science, administration, marriage, parenthood and of course teaching itself, the message soon acquires the aura of a universal and unquestionable truth. Few young people pause to ask whether it is in fact either: whether, in particular, it applies to artistic creation.

There is another reason why communication skills are so persistently plugged by educators. Parents and teachers teach not what they should but what they can. To teach communication skills is difficult enough: it needs flair and strenuous application, the more so since to children the inherent merits of these skills are rarely obvious and may even seem faintly distasteful. But to teach self-expression needs little less than genius. Surprisingly perhaps, since the chances of being born a genius in two separate fields – art and teaching – are against the odds, several masters fancied themselves as inspired pedagogues. Their students rarely agreed with them. Turner's stentorian clearings of his nasal passages and occasional swigs from a hip-flask during lectures probably kept his audience entranced, but few, apart from Turner himself, shed a tear when he retired from his chair at the Royal Academy. Ingres, a dedicated teacher, never learnt that sarcasm, however illuminating in theory, rarely endears the instructor to his pupils and almost never achieves its intended purpose. Rodin captivated most visitors to his studio with his natural charm; but few prospective pupils stayed for more than one lesson (at least for reasons of artistic instruction);[2] and his formal lectures were studiously avoided by all who had attended one. (He was proud of his acceptance speech of the honorary doctorate bestowed on him by the University of Oxford and even had it printed;[3] but his fellow-honorand, Camille Saint-Saëns, told his friends that the Prince of Wales thought that the artist had spoken in French, the French ambassador congratulated Rodin on the fluency of his English, and the Professor of Modern Languages was stunned by his command of Latin.) Klee, one of the best-loved personalities at the Bauhaus, spent many hours preparing his every tutorial but his appearance could empty a classroom within minutes.[4] The studios of most Venetian masters were kept in business by their pupils after the masters' deaths; but none produced notable original works without the masters' presiding presence. Bernini's studio was visited by admiring young men from every part of Europe for fifty years, but none later claimed to have been his pupil.[5]

---

[2] Camille Claudel and Gwen John among numerous others stayed as his mistresses; they did not become his pupils.

[3] Two years after Glasgow but a year before Jena in Germany. A framed copy hung in his bedroom in Meudon.

[4] A flexible timetable was one of the joys of the Bauhaus. Students never knew who would turn up to lecture them.

[5] His legendary temper could have had something to do with it, but that was vented more often on overbearing cardinals and silly principessas than on pupils or apprentices.

Indeed, of great artists who reached old age, only Kandinski shone in both capacities, perhaps because to him teaching was always as much a voyage of discovery as it was to his students. He was also, with his thick glasses, eclectic accent and gravely courteous manner, an irresistible target for leg-pullers; and his audience watched agog how, without seemingly realising that he was participating in a contest, he usually got the better of his mockers.

After a spell-binding but abstruse lecture about the spiritual significance of colours (the painter Béla Czobel was to recall) one of his students approached Kandinski with a blank canvas. "Team-leader", the student addressed him while the rest of the class watched transfixed, "I have at last succeeded in painting an absolutely pure picture of absolutely nothing." Kandinski spent some minutes scrutinising the canvas. "Yes, the dimensions are right. But why did you choose white? Nothingness is a great deal. Remember that God created the Universe from Nothing. I see it more as a red with a few other colours." He took a brush and painted a large red spot near the middle of the field. Then he painted smaller blots and lines with blue and yellow. He then glazed in a bright green shadow at the side. And "suddenly a picture was there – a magnificent though mysterious abstract painting". Kandinski handed the canvas back to the student. "I congratulate you", he said with the utmost seriousness.[6]

Even if art teachers of genius are rare and art teaching is often misconceived, it might be thought that, once out of art school, most pupils would quickly realise that communication skills are not all. Unfortunately, in art as in other fields, one is faced with the gruesome fact that the grip that acquired knowledge exercises on the mind depends not on its intrinsic worth but on the suffering involved in its acquisition.

Charles Gleyre was a sturdy Vaudois, and a mediocre painter in the Orientalist vein, who migrated to Paris and opened a painting atelier.[7] For reasons which remain somewhat mysterious, but mainly perhaps because he inherited most of the students of Delaroche who himself had inherited his atelier from Baron Gros, the institution flourished. It was particularly popular with foreign students who could join for short courses: many came from as far afield as Russia and the United States.[8] Monsieur

---

[6] Czobel, one of the foremost Hungarian Expressionist painters of the interwar years – he died in 1976, aged eighty-nine – described the incident in a radio interview on Radio Geneva on a visit to Switzerland in 1947 and briefly in an interview with the *Tribune de Genève*, 7 July 1947.

[7] He is still held in some esteem in his native Switzerland or at least his native canton.

[8] Apart from the Impressionists, Whistler, Sargent, George du Maurier and a future President of the Royal Academy, Edward Poynter, were among his pupils and remembered their sojourn in Paris fondly. Gleyre's posthumous reputation also benefited from a sympathetic "definitive" biography, C. Clement, *Gleyre* (Paris, 1878).

Gleyre, who never forgot his own struggles as a youth, was also less rapacious then many other *patrons*. Nevertheless, Renoir and Monet, both in their twenties and penniless, made great sacrifices to enter;[9] Renoir in particular gave up a well-paid job to do so. Neither he nor Monet were clear about what they hoped to learn. It was perhaps more a statement of intent, their way of proclaiming their commitment to the idea of becoming professional artists. At the school they met Bazille, Lepic and Sisley, who had already enrolled to sit at Monsieur Gleyre's feet. The latter were not, in fact, much in evidence. Tasks, usually the drawing of plaster casts of classical statuary or the painting of a bouquet of artificial flowers in a Delft vase, were set and explained to students by assistants. Occasionally live models were hired, always decorously draped. At the end of the sessions Monsieur Gleyre made a brief appearance and inspected the students' efforts. He rarely made a comment beyond nodding benignly. He was never scathing. He invariably congratulated lady students on their attire. He commented from time to time that art was a matter of copying nature. This was best done one step removed from reality by copying old masters "who knew their job better than you or even I". His letters of commendation which accompanied submissions of work by his students to the Salon were treated with respect by the jury. "His only merit", Monet wrote, "was that, once we had paid our fees, he did not mind if we played truant. So we [Bazille, Sisley, Renoir, Monet, Paal and a few others] would decamp to Fontainebleau to paint the forest." [10] And yet, long after liberating themselves of any lingering influence of Monsieur Gleyre's precepts, neither Monet nor Renoir could bring themselves to admit that their pupillage had been a waste of time, money and effort. "It was a dismal old place and perhaps I hated it at the time", Renoir told his son, Jean, "but Gleyre taught me how to draw." This was of course nonsense and both Renoirs knew it: the father was taught to draw (in so far as he needed much teaching) in Monsieur Lévy's pottery shop decorating plates with garlands of roses and portraits of poor Queen Marie-Antoinette.[11]

A no less depressing reason for the increasing importance of communication skills is that even creative artists must eat. The adulation which is now heaped on Van Gogh, Cézanne and Csontváry and the prices paid for their work are strictly posthumous tributes to their single-minded determination

[9] Monet had just completed the two years of military service in North Africa his father insisted on as a condition to giving his reluctant blessing to his son's career as a painter.

[10] Monet's letter to Marcel Pays, quoted in *The Impressionists at First Hand*, edited by B. Denvir (London, 1987), p. 24.

[11] See above, Chapter 8, p. 109.

to express their vision:[12] in life they had to pay a heavy price for their obstinacy. Van Gogh never sold a picture except in barter for food and fuel; Cézanne would have starved without the nest-egg bequeathed to him by his banker father; and the mad Csontváry's entire oeuvre would have been sold as a job-lot of sacking (reduced in value because of its contamination with paint) but for the presence at the auction of an eccentric collector.

Happily or not, the reverse is also true. Academic artists dedicated to communication may have nothing to say, but they may say nothing well; and for their efforts they may be richly rewarded.[13] It is true that communication without content is rarely memorable and its products are soon forgotten; but most artists – like most dustmen, doctors, lawyers or teachers – would rather survive than be remembered.

There is, one must hasten to add, nothing wrong with communication. In science, where progress depends on the stepwise development of ideas, communication is essential. A scientific paper may embody observations of revolutionary significance, the fruit perhaps of a lifetime's labour; but if it remains unpublished, or is published but not read, or is read but not understood, it might never have been written. In this respect at least artists are fortunate, even if, driven to madness or suicide, they may be forgiven for not appreciating their good fortune. A rediscovered medieval monkish manuscript establishing Newton's laws of thermodynamics, describing the healing powers of the mould *Penicillium notatum,* or anticipating Rutherford's discovery of atomic structure, would be of historical rather than scientific interest: no practising scientist would want to read it in preference to last

[12] Tivadar Csontváry was born in Kisszeben (Sabinov) in what was then northern Hungary and is today the Slovak Republic in 1853, the same year as Van Gogh. By profession he was a pharmacist, but he always regarded himself as a painter. He was a mystic and a visionary and more than slightly mad; but his huge canvases are aglow with colour and induce a trance-like state in his devotees. He never sold a picture in his life; but today a whole new gallery is dedicated to him in his native Hungary. One of his smaller pictures, *The Lonely Cedar Tree,* has become the Hungarian equivalent of Van Gogh's *Sunflowers.*

All Csontváry's work would have been destroyed after his death in 1919 but there was, in the aftermath of the war, a great shortage of sacking (among many other commodities). To pay his debts, his rolled-up canvases were put up for sale per square metre, together with his other meagre effects. They were bought by Lajos Gerloczy (still insufficiently honoured in his country), who exhibited them from time to time in the 1920s and 1930s. International acclaim came after 1958 (twenty-nine years after Csontváry's death) when the jury at the exhibition of Fifty Years of Modern Art at the Brussels World Fair awarded his *Riders by the Seashore* the *grand prix;* but the first T-shirt with *The Lonely Cedar Tree* was not on sale in Hungary till the late 1970s.

[13] Boardroom and royal portraiture, though probably the most lucrative branch of painting, is difficult to classify. With few exceptions it neither communicates nor expresses anything other than the superiority of photography.

week's *Nature*. Great paintings or sculptures, by contrast, can moulder in an attic or remain buried underground for centuries without losing their appeal or their so-called relevance.

But as the chief driving force of either artistic or scientific creation, indeed as the chief motivation in any pursuit other than advertising, communication is inadequate or worse. After decades of struggling against incomprehension and ridicule, creative artists in middle age may decide that they have starved for long enough, forget about expressing their inner vision, and begin to concentrate on communicating. The results may surpass their wildest dreams. Suddenly their talent may be recognised. Their works may begin to sell. They may be invited to lunch with the Queen. And their long-suffering families may watch them with pride when on television they expatiate on the purpose of the universe, the future of mankind and other subjects of burning topical interest. In this happy denouement there is only one snag. To the consternation of their admirers and their own mortification, they may find themselves incapable of further creation. Those who have experienced such a crisis find the memory more painful than almost any other: it is rarely recalled in ghosted memoirs (or even in private journals), and it never becomes the stuff of coffee-table books. Yet many artists were nearly destroyed by it.

Jean Renoir's biography of his father illuminates almost every aspect of the painter's life – except one. There is no mention of the depressive crisis the artist suffered in his fifties; of the occasions when, after months of intensive labour, he would destroy all his work, sometimes dozens of canvases; of the times when he would take off for weeks on his own, leaving Aline and Pierre without an explanation or a forwarding address, though never without funds.[14] Nor was he questioning his talent, he was too intelligent to do that. His doubts were about the validity of what he was doing with that talent:[15] the crisis was a crisis of success, not of failure.[16]

[14] See above, Chapter 7.

[15] For some years, his "dry period" according to art historians with a compulsion for labels, he tried to combine the freedom of Impressionism with the austere draughtsmanship of Ingres. Some of his creations in the style – like *Les Parapluies* and the *Dancers* – have become famous and justly so. But they are not the essential Renoir.

[16] This is how Franz Werfel described it in one of the best-documented cases outside the visual arts. After the international success of *Aida*, first performed in 1871, Verdi virtually stopped composing. He was fifty-eight; and, though widely revered as the greatest operatic composer of his day, his day was regarded (not least by Verdi himself) as passed. Then, at the age of seventy-eight, he began to compose his two greatest operas, *Otello* and *Falstaff*. In Franz Werfel's biographical novel, a penetrating study in fiction of the mid-career crisis, it is the death of Wagner at seventy (both composers having been born in 1813, a good year) which releases Verdi's creative energy.

A similar crisis in Munch's life was the most clinically apparent: it too struck him as he was beginning to be internationally recognised and celebrated. Since he never learnt to drive, he hired a taxi and spent his sixtieth birthday being driven around Oslo in an attempt to avoid well-wishers and celebrations. But there was no escape. Returning to Ekely about midnight, he was ambushed by a lurking reporter. "Only one question, please, master!" Incorrigibly polite, it was not a request Munch could refuse. "It is well known", the reporter went on, "that you are still reworking your most famous images. Like *The Scream.* Or *Jealousy.* Do you think that with the wisdom of age you can improve on them?" Munch was horrified at the suggestion. "No, no, no, of course not! The first versions are always the best." "Why then are you always reworking them?" There was a long, almost embarrassed pause. "Often nothing more ... challenging ... comes to my mind", the tentative answer eventually came.[17]

It was Bonnard who best summed up the experience in his clipped schoolmasterly manner. "Suddenly", he wrote to his friend, Joseph Rippl-Ronai, about his fifties,

> I was famous. I could sell anything, however repetitious. People sidled up to me on the beach and at the racecourse to assure me that they understood what I was trying to say. I thanked them politely, as one does, but in reality I no longer wanted to say anything. I had nothing to say. It was very vexing. At last I had succeeded in making myself comprehensible and I no longer wanted to be comprehended. What was I to do? Perhaps suicide was the answer. But who then would look after Marthe? [18]

Fortunately the crisis of success is like the crisis in old-fashioned lobar pneumonia. After a few days of worsening illness and an hour of terrible suspense the patients often died. But if, at the end of the critical hour, they showed even a flicker of improvement, they would continue to improve and would recover fully. Similarly, if and when great artists survived their crisis of success, the prognosis was excellent. In Renoir's case the recovery came – coincidentally or not – with the onset of his physical illness. To Bonnard it came after he moved to the south of France. To Munch it would come when he began to be haunted by a new ghost. In each case the recovery represented another shift in the balance between the two mainsprings of creation. Just as in childhood and middle age the drift was always and almost inexorably from self-expression to communication, so with the approach of old age the balance began gloriously to tilt once again in the opposite direction.

[17] Based on an account given to the writer by Axel Shon; also referred to in H. E. Gerlach, *Edvard Munch: sein Leben und sein Werk* (Hamburg, 1955).
[18] M. Marton, *Rippl-Ronai Jozsef* (Budapest, 1982), p. 124.

# A Second Childhood?

Does the tilting back of the balance toward self-expression mean that artists in old age revert to the creative innocence of childhood? Surely not. Artistic techniques, the tools of communication, cannot be unlearnt any more than one can unlearn riding a bicycle. Nor is it possible to shed decades of experience at will. Nor indeed would any creative artist want to try. But there are echoes.

Some great artists achieved fame and fortune in old age, others died in relative obscurity. But all, as they progressed through their sixties, seventies and eighties, became less and less impelled to surprise, shock, dazzle or disturb: they paraded no messages and had no weighty lessons to teach; they wished neither to flatter nor to excoriate; their work did not try to exhort, soothe, inspire, exalt or stimulate. Often they did not even try to please. Why then, often in the face of great physical difficulties, did they continue to paint or sculpt? A child asked to explain the inexplicable would probably say: "I paint because I like to." Monet's answer in his eighties, when pestered why in defiance of doctor's orders he was still at it, was not very different: "I paint because I breathe."

The products are of course different. In children's art the sheer exuberance of self-expression has to compensate for the artist's indifference to communication. The non-communication of great artists in old age is of another kind. They do in fact communicate – indeed, one often senses their mastery of communication – but they are difficult to understand. This may seem self-contradictory but it is not. In its adult form communication tends to mean not a speech, a sermon or a lecture but a two-way exchange. Great actors, preachers and teachers can of course achieve this without their audience uttering a single word: their seeming monologue is in truth a continuous exchange of thoughts and feelings, questions and responses.[1] The totally deaf, by contrast, can utter commands and express their thoughts; but they cannot engage in a verbal give and take; and without such an exchange their communication is rarely satisfactory. But is one's

[1] Second-rate performers or worse can do this only by relying on their every utterance being responded to by sustained laughter or applause.

lack of understanding of great artists in old age like a conversation with the deaf?

Of all great artists Goya was the one who most frequently and most passionately extolled "reason", yet the one whose motives are often the most difficult to divine. When, at the age of seventy-four, he left his comfortable town house in Madrid and moved to an isolated *quinta* on the outskirts of the city, he had every reason to be disgusted with the political and social climate; but that had been the same in Spain for most of his life. His personal position as the King's First Painter was secure and his family were doing well (or at least were temporarily keeping out of scrapes). He was totally deaf but by now he must have got used to it.[2] Yet, in a frenzy of loathing, he covered the walls of two rooms of the house with the most terrifying images of the private obsessions, fears and fantasies of any artist. These Black Paintings (Plate 7), black almost in colour as well as in content, were not meant for public viewing. They were not in fact seen for fifty years except by later tenants of the *quinta*. (They must have had nerves of steel if they could consume their morning *chocolat* and brioches contemplating Saturn devouring his offspring or the idiot grimaces of the pilgrims of St Isidore.) When the building was due to be demolished to make way for a cemetery, the frescoes were declared to be of no realisable value and condemned to go the way of bricks and mortar. They were saved just in time by Baron Emile d'Erlanger of the French banking family. Having purchased them for an exorbitant sum – the paintings acquired great value as soon as the Baron's intentions became known – he planned to show them at the Paris World Exhibition of 1878 and then to present them to the Louvre. Outrage and horror (which came as a shock to d'Erlanger) greeted their unveiling. P. G. Hammerton, speaking for the British contingent of experts, described them as "the vilest abortion that ever came from the mind of a sinner"; and Jean Barbès wrote that "if these are paintings, then they are the end of painting as an art". If he meant painting as practised before Goya and for decades still to come he was nearly right. But if the paintings were an end, they were also a beginning: only it took time for their language to be understood. When it happened, they spoke not only to painters but also to artists in media unknown to Goya. He inspired pioneer film makers like Pabst and Buñuel, and almost nightly one can see his images flickering on one's television screen, though with the enjoinder that viewers who find torture, mass starvation, mutilated bodies and genocide disturbing should look away.

Such reappearances long after the death of the artist make one realise that, except in the physical sense, old artists like Goya were not deaf, nor even

[2] See above, Chapter 5, pp. 63–65.

hard of hearing. But often they were hard of listening to what they did not want to hear. Sometimes it was the harmless chatter of their friends, neighbours and families. More often it was the portentous but even more vacuous noise of public figures. But the communications of the creator of the Black Paintings were never a one-way process, any more than were the communications in the same decade of the physically equally deaf composer of String Quartets Op. 127, 130, 131, 132 and 135. Only they often conducted their exchanges with voices of the past and of the future; and their sparring partner was often a cantankerous God.

Complexity and obscurity were not always the hallmarks of old masters. Any schoolchild can copy Matisse's last cut-outs without difficulty. Only the products, if faithfully reproduced rather than freely paraphrased, would portray not the child's but Matisse's vision. And, in contrast to the creations of childhood, the simplicities of aged masters tend to grow in interest rather than pall with the passage of time.

But not all differences between the very young and the very old redound to the latter's credit. In children the urge to express themselves without any concern for communication goes hand in hand with a blissful indifference to the fate of their creations. This is as it should be. Let Mother preserve their flashes of artistic insight if she wants to: maternal motives are unfathomable. But discovering their insights in the recycling bin a few months later does not, as a rule, lead to more than a perfunctory show of anguish. Old masters may have been similarly indifferent to the opinion of the contemporary world; but they were rarely indifferent to the future of their creations. Their concern was not, of course, always translated into practice. Turner, one of the most persistent and least effectual of will-makers,[3] was obsessed with how and where his collection of paintings bequeathed to the nation would be displayed; yet fifty years after his death, when Matisse took his bride on their honeymoon to London "to look at the Turners", they were amazed to find that no more than half a dozen of the treasures were on public display;[4] and when Kenneth Clark took over the directorship of the

[3] He was too parsimonious to employ a competent lawyer, and his much-codicilled will, tenaciously contested by a pack of distant relatives (who claimed that he was "patently" of unsound mind), was eventually declared invalid.

[4] Successive government committees pondered gravely and at length how to build a one-man museum worthy of England's greatest artist, occupying no space and costing no money. Their deliberations proved fruitless except in terms of knighthoods for the deliberators. When eventually a worthy gallery was built, it was financed and named after a take-over tycoon who prospered mightily in the aftermath of the Second World War. A nation of shopkeepers? Matisse would have been too polite to do more than smile enigmatically.

National Gallery in London in 1939, fifty rolled-up Turner canvases were discovered in the museum vaults labelled "tarpaulins". Turner would also have been horrified at the idea of his high-minded young friend, John Ruskin, acting as a moral censor over some of his legacy.[5] Characteristically, Corot brushed aside warnings that his too easily forged signature and easy-going benevolence was spawning an industry of forgeries. Ingres, by contrast, was tormented by the nightmarish thought that unsigned and inferior paintings by his students might one day be mistaken for his own (as indeed they were and still are, despite his obsessive cataloguing). David, apostle of the Revolution, fussed like an old hen when he learnt in exile that a few of his sketches, dating back to the darkest days of the Terror (when, with patriotic fervour, he helped to send thousands of innocent people to the guillotine), had unaccountably gone missing.[6]

Yet for almost every important difference between the very young and the very old one can point to a small similarity. Only young children in the throes of creative work can cut themselves off as completely both from the outside world and from inner needs as did the old masters. Domenico Bernini related that his father in his last years would go for days – or try to – without food or rest while working on a marble or an architectural design. Family, friends, visiting cardinals, even messengers from the Queen of Sweden, were ignored. When they became too intrusive, he would greet them by the wrong name, the wrong sex or, most effectively one would imagine, by an inappropriately lowly title.

Dr Mawas, Monet's clever young oculist, had a similar tale to tell. Arriving in Giverny a little earlier than had been arranged, he reassured Blanche Monet that he did not wish to disturb the Master whom he had espied working in his studio. Blanche laughed. "That would be impossible, doctor. You could

[5] Ruskin spent many months of dedicated labour going through Turner's "boxes", left in his studio in Queen Anne Street, saving hundreds of jottings and water-colours, many in a parlous state. Sadly, he blotted his copybook by coming across a box or two of "obscene drawings ... of the most degrading kind". See A. Bailey, *Standing in the Sun* (London, 1998), p. 406. Taking a leaf out of Pontius Pilate's book, he instructed his associate, R. N. Wornum, to burn them. This was eventually revealed – or half-revealed – and caused great consternation among the cognoscenti. Continental art-lovers had a field day gloating over philistine Anglo-Saxon hypocrisy. (Many French, Dutch, Italian and Spanish masters, including the divine Ingres, were enthusiastic collectors of pornography and contributed their share.) Turner was not a great figure painter, and his few surviving pornographic sheets (most of them in the special collection of the British Library) do not make one palpitate for more. Of course the act was barbarous (the burning, that is) and unforgivable; but to many the most intriguing question is how Ruskin knew what was and what was not obscene.

[6] Including not only many of his most generous former patrons, notably Lavoisier, but also France's greatest poet, André Chénier.

dance around him naked, brandishing an assegai, and he wouldn't notice you if he didn't want to."[7] Even more remarkably, when painting and only when painting, the Master would sometimes forget to roll and light a fresh cigarette from the stub of the last and, bereft of matches, he would occasionally delay by as much as a quarter of an hour going in search of a fresh supply.

Like young children, Bernini, Monet and other great artists in old age learnt to create solitude, perhaps by the same means and for the same end. Solitude must not of course be confused with loneliness. Loneliness implies a sense of deprivation and is as sterile as hunger.[8] Solitude, "the school of genius",[9] always implies the invisible, intangible and inaudible but positive support of others. Small children who are part of a loving family sense it and create happily in solitude without feeling in the least lonely. The same kind of unobtrusive support sustained many old masters in creating their late masterpieces.

This may be a suitable point to refer back to an earlier statement and qualify it. Dismissing the notion that creative work might act as a "preservative" against the ravages of time, it was suggested that neither in their physical frailty nor in their mental fragility were aged geniuses different from their less spectacularly gifted contemporaries. Perhaps this is not quite true. They did share a quality which is generally thought to be more closely associated with childhood than with old age. They were often irrationally – and sometimes even rationally – loved.

Maillol was seventy-three when in the spring of 1934 his friend, Dondel, suggested that he might like to make the acquaintance of a vivacious and gifted young woman, Dina Vierny. She was fifteen and overawed to meet one of the grand old men of French culture. Nor was their first encounter entirely propitious. But their friendship blossomed and she became his muse and the inspiration of his greatest works.[10] Maillol's experience was remarkable but not unique. Tintoretto and Claude in their old age were surrounded by a numerous and loving family. Domenico Bernini's description of his father's last illness might raise a disapproving eyebrow among medical and nursing experts today; but to the Berninis, assembled in force around the dying man's bed, the "continuous flux and reflux of the most conspicuous personages of the city – cardinals, not one but several every day, princes,

---

[7] Unpublished anecdote recounted by Dr Mawas. See also J.-P. Hoschedé, *Claude Monet, ce mal-connu* (Geneva, 1960).

[8] Knut Hamsun's famous novel by that name was written years after experiencing hunger himself.

[9] Gibbon's memorable phrase.

[10] See above, Chapter 8, pp. 133–38.

ambassadors, emissaries of the Queen of Sweden and chamberlains of the Holy Father bringing his pontifical blessing every morning – as well as of many common people and usually their wives and children and even their babes in arm who wished to see him and ask for his blessing" was a matter of pride and satisfaction.[11] Many brought and recited "specially composed eulogies, sonnets, poems, erudite verses both in Latin and in the most ingenious vernacular in praise of the world's greatest and most noble artist". On his last day, the choir of the church of San Filippo Neri came to sing at his bedside. There was also a large concourse of his family, some greatly loved and esteemed, others perhaps only greatly loved. All received the dying man's parting benediction. As his last breath drew near, his nephew, the Oratorian priest Father Marchese, who throughout his illness had not left his bedside, asked him if there was any small thing that was still troubling him. The dying man pointed to a note which he had dictated a few weeks earlier. "Father, I shall soon render my account to a Lord who does not count in halfpennies." "He died", in Baldinucci's words, "in his prayer. As the news spread, Rome wept." [12]

Kandinski was fifty-one when, in the seismic year of 1917, he met the eighteen-year-old Nina de Andreevski at an exhibition in Moscow. They fell in love and married; and she remained his loving and irrepressible companion and support for the rest of his life.[13] Emil Nolde's first wife, Ada, died in 1946. A year later he married Jolanthe Erdman, the twenty-six-year-old daughter of a friend and a gifted artist. His last eight years were blessed by their happy marriage.

Ingres proposed to Madeleine Chapelle by letter, never having met her, while he was eking out a precarious living in Rome, and married her there a month later. It proved to be a marriage of great happiness which lasted thirty-five years: even those who find his oeuvre generally unpalatable are won over by his tender portraits of her. He was devastated by her death in 1849 from cancer; but two years later, when he was seventy-one, he married Delphine Ramel, a buxom forty-three-year-old spinster. This marriage too was idyllically happy; or, to use his own characteristic words, she became an "excellent minister of the interior". His portrait of her, his last work, is charming.

---

[11] Bernini's last illness and death was vividly described in Filippo Baldinucci's contemporary *Vita de Bernini* (Florence, 1682), translated by C. Enggass (University Park, Pennsylvania, 1966), and in the biography of the artist's son, Domenico Bernino's *Vita del Cavalier Gio. Lorenzo Bernino* (Rome, 1713). Based on these accounts, the events are well described in H. Hibbard, *Bernini* (London, 1965).

[12] Baldinucci, *Bernini*, p. 128.

[13] See above, Chapter 11, pp. 165–77.

In more orthodox style the Davids had a crisis in their marriage when the painter's involvement with the Committee of Public Safety became too much for Mme David. They separated after he openly declared that if he had to choose between domestic felicity and the lofty ideals of the Revolution (as propounded by his current idol, Robespierre) there could be no question which one he would choose. But when, after the fall of Robespierre, he was temporarily imprisoned in the Luxembourg, Mme David was among the first to visit him. A reconciliation swiftly followed and the marriage happily survived the rise and fall of David's next hero, Napoleon, and exile in Brussels.[14] Corot, a bachelor, had (so far as is known) no consuming passions; but in his last illness he was surrounded by a circle of devoted young friends of both sexes and from all walks of life.[15]

The aged and intermittently paralysed Hokusai was lovingly nursed by his daughter O Ei, and Monet by his daughter-in-law Blanche Monet. Both women were gifted artists who seem to have put their own careers second. Neither expressed any bitterness or regret. Aline Charigot was seventeen when she caught her first glimpse of – and instantly fell in love with – the fifty-two-year old Renoir.[16] It was to be a wonderfully happy union.

Unlike Renoir, Goya was a crusty and demanding old roué; but he too had Dona Leocadia Weiss to share his bed in his seventies and eighties and to present him with the joy of his last years, Rosarito.[17] Half a century later Turner, irascible to the end, had the much younger Sophia Booth to take his mind off the miseries of his edentulous old age.[18] Bonnard's artistic and intellectual friends never had a good word to say about his mistress and later

---

[14] See above, Chapter 6, pp. 86, 87, 90.

[15] Countess Juliette Pálffy recorded that "all the models and midinettes of Paris seem to have assembled round his sick-bed in the Rue Paradis Poissonière", as well as a fair sprinkling of fellow artists, writers and aristocrats. See J. Pálffy, *Parisi Emlékek* (Budapest, 1932), p. 248.

[16] See above, Chapter 8, pp. 113, 114, 117, 118 n.23, 119, 120, 121.

[17] See above, Chapter 5, pp. 73, 75, 76.

[18] They met at the boarding house run by the Booths in Margate, and, after Mr Booth's death, came to "a mutually satisfactory arrangement". In Chelsea, Turner became known locally as "Mr Booth" or, by some, taking their cue from the marine clutter in the house, as "Captain" or even "Admiral" Booth. Sophia was a kindly, hard-working woman, at least twenty years younger than him, who, admiral's wife or not, kept the home shipshape. But this was the dawn of the Victorian age and an unrelated Mr Turner expressed the view of many of his genteel friends when he deplored "that a man so great in talent should not have had a more lady-like companion. He could never have introduced her to society without embarrassment", A. Wilton, *Turner*, p. 246. It did not seem to worry Turner in the least.

wife, Marthe;[19] but, if she seemed a millstone to the outside world, she was also his love, his muse and his fulfilment.[20] "The light has gone out of my life", he wrote to Matisse when she died in 1942;[21] and nobody doubted his sincerity. And Matisse himself in his eighties had the young and self-effacing Lydia dedicated to his comfort and happiness.[22]

And what about the greatest lover of them all? Through all his innumerable infidelities, Rodin had his "Rose toujours", who never for a moment wavered in her love for him. Or, in his own way, he in his for her.[23] The relationship had a happy ending of sorts. After the break-up of his last *grande affaire* with the Duchesse, some of his admirers conceived the idea of preserving his studio at the Hôtel Biron and transforming it into a Musée Rodin. Rodin undoubtedly loved the house: nowhere, he declared, did he feel so much at peace with the world. But it was not going to be easy. The building had once been a convent school and now belonged to the state;[24] and its conversion

[19] Her real name was Marie Boursin but, for reasons never revealed, she preferred to call herself Marthe de Merigny. She was sixteen when Bonnard met her, not entirely uneducated but without any visible background. Like thousands of young women in and around the artist cafés of the *quartier*, she offered her services as a model, though, according to Vuillard, she was too shy for the job. At least she appeared to be shy: she would never join a light-hearted conversation until suddenly she put a stop to it with a feverish outburst of passionate approval or disapproval. Later Bonnard's charitable friends described her as "highly strung", R. Coignat, *Bonnard* (Milan, 1968), p. 87. The less charitable described her less charitably. But if her behaviour often seemed outrageous to others, fussing over her exotic ailments was his happiness.

[20] They married in 1925 and moved to the south of France for its milder climate.

[21] See Coignat, *Bonnard*, p. 126.

[22] The Matisses' marriage held (despite his serial infidelities) until the Second World War. Then Mme Matisse became active in the Resistance (and was saved from deportation to Germany only by a timely air raid), whereas he deplored all forms of "unnecessary provocation". See J. Guichard-Meili, *Matisse* (London, 1954), p. 256.

[23] It may have been the Duchesse's demand that he get rid of "that peasant" which precipitated their final break. A peasant perhaps, but she made the best onion soup with croutons, which he rightly regarded as one of the three glories of France. (The other two were its women and its cathedrals.)

[24] It had been built in the late eighteenth century by Jacques-Ange Gabriel, architect of Le Petit Trianon, and had once been among the stateliest mansions of the Faubourg St-Germain. (It took its name from Louis de Gontaut, Duc de Biron, Marshal of France, who was among its many famous tenants.) The school was closed by the virulently anticlerical government of Combe in 1904. While the authorities bickered about what do with it, the official liquidator rented out rooms at a peppercorn rent to anybody who took a fancy to the place. Among them was the poet, Rainer Maria Rilke, who, for a few months, had worked as Rodin's "secretary". (None of Rodin's secretaries lasted for long – he never knew what to do with them – but, like his discarded mistresses, most of them preserved a fond memory of him.) Rilke recommended the place to his former master, who immediately fell in love with it. The splendid garden in its former state of benign neglect must have been particularly

was going to require the ratification of the Chamber. The Catholic lobby would strenuously oppose the scheme: to display the shamelessly erotic images of a self-confessed agnostic in a building that still had a consecrated chapel in its grounds was nothing short of blasphemous. The gutter press could be relied on to throw up their hands in horror.[25] But the scheme also had influential backers; and the outbreak of the war probably worked in its favour.[26] Of course there could be no question of pressing forward with the necessary legislation while the Germans were on the Marne; and in the meantime the problem was the old man himself.

His break with the Duchesse left "decency" triumphant but the protagonist a broken man.[27] This might not have mattered to his high-minded backers if his more mundane affairs had not been allowed to lapse into chaos. But he was being plundered. Even in wartime there was a constant stream of visitors tramping round both the Hôtel Biron and the Villa des Brillants,[28] ostensibly to visit him and pay him homage but in reality to

lovely; and few artists have ever had such a beautiful studio as Rodin had on the first floor. It is here that he created most of his "One-Minute Drawings". During his *affaire* with the Duchesse he hardly went near his home, the Villa des Brillants in Meudon.

[25] One of the scheme's most vituperative opponents, Gaston Calmette, fell victim to a well-timed shot by Mme Caillaux, furious at the scandalous and, as it happened, groundless, insinuations against her husband. Mme Caillaux was acquitted of murder by an all-male jury and Charles Ricketts perceptively commented that "the French system of having the tyranny of the gutter press tempered by assassination seems to me admirable". C. Ricketts, *Self-Portrait* (London, 1905), p. 348.

[26] The "Union Sacré" between parties, proclaimed by President Poincaré in 1914, held until 1917.

[27] He never quite recovered his youthful energy, and was confused and saddened by the outbreak of the war. He tried to escape from the war-fever in Paris, first to England (where he and Rose spent some months in Cheltenham at a private hotel for retired Indian Army officers run by Mrs Priscilla Grundy, where Rose explained to everyone who would listen that she was not entitled to be called Mme Rodin), and then to Rome. The Roman trip too was a failure.

[28] He had acquired the villa (now a second museum dedicated to him) after his break with the beautiful Camille Claudel. It was here that he kept court for many years to a constant stream of celebrities and it was to here that he returned after the break with the Duchesse. The place was crammed with a mixture of junk and priceless works of art – Egyptian mummies, Roman statuary, fake Japanese vases, medieval stained glass, Indo-Chinese bronzes, Persian miniatures, and a Gothic Cross (in his bedroom), as well as several fine Renoirs and Van Gogh's *Père Tanguy*. Some of his visitors would catch a glimpse of Rose scurrying to the vegetable garden or the chicken run and would ask to be allowed to pay their respects to *Madame*. "Mais elle est une sauvage", Rodin would expostulate; but, if his guests insisted, Rose would be summoned, wipe her hands on her apron, say good morning and then disappear again. Grunfeld, *Rodin*, p. 465. The main drawback of the house was the lack of heating and the paucity of any seating accommodation. Neither worried Rodin.

acquire a little something – a few drawings perhaps, or a bronze or two, or perhaps a small marble ... or could the *cher maître* make it two marbles? The *cher maître* usually could. Nor would Rose ever dream of questioning his actions. Unscrupulous and rapidly changing servants amassed a fortune selling anything that bore the Master's signature.[29] To cap it all, the Master had developed the distressing habit of making and remaking his will, often in response to blatant flattery and in favour of such frivolous causes as a home for indigent artists or a new Musée Moderne. Without his estate, consisting not only his own creations but also the works of art and antiquities he had accumulated as a collector, the chances of creating a Musée Rodin were negligible. It was not enough to post guards on the gates and inside the building and have the Master discreetly shadowed by a bevy of muscular secretaries: his whole estate had to be immediately transferred to the state.

Few of those who listened to the long and complex document being read out at the Villa des Brillants understood its provisions; the testator himself (in one of his "withdrawn" moods) certainly did not. But he had never been much interested in money or in the disposal of his artistic legacy; and he was happy to leave such tiresome matters to experienced friends such as Judith Cladel and Etienne Clementel. Having revoked all previous wills and bequests, and excepting a small annuity for Rose "in recognition of fifty years' faithful service", every scrap of paper and every object he possessed, all his property and the copyright of all his works, were unconditionally transferred to the state.[30]

After the document was signed and witnessed (and the huge estate was

[29] Perhaps they were helped by Auguste Beuret, never legitimised, who had moved into the garden lodge. Rodin had never been unkind to him; but he had no paternal feelings and Rose had always made it clear that in her book "Monsieur Rodin" always came first.

[30] The event, as well as the subsequent wedding, was recorded by two eye-witnesses: J. Cladel, *Rodin* (London, 1953) and M. Tirel, *Rodin intime* (Paris, 1923). Judith Cladel was besotted (in a Platonic way) with Rodin or at least with the image of what she considered a genius like Rodin ought to be like, and saw herself as the one reliable, selfless and practical guardian of Rodin's welfare and reputation. She loathed the Duchesse, whom she considered to be Rodin's evil genius and who barely rates a mention in her book; but she approved of Rose, who was sufficiently doglike in her devotion both to Rodin and to Judith Cladel. She was probably not a deliberate liar; but her accounts of events witnessed by her rarely sound wholly believable. Marcelle Tirel, on the other hand, was no great writer but she was transparently truthful: a relative of the Duchesse's dressmaker but no great admirer of the Duchesse, she joined the Meudon household as Rodin's secretary in 1906 and, as an exception to the rule, stayed till after Rodin's death. She was a more reliable witness than Cladel (who did not see much of Rodin after Rodin's estate was safely in the bag and he was known to be ill). The account here is largely based on Tirel's book and on F. V. Grunfeld's excellent biography, *Rodin* (London, 1987).

safely in the bag), Judith Cladel turned to him. "Would it not be appropriate, Master, if you gave Rose your name legally?" "Ah yes: you always have such good ideas", he replied.[31] It was quickly arranged. The ceremony, attended by a few close friends and relatives, was performed by the Maire of Meudon in the drawing-room of the villa (unheated as usual) on 19 January 1917. Rodin wore a frock-coat and a large red velvet beret and kept repeating that he had never felt better. Rose was soberly dressed and behaved with great dignity despite the pains that already racked her chest.

To the prescribed questions he replied a resounding "Oui" and she a whispered "Oui, Monsieur le Maire, avec tout mon coeur". Tired by the ceremony, she then retired to her bed. Years of suffering had reduced her to a shadow, but her last days were serene. On her last morning, twenty-five days after the wedding, she kissed her husband before he went out for his morning walk and told him that he had brought her great happiness. Later, as he sat at her bedside looking at her face, tranquil in death, he murmured over and over again: "How beautiful she is. As beautiful as a statue." [32]

Love is not an aspect of old age – or of any age – susceptible to statistical analysis; but if the breed of old masters differed from their less gifted contemporaries in any respect other than their talent, it was in their ability to kindle and sustain the love of partners often many years younger than themselves. Was this a side-effect of their continued creativity? It is impossible to say; but Rose Beuret – or, to give her her proper name, Rose Rodin – totally ignorant though she professed to be about matters artistic, might not have suffered in silence Rodin's philanderings had he been, like his father, a low-grade clerk in the police. Yet her love, and the love of all her sisters in

---

[31] Cladel, *Rodin*, p. 202.

[32] Rodin survived her by only a few months and they must have been horrible. Lorries arrived at the Villa des Brillants to cart all his valuables to the Hôtel Biron: now that they belonged to the state, their safety had to be ensured. The removal of the Gothic Cross from his bedroom threw him into a rage and may have hastened his final collapse. It was as if his wonderfully devoted friends, so anxious to preserve his life's work, were now trying to kill him off as expeditiously as possible. His nurses had strict instructions not to let him have pencil and paper in case he tried to make another will. During his last days his hands were groping for clay; but that was deemed too messy.

He died at a moment when France's fortunes in the war were at their lowest ebb and only a junior minister could be spared to attend the funeral. The coffin was laid to rest next to Rose's, in front of the façade of the Château d'Issy which, many years earlier, he had helped to save. There the graves remain. Over them crouches the bronze effigy of a strange figure, originally conceived for the never-finished *Gates of Hell* and called *The Great Shade*. In innumerable reproductions and distortions the large head resting on the knuckles of the right hand, the bent knees and the curled toes were already famous. Over the century it would become still more widely known, an icon representing one of the world's most endangered species.

destiny, was deep and true, not the spurious "aphrodisiac effect of power" extolled by vulgar twentieth-century arrivistes. Creative geniuses are often represented as self-centred monsters, and many undoubtedly were and are. But they were never dull; and their self-centred monstrosity, like that of children – at least one's own – was, for some reason, always worth suffering.

So the confident "surely not" in answer to the question whether the old age of great artists was like a second childhood should perhaps be toned down. Among the few basic – though rarely mentioned – differences between humans and their closest evolutionary cousins is the way in which, all through life, humans retain some of the characteristics and responses of childhood. This does not seem to happen in the rest of the animal kingdom. Chimpanzees develop in the womb, grow up and then grow old. Humans too develop in the womb and they too, alas, grow old: but they never quite grow up. This is near the root of what one perceives as the kinship between the exuberant creativity of children and that of creative geniuses in old age.

# 19

## *Style*

The term "soaring" has been used in an earlier chapter to describe the art of old masters. But what does the term mean? Uncontentiously, it implies an upward displacement; and, by some atavistic convention, upward displacements are generally interpreted as improvements. So was Michelangelo's last unfinished *Pietà* an improvement on his first?[1] And were Titian's late *poesies* improvements on his great *Assumption* in the Frari?[2] No art-lover can subscribe to that great discussion stopper, "there is no arguing about tastes". To the present writer Adolf Ziegler's *The Judgement of Paris* (which Hitler chose to hang over his desk) is infinitely inferior to Rubens' treatment of the same subject. But when it comes to comparing early and late Michelangelo, or early and late Titian, or early and late any of the long-lived old masters, the answer is not so simple. Most of the late works are not more accomplished, not more beautiful, not more important historically and certainly not more liveable with. In many respects indeed they are patently less good. But are they "greater"? If pressed, my answer would have to be "yes" – but that is no answer. Greatness in art is ultimately undefinable. Less ambitiously then, one can try and see in what way their style, technique and subjects were *different*.

Much has been written, especially by German scholars, about the *Spät-Stil* of great artists. The bait is the family resemblance between the broad, sweeping brushstrokes, often seemingly uncontrolled and yet extraordinarily powerful and expressive, of old Titian, old Hals, old Goya and other old masters. The snag is that Ingres' increasingly lacquered surfaces were no less his apotheosis and Turner's vaporous blotches his. Matisse's style in old age became simpler, Tintoretto's more complicated, Renoir's more earthy, Bernini's more spiritual, Donatello's more haunted and Claude's more serene. All that these *Spät-Stile* had in common was that their only purpose was to convey in the most direct way the artist's personal vision.

---

[1] The first, now in St Peter's behind bullet-proof glass, was the only sculpture signed with his name. The last, known as the *Rondanini Pietà*, is now in the Castello Sforzesco in Milan.

[2] Titian called his late mythological paintings destined for Philip II *poesies*. It is not clear what exactly he meant by the term.

This may not seem much; but it is. Inevitably an artist's style is hemmed in not only by the conventions of his age, his background, his training and the taste of his public, but also – and most compellingly – by the rules he lays down for himself. Monet decided as a young man that it was impossible to paint a sky inside a studio, while Degas succinctly described the idea of *plein air* painting – "making art into a sporting event" – as "*idiot*".[3] Both remained true to their magisterial pronouncements until they jettisoned them in their last years because they no longer served their purpose. Monet laboured long and half-blind on his skies (and, even more elusively, on his skies as reflected in water) inside his studio (Plate 15); and Degas created many of his last, haunting landscapes in pastels looking out of the window of a railway carriage.

During his Bauhaus period Kandinski maintained that any literary content ruined a painting.[4] "Let us take this little pencil for a walk", he said to a new student one day. (It was an old joke but everybody loved Vasili and the class dutifully laughed.) Aimlessly the master (or "team-leader" as a professor was called at the Bauhaus) allowed his pencilled line to meander over the blank sheet of paper. Then he looked up at the student expectantly. The student, a country lad from Hungary, contemplated the line for a minute or two in painful concentration; then his face lit up. "Ah ja! It is perfect. The flight of a swallow." Vasili stared at his handiwork in consternation. Then he crumpled up the "abstract" and threw it away in dismay.[5] But fifteen years later, as Europe was plunging into the darkness of war once again, he populated his last luminous skies with creatures which could be swallows, eagles, bees, mosquitoes or influenza viruses, but which, whatever they are, are undoubtedly alive and bouncing.

Titian has always been one of the challenges to art-historical pigeon-holers. By the 1560s, whether it was his eighth or ninth decade,[6] his technical command was complete. This did not mean that he could paint anything he liked; no artist can do that. But he knew how an amorphous patch of heavy impasto or a few layers of transparent glaze would appear in the

[3] A. Vollard, *Recollections of a Picture Dealer*, translated by V. M. Macdonald (London, 1936), p. 128.

[4] See above, Chapter 11, pp. 167–71.

[5] A. Balzsa, "Látogatás Kandinskinél" (Visiting Kandinski), *Müvészet* (Budapest), 3 (1963), p. 82. To illustrate Kandinski's commitment to abstraction, the author of the article also describes a hearsay anecdote. When, visiting the Sistine Chapel, Kandinski was told that the ceiling was originally sky blue with dotted stars. His comment was: "And then Michelangelo came and ruined it."

[6] His date of birth remains controversial.

finished painting without a moment's thought or hours of experimentation. And, armed with this knowledge, he could – or thought he could and certainly did – ignore much of the painter's traditional craft.

Traditionally the bulk of individual brushstrokes in a painting serve a mimetic purpose: they define outlines, accentuate highlights, chart spatial relationships and give solidity to three-dimensional objects. In translating an artist's vision, these are pedestrian tasks which nevertheless absorb much of the painter's time and energy. Often – sadly – they become the painting itself. In old age Titian achieved his mimetic objectives automatically; or, when he did not, he ignored them. And, relieved of their traditional functions, his brushes were free to pursue different goals: they created space, air, movement, tension and, above all, a dark and totally pervasive mood. His Vienna *Nymph and Shepherd* could have been a simple idyll;[7] but nothing in his old man's world was simple or idyllic any more. His lovers inhabit a landscape of molten passion. A stag in the background savagely tears at a partly destroyed tree. Everything – the sky, the distant hills, the foliage, the grass, the spotted fur on which the nymph reclines and the pale glow of human flesh – contributes to the feeling of betrayal and disaster. What do details like the shepherd's three hands or the obscurity of the storyline matter?[8]

Even in his last decades Titian could tease his future interpreters by modulating in the same painting from a finely modelled, almost Florentine, head of Judith to a boldly sketched (as well as severed) head of Holofernes. Or repaint an earlier work and imbue Arcadian bliss with a mysterious sense of unease. The composition known as *The Pardo Venus* was probably begun when he was in his fifties but finished (or repainted) twenty years later.[9] It is impossible to say what the picture is about or even if it is about anything in particular.[10] In an idyllic landscape there is only a half-sleeping naked goddess, if indeed she is a goddess and if indeed she is half-asleep rather than provocatively half-awake, surrounded by satyrs, Cupid, hunters and hounds. Other figures are distantly glimpsed. The colouring is muted. No drama is being enacted. What then causes the unease? Of course there is the mystery of the storyline. Great narrative paintings exist in time as well as in

[7] Or perhaps *Paris and the Nymph Oenone*. See E. Panofski, *Problems in Titian* (New York, 1969).

[8] It was one of the paintings found in his ransacked studio after his death; and perhaps he meant to paint out the third hand. But what fun for children of all ages to discover the fault.

[9] Named after the palace of El Pardo in Madrid where it once hung.

[10] Titian may have referred to the work in a letter mentioning a nude in a landscape with a satyr. It is possible that he was deliberately trying to revive a genre of mythological compositions without any specific storyline.

space. They grip not only because of the frozen moment of action but also because one's mind experiences the minutes or seconds that have led up to that moment and the minutes or seconds which must surely follow. This is particularly true of Titian's late representations of horror. The single image of *The Rape of Lucretia* conjures up a tumultuous sequence of lust, violence and murder more vividly than Livy's flat narrative.[11] But there is usually a clue, even in such seemingly hopelessly confused works as *The Flaying of Marsyas*.[12] There is none in the *Pardo Venus*. What then causes the disquiet? Like all great artists, Titian spoke differently to different ages; and most generations find the responses of their predecessors a little quaint. But perhaps the no longer fashionable Walter Pater, writing in the hothouse atmosphere of mid-Victorian aestheticism, got it right when he suggested that it is not the shapes, the colours and the story which bring Titian's late mythologies alive but the sounds.[13] Only he must surely have been thinking not only of the musical sounds of the flute or the hunting horn but also of the rustling of the brook, the song of birds, the sussuration of the wind in the trees, and the gentle rhythm of a woman breathing in her sleep. Added to that, in Titian's old age there was always a slow and yet urgent obbligato throb, audible perhaps only to the old, of time relentlessly passing.

Perhaps the oddest and certainly the most paradoxical aspect of *Spät-Stil* is that its flaws often add rather than detract from the work's impact. Palma Giovane, one of Titian's last and most gifted pupils reverently patched up his master's unfinished *Pietà* and is often blamed for its faults.[14] That is unfair. The faults are recognisably, even characteristically, Titian's in his last years.

[11] In a nutshell: Lucretia, a virtuous woman and wife of a nobleman, is visited in her chamber by Sextus, the son of Tarquin the Proud, Rome's seventh and last king. He threatens her that, unless she yields to him, he will kill her and cut the throat of a slave and lay his body beside hers, making it appear that she had been caught by Sextus in adultery with a servant. She gives herself to him and then, having informed her husband and father of the truth, kills herself. Her death precipitates a rebellion, led by Brutus the Elder (sculpted by Michelangelo among others), which forces Tarquin and his awful brood into exile.

[12] In Ovid the story is ghastly but simple. Piqued at being almost defeated in a musical contest by the bumptious faun, Marsyas, Apollo flays him alive. In the painting there are several characters who *could* be the god but none of whom convincingly is. There is also a faun, carrying a bucket, a horrible child leading a slavering hound, a Midas character contemplating the proceedings with apparent boredom, and the most revolting lapdog Titian ever painted, gorging itself on Marsyas's dripping blood. The painting was bought in Italy by Lady Arundel in the 1620s but was later won in a lottery by Prince Karl von Liechtenstein, archbishop of Olmütz (now Olomuc) for the archiepiscopal palace of Kromeriz, now in the Czech Republic. Much ink has been spilt trying to interpret the picture.

[13] W. Pater, *The Renaissance* (2nd edn, London, 1877), p. 54.

[14] Grandson of the more famous Jacopo Palma or Palma Vecchio. He died in 1628, aged eighty-four.

And they are numerous. Even at a glance the proportions are all wrong. The figure of Christ is too small. It is also rather laboured. Mary Magdalen, ominously waving her poorly articulated limbs, is gigantic. St Joseph of Arimathea – if it is he – is little more than a tortured symbol.[15] Moses and the Hellespontic Sybil are poorly balanced. The elaboration of the pigment in some areas conjures up the image of an artist feverishly belabouring small details while losing sight of the whole. Time and neglect have added their toll. The paint along one edge is recent. The original canvas seems to have rotted away from its stretcher and has sagged on itself. The damage has been patched up with astonishing incompetence. The tonality of the whole is a dull, greenish grey, the colour of ashes. And yet, for every fault one can point to a stroke of inspiration: while deploring the overall dullness one could rhapsodise about the flashes of colour. But to draw up a balance sheet would be an exercise in futility. This is not, one feels, an ordinary picture which has been pondered, planned and painted. It is a vision which has been captured but which at any moment might disappear. And to many it remains, with all its mistakes (or perhaps because of them), one of the sublime visions in art.[16]

Great artists' *Spät-Stile* sometimes puzzled and even dismayed their contemporaries; and in some cases their regretful dismissal became the received wisdom of art history. Donatello's sublime last bronze reliefs were not installed in San Lorenzo's in Florence until a hundred years after their completion; and they still do not feel at home. The panels are not at the same height and the surrounds have no unifying theme. The artist's austere late style was already out of fashion among Florentine *cognoscenti* by the time of his death, and one cannot help feeling that his legacy presented his executors and the authorities of San Lorenzo's with a not uncommon problem: what to do with works of art which cannot be disposed of but are out of tune with current taste.[17] Four hundred years after Donatello, David too horrified his admirers with the "novel style" he adopted in many of his last paintings; and contemporary judgement was widely accepted for over a hundred years.[18]

---

[15] But perhaps the aged Titian's last self-portrait.

[16] According to tradition, Titian had applied to the friars of the Frari some years before his death to be buried in their church under a monument of his own design. The friars, one can readily imagine, were less than enthusiastic. They were a mendicant Order, and, while Titian's earlier altar-pieces were rightly admired and drew the crowds, they were arguably out of tune with the Franciscan ethos. The *Pietà* may have been begun as a pious bribe. It was another of the paintings found in the artist's studio after his death; it is now in the Accademia.

[17] See Biographical Appendix, "Donatello", below, pp. 319–22.

[18] See above, Chapter 6, pp. 89–93.

Even if the *Spät-Stile* of the masters were as individual and varied as their style in youth, one can detect – or suspect – at least two shared characteristics. Most of the old artists seemed to achieve their objectives with extraordinary economy. This was not the Victorian virtue of thrift, an admirable characteristic perhaps but entirely contrary to Nature;[19] nor did it ever draw attention to itself. Often it shows up in seemingly unimportant details.

Today the modelling of drapery in stone is a lost art, neither practised nor appreciated. To Bernini's contemporaries it was the yardstick of a sculptor's competence. Connoisseurs and prospective patrons judged its quality at a glance. To pass muster it had to be realistic, a credible representation of the varying degrees of inertia of different materials, and of forces and currents of air set up by different kinds of movement. To be commendable it had to emphasise – though unobtrusively – the hollows and swells of the body underneath. But, for perfection, it had to serve as the visual equivalent of the Greek chorus and convey, as appropriate, majesty, power, holy exaltation, inner torment or an atmosphere of contemplation and repose. In his twenties and thirties Bernini was already acknowledged as a virtuoso; but at the height of his physical powers – the decades of the great sepulchral monuments, the fabulous fountains, the Cornaro Chapel and the Cathedra Petri – his pre-eminence was unquestioned even by his enemies. Take away the faces, the hands and the feet, and the flowing and fluttering garments of his popes, saints, prophets and angels would remain almost as eloquent. In his late seventies he was still a prodigious worker. Perhaps it was a form of escape. Rome in decay was not without charm; but the charm was not of the kind to gladden his heart.[20] Yet he surprised his friends when he accepted a commission to carve a monument to the Blessed Ludovica Albertoni.

[19]  Anything remotely damaged, worn or time-expired, whether a molecule, a cell or an individual, Nature discards and replaces rather than repairs. Physiological repair or "preservation" does of course happen but it is not the norm. Perhaps this is what makes it so difficult to inculcate the need to preserve damaged or even used objects in young children.

[20]  After the religious settlement of 1648, Rome stopped drawing tens of thousands of pilgrims every year: the churches were empty, and there was no dawn crush in front of St Peter's on high feast days to wait for the pontifical blessing. Ironically, the pilgrims who still came – and indeed came in greater numbers than ever – made the pilgrimage to visit the workshops, not the churches. The cities and courts of Europe, slowly recovering from the depredations of the religious wars, needed to relearn the skills of a departed age; and the modellers, carvers, gilders, founders and chisellers of Rome were still unsurpassed. Conceived to celebrate the timeless and the universal, the broken pediments, the flying draperies, the convulsive gestures, the *trompe l'oeil* ceilings and the marble waterfalls would be adapted to exalt the flotsam of the passing scenes – emperors, kings, generals, prince archbishops, rich merchants, political adventurers and their wives, mistresses and pets.

The Blessed Ludovica was not, like St Theresa of the Cornaro Chapel,[21] a cult figure. Also, she had been a Franciscan nun and Franciscans were not an Order smiled upon by Bernini's friends, the Jesuits. It is still sometimes suggested that the reason for his acceptance was a combination of opportunism and family obligation. Cardinal Paluzzi degli Albertoni's favourite nephew, Gaspare, had married the niece of the reigning Altieri pope, Clement X, sufficient reason for honouring an aunt's memory. And, after another alleged escapade by a high-spirited nephew, the aged master is said to have thought it politic to placate the most ambitious tribe in the Vatican. The story is not entirely convincing. Bernini was the concerned uncle of many nephews and nieces (and their complex ramifications), but in his seventies he was quite capable of resisting pontifical blandishments. It was probably the theme – or the lack of it – which attracted him. The Blessed Ludovica had no doubt been a woman of exemplary virtue; but her main claim to beatification (other than her pushy kin in the Vatican) had been her patient suffering and the devout manner of her dying. It was this *Bona Mors* or Good Death which Bernini, speaking not the language of medieval mysticism and even less the confused jabber of the twenty-first century, set out to carve into marble.[22]

The sculpture is reminiscent of, but also strikingly different from, Bernini's earlier monuments to the dead.[23] Once again it is the drapery that tells the story as much as the face and the hands; but the message is not about power and glory but about redemption through suffering. Gone are the sweeping curves and bold diagonals, Bernini's vehicle in youth of intense emotions. The resulting angularity is softened only by the extraordinary delicacy of the carving. But, as in earlier works, every highlight and shadow tells. The dying woman raises a small, nearly vertical fold with her right hand. It is an unobtrusive feature, like a tiny exclamation mark. It surely marks the very moment of the Good Death or rather the beginning of a Better Life

[21] One of Bernini's supreme masterpieces, the Cornaro family's memorial chapel in the Carmelite Church, Santa Maria della Victoria. The family's patron saint, St Theresa of Avila, was a mystic and a visionary but also a superb organiser who founded the Reformed Carmelites, the nearest among female Orders to the Jesuits.

[22] The idea of the Good Death was of medieval mystical origin but was revived and widely propagated during the Counter-Reformation by the Jesuits and the Oratorians. It had a large literature to which Bernini's nephew, the Oratorian priest, Marchese, contributed a powerful work, *Unica speranza*. Bernini's own death was as near perfect an enactment of the ideal as it is possible to say from this side of the divide.

[23] His papal tombs in St Peter's – imperiously commanding for Urban VIII and quietly prayerful for Alexander VII – were acclaimed as being among his loftiest creations.

after Death. Has any sculptor, even Bernini's younger self, ever expressed so much with so little? One doubts it.

Yet Bernini's artistry in conveying profound emotions by the simplest means was carried even further in what was almost certainly his last memorial carving. The subject, Gabriele Fonseca (Plate 4), was a fashionable physician of Portuguese extraction who may have looked after Bernini (as well as a succession of holy fathers and their kin) with great skill and devotion, but who seems to have fallen out of favour in his last years.[24] His image in the family's chapel certainly portrays deep spiritual anguish. He leans forward from a roundel as if gazing out of a window. One hand is convulsively pressed against his chest. The other clasps a rosary. It is the grip of a drowning man or of one seized by a major coronary occlusion. Colour could add nothing to the illusion of cold sweat. The neatness of the hair and moustache only emphasises the desperation in the eyes. And the dark shadows and flickers of light of the deeply undercut folds of the gown seem to anticipate by three hundred years the electrical record of a terminally fibrillating heart. But Bernini's figures, even his last unadorned portrait busts, never exist in isolation. Fonseca's eyes do not just stare into space (as they seem to on photographs). In the Fonseca Chapel they are fixed on the image of the Annunciation carried by angels above the altar.[25] The look may seem despairing but it is still that of a supplicant; and, so long as there is supplication, there is hope.

The same trend towards expressive simplification marked Bernini's last contribution to St Peter's. By the 1660s angels had become the resounding cliché of the Baroque. They were pretty in a sexless – or rather bisexual – way, their cheerful tumbles during overlong services providing a pleasant

---

[24] It seems that he was accused by jealous colleagues of too close links with the city's Jewish community. This was unusual. By nature, indolence or necessity Rome had always been a tolerant city. To Romans the blood laws of Spain were a joke. (Every Spaniard, they maintained, not least the sainted Borgias, had Jewish or Moorish blood in them, probably both.) But the pilgrim trade was drying up and somebody had to be blamed for the unprecedented slump in the price of holy relics and other profitable objects of adoration; also for recent outbreaks of the plague, the soaring food prices, increasing crime and vice, and the uncouth manners of the young. The 1660s witnessed in Rome (as in other Catholic places of pilgrimage) a violent upsurge of antisemitism. Bernini was no liberal. He abominated heresy. He firmly believed in witches. He had no patience with clever boffins like Galileo who professed to be Christians but always knew better. But, like his mentors, the Jesuits, he regarded racism as an outrage against God's universal church and antisemitism as an affront to Jesus Christ. This may have been the reason why, a year or two after Fonseca's death, Bernini undertook the task of carving the memorial.

[25] The chapel itself in San Lorenzo's in Lucina was designed by Bernini some years earlier. The altar-piece is by Guido Reni.

distraction. For the Chapel of the Blessed Sacrament Bernini had originally envisaged a heavenly host cascading down from the walls and the ceiling, a riot of coloured marble, gilt and fresco to rival the inspired theatricality of the Cornaro Chapel. This would have kept the whole workshop busy, a chance to demonstrate once again that it was still the best in Rome. But he discarded the design in favour of two angels only, to be carved entirely by himself. It was a risk; but Bernini was one of the few artists left who could still portray these semi-divine creatures as truly superior beings. His last pair he placed on either side of the tabernacle. They are without frills and indulge in no dramatic gestures; but, absorbed in silent adoration, they radiate immutable happiness.

Faced with Bernini's last works one recalls with a sense of shock his dismissal by high-minded Victorians.[26] "It is impossible", John Ruskin said with a vocal shiver (and nobody could shiver more vocally), "for false taste and base feeling to sink lower than Bernini." [27] Of course he was identifying Bernini with the Roman Baroque, the Roman Baroque with the Jesuit ascendancy, and the Jesuit ascendancy with the crimes of the religious wars.[28] To him, as to other prophets of a more civilised age, looking forward to uninterrupted progress based on the blessings of science, the horrorscape was indivisible. Bernini's chapels were not gorgeous inventions uniting all the arts in celebration of God but sinister instruments of deceit, very nearly the Inquisition carved in marble. Professional aesthetes too tended to be scathing. In the shadow of the great Winckelmann, the twisted columns of the Baldacchino in St Peter's were not sculptured fanfares but outrages against the canons of beauty as promulgated for all eternity by the builders of the Parthenon. These were not ignoble sentiments. Ruskin and his fellow Victorians had not seen (as their great-grandchildren would) the horrors of the religious wars easily surpassed without any help from organised religion but keenly supported by the advances of science. Perhaps the Age of Faith had much to answer for; and that Faith was undoubtedly Bernini's inspiration. But as an old man he no longer represented triumphalism of any sort.

[26] Bernini clearly foresaw that his reputation, rooted in the Age of Faith, would plummet after his death. It is still far from secure.

[27] Quoted by R. Wallace, *The World of Bernini* (London, 1970), p. 9. Like many of his judgements, Ruskin's view of Bernini can only be described as asinine, but who would be without his heavenly diatribes?

[28] The link between Bernini and the Jesuits was real; even his detractors (then as today) never doubted his piety. For seventy years every morning he would go to Mass and recite the Little Office. Every evening he would walk to Della Porta's triumphal new church, Il Gesù, and spend half an hour there in silent meditation.

With incomparable technical mastery and the simplest of means, he expressed only his hope in Divine Mercy.[29]

If, by its very nature, simplicity does not draw attention to itself and is
therefore not an easy quality to demonstrate, the second shared characteristic
of the late style of old masters is even more elusive. Degas maintained that
there was only one useful piece of advice he had ever received about painting.
"Cherish the accidental", an old artist teacher had advised him.[30] Of course
even young artists make use of serendipity – the running of a colour producing
a dreamlike effect never in fact dreamt of, or a dramatic break in an uninteresting flat field produced by a hidden irregularity in the canvas; but it is
in the last works of the masters that one senses the ultimate virtuosity. One
cannot put it higher than "sense": if the underlying accident is obvious, its
exploitation is no longer a success. It is probably Nolde's "unpainted pictures",
the fruit of his wartime prohibition from painting, which provide the nearest
to what might be described as evidence. This is partly because their technique
– or lack of it – was so obviously improvised and haphazard;[31] but also because
Nolde was a man of unsophisticated honesty. Often, to the consternation of
his minders, he would boast that his "unpainted pictures" were literally

---

[29] As an architect he moved in the same direction. The last church he built in Rome, Sant'
Andrea al Qurinale, became his own favourite, as it was to be Cardinal Newman's and that
of many other pilgrims to the city. It is one of his loveliest and simplest conceptions, departing
from every traditional device, yet striving for no effect other than that of a profound spiritual
experience.

[30] M. Guérin, editor, *Lettres de Degas* (Paris, 1945), p. 192.

[31] Although Nolde started the series as a substitute for oil painting (and he used some after
the war as the basis of larger and usually inferior oil paintings), they are in no sense sketches.
Though quite small, rarely more than 10 x 10 inches, they are intensely formed paintings in
a mixture of chalk, water-colour, varying other colouring matter and dirt. Most of them he
began by allowing wet pigment to flow over scraps of rice-paper, partially controlling the
flow with balls of cotton wool, and sometimes reinforcing colours or outlines with ink. He
broke all the rules. The variable density and translucency of the paintings is due to multi-
layering and several reworkings, often over weeks or months. Sometimes he applied paint
from the reverse side of the paper; and, because he was always short of material, he occasionally
cut up and overpainted earlier pieces. The new pictures then became different images but
haunted by the ghosts of their predecessors – small shadowy figures, for example, dwarfed
by huge flowers. They were – as such improbable works usually are – a reconciliation between
two seemingly irreconcilable opposites. On the one hand, the paintings were deliberately the
products of "passive creativity": in Nolde's words, "when a picture looks as if it had painted
itself, that is the moment I am looking for ... that is the moment to stop". Quoted in
W. Haftmann, *Emil Nolde: Ungemalte Bilder* (Cologne, 1971), p. 68. On the other hand, the
more one seeks and finds that accidental moment, the more one is in truth depending on
one's knowledge of the properties of the paper, the paint, the brush, the solvents and, above
all, their time-dependent interaction.

nothing more than *kleine Unfälle* – little accidents. And this was true, up to a point. One can believe that some of his blazing orange skies did indeed remind him of days when he had run out of blue paint. *Wunderbares Glück, nicht wahr?* – wonderful luck, wasn't it? [32] But nothing was pure *Glück* in the happily accident-prone art of the old masters; or one would have to play about with paints, brushes and scraps of paper for a very long time before being able to duplicate hundreds of such lucky dips.

Nolde in his seventies became a master of accidental art; but he was not the first or the oldest. Goya's technique in his eighties in painting his miniatures on ivory remains both mysterious and controversial. He seems to have had no intention of selling the products; yet he was immensely proud of them, writing to his friend Ferrer that they made use of a technique never tried before.[33] The works are small, measuring less than three by three inches, and show one or two figures only. Some depict popular types introduced into earlier paintings – celestinas, majas, grotesques – others recall the *Witches' Sabbath* and other nightmares of the Black Paintings. The claim of novelty was subsequently explained by Laurent Matheron, who described his reconstruction of the method.

> Goya blackened the ivory plaque and let fall on it a drop of water which, as it spread out, lifted away part of the black ground, leaving random light spots. He then made use of these bare spaces, always turning them into something unexpected and original ... He wiped off many which did not please him to economise on the ivory.[34]

The surviving works are so brilliantly expressive that the description of what amounted to the exploitation of "happy accidents" was questioned. But a few years ago experiments carried out with ivory coated with a binder and carbon black (which had been the pigment used by Goya) confirmed Matheron's account: despite the clarity of the contours, the figures were indeed "lifted out" of blackness by the haphazard flow of drops of water.[35] Goya may have been physically enfeebled in his last years, but physical frailty had not dimmed his capacity to surprise, provoke and delight future generations.

---

[32] W. Haftmann, *Emil Nolde*, p. 72.

[33] C. Lopez, editor, *Goya, diplomatorio*, p. 389. See also above, Chapter 5, pp. 75–76.

[34] Cited in E. Sayre, "Goya's Bordeaux Miniatures", *Boston Museum of Fine Arts Bulletin*, 64 (1966), p. 108.

[35] J. Tomlinson, *Goya* (London, 1994), p. 432.

Goya, like most great artists in old age, frequently reused canvases too. (The ghost of a bearded head is now visible in his very last painting, *The Milkmaid of Bordeaux*.) The motives were probably mixed: economy, of course, but also a disinclination to leave behind works which did not please him.

# 20

# *Technique*

Even if style, an elusive characteristic, does not change in an uniform way in old age, basic technique might be expected to. It does at the other extreme of life. Children's paintings can be as varied and as individual as the work of adults; but their basic technique tends to establish at a glance the approximate age of the artist. The causes are complex and imperfectly understood; but in everyday language they are often described as "part of growing up".[1] The changes associated with "growing old" are no less complex or better understood; but, by analogy with childhood, one might expect them to have a similarly recognisable effect. This should apply particularly to the influence of a function which is both invariably altered in old age and critically important in practising any of the visual arts.

All the artists who reached old age must have suffered from some degree of visual impairment in their last years. For the distant past medical details are lacking; but even there one has pointers. There was surely a grain of truth in old Titian's "blindness", even if his sight was less impaired than malicious gossips insinuated. More than one testimony refers to the "dimness" of Hals's vision in his eighties. The spectacles perched on Chardin's nose in his last self- portraits seem quite strong.[2] Goya too wore spectacles as early as his fifties, and his nose almost touched the canvas (according to his friend Moratín) as he belaboured his last paintings in his eighties. Turner's preserved glasses are weak; but he may not have troubled to obtain stronger ones. Clinical details are more readily available as one approaches modern times. Kandinski was extremely short-sighted, at least since his Munich days; and Nina always explained his aloofness by the fact that he did not recognise friends and acquaintances unless they came quite close or spoke to him. (His hearing was acute and he had perfect pitch.) Munch developed a vitreous opacity in the better of his two eyes – as did Reynolds a century earlier – and even "drew it in" in his last sketches in the form of a grotesque beaked bird. (Both artists were much exercised by the fear of blindness.) Degas'

---

[1] Humans have the longest postnatal development among mammals relative to their average life-span, size and period of gestation.

[2] They were also of high quality, probably imported from England.

blindness, due to slow retinal degeneration, is relatively well documented though its cause remains obscure. Most famously, not only Monet but also Daumier, Pissarro, Mary Cassatt, Reti and many near-contemporary artists suffered from progressive "senile" cataracts for many years before they were operated on, went blind or died.[3]

Many of these disabilities should be traceable in the last works of long-lived artists; and not a few biographers oblige. "The tell-tale signs of a cataract are already apparent in Monet's Venetian paintings" (in the 1890s), one Monet scholar has recently written; and one can but marvel at his clinical acumen. It is not that one cannot interpret Monet's pictures – Venetian or even earlier – in terms of visual disturbance; but if these disturbances are "tell-tale", then the tale they tell is very *nouvelle vague*. An artistically inclined professor of ophthalmology could give a lecture on the characteristic colour changes of cataract based on the changes of Monet's palette; and he might follow this up with two similar lectures based on the cataracts of Pissarro and Mary Cassatt; but these changes were so different that he could not use all three examples in the same lecture without risking making a fool of himself. And one doubts if even the most sagacious diagnostician conducted round the *Water Lilies* in the Orangerie would guess without foreknowledge that they represent the world seen through "blunted sight".

More precise near-contemporary testimonies from artists underline the unpredictability of the effects. Sir Matthew Smith had his cataracts removed about the same age as Monet and noted comparatively little change except that "some of the colours became a little brighter and the details a little clearer". But Edward Ardizzone saw through his operated eye (after his first operation)

> a much colder brighter world in which reds became pink, the greens became greener and blue was more intense ... Everything looked bigger too and closer, harder and brighter. In looking at a face I saw too much – the down on the lip, every wrinkle and pimple and all the stubble of the beard. I am rapidly getting used to the new vision and am unconsciously making all sorts of adjustments ... All the same, when my second eye is operated on, I am going to miss the smaller, kinder if rather mistier world I have loved so well.[4]

To this it has to be added that to one admirer at least of both artists the effect of the operation remains wholly undetectable when works painted before and after are compared. In the same inconclusive vein one can

---

[3] The effect or lack of effect of visual disturbances on painting is discussed by Patrick Trevor-Roper, a distinguished London ophthalmologist, in *The World Through Blunted Sight* (2nd edn, London, 1988).

[4] Edward Ardizzone, ibid., p. 96.

point to the short fine brushstrokes of the aged Goya or the lumpy sweeps of the old Hals's brush as "diagnostic" or even "tell-tale" – but surely not simultaneously to both.

This does not of course mean that the techniques of old artists did not change as a result of old age; nor even that one cannot sense in the late works the unforgiving weight of passing years. Drawings are often more revealing in this respect than paintings. Claude started to sketch in his *Liber veritatis* with pen or pencil while he was still an apprentice, and he never stopped. Probably all his oil paintings were planned in this way before they were committed to canvas, and many of the preparatory sheets are of great though unplanned beauty. In his seventies he developed a technique of short penstrokes that created an effect of vibrant light and almost Rococo grace. In his very last sketches these penstrokes as well as the brushstrokes became noticeably shaky; but their tremulousness under the blue, grey and green washes gives them a delicacy even he had never achieved before.[5] One witnesses a similar kind of dissolution in Michelangelo's last drawings. Their hesitancy is a pale reflection of his once imperial command of line; but genius battling with and transcending physical frailty is a unique, awesome and uplifting experience.[6]

The last example may point to a more generally valid reason why physical handicaps could impair technique but never obliterate creative talent. By the time artists reached their sixties, seventies and eighties, they must have mastered three extremely complicated processes. First, they must have learnt to *see* in the real world the raw material of their future paintings, drawings or sculpture. Secondly, they must have learnt to *transform* what they saw in their minds into the works of art they were about to create. Thirdly, they must have been able to *translate* their mental images into actual paintings, drawings or sculpture. Defects of vision and other physical disabilities merely added a fourth skill to be acquired. They now had to learn to circumvent, overcome or cheat the newly imposed limitations. This was not always easy – sometimes it must have been fearfully difficult – but, compared to the other three, it was child's play.

The magic of Michelangelo's and Claude's last drawings raises another remote but possible explanation for the often brilliant artistry of old age. Death can cut short the career of an artist at any time, and many gifted youths have left behind little more than a few bold beginnings. But, when

---

[5] H. Langdon, *Claude Lorrain* (London, 1989), p. 121.

[6] The last black chalks of the *Crucified Christ* and of the *Madonna* in the British Museum are particularly eloquent.

it comes to unfinished fragments, one might expect the legacy of the very old to be a particularly rich source. There is the proverbial forgetfulness and supposedly enfeebled grip on practicalities of the aged and infirm: they might start something one day and forget about it the next and perhaps start something new or even the same thing all over again. And even formerly obsessive workers might no longer fret if some of their products did not receive "the last solemn rites of our sacred craft".[7] Far from regretting this, some critics have detected in the unfinished state the very secret of the extraordinary impact of the late creations, what Max Liebermann movingly described, approaching his own harassed old age, as "the mysterious beauty of the sketch".[8]

Michelangelo has long been the tutelary deity of this school of thought; and his three sculpted *Pietàs*, spanning virtually the whole of his career, provide it with titanic support.[9] Millions gaze at the first and most famous one every year in St Peter's Basilica in Rome. It was the creation of his twenties and must be one of the most sheerly beautiful works ever carved in marble. Before him, to most of his contemporaries in Italy the idea of a frail, grief-stricken Virgin holding the dead body of a grown man in her lap was an awkward, even grotesque, idea;[10] indeed, the reluctance of established masters to tackle the theme in the way the French Cardinal de la Groslaie wanted it may have been the reason why the aged prelate entrusted the task to the still comparatively unknown young Tuscan.[11] To Michelangelo, too, combining pathos and beauty must have been a challenge; but such challenges were his life-blood. The result was a triumph. After the unveiling people felt that they

[7] Ingres: who else? Quoted by J. Billaux, *Ingres immortel* (Paris, 1932), p. 82.

[8] M. Liebermann, *Gesammelte Schriften* (Berlin, 1922), p. 220.

Max Liebermann advanced from the Naturalism of Bastien-Lepage, fashionable in the 1880s, to become the leading German Impressionist. In all styles, but especially in the last, he created beautiful works. He was also a distinguished portraitist. In his last years – he died in 1935, aged eighty-five – he saw his paintings ridiculed by the Nazis and removed from museums and even destroyed.

[9] Four if one includes the lovely but probably unauthentic *"Palestrina" Pietà*. The name derives from the town where, in the Barberini Chapel of the church of Santa Rosalia, the sculpture stood for many years. It is of the yellow marble-coloured limestone found in the region. It did not begin to be attributed to Michelangelo until the eighteenth century.

In addition to the sculpted *Pietàs* there is also a drawing, dedicated to Vittoria Colonna, to whom he also dedicated many of his late sonnets.

[10] It was a northern theme: French and German artists could exploit the "grotesqueness" to add pathos to their creations.

[11] The Cardinal (who represented the King of France at the Curia) specified that there should be only two figures, the Virgin and the dead Christ. The work was intended for his own tomb – he never saw it completed – and it did in fact stand in the French Chapel in old St Peter's before being transferred to its present position.

could refer to the artist as "Il Divino" without being guilty of blasphemy. Nobody expected the work to be surpassed even by its young creator. Yet the theme of heavenly love continued to stir in the artist's mind.

He began his second or Florentine *Pietà* in his early seventies, perhaps intending it for his own tomb.[12] As the work neared completion, a vein of emery exploded in a shower of sparks and the enraged artist destroyed much of what he had already carved.[13] But the unfinished sculpture still stops one's breath. The mutilated Christ sags lifelessly, the head falling toward the face of the Virgin. Hers is a figure compounded of love and grief but also of strength, perhaps born of the remembrance of the artist's own mother. The hooded figure of Nicodemus,[14] the face fraught with fatigue and suffering, the half-closed eyes dulled with pain, is almost certainly a self-portrait. A pupil and assistant, Tiberio Calcagni, reverently assembled the pieces and

[12] The work did not arrive in Florence (in its reconstructed state) until a hundred years after the artist's body had been laid to rest in the church of Santa Croce (as had been his wish) under a mediocre monument by Vasari. His own *Pietà* was therefore placed first in the vault of San Lorenzo's and later behind the high altar of the Duomo. It is now in the Museum of the Opera del Duomo.

[13] The block of marble was a present from Pope Paul III Farnese and had been recovered from the ruins of a Roman temple. Despite the unbounded reverence professed (and no doubt felt) by Renaissance popes, princes, scholars and artists for the masterpieces of Antiquity – the discovery of a previously unknown manuscript by a Greek or Roman poet or philosopher was hailed as an event surpassing in importance minor wars – their treatment of lapidary remains would horrify a present-day conservationist. Nicholas V, one of the most learned of Renaissance popes, had 2300 wagon-loads of marble removed from the Colosseum in a single year, as well as quarrying from the Circus Maximus, the Forum and the Temple of Venus for the construction of his new palace in the Vatican; and that great patron of art, Sixtus IV, had a whole temple of Apollo demolished to provide material for building the famous chapel named after him. Nor were professional sculptors and architects more conservation-minded. Brunelleschi was one of the few who is known to have made measurements of architectural remains to calculate effective proportions. Others, including Michelangelo, were merely inspired to brood poetically over the impermanence of earthly power and glory while using blocks of antique statuary for their own work. The damage done to imperial Rome by the Renaissance was probably far greater than that inflicted by barbarian hordes.

[14] Pedantically speaking it is a "Deposition" rather than a "*Pietà*" (as are many other Renaissance *Pietàs*, similarly misnamed), the latter title being canonically reserved for two-figure compositions of the Virgin and the dead Christ. In the same spirit, although Nicodemus, the Pharisee, is often shown carrying or supporting Christ's body in Renaissance entombments, there is no biblical authority for his presence. But, according to St John (3: 1–21), he did visit Christ in the night and Christ said to him: "Verily, verily, I say unto thee, Except a man be born again, he cannot see the kingdom of God ... For God so loved the world, that he gave his only begotten Son, that whosoever believeth in him, should not perish, but have everlasting life ... He that believeth in him is not condemned ..." The passage so closely embodies Michelangelo's and the Catholic Reformation's basic doctrine that they make any alternative identification unlikely.

for structural reasons even added a Magdalen of his own. The figure is a respectable piece of funerary stonemasonry, but as part of a group carved by Michelangelo it is pathetic.

Nobody ever dared to touch Michelangelo's third and last *Pietà*.[15] It is indeed still almost as much a natural formation as an artefact, the beginning of sculpture as well as one of its peaks. The artist probably began it in his late seventies and was still working on it a week before he died. In some preliminary sketches he seems to have envisaged a complex three-, four- or five-figure composition. Eventually he eliminated all but two. But is it two? It is almost impossible to visualise a clear line of division between the figures of Christ and the Virgin. Nor can their union be understood in purely physical terms. Christ's angular and attenuated body cannot gravitationally be supported by its legs. Yet not only is it supported but it itself becomes the support of the Virgin. And not just physical support; she seems to draw strength from His inert figure – as the living can still draw strength from the dead.

Could Michelangelo have finished the work given another year – or ten years?[16] Did he expect to finish it? He had always lived a frugal life and in his eighties he was still reasonably fit. But as a young man he had listened to the scorching message of Savonarola – and had for many years ignored it. A little book by the heretical – or martyred – friar nevertheless remained his nightly reading.[17] *About Prayer* is a work as simple as it is profound. One passage compares "inward prayer" to an artist trying to mould in clay the image of God. Savonarola adds the warning: "to aim at finishing such a work would be like some showy outward ceremony ... palliative but self-deceiving for a soul without faith".[18] In youth and middle age Michelangelo had often

[15] Named "Rondanini" after the palace in Rome in whose courtyard it stood for centuries.

[16] The concept of the "unfinishable" work of art was developed by H. von Einem, *Das Unvollendete als künstlerische Form* (Berlin, 1959), p. 69, and is learnedly discussed by E. Wind, *Art and Anarchy* (London, 1963), p. 124.

[17] Few religious reformers have had such a bad press from historians – both Catholic and Protestant – as this saintly and learned Dominican. It was his misfortune to become a political figurehead and eventual scapegoat in the infighting of the political factions in Florence. Although his flock was responsible for the destruction of some objects of beauty (as well as of luxury), he himself was no enemy of the arts and learning. When, after a period of high popularity, Florentines tired of him, they readily collaborated with a servile clergy and a vengeful papacy in having him tortured, hanged and burned. Savonarola was forty-six, and the date, 1498, marks the end of Florence's intellectual and artistic leadership of the Renaissance. Savonarola was not a great thinker but a man pure in soul whom not only Michelangelo but also other great artists like Botticelli loved and admired. Despite the flagrant injustice done to him, he has never been rehabilitated by the church.

[18] G. Savonarola, "About Prayer", in *Selected Works*, translated and edited by J. Mercier (London, 1895), p. 328.

proclaimed his intention of storming the heavens: "Al cielo aspiro ... Al ciel sempre son mosso." At nearly ninety – "si presso a morte, e si lontan da Dio" – he had no such aspirations.[19] He was seeking, not storming, a sinner tormented by fears and doubts but surely not lacking in faith.

Unfinished or unfinishable? Goethe would have been in no doubt that the last *Pietà*, like *Day* and *Night* in the Medici Chapel in Florence, were not only *unvollendet* but also *unvollendbar*; and Henry Moore, not given to swooning over mysterious beauties, not only regarded the late "unfinished" *Slaves* in Florence as superior to the earlier "finished" ones in the Louvre, but also suggested that the former should not be called "unfinished":[20] Michelangelo, Moore maintained, had clearly never intended to "finish" them.[21] Perhaps not. One great artist never explains another; but possible analogies – in this case between the unfinished works of Michelangelo and of Rodin – are sometimes illuminating.

Rodin loved ruins, partly for their Romantic resonance but also because unplanned physical damage sometimes added what he described as a special radiance to the surviving remains. In pursuit of this magic he occasionally tried to enhance his own creations by exposing them in a few minutes to the battering of centuries.[22] The experiments were worth trying but never really worked. His artificial fragments look like artificial fragments; and one sometimes feels an unworthy urge to chop off large lumps of functionless marble from his deliberately unfinished pieces. But this is never true of the works which were conceived as torsos from the start and for a purpose.

A comparison between his late *Marching Man* and his early *St John* is instructive. *St John* is a complete figure,[23] seemingly propelled forward by the inner force of faith. The *Marching Man* is headless and armless and has

---

[19] J. A. Symonds, translator, *The Sonnets of Michelangelo* (London, 1950; first published in 1878), pp. 45 and 180. More recent works, in particular G. Creighton and R. N. Linscott, translators, *Complete Poems and Selected Letters of Michelangelo* (New York, 1965), give English texts only.

[20] The Florentine figures were probably meant for the tomb of Julius II and there is no good reason to doubt that they were intended to receive the same finish as the completed supporting figures, Leah and Rachel.

[21] P. James, editor, *Henry Moore on Sculpture* (London, 1986), p. 183.

[22] Vollard among others claimed to have seen Rodin smashing up statues to obtain "evocative fragments"; and Rilke for one heartily approved. See R. M. Rilke, *Auguste Rodin* (Berlin, 1903), p. 68. But Anatole France, more down to earth, disagreed: "Rodin collaborated too closely with catastrophe", he was quoted as saying. See G. Apollinaire, *Chronique d'art* (Paris, 1934), p. 430.

[23] The model for it was an old Italian peasant who wandered into Rodin's studio, a disused shed in the Rue de Furneaux (now the Rue Falguière) near the Luxembourg, in search of shelter.

no spiritual dimension.[24] The latter does not eclipse the former; but for sheer *élan* (to use one of Rodin's favourite expressions) it is undoubtedly superior. Rodin's own explanation, that one needs neither a head nor arms to march, is sometimes quoted as evidence of his sense of humour; but he was probably serious and the statement is certainly valid. Similarly the impact of *Balzac*'s finely carved head is enhanced by emerging from an amorphous, rocklike body; and *The Thinker* owes its evocation of concentrated thought as much to the cursorily modelled small head as to the brilliantly detailed feet.[25] But these "unfinished" effects were not designed to give a false impression. The *Marching Man* does not pretend to be a male *Venus of Milo*, and *Balzac* and *The Thinker* are not petrified sketches. The same is probably true of most other "unfinishable" works.

In an account of the death of Michelangelo in Rome the Florentine envoy reported home that the master had burnt all his unfinished drawings before he died, "not wishing that posterity should dwell on incomplete and tentative adumbrations".[26] It does not sound like the action of a man bent on leaving behind an oeuvre of unfinished works. Yet there is some truth in the "unfinishable". The *Florentine Slaves, Day and Night* and the *Rondanini Pietà* are unfinishable in the sense that nobody after Michelangelo's death could have finished them. Nor could the artist in his eighties and nineties realistically hope to bring them himself to their final state of perfection. In making his progress unhurried, despite the pressure of time, he was also probably influenced by the pieties of the Catholic Reformation.[27] But acquiescence in works never being completed is not the same as planning them to remain incomplete. And to suggest that Michelangelo could not have finished his unfinished works is as fatuous as to suggest that Mozart reached such perfection by the time he died at thirty-five that he could not have progressed further had he lived, like his old friend Haydn, another fifty years. Such

---

[24] By the time he completed it, Rodin was recognised as a "representative" French master, and the work was purchased by the state to be installed amid suitable festivities (superintended by the Duchesse de Choiseul) in the courtyard of the Palazzo Farnese, the French embassy in Rome. The ambassador, the Marquis de Lande, hated it from the start: he was, he maintained, surrounded by quite enough people who had lost their heads without this "awful permanent fixture" and threatened to demolish it with his ambassadorial Hispano-Suisa. The Duchesse prevailed for a time but the Marquis had his way in the end; though not actually demolished, the original statue was returned to France in 1918 and is now in the Musée des Beaux-Arts in Lyon. (Its positioning, on top of a Corinthian column, greatly reduces its impact.)

[25] Or, as Rilke put it, "his feet look more intelligent than his face", Rilke, *Auguste Rodin*, p. 254.

[26] J. A. Symonds, *The Life of Michelangelo Buonarroti*, 2 volumes (London, 1893), p. 321.

[27] See above, Chapter 2, p. 22 and nn. 33–35.

speculations cannot be disproved but all circumstantial evidence contradicts them.[28]

What was true of Michelangelo and Rodin was also true of other old artists. Titian's last *Pietà* and Maillol's *Harmony* are great works of art despite the fact that they are unfinished, not because of it. Kandinski, Bonnard and Munch died after years of more or less enforced isolation; but their legacy was not a clutter of doodles, sketches and forgotten beginnings. Of course they were interrupted – Kandinski's last painting, like Chardin's, was on his easel when he died – but their studios were in a state no different from that of a busy young artist putting his brush down for a moment to answer the door-bell.

[28] Neither Haydn nor any other long-lived great composer began to decline in his mid-thirties (except as a result of physical or mental breakdown due to illness); and the same is true of visual artists.

# 21

# *Themes and Prophecies*

If there was no universal late style and no universal late technique, one would hardly expect to discover a universal late theme; nor was there one. But one can point to something that almost amounts to an exception. While commissioned portraits have always been a popular and remunerative branch of the visual arts, this has never been true of self-portraits. Few of Rembrandt's fascinating series sold in his lifetime (except as bonuses to accompany other commissioned work); and, until the seventeenth century, when one of the more imaginative of the late Medicis, the Cardinal Leopoldo, started his collection in Florence,[1] even celebrated contemporary artists were rarely paid to commemorate their own likenesses. Lack of outside interest did not of course stop artists from turning to the mirror for inspiration. Most young people, embarking on or even contemplating a career in the arts, still find the challenge irresistible.[2] But other subjects soon claim their attention; and self-portraits in middle age tend to become an occasional indulgence. There is then a reversal of the trend. No longer concerned with selling their products, dazzling their admirers or hitting the headlines, many long-lived artists produced in old age a remarkable crop of self-revelations, including a few virtual firsts and several masterpieces of the genre.

Was Bellini's Noah in one of his astonishing late works, *The Drunkenness of Noah*, a self-portrait? There is no documentary evidence for it but he had never painted a naked old man before and he must surely have been influenced by what he saw in the mirror.[3] His successor as First Painter to the Serenissima, Titian, was temperamentally disinclined to paint anything for

---

[1] Now housed in the Vasari Corridor, linking the Uffizi with the Pitti Palace. The collection was continued by the Medici archdukes of Tuscany, the Habsburg-Lorraine archdukes and the Italian state and is still being added to. It now contains self-portraits by Leonardo da Vinci, Michelangelo, Fra Angelico, Rubens, Vasari, Bassano, Andrea del Sarto, Veronese, Rosalba Carriera, Correggio, Carracci, Batoni, Rembrandt, Raphael, Velasquez, Bernini, Titian, David, Canova, Delacroix, Corot, Ingres, Puvis de Chavannes, Ensor and Chagall, among several hundred others.

[2] Even the young Corot and Turner, neither of them particularly interested in faces, did.

[3] The scene, described in Genesis 9:20–27, is potentially tragic, as Michelangelo depicted it on the ceiling of the Sistine Chapel, or broadly comic; but Bellini's *Noah* is neither. The three sons (Ham who mocked, Shem who looked on, and Japhet who covered his father) are

which there was no buyer waiting in the wings;[4] but he too painted himself more than once during his last twenty years. In the Berlin portrait his beard is still black, his face is vigorous and there is swagger in his display of the golden chain of knighthood bestowed on him many years earlier by the Emperor, but the painting is unfinished. His Prado self-portrait dates from several years later. Here he is an old man, grey-haired, pale, tired-looking but still at work (Plate 2).[5] In the still later triple portrait of his elder son, Orazio, his *nepote*, Niccolò, and himself, known as *The Allegory of Prudence*, he looks ancient, but fierce. But most movingly he is probably the supplicating emaciated figure of St Joseph of Arimathea in the last *Pietà*.[6] The third artist in the great Venetian succession, Tintoretto, painted a glowering image of himself as a young man but thereafter, for fifty years, one glimpses him only occasionally as one in a crowd.[7] But in old age he painted a mesmeric full-frontal portrait of himself as well as appearing in his last *Pietà*.[8]

Michelangelo's distorted face looks out from the flayed skin held up by St Bartholomew in the *Last Judgement* in the Sistine Chapel; and he is almost certainly Nicodemus in the Florentine *Pietà*.[9] Bernini painted himself as a darkly handsome youth at sixteen, and began to explore his own features regularly in his sixties. As befits a man who made almost a cult of his own modesty, Chardin did not paint himself until his seventies (or at least none of his youthful essays in the genre survive); but then he created in pastels a series which a hundred years later sent the Goncourts into raptures (Plate 6).[10] Goya's last self-portrait in his seventies was not only his best but also the most memorable depiction in art of a diagnosable acute medical condition (Plate 8).[11] A

stock characters and a little squashed but the Patriarch is unlike any other Noah painted before or since. He is neither a neglected geriatric nor a drooling drunk: yet he is very old and frail and not just because of his beard and thin white hair. Every square inch of his almost transparent skin, his every muscle and his every bone proclaim his age (especially the superbly modelled "Pagetoid" bowed and thickened right thigh; a common medical condition in the elderly described by Sir James Paget of St Bartholomew's Hospital, London, in 1877, and named after him), but he is also cuddly as a baby and spotlessly clean.

    [4] See above, Chapter 2, p. 17.
    [5] He also painted himself into the great *Trinity*, commissioned by Charles V, which the Emperor took with him to the monastery of Yuste after his abdication and which he ordered to be brought to him before retiring to his death-bed. The artist is shown on the extreme right under the portrait of Philip.
    [6] See above, Chapter 19, p. 271 n. 15.
    [7] As in *The Miracle of St Mark Freeing the Slave*, where he is the rather smug-looking onlooker near the right margin.
    [8] See above, Chapter 2, p. 29.
    [9] See above, Chapter 20, p. 283 and n. 14.
    [10] See above, Chapter 4, pp. 54–57.
    [11] See above, Chapter 5, pp. 72–73.

sensitive and revealing self-portrait was one of Ingres's last works (to contrast with the accomplished but arrogant image he painted of himself in his early twenties);[12] and a self-portrait was one of Nolde's last oil paintings. Käthe Kollwitz too recorded her grief-lined but still beautiful face in her seventies. Even Hokusai, an unashamedly commercial artist whose physiognomy was no saleable commodity, painted himself more than once as he approached the end of his long life.[13] In more modern times it was Munch and Bonnard who created, within the limits of the genre, something more than a personal record.

Munch recorded his fight with the ghost of old age.[14] Bonnard's motives are more problematic (Plate 17). He never regarded himself as a portraitist. Before the First World War he regularly refused commissions even when he was hard pressed financially; and though he gave in to Vollard's insistence, and Vollard professed to prefer Bonnard's portrait of him to sparkling likenesses by Renoir, Braque, Cézanne and Picasso, the painting is no more than respectable. But from middle age onwards, and with increasing frequency, Bonnard painted himself: the oddest series of self-portraits in twentieth-century art. In all he is turning his back to the light, his features barely visible within the egg shape of the head. It feels as if he was reluctantly being dragged into the limelight and fearful of what it might reveal. But who was doing the dragging? And if detailed revelations might embarrass him, why did he choose to reveal himself at all? Perhaps he felt that the hiding and revealing but not revealing was itself part of his personality, a Greta Garbo act without the hankering for publicity. It was in the years after Marthe's death that the act reached its apogee; in the end his face became no more than an Oriental mask, enigmatic, mocking, mysterious and tragic.

Of course there are lacunae. Turner painted himself in youth once – handsome, intelligent and confident – but never afterwards. There is no authentic likeness of one of the greatest of all portraitists, Hals; and only one self-portrait of another, David.[15] But occasionally the "self-portrait" took an odd form.

"Surtout il ne faut jamais mourir", Matisse told Françoise Gilot in his eighties, perhaps half-jokingly.[16] But, coming from him, it was a profoundly revealing remark. His career had spanned two world wars, revolutions, mass murder, the Holocaust and the collapse of man's faith in progress.

[12] He repainted it in his seventies, changing the dress and the background, making himself look even more like an all-conquering hero.

[13] Most memorably at eighty-three, on the margin of a letter written to his publisher, now in the Ethnographical Museum, Leiden, Holland.

[14] See above, Chapter 10, pp. 151–53.

[15] In the Uffizi collection of self-portraits.

[16] F. Gilot, quoted in J. Flam, *Matisse* (New York, 1988), p. 387.

Throughout that time he had celebrated the most mundane blessings of life: sunlight, flowers, women, fruit and sleep. In the doom-laden 1930s he had been apostrophised by the politically committed avant-garde as the painter who pandered to frivolous luxury, the "king of escapists", a "sedative for exhausted brains" and, most famously, "an armchair for tired bourgeois".[17] Unfavourable comparisons with the socially aware Picasso were hurled at him by youngsters who had been yet unborn when he was already leader of the Fauves.[18] None of this stopped his fame from spreading, but at times even his admirers were irritated by his apparent lack of an ideological programme. He never explained and never apologised. Neither in the 1930s nor after the Second World War, emerging as one of the cultural icons of the century, did he feel under any obligation to paint what was cruel, stupid or hideous in the world. Then, at the age of eighty-two, he surprised his friends (and perhaps himself) with *The Sadness of the King*, as near as he ever got to a full-scale "self-portrait" after youth.[19] In this remarkable "confession" black savages white, blue attacks orange, magenta and purple bite yellows, greens strangle reds. The monumental stability of his earlier paintings, even those seemingly most violent and disorderly, is gone: drunkenly the whole composition leans to the left, the black window of death lurking in an upper corner. Elements of vegetation seem to flutter in the air or creep around the throne; a musician strums a guitar; a dancer whirls in the foreground. None of those can dispel the pervasive pathos or relieve the despairing posture of the King himself. "Never before", wrote Françoise Gilot,

> had Matisse allowed one of his paintings to reflect a feeling so far removed from exultation and joy. For once the pride of the ageing genius has melted away and

---

[17] Ibid., p. 243.

[18] Or "Wild Beasts". The name was given by a critic, Louis Vaucelles, to the group of young artists around Matisse (Valtat, Manguin, Derain, Vlaminck, gifted but none in Matisse's class) who exhibited together in a room ("la cage des fauves") in the Third Salon d'Automne in Paris in 1905 and scandalised both the public and the critics with their violent colours and contrasts. But in private life Matisse was anything but a savage beast and never gloried in the role. "Please tell the American people", he said to Clara MacChesney, "that I am a devoted husband, that I have three fine children, that I go to the theatre, that I enjoy horseback riding, that I have a comfortable home and a nice garden and that I love flowers like any normal man." See Flam, *Matisse*, p. 32. And Mrs MacChesney, horrified as she was by the threat Monsieur Matisse and his fellow wild beasts posed not only to art but "to the very fabric of our civilisation", had yet to admit that, as he said good-bye to her and invited her to come again, "he seemed like a perfectly polite and ordinary gentleman". Ibid., p. 33. In the event and within a few years it did not need a few lumpen artists to destroy the fabric of the civilisation Mrs MacChesney and others felt so concerned about.

[19] He had occasionally sketched himself in a more orthodox manner: a pen drawing he gave to Dina Vierny is now in the Musée Maillol in Paris.

he confided ... sharing his sentiments about the impermanence of all things physical, giving voice not to fear but to a deep sorrow at the thought of parting from this world.[20]

The lack of a universal late theme did not mean that individual artists in old age did not discover themes which they had held in contempt for most of their lives. Wandering through the echoing and thoroughly looted marble halls and corridors of the Casita del Principe, formerly a royal hunting lodge on the slopes of El Escorial, Goya discovered a cache of paintings by Luis Melendez. Melendez had been one of the casualties of the savage art-political war in which Goya was a natural winner;[21] and thirty years after his death he was virtually forgotten. But he had left behind an astonishing group of still lives: dense, crowded, monumental and sometimes permeated with an air of decay – mouldy bread, fruit with worm-holes, chipped faïence and dead birds stiff in their last agony. The paintings had understandably not tempted the officially appointed thieves of King Joseph Bonaparte, or even the more discriminating amateur competition, but they fascinated Goya. He may of course have seen them before – the social and artistic circles revolving around the royal court were small and incestuous – but, soon after witnessing some of the scenes of horror he was later to depict in *The Disasters of War*, the genre must have struck him with hitherto hidden possibilities. In the past he probably regarded it as the province of hacks and even of craftsmen painter-decorators. It was also going out of fashion. But it was always when he was selling himself most clamorously in the market place (as he was doing at the Bonaparte Court) that he also created his most private pictures. He never expected to sell his still lives; nor did he. His *Dead Turkey*, though almost certainly inspired by Melendez, is more stark, gruesome and grand. The image of the murdered creature, its outstretched neck still straining against death, one wing still almost aflutter, inhabits a different world from that of the elegantly unprotesting fowl of Oudry and Chardin, let alone their numerous second- and third-rate imitators. The chasm expressed the difference between the gentle if at times insipid eighteenth-century grace of Goya's youth, depicted on his tapestry cartoons, and the all-too-sipid

[20] F. Gillot, *Picasso and Matisse*, translated by N. A. Talese (London, 1990), p. 178.

[21] Melendez's father, a gifted miniaturist, was a founder of the Academia de Bellas Artes de San Fernando, the Royal Academy of Spain, but an apparently quarrelsome and difficult character. He carelessly aroused the disfavour of Philip V's court painter, Van Loo, and was expelled. The son may have inherited some of the paternal quirks: after a promising start he too fell out of favour at Court and, despite repeated efforts, did not succeed in ingratiating himself again until a few years before his death. During his last years he painted a series of still lives for the Casita del Principe, the villa used by the Prince of Asturias, the future Carlos IV. Melendez died in 1780, aged sixty-four.

nineteenth century which was buffeting him in old age.[22] A few more still lives followed, all during the blood-soaked years between 1808 and 1812.[23] His dead fish, their scaly bodies glinting in the moonlight, stare at the beholder as if startled by their sudden transition from life to death. His pair of dead woodcock, thrown into a heap, embrace each other tenderly in death. His rib, loin and head of mutton (with the brain removed) is like a monstrous guffaw at the butchery of life: animal or human, what's the difference? The artist signed his name under the sheep's head with red paint as if in blood.[24]

There is one other aspect of the art of old age which is not style, technique or theme but a bit of all three. Art historians sometimes describe the late works of the masters as "prophetic". Late Donatello is said to foreshadow not only Michelangelo but also Rodin. Late Bassano is said to foreshadow El Greco. Late Claude foreshadows Turner. Late Turner foreshadows Monet. Monet of the last *Water Lilies* foreshadows everything that has been painted since. Such lineages are fun to trace (as are most kinships) but often they are figments. What seemed prophetic to later generations was usually not a particular style but the freedom of old masters to jettison rules and paint in the style that best suited their purpose. Young artists of a later age would respond to their predecessors' sense of liberation and would at times mistakenly adopt their manner and mannerisms. The results were often poor; but the impulse was right. With luck and perseverance the young artists would eventually discover *their* personal style and, with it, their own path to freedom. Yet no generalisation about art is entirely true, not even one's own. Great artists in old age did sometimes achieve what was in a sense "prophetic", their last works casting a shaft of light far into the future. But this had little to do with brushwork, colour schemes, composition, subject or any technical device.

Bellini, the greatest of the *Madonnieri*, was a spiritual painter, the child of an age in which the arts were still handmaidens of faith. He was also, like

---

[22] Tapestry cartoons were always idealised. The idyllic harvest scene showing merry peasants having a well-earned rest with the corn piled up around them was painted in 1786, the year of one of the worst famines in eighteenth-century Spain. Winter was portrayed as peasants huddling around a fire in a snowstorm; but they are warmly clothed and are taking a pig home.

[23] The chilling resonances between the still lives and some of the most gruesome sheets of the *Disasters of War* were pointed out by J. Lopez-Rey, *Art Quarterly*, 44 (1948), p. 251.

[24] Goya's masterly brushwork, ranging from thin films to thickly built-up impasto, was rarely more in evidence than in these relatively little-known dead animal paintings. The single brushstrokes of black, ochre and grey which create the turkey's wings and tail are stunning. After Goya's death the unsold still lives passed to his son, Javier, and then to his grandson, Mariano, whose gambling debts they eventually helped to pay.

most innovative geniuses, a firm traditionalist.[25] But as a new and more secular age dawned, painters of Madonnas were no longer judged exclusively by the pious sentiments they kindled; and Bellini responded to this too. His Madonnas and female saints, though always pure and serene, were also beautiful: any normal male could fall in love with them. It was this concession to human interest, perhaps even to animal longing, which allowed religious art to survive through centuries of irreligion. But it was the less obvious complementary truth which was Bellini's most prophetic achievement.

The Feast of the Gods, one of the works Bellini completed in his late seventies, seems to be a little confusingly based on two amalgamated scenes from Ovid's Fasti.[26] Its exact origin, especially by whom and for what occasion it was commissioned, has been the subject of much learned but inconclusive debate.[27] No less intriguing is why part of the background was repainted by Titian.[28] But most puzzling is the theme and the mood. All Bellini's earlier work had been transparently chaste. No doubt this was expected from a celebrated painter of altar-pieces; but it was also the style of his generation. Erotica and pornography probably flourished in the Venice of his youth, as always and everywhere; but they were no part of art as Bellini's contemporaries

[25] Almost every detail of Vasari's vivid account of the adoption of oil painting by Venetian painters has been questioned by art historians, and there may well have been desultory experiments in Venice (and elsewhere in Italy) with oil-based pigments for at least a hundred years before Bellini. Yet the decisive events were probably the arrival in Venice of the Neapolitan painter Antonella de Messina (who may have learnt the technique in Flanders from its possible inventors, the Van Eyck brothers), and the adoption of the new medium by Bellini and his workshop. New media do not of course generate masterpieces – very soon oil paints would be responsible for more bad painting in Italy and elsewhere than all other media put together – but intuitively Bellini and his pupils grasped its essence. It was (as it still is) a language of individual brushstrokes. Of course it provided scope for washes and blobs and smudges – spoken language too would be impoverished without its groans, grunts, sighs and clearings of the throat – but, just as the value of speech ultimately depends on individually articulated single words, so the message of oil painting depends on individually smeared single brush-loads. By the end of Bellini's long life that knowledge was to carry Venetian painting to its summit.

[26] The first scene is set at the biennial festival of Bacchus, attended by gods, satyrs, Pan and Silenus and his ass. When all are drowsy on wine, Priapus tries to assault the sleeping nymph, Lotis; but she is awakened by the braying of Silenus's ass and escapes Priapus's unwelcome attention. The second scene is the feast of Cybele where Priapus again, this time a gatecrasher, attempts to rape Vesta herself. None of the characters quite fit either scene.

[27] E. Wind, in Bellini's Feast of the Gods (Cambridge, Massachusetts, 1948), suggested that the painting may have been commissioned to celebrate the wedding of Alfonso d'Este and Lucrezia Borgia and identified several prominent guests among the characters in the painting.

[28] Titian's landscape backgrounds are always worth having; but X-ray studies suggest that Bellini's original was just as good and perhaps more appropriate.

understood the term. But by the second and third decade of the next century perceptions of what was and was not proper changed (as they still do every generation or so), and with it came a growing demand for paintings of a more relaxed and sometimes frankly titillating kind. The demand was well catered for by Bellini's pupils, Titian and Giorgione among them, but nobody expected the patriarch himself to embrace the new permissive world of young trendies. Nor did he. That his painting depicts highly questionable goings on is certain. There is the crude gesture of the central character, for example, and the priapic state of Priapus himself.[29] And yet, in contrast to Titian's contemporary *Bacchanal,* an unblushing celebration of carnal pleasures, the overall mood of *The Feast of the Gods* is blissfully, even a little wistfully, Arcadian; a page from Virgil rather than from Ovid at his steamiest.[30]

At a glance the master's last altar-piece in San Giovanni Chrisostomo, one of Venice's homeliest churches, is a less startling departure from convention. The conception is harmonious and the background is of a dreamlike beauty; but these had been attributes of Bellini's altar-pieces for half a century. But here, for the first time, the architectural framework has become part of the devotional message. The two flanking saints, St Christopher and St Louis of Toulouse, are inside the picture but are also stepping out of it: they seem about to join the congregation to seek out and to bring comfort to those troubled in heart. The departure from established format may seem trivial today but it represented a significant shift in the relationship of the church to the faithful; a greater intimacy but also a staginess that pre-echoed Bernini.

The most surprising – and beautiful – is what may have been Bellini's last painting (Plate 1). Who was *The Lady at her Toilet?* She is not a goddess but nor is she quite an ordinary mortal. A naked and luscious young woman gazes into the mirror with the serenity of a Madonna. She adjusts her hair in preparation for – what? The image is more sensuous than anything Bellini had ever painted before; but there is about it no more than a soupçon of impropriety. Yet it is there. And of course the figure is only part of the whole. As in all of Bellini's late works, the parts – the purple damask of the headdress, the green of the curtain, the soft pink of the drapery, the receding landscape, the luminous sky and the pearly flesh-tones – fuse in perfect harmony. At one level, then, a desirable naked young woman is readying

[29] Even if one could overlook Neptune, alias Alfonso, stroking his bride's thigh with one hand in anticipation of his conjugal rights, one can hardly condone his pinching Ceres's bottom at the same time with the other. There is clearly room here for more art-historical research.

[30] Not surprisingly, it was lovingly copied by the greatest of Arcadians, Poussin, a century and a half later.

herself for an assignation or just ministering to her own vanity. At another level it is an almost virginal celebration of female beauty, one of God's gifts to mankind.

Of course the verbiage – celebrations of art, beauty, nature, love, God, this, that and the other – is familiar from the mouths of pornographers and trash merchants. But *The Feast of the Gods* and *The Lady at her Toilet* are neither pornography nor trash. Bellini's contemporaries recognised them as works of art and they have been cherished as such ever since. And if it was the introduction of a carnal element which allowed religious art to survive, the reverse is no less true. Without a whiff of Bellinian holiness that can emanate even from the most fleshbound creations, secular art would surely have withered. Perhaps this was an inevitable historical development; and, if he had died at seventy, another great artist, or several, would have established it. But it was Bellini who in his astonishing old age actually did so.

# 22

# *Exceptions*

If exceptions are the touchstones of norms, then the long-lived artists in this study are something of an embarrassment. None truly qualifies as an exception. To find examples, it is necessary to look among painters and sculptors who would not perhaps be generally regarded as being of the first rank.[1] This is not to suggest that artists of lower rank are (or were) more likely to decline or stagnate. Perhaps, perhaps not. The two groups are not comparable on grounds of numbers alone.

Turner was the only English-speaking artist originally included. Relaxing the rank qualifications even slightly, the numbers start mounting at once. Stubbs and Sickert, both of them over eighty when they died, are but two of the well-loved and excellent painters who would be added.[2] They would not be the only ones. Between its foundation in 1768 and 1960 the Royal Academy of Arts of London has had 464 fellows of whom no less than 182 lived to seventy-five or over. Of the fifteen presidents seven did. Royal Academicians have included a number of gifted painters and sculptors (though rarely, after the generation of Turner and Constable, the most gifted ones of any period); and not many of the fellows and presidents were entirely innocent of talent. There would therefore be well over a hundred artists to be included in any long-lived series just below the top rank from England alone. Considering that until the present century the English-speaking people hardly shone in the visual arts, the inclusion of artists of comparable stature from the rest of the world would present one with a case material of thousands. To try to compare such a crowd with a select list of thirty would be absurd. Less ambitiously, one can look for a few exceptions simply to make the late flowering acceptable as a norm.

Inevitably one looks with keenest interest at artists whose career was

---

[1] It may be recalled (see above, Chapter 1) that the other criterion for selection was longevity to seventy-five years or over; and that artists still alive or those who have died within the past forty-five years were to be excluded. Breaking one condition was bad enough: looking for exceptions among lower "ranks", the lower age limit of seventy-five and the exclusion zone of forty-five years were to be meticulously observed.

[2] George Stubbs was eighty-two when he died in 1806; Walter Sickert was eighty-one when he died in 1942.

interrupted in midstream by some historical or social cataclysm, not too recent but not lost in the dim distant past either. The French Revolution and its Napoleonic aftermath might have been staged for that purpose. David was a young lion patronised by royalty and the highest aristocracy when the Revolution erupted.[3] He survived and indeed flourished under both its high-minded beginnings and the Terror. Robespierre's fall left a temporary vacancy in his niche of heroes, but it was quickly filled by the young General Bonaparte.[4] The artist survived the rise and fall of Napoleon, too, and found what was arguably his best artistic incarnation in old age.

Not all were so lucky. At a distinctly lower level of achievement, Jean-Baptiste Greuze made his name at thirty with a well-painted and hugely sentimental genre piece, *Grandfather Explaining the Bible to his Family*. Financially outclassing far better painters like Chardin, he became the darling of a society steeped in the lachrymose rustic simplicities of Jean-Jacques Rousseau. To the young Queen Marie-Antoinette and her friends, too, playing milkmaids and shepherds in the glades of the Petit Trianon, his confections of bashful eroticism provided the perfect backdrop and inspiration; and prints of his *Broken Pitcher* broke all records in popularity. But, despite his frantic efforts to adapt his talent, such as it was, to the new dispensation, the Revolution ruined him both financially and morally. Napoleon and his scatterbrained but tender-hearted siblings, brought up among Greuze prints in faraway Corsica, continued to provide him with charitable commissions. He painted the future Emperor himself, still as First Consul, about the same time as did the young Ingres. Even without making a devastating comparison with Ingres' portrait (the best of Bonaparte and certainly of Bonaparte at his best), Greuze's effort was shockingly bad.[5] Many of his late paintings survive – he was eighty when he died in 1805 –

[3] Not only the King, Louis XVI, who commissioned *The Oath of the Horatii*, but also the Duke of Saxe-Teschen, the Duc de Noailles, the Marquis de la Motte and the King's younger brother, the Comte d'Artois (the future Charles X), were among his patrons.

[4] David's most famous image of the future Emperor, *Bonaparte Crossing the Alps*, commemorates the campaign that ended in near-disaster but ultimate victory at Marengo. Ironically, the best of the five copies (now at Malmaison) was commissioned by Carlos IV of Spain, a temporary ally soon to be bundled off his throne by Napoleon.

[5] The year was 1803 and Bonaparte was at work on his Code Civil. The once untidy and emaciated-looking general had had a much-needed haircut but had not yet put on an ounce of flab. Ingres' portrait was commissioned by the city of Liège in recognition of the First Consul's grant of 30,000 francs for the reconstruction of the suburb of Amercour, destroyed by Austrian bombardment and seen through the window. It is infinitely superior not only to Greuze's terrible effort but also to Ingres' later ridiculous portrait of the Emperor posing as Jupiter.

and periodic attempts to elevate him among the masters founder (unfairly perhaps) on their dreadfulness.[6]

The personal fate of another royal favourite, Mme Marie-Louise-Elisabeth Vigée-Lebrun, was happier. Summoned to Versailles in her twenties (perhaps on Greuze's recommendation), she became the Queen's confidante as well as her official painter. Her charmingly relaxed and yet dignified portrait of Marie-Antoinette with her three children (to be endlessly copied on fans, vases, jewellery and every conceivable furnishing of a lady's dressing-table) was painted for the express purpose of restoring her mistress's frayed reputation as the embodiment of wifely, motherly and royal virtue.[7] In this objective it was at best a qualified success; but it secured for the painter membership of the Académie and a position as a leading society hostess.[8] At the outbreak of the Revolution – she was then thirty-four – she emigrated to Italy and then to Vienna, Prague, Dresden and St Petersburg. She returned to Paris in 1802; but, finding the "Merveilleuses" and "Epouvantables" unspeakably vulgar (as indeed they were),[9] she left again, first for England and then for Switzerland. She returned to France for good after the Bourbon Restoration, when she was fifty-five. Her occasional portraits of aristocratic ladies and their daughters were never less than accomplished and remained popular – a few have found their way into public collections – but she never recaptured the glories of her prerevolutionary days.[10] Her essays in landscape and genre painting were not notably successful. To better effect, she published two volumes of delightfully catty memoirs in 1843, when she was eighty.

A greater artist than either Greuze or Mme Vigée-Lebrun, and the most enigmatic casualty of the Revolution, was Jean-Antoine Houdon. Born in 1741, his talent at catching people's likenesses in clay was quickly noticed, and, in the decades before the Revolution, he created an unique visual and artistic record of the Age of Reason in its final and finest flowering.[11] His

[6] But prints and reproductions of his paintings remained immensely popular well into the twentieth century. His *Young Girl Weeping over a Dead Bird* was the last Tsarina's favourite painting.

[7] By young Renoir among others.

[8] Her husband, Jean-Baptiste Pierre Lebrun, was an art dealer, which, by the rules of the Académie, should have barred her from membership. But the Queen expressed her displeasure at such outdated practices and the rules crumbled.

[9] After the fall of Robespierre and under the Directory, France (or rather Paris) plunged into an orgy of merry-making. The ludicrously dolled up and affected fashionable young were called after their endlessly parroted exclamations of surprise.

[10] A particularly charming one of the Countess Golovin, which she painted in St Petersburg, is now in the Barber Institute of Fine Arts, Birmingham.

[11] Turgot, Rousseau, d'Alembert, Diderot, Buffon, the Montgolfier brothers, Lafayette, Mirabeau, Benjamin Franklin, Necker and, most famously, Voltaire were among his sitters.

affectionate and intimate portraits of his family and friends are no less cherishable. He was also the first European artist to be, at Thomas Jefferson's recommendation,[12] invited by the young United States of America to cross the Atlantic and fulfil official commissions.[13] His full-length portrait of George Washington is still the image by which the First President is best known today.[14] Back in France he escaped the Terror (by withdrawing from Paris and going into hiding), to be revered both by Napoleon and later by the restored Bourbons. But his last portraits – of Laplace, Andrew Fulton and Napoleon himself – are among his least successful ones; and, even allowing for the inhospitable setting and the atrocious lighting, his standing Voltaire in the crypt of the Pantheon does not compare with his earlier depiction of the sage sitting in an armchair.[15] And though the artist, a small wiry man who took pride in his peasant origins, remained an active and indeed contumacious member of the teaching staff of the Ecole des Beaux-Arts into his eighties, he created no more works of distinction after the age of sixty-two.[16]

It is to this cluster that an artist of the first rank who died just short of his seventy-fifth birthday belongs. Talleyrand, probably history's greatest authority on *douceurs* of every kind,[17] maintained that nobody who had not lived

[12] Jefferson recommended him to the Assembly of the State of Virginia as "the artist who is resorted to for portraits by most of the sovereigns in Europe". See H. H. Arnason, *Houdon* (London, 1975) p. 191. It was an excellent choice; but, knowingly or not, the claim was over the top. Houdon had carved busts of minor royalty, but the only two crowned heads he sculpted – Louis XVI and Catherine the Great of Russia – were *after* the commission from the United States.

[13] Houdon had been a great admirer of General Washington from afar and originally planned an equestrian statue in the manner of Falconet's monumental *Peter the Great* in St Petersburg. The General set his mind against such "ridiculous flamboyance" (as he did against wearing a Roman toga) and got his way; but Houdon's insistence on Washington sitting for him personally rather than sending "likenesses" was accepted. The long and elegant correspondence between Houdon, Jefferson, Patrick Henry, Governor of Virginia, and Henry Macon of the Assembly of Virginia still exists and is an excellent contemporary source. Eventually a fee was agreed, a time-scale set (three weeks in Mount Vernon to make clay models and three years back in France to carve the final marble) and an insurance for the artist's life crossing the Atlantic. The Assembly also agreed that the artist would bring with him one or two subordinate workmen who, Jefferson assured his friends, "would of course associate with their own class only" (quoted by Arnason, *Houdon*, p. 194).

[14] The original marble signed 1788 is in the Capitol of the State of Virginia in Richmond. The bronze in front of the National Gallery in London is a copy.

[15] Now in the foyer of the Comédie Française.

[16] He died in 1826, aged eighty-seven.

[17] No politician, let alone ex-bishop, amassed such a vast fortune in bribes from so many conflicting interests, or fathered such a brilliant brood of bastards (Delacroix among them). But more than once he was his country's saviour and even (over the Belgian crisis of 1830) the saviour of the peace of Europe.

during the *Ancien Régime* could have any idea of the meaning of the term *douceur de vivre*. One would not wish to argue with an expert, but there is nothing to stop one from savouring the sweetness of the period by looking at the work of Jean-Honoré Fragonard. Fragonard was of course more than the master of the stolen kiss, the rumpled bed and the treacherous glade; even his frothiest confections are suffused with lyricism, grace and elegance. He was only sixty when his world collapsed around him and his last patroness, Mme du Barry, lost her still beautiful head on the guillotine.[18] The artist withdrew for a time to Grasse, his birthplace, but then returned to Paris. David, who held Rococo artists of the *petit style* like Boucher, Lancret and Nattier in contempt,[19] had a high regard for Fragonard and found a post for him in the new museum service, and even a small apartment in the Louvre. But repeated attempts to recruit him to join in the celebrations of Republican virtue or later in the apotheosis of Napoleon proved vain; whether Fragonard ever tried and failed or never even tried is not known. Napoleon needed Fragonard's apartment in the Louvre – or so he said: he could be generous but also petty. In 1804 the old man was moved into a leaking garret in the Palais Royal and forgotten. A year and a half later, eighteen years after he completed his last signed and dated painting, he collapsed in the street and died a few days later. In the year of the French victory of Jena, the crushing defeat of Prussia and the ignominious demise (after 800 years) of the Holy Roman Empire, the event passed without even a ripple of public interest.

A sharp decline in creativity with advancing age may reflect private changes as well as historical upheavals. Augustus John hit the London art scene at a time when the visual arts in England were touching the rock bottom of dreariness.[20] He was spectacularly gifted, and had a flamboyant character and a reputation for leonine sexual prowess to match; and well into middle life his paintings and especially his drawings dazzled both professional critics and the picture-buying public. But this was not yet the dawn of the British artistic Renaissance of the twentieth century. By the time honours began to be heaped on him – a one-man retrospective exhibition at the Royal Academy (who cherished him as their tame lion), the presidency of the Royal Society of Portrait Painters, the Order of Merit, and, in 1941, a commission to paint

---

[18] She was Louis XV's last mistress and forty-six when she was arrested in 1793, on her return from England, and sentenced to death (on no grounds whatever, so far as one can tell, except for being rather silly). David enthusiastically welcomed the sentence.

[19] David and Fragonard came from the same background of respectable craftsmen, the backbone of the Third Estate, as did all the outstanding French artists of the eighteenth century. Fragonard's father was a glovemaker.

[20] He was born in 1878 and first exhibited at the Royal Academy in 1910. He died aged eighty-three.

a portrait of the Queen – his never very robust talent was near or even past exhaustion.[21] He himself was well aware of this. The question whether it was his unavailing search for the lost glories of youth which drove him to drink or the other way round remains unanswerable. Whereas his portraits of the 1930s were at least passable likenesses, even if not a patch on his work before the First World War, almost everything he painted after the Second World War, including an unintended caricature of Field Marshal Viscount Montgomery, was embarrassingly bad. The tragic spectacle of his final decline is relieved only by a last glimpse of him shakily descending the steps of the National Gallery in Trafalgar Square to join his fellow nonagenarian, Bertrand Russell, in the pelting rain in a sit-down protest against the nuclear posturings of the government of the day.

Gentlemanly stagnation has been – as it still is – more common than a sharp or even gradual decline. Of course, for a happy and prosperous bum-bledom in old age, artists need a stable society in which art of a safely traditional kind has a small but secure place; and such a state of affairs is not easy to conjure up today. But most of Europe and England in particular provided just such a setting (with brief interruptions) between the Napole-onic conflicts and the First World War; and for every revolutionary trail-blazer who outraged respectable opinion in his day and is a star of the auction rooms today, there were thousands who took advantage of this happy dispensation. What is more disappointing – perhaps unreasonably so – is how many of the elderly and prosperous art merchants of the late Victorian and Edwardian scene had shown creative talent in their younger days.

Sir Luke Fildes painted his heart-rending *Applicants for Admission to a Casual Ward* when he was twenty-six. Exhibited at the Royal Academy, it caused a sensation: critics hailed him as the Dickens of painting. Such epithets are rarely meaningful; in this particular case the claim proved to be particu-larly hollow. Social comment was useful for attracting attention, but not for bringing in money. Fildes soon moved on to middle-class genre scenes (some not without charm),[22] then to dulcet Venetian views, both lucrative and popular, and last to commissioned portraits. Comfortably established in a mansion in Kensington (designed for him by Norman Shaw), he crowned his long career with a succession of royal portraits of surpassing banality and the obligatory knighthood. He died in 1927, aged eighty-three.

Treading a somewhat similar path, William Powell Frith painted his lively *Railway Station* when he was twenty-nine and *Derby Day* a decade later. Both were popular successes and earned him Turner's chair in the Royal

---

[21] Later Queen Elizabeth the Queen Mother.
[22] Like the much-reproduced *The Doctor's Visit.*

Academy. Alas, "you cannot put titles into a stew". After his forties his subjects became increasingly moralising and derivative, his style shiveringly drab. Pictorial sermons like *The Road to Ruin* shamelessly echo Hogarth without the Hogarthian wit; but they firmly established him among the great and the good. Bedecked with honours, he also churned out much-praised canvases on historical subjects; and many commented on his uncanny gift for capturing the likenesses of the Prince and Princess of Wales's wax effigies at Mme Tussaud's. He died at ninety, having produced not one memorable picture for fifty years.

Rumours that the dealer Flotow had paid Frith the highest price ever for a "modern" painting were silenced when it transpired that Flotow's rival, Gambart, had paid William Holman Hunt 5500 guineas for the painting and copyright of *The Finding of the Saviour in the Temple*. "Verily", *Critic* commented in the *Morning Post*, "these are piping times for modern painters, especially for painters of sacred subjects extolling the virtues of meekness and poverty." [23] Hunt was not devoid of talent and *The Scapegoat*, for which, at the age of twenty-nine, he undertook a much-publicised pilgrimage to the Holy Land, still exercises a certain horrible fascination. But after his greatest success, *The Light of the World*, he went on repeating himself year after year with ever-diminishing conviction and an ever-increasing dose of holy saccharine. Nevertheless, he died at eighty-three, a Knight of the British Empire and a millionaire.

Many others who dotted the Victorian landscape had been only marginally less gifted in their usually impecunious youth and became only marginally less successful and mediocre in old age. Thomas Sidney Cooper, one of the most promising students in his year at the Royal Academy School, became an accomplished painter of sheep, goats, horses, dogs and especially cows, continuing his pictorial husbandry well into his nineties. Tino Conti, another outstanding student, later specialised in dashing cavaliers and carousing cardinals and was still doing a brisk trade in them after the First World War. King George V had one of his works adorning his study at Sandringham. Conti died in 1924, aged eighty-two. Among topographers Peter Graham shared his deep and unvarying affection for Highland scenery with his Queen, who purchased several of his deer; and Benjamin William Leader found inexhaustible inspiration in the hills and valleys of Wales. Graham died in 1921 aged eighty-two and Leader two years later aged eighty-five. After a promising start Erskine Nicol discovered his *métier* in depicting nearly indistinguishable episodes from the life of Scottish fishermen; and the restless and brilliantly gifted youth, Briton Riviere, became well known as a whimsical

---

[23] Quoted in J. Chapel, *Victorian Taste* (London, 1982), p. 82.

painter of farmyards, branching out occasionally to add to his menagerie *Daniel in the Lions' Den* and contributing to *Punch*. Nicol died in 1925 aged seventy-nine and Briton Riviere in 1920 aged eighty.

None of these successful careers could compare with those of two princes of meretriciousness. Sir Lawrence Alma Tadema began as an outstandingly gifted painter of landscapes but soon found the rewards of depicting Victorian maidens coyly draped in Graeco-Roman shifts (or whatever) more commensurate with his talents. He continued to paint classical confections, peopling marble frigidaria with chlorotic virgins until his death in 1912 at seventy-six.[24] Sir Edward Poynter, a fellow student of Renoir, Monet, Sargent and Whistler at Monsieur Gleyre's atelier in Paris, succeeded Millais as President of the Royal Academy. After a promising – or not wholly unpromising – start, he found his vocation in catering for the British passion for sprays of sea-water combined with a more cosmopolitan taste for naked young ladies in poses of picturesque abandon. He died in 1929, aged eighty-three.

It must not be thought that, after recovering from the troubles of 1848 and the contretemps of the Franco-Prussian War and the Commune, the continental panorama was significantly different. Probably not more than one in ten thousand gallery-goers in the 1870s was even dimly aware of the Impressionist conspiracy in their midst. It was the latest offering of the divine Monsieur Meissonier, as active as ever in his seventies and recently created the first Grand Commander of the Legion of Honour among painters, which was the sensation of the salons; and it was not the colossal sum of 200 francs paid by a certain Mr Benjamin Gould of Philadelphia for the latest daub of the wholly unknown Auguste Renoir but the 850,000 francs paid by the dealer Chenard for the Grand Commander's *1814* which dazzled the frock-coated, top-hatted connoisseurs of the Bourse.[25]

It is a common fallacy to imagine that even among the avant-garde Monet, Renoir, Sisley and their Impressionist friends were acclaimed as the leaders. In fact, for several decades they were no more than a barely visible fringe group among artists who claimed to represent the future and who drew the fiercest disapproval of the Beaux-Arts establishment. (Such disapproval was always regarded as the highest accolade among artists in Bohemia.) At least until the 1890s the recognised "moderns" (and therefore acceptable though speculative investments) were the Naturalists, with the the Symbolists for a time hovering in second place. They emerged about the same time as the

---

[24] He was severely rebuked by the critic of *The Times* for painting his one undraped nude. He repented and did not reoffend.

[25] Jean-Louis Ernest Meissonier specialised in historic canvases from the Napoleonic age. He died in 1891, aged seventy-six.

Impressionists and were just as contemptuous of academic bombast and the mythologies of Monsieur Bouguereau and the historical tableaux of Monsieur Meissonier as were Monet and his small band of rebels.[26] That Naturalism was essentially a literary rather than an artistic idiom was for a time obscured by the sheer talent of the young generation of artists who adopted it. Only – sadly – most of the gifted and adventurous pioneers ran out of steam in their thirties and forties, victims of the new art of photography, and never progressed once they had established themselves in the market.

The young Pascal-Adolphe-Jean Dagnan Bouveret, now barely remembered, was the recognised heir in France to Jules Bastien-Lepage, the charismatic founder of Naturalism in the visual arts.[27] Like his mentor, he painted in the 1870s and 1880s powerful and to many traditionalists shockingly unvarnished scenes of peasant life. But after his rise to academic eminence he went on painting in the same vein but with diminishing punch till his death in 1929, aged seventy-seven, execrating the Impressionists, the Expressionists, the Fauves, the Cubists and other "charlatans" impartially; and watching outraged as his once-celebrated canvases – the famous *Horses at the Watering Trough*, *The Wedding Party* and others – were stealthily removed from the Gallerie d'Honneur in the Luxembourg to provincial museums.

The long careers of Jules-Alexis Muenier, Emile Friant, Fernand Pelez, Jules Adler, Victor Gilbert and other early Naturalists developed along not dissimilar lines. Coming across in private collections the young Muenier's poetically evocative scenes of his native Franche-Comté, one immediately assumes that so gifted and yet so forgotten an artist must have died young, But he went on painting and haranguing his colleagues at the Institut, and indeed anybody who would listen, about the iniquities of all post-Naturalist conspiracies till shortly before he died in 1942, at the age of eighty-two.

---

[26] William Bouguereau was the "pope of the *pompiers*", his *Birth of Venus*, *Remorse of Orestes*, *The Childhood of Bacchus*, his *Nymphs*, and his adorable (to his obituarist in the *Moniteur*) *Madonnas*, see J.-L. Ferrier, *Art of the Century* (New York, 1989), p. 67, the most famous and in their terrible way the most accomplished products of French academic art of the nineteenth century. Many years before the development of his cataracts, Monet was diagnosed as suffering from moderate myopia and his friends suggested that he should wear glasses. When the first pair was tried on he exclaimed in horror: "Take them away! They make me see the world as if it had been painted by Bouguereau." Bouguereau was a kindly man who never said a harsh word about the Impressionists or even about Matisse. He died in 1905, aged eighty.

[27] He inspired generations of artists who flocked to Paris in the 1870s and 1880s in search of "modern art" from England, Scotland, Russia, Scandinavia, Germany and Hungary. They virtually ignored the Impressionists but were captivated by the real-life rural Naturalism of Bastien-Lepage and his circle. Bastien-Lepage died of cancer of the stomach in 1884, aged thirty-six.

(Consolation came in his last years when some of his canvases proved popular with, and were eagerly bought by, the artistically inclined members of the occupying Wehrmacht.) Friant's moving *All Saints' Day*, painted in 1888 when the artist was twenty-eight, inspired and influenced good artists in Russia, Poland, Hungary, Scandinavia and Britain;[28] but he never advanced beyond his early promise and still painted and mostly sold photographic genre scenes of a vaguely *fin-de-siècle* flavour in the early 1930s. He died in 1934, aged seventy-seven. Jules Adler's early Parisian down-and-outs are as powerful as Luke Fildes's *Applicants for Admission to a Casual Ward*: inspired perhaps by Zola's *L'Assommoir*, *The Weary*, showing the Parisian proletariat trudging to work in the grey dawn of a cold winter day, was painted in 1897 when he was thirty-one, a blazing talent in the making. But it never got made. He moved from representations of the less *belle* face of *Belle Epoque* Paris – *The Street* and the *Miners' Strike* were other powerful social documents – to more saleable theatrical scenes, popular with lovers of Gay Paris, and made a comfortable living churning them out until his death in 1952, aged eighty-nine.[29]

The pattern was similar outside France, though in artistically more backward countries, where Naturalism did not have to compete with Impressionism, Expressionism and other more revolutionary movements, it remained vital and modern for longer. In Denmark Ejnar Nielsen painted his shattering *The Sick Girl* in 1896, when he was twenty-six; and the sick, the crippled and the dispossessed remained his artistic preoccupation for many years. But though he lived and worked on till 1952 (when he died aged eighty-two), he never regained the power of his creative youth. In Russia the depressing late decline of Ilya Repin, perhaps the most gifted of east European Naturalists, remains something of a mystery. After a successful career under the last Tsars – he was seventy-one when Nicolas II abdicated in 1917 – he was revered in Leninist and even in Stalinist Russia as the "Father

---

[28] George Clausen in England and János Thorma in Hungary were among those who painted celebrated canvases on the same theme, directly inspired by him.

[29] His best paintings, all dating from the 1880s and 1890s, are in provincial French museums, mainly in Castres, Besançon and Amiens.

This almost random selection of long-lived artists whose revolutionary early style simply went out of fashion and who never fulfilled their youthful promise ignores such influential and good artists as Jean-Eugène Buland, who died in 1929 aged seventy-six, and that sensitive painter of children, Henri-Jules-Jean Geoffroy, who died in 1926 also aged seventy-six. It passes over a generation of American expatriates who created their best work as young men and women painting in France in the Naturalist idiom of Bastien-Lepage – among them Alexander Harrison who died in 1930 aged seventy-eight, Gary Melchers who died in 1932 aged seventy-six, Daniel Ridgway Knight who died in 1929 aged ninety, and that perceptive artist at her best, Elizabeth Nourse, who died in 1937 aged ninety.

of Social Realism": a reproduction of one of his early works (usually *The Unexpected Arrival* or the *Volga Bargemen*) in classrooms in art colleges was as compulsory as was a cage with a token Pavlov dog under a portrait of Stalin in medical laboratories. It was the kind of reputation which did him neither good nor justice. According to Soviet commentators, he spent his last years in Finland, pining to return to his native Ukraine. But if he did, why did he not? He lived on till 1930, when he was eighty-four, apparently working till his last days; but only a few of his late works are known in the west. They are extraordinarily bad. Glasnost has not yet dispelled the fog surrounding this period of his life, though the village in Karelia where he lived after 1916, and which Finland had to cede to Russia after the Second World War, has been renamed Repin in his honour.[30] Such broken or slowly declining careers among long-lived Naturalists whose work had started full of promise could be traced in most central and eastern European countries. The idiom began as one of the most exciting but became, after its initial flowering, one of the most barren in European art, ending in the graveyard of Nazi and Stalinist Socialist Realism.

Just as one can find cases of decline in old age among thousands of promising artists of the second and third rank, so even a cursory glance reveals examples of creative talent giving up in despair in the face of public incomprehension, ridicule or, most commonly, simple indifference. Let the memory of just one be resurrected to serve as an example.

Compared to grandees like the Princes Eszterházi and Counts Károlyi, the Szinyei-Merses of north-eastern Hungary were neither rich nor famous; but, with their roots lost in medieval Magyar mists, they looked down on the Eszterházis and Károlyis as poodles of a foreign dynasty, and regarded the Habsburgs themselves as rootless matrimonial adventurers.[31] Their history was rich in eccentrics and when Pál, heir to the family estates in the 1880s, announced his intention to become a painter rather than a breeder of racehorses, an amateur poet or a digger of canals, it was accepted without unseemly fuss. Munich was inevitably his destination. Hardly a name of that once-famous school of painting, dedicated above all to historical panoramas and allegorical compositions suitable for the ceilings of opera houses, survives today; and, a decade or two after Pál's arrival, it would be overshadowed by Vienna and Berlin and then by the emerging avant-garde and *Sezession*. But

[30] The only occasion, so far as the writer is aware, of a town or village having its name changed to that of an artist rather than the other way round.

[31] "Bella gerant alii: tu, felix Austria, nube" (Let others wage war: you, happy Austria, marry) was a saying attributed to King Matthias Corvinus of Hungary, referring to the complex web of matrimonial alliances woven by the odious but clever Emperor Frederick III.

in the 1860s Munich was still where budding artists from eastern Europe flocked to learn not only the rudiments of their craft but also a properly Bohemian (but not too Bohemian) life style. It had everything or almost everything: a superb collection of old masters (the best north of the Alps and east of the Rhine), a famously atmospheric artists' quarter, a tradition of beery *Gemütlichkeit,* a verdant lake-studded countryside and a crazy art-loving dynasty. What it lacked (without it being much missed) was anything that could be remotely described as modern art.[32] Since the tradition of the old and prestigious School of Fine Arts rigorously excluded anything that smelt of grass, hay, trees or anything found in the great outdoors, the question of what drove young Szinyei-Merse into the countryside to paint at about the same time as Renoir, Monet, Sisley and Bazille decamped from Monsieur Gleyre's atelier to the Forest of Fontainebleau remains a mystery.[33] But something in the beautiful month of May did and what he painted was his friends and their lady-friends having a glorious picnic under the spring sky, complete with hamper and a bottle or two of wine. All remained decorously dressed; there was nothing remotely improper about the proceedings to provoke an outcry. But provoke an outcry it did, almost as shrill as that which greeted Manet's far more audacious *Déjeuner sur l'Herbe* about the same time in France. The unashamed celebration of youth, spring and the joys of the countryside was, it seems, reason enough.

One wonders if even young Monet, supremely confident though he was of his own talent, would have persisted in his crazy experiments had he not been one of a lively band of like-minded young men and women. There was no such band in Munich, Vienna or Budapest to sustain a well-heeled sprig of the aristocracy whose artistic pretensions were tolerated but only as a harmless eccentricity. Uncomplaining, Szinyei-Merse retired to look after his family estates; and for the next thirty years he painted hardly anything other than tender portraits of his wife.

[32] Even by the dismal standards of other royal, imperial and national academies, the Royal Munich Academy was the epitome of hidebound repression. Fortunately, there were plenty of alternative outlets for young artists. Schwabing, Munich's artistic and student quarter, had a *Bierstube* combined with a gallery of sorts on every street corner; and among Szinyei-Merse's friends were the officially outcast but delightful Carl Spitzweg, the animal painter Friedrich Voltz and Moritz von Schwind. The dynasty too was an asset. The more eccentric the ruling monarch (and his current mistress), the more enlightened was their art patronage; and, by the time Szinyei-Merse arrived in Munich, the Wittelsbachs were very eccentric indeed.

[33] It would be as misguided to attribute the spread of *plein air* painting to technical improvements as it would be to explain Bellini's late masterpieces by the adoption of oil painting; but the invention of collapsible paint-tubes around 1850 (to replace pig's bladders), and an array of wonderful new synthetic colours which did not dry out so quickly as many of the old paints, did make the setting up of an easel out of doors easier.

In 1897 Hungary celebrated with all the pomp, bombast and panoply of that supremely self-satisfied age its "Millenary Year", commemorating the conquest by nomadic Magyar tribes of what was to become the kingdom of St Stephen;[34] and, somewhat short of material to illustrate modern Magyar art, the early works of Szinyei-Merse were included in an official retrospective exhibition. To a new generation of gallery-goers – artists, critics, collectors, rich urban industrialists who travelled regularly to Paris and London – *The May Picnic*, painted more than a quarter of a century earlier, was a revelation. Could it be that, unrecognised by the world at large, but like most great achievements of the human race, even modern art had been invented by a Hungarian? Looking at the mellow beauty of the Nográd countryside under the May sky conjured up by the young Szinyei-Merse, the proposition could not be doubted.[35]

The artist was persuaded to emerge from his retirement and even accepted – on condition that the post during his tenure would remain unsalaried – the directorship of the Budapest Academy of Fine Arts. The avant-garde, mostly painters in the Naturalist manner of Bastien-Lepage, welcomed him as a future patron and guarantee of progressive values. The establishment appreciated his table manners. Both camps were to be disappointed. In peacetime he might have become a happily ineffectual but privately generous figurehead. During the First World War, and even more during its hectic and bloody aftermath, his lack of training as an adventurer, politician or crook proved disastrous. But amidst the ruin of his country's and his personal fortune, he was, for the first time in decades, painting again. The creations of his old age, little known even in Hungary, were mostly sad, beautiful landscapes, in the tumultuous postwar years dominated in the arts by Expressionism and other more or less violent styles, as out of tune with the times as his *May Picnic* had been fifty years earlier. Although retired to his beloved Merse, he was still patron of the Society of Modern Artists, soon to be named after him; and under a pseudonym he regularly submitted works for their annual exhibition. They were no less regularly rejected. But he went on painting till he died in 1921, aged seventy-five.

Such case-histories show that decline, stagnation and paralysing despair in old age are possible among artists. They do not prove or even suggest that

---

[34] In 1001. The coronation scheduled for a year earlier was postponed because of the widespread fear that the year 1000 would mark the end of the world and the Second Coming.

[35] But a little mystery still lingers about *The May Picnic*. The work is dated in Munich where it was undoubtedly painted; but the countryside breathes the air of County Nográd in northern Hungary. But if he painted the skies and meadows of his childhood wherever he painted, Szinyei-Merse would not be the first (or last) expatriate artist to do so.

they are common among the sub-genius class but not among artists of the first rank. For every exception mentioned here one could summon up the memory of a dozen artists whose modest but genuine talent blossomed in old age as richly as did Michelangelo's or Titian's. The exceptions merely validate the opposite.

Or do they? The knights and knight commanders of the Victorian and Edwardian art scenes were mostly competent and often industrious producers of painted canvases; but, after early middle age, they were no longer creative artists. This is not said in disparagement. One does not expect successful teachers, doctors, greengrocers, bankers or safe-blowers to continue to "develop" after they have learnt their craft; why then painters and sculptors? Yet those who do should not be lumped together with those who do not, whether the former are incandescent geniuses or artists of modest talent. Developing creativeness – the searching and the finding – not "greatness" is the divide; but a divide it undoubtedly is. At times the two sides seem to belong to different species, neither capable of validating the other.

# 23

## *The Imprint of Age*

There are as many different five year olds, thirty-five-year-olds and seventy-five-year-olds as there are individuals who are five, thirty-five and seventy-five; but there is also a modulator which imprints itself on every age, a characteristic shared by all those who are five, thirty-five and seventy-five. This characteristic, the imprint of age, is the opposite to the other defining aspect of personality, the continuity of self. It is the continuity of self which makes one exclaim on meeting a childhood friend after many years: how little he or she has changed! The years have passed but their personality – and, no less significantly, one's own response to it – has remained the same. Both characteristics – the imprint of age and the continuity of self – are immensely complex and deeply mysterious. The continuity of self depends on the unchanging genetic constitution of a person in a constantly changing environment. The imprint of age depends on the experience shared by millions of individuals of something almost indefinable, the passage of personal time.[1]

With so many mysteries and indefinables, it is hardly surprising that to recognise the imprint of age – or rather, the interaction of the imprint of age with the continuity of self – in great art is far from simple. But it is not impossible. In some respects "old" applied to human age is like those generalisations one pins to different countries, races, cultures, historical periods and other troublesome abstractions. One realises of course that they are only labels, intellectually false, politically incorrect and morally often reprehensible: yet one goes on believing that there is an obvious difference between "the French" and "the English", between "the Victorians" and the children of the third millennium, or between "the male" and "the female" characters. Only the "obvious" needs to be qualified. No learned academic study, practical guide or witty travelogue – and there have been thousands – has ever succeeded in defining the difference between "Frenchness" and

---

[1] Personal time is different from both chronological time, a physical concept of no great interest, and from biological time, the measure of objective biological changes like the loss of hair. The moment when a man or woman suddenly feels old – and almost always it is moment, not a week, month or year – is an event on the individual's personal time-scale.

"Englishness". Yet the difference is perceived as clearly as the difference between sweet and sour by every day-tripper to Calais or Dover. But, as with sweet and sour, experiencing the difference is essential. It is this which puts the imprint of age into a special category.

National characteristics are recognisable by travellers crossing the Channel or a land frontier *either way*. With the imprint of age experience can work only in one direction. As Sebastien de Chamfort observed: "We arrive as novices at every age of our life." Forty-year-olds have experienced their twenties and sixty-year-olds have lived through their forties. However uncertain their recollections and mistaken the lessons they have learnt, the experience provides a framework of reference. The reverse is never true: no twenty-year-olds have lived through their forties and no forty-year-olds have experienced their sixties. In a similar way, one can usually recognise the continuity of self in a great artist at ninety. It is an unchanging quality. The imprint of age, by contrast, to anyone younger than ninety can only be guesswork.

Titian was probably in his late teens when he arrived in Venice. He seems to have been poor and without many useful contacts. He conquered the city, then Italy and finally Europe by sheer talent. Whatever he painted afterwards – nudes, mythologies, kings, doges or dogs – the theme of conquest resonates in almost every picture.[2] Of course the message is not always explicit and not always physical. Imaginary trumpets sound to celebrate military conquest in the great equestrian portrait of the Emperor Charles V. That was in 1548 and Titian was recognised as the greatest – and most triumphalist – painter in Europe. The Emperor too had reached the peak of his own and his dynasty's power.[3] The aura of physical conquest also radiates from the commanding posture of victorious generals. But, in their different ways, Titian's Venuses – indolent and a little bored as they survey their past or

[2] The variety of breeds he painted deserves a monograph by an expert. His horses were good too but less individually characterised. He seems to have had no interest in cats.

[3] The portrait is a *tour de force*. Charles V was the most uncharismatic of men. He was neither a great soldier nor a great administrator. His appetites were vast but coarse. Even for a Habsburg, he was unprepossessing to look at. Titian disguised none of these deficiencies: it is the lack of heroics which invests his subject with majesty. The long spear recalls the antique image of Marcus Aurelius, the wisest of Roman emperors. The armour celebrates the Emperor's recent victory over Germany's Protestant princes. But there is no allegorical clutter: no beaming angels, cherubs or Olympian divinities detract from the awesome solitariness of the monarch. He gazes into the distance without any visible emotion. And yet, in this moment of triumph, there is no hint of triumphalism. A scarlet glow suffuses the horizon. The air breathes the impermanence, even the menace, of an electrically charged summer evening. Seven years later Charles abdicated, a tired and disillusioned man.

future lovers – portray sexual conquest no less explicitly.[4] And, in his greatest altar-piece, the Virgin rises above her subjects like a vision of victory. Then, perhaps soon after the Augsburg portrait of the Emperor, the artist's world suddenly changed. Or, more likely, he did. He was an old man.[5]

In old age Titian's chief theme – or obsession or preoccupation – remained the same. It was still conquest. That would never change. It was in Titian's art the continuity of self. But something else did change. In his last altar-pieces, mythologies and *poesies* he no longer celebrated the joys and exhilarations of conquest. What he conveyed is its deep and horrible core of pain. It permeates all his last great paintings. Adonis, impatient to follow the call of the hunting horn, shakes off the clinging Venus with a brutality that is not implicit in Ovid. Diana transforms Actaeon into a stag and has him torn to pieces by her hounds for the venial sin of having unwittingly espied her naked. In a fit of temper she orders her gaggle of nymphs to kill the innocent though foolish Callisto.[6] There will to be no fun and games at the end of screaming Europa's ride on the back of the slavering bull.[7] Sextus's knife glints murderously as he rapes Lucretia.[8] Apollo seems to be experiencing a frisson of pleasure flaying Marsyas. But rape and abductions are about violence. The Annunciation is not. Indeed, it is one of the few wholly

---

[4] Fat, flabby, female, fertile and forty were the five fs which the eminent surgeon, the first Lord Moynihan, pronounced in 1921 to define those most likely to develop gallstones. Some of Titian's Venuses look at risk.

[5] Little of this showed on the surface. The artist remained a celebrity, an ornament of the republic. Distinguished visitors called on him as a matter of course. He sat on every important artistic jury. In his Casa Grande a cohort of apprentices under the watchful eye of the worthy Orazio were occupied in copying his middle-period paintings. His beautiful and erotic Magdalen (with or without bosom exposed) was still in demand by princely collectors from Poland to Portugal. He would often append his signature: it was already worth a fortune. But his autograph pictures – and in the privacy of his studio he was often at work on several vast canvases – would not even be seen by Venetians. On most of his last paintings the varnish can hardly have been dry when they were rolled up, crated and dispatched to El Escorial. There Philip II, known to begrudge every minute he could not devote to his files, his roses or his *autos-da-fé*, would spend hours in rapt contemplation of the old artist's blood-soaked narratives.

[6] Callisto, one of Diana's nymphs (expected to remain as chaste – or as frigid – as their mistress) was made pregnant in her sleep by Jupiter who had disguised himself as Diana. Having chastised her, Diana transformed Callisto into a bear and was about to have her torn to pieces by her nymphs and hounds when Jupiter whisked his victim away to an unspecified but presumably safe place on the slopes of Mount Olympus.

[7] Another of the versatile Jupiter's disguises. How different Titian's abduction is from the stately procession depicted by Veronese about the same time.

[8] He seems to have repainted the tip of the knife many times while leaving other parts of the picture (like Lucretia's left foot) somewhat unfinished or not quite well drawn.

joyful episodes in the Gospels. The news the angelic messenger brings is – or should be – the happiest in a woman's life. Of course it is tinged with anxiety: what human happiness is not? But to share in the moment's rapture needs neither theological training nor mystical transport. According to tradition, Luke who related the event, was a painter. Perhaps the scene was his gift to future painters as a subject for scriptural joy. It was certainly seized in this spirit – as it still is – by countless followers of the Evangelist. But not by Titian in his seventies. At first glance his altar-piece in the church of San Salvatore does not depart from orthodox images. That makes it the more disturbing. His archangel is a huge feathered hulk with broad hips and a bull neck. His advance is more an assault than an annunciation. Not surprisingly, Mary raises her cloak more in defence than in greeting.[9] And the scene is bathed not in the dewy morning light of Florentine Annunciations, or the clear radiance of noon favoured by older Venetian masters, but in a metallic glow that barely penetrates through the menacing cumulus of clouds and a disorderly concourse of angels. It is a scene of conquest but also of terrible menace. And a short earthly lifetime after the Annunciation, the sublime spiritual triumph of *The Crowning with Thorns* is almost unbearable in its portrayal of human cruelty.[10]

After trying to survey the seemingly endless individual variations in the art of old age, only three generalisations appear to be justified.

The first is the sense of liberation which came to many great artists in their last decades. Whatever and however fierce had been the ogres of childhood, youth and middle age – the social shibboleths, the ambitions, the frustrations, the inhibitions, the envies and the self-imposed imperatives – they were dead, in retreat or transformed into harmless, almost likeable pets. It gave their art a freedom which it had never possessed before.

The second is a commitment to truth. Of course in everyday life old artists were probably as prone to pretence, posturings and perjury as any other old man or woman (or man or woman of any age). No doubt their confabulations, repetitiousness, wishful thinking and romancing were, at times, a trial to their families. But they spoke the truth in their art – or the truth as they knew it. Why should they not? Nothing else made it worth suffering the adversities of age and the pangs of creation.

---

[9] But perhaps the gesture is symbolic, signifying her impregnation by the Holy Ghost through her ear – that is by word rather than deed.

[10] How remote is the sound of the angelic choir: "Christus vincit. Christus regnat. Christus imperat." Yet the Crowning was still to become the beginning of a conquest, one of the most remarkable in history. Like the last *Pietà*, this shattering work was found unfinished in Titian's looted studio after he died during the Great Plague of 1576. It was bought by Tintoretto.

The third and last is not a characteristic of the art of old age but of one's response to it. On first acquaintance there is hardly a work of an old master which does not demand – or at least invite – a plea in mitigation. Their technique was often clumsy. Their paintings may be packed with confusing and unnecessary detail. They may, on the other hand, be uncomfortably empty. In either case they may lack coherence. They may be unbalanced. The storyline may make no sense. The presentation may be muddled. They may appear unfinished. But since the master's past record commands respect, even admiration, one begins to search for extenuating circumstances. One points to the master's physical or mental frailty at the time the work was completed. A specific infirmity may be worth special emphasis. One recalls, when appropriate, the master's material difficulties. In a more positive vein, one praises his or her indomitable (if perhaps slightly misguided) spirit. Then suddenly the futility of the enterprise hits home. It is the works themselves which bring belated but blinding illumination. Whatever else they need, they do not need extenuation and apology. Their offences against conventions show up conventions for the vanities and artefacts they are. Their faults by ancient canons make ancient canons look foolish. Their disregard of the "cans" and "can'ts" of art reveal the "cans" and "can'ts" as the arid pedantries of hopelessly prosaic minds. To try and apologise for such "errors" is not only futile, it is inane. The realisation is humbling but inescapable. The master in his eighties may have been physically frail and mentally odd. He may have been three-quarters blind. His memory may have become like a sieve. His grasp of detail may have become non-existent. His sense of form, colour and balance may have become bizarre. His command of line may have gone by the board. One could go on. But in some way, in some miraculous way, none of these shortcomings suggest decline and decay. On the contrary, they bear witness to human creativity at its most indestructible and at its most sublime.

# BIOGRAPHICAL APPENDIX

## Other Long-Lived Artists*

DONATELLO (Donato di Niccolò di Betti Bardi) (died in 1466, c. eighty). For long Donatello was overshadowed by the giants who crowded in his footsteps.[1] All acknowledged him as their forerunner; but, a few centuries after his death, Goethe and Stendhal, both enthusiastic travellers in Italy and cultural oracles in their respective countries, barely noticed him. He is still regularly being rediscovered by artists and art lovers who approach him as a pioneering historical figure rather than as one of the greatest sculptors of any age.[2] He was of course not what the Romatics dubbed a "Renaissance Man". He could turn his hand to bronze founding, stucco, furniture, jewellery, stained glass and military fortification; but most fifteenth-century Florentine painters and sculptors could do that. There is no record that he composed music or wrote sonnets like Michaelangelo; he did not invent the unflying aeroplane like Leonardo; and he was not an irresistible charmer like Raphael. Numerous anecdotes testify to his generosity and wit in youth;[3] even his occasional testiness was later acclaimed as endearingly Florentine. But, like his close friend, Brunelleschi, he was unmarried, probably homosexual;[4] and, after Brunelleschi's death, he strikes one as a grave and lonely

---

* Biographical notes in chronological order of birth on long-lived artists not included in Chapters 2–11. See Table, above, p. 5.

[1] Outstanding monographs of his life and work are H. Kaufmann, *Donatello: eine Einführung in sein Bilden und Denken* (Berlin, 1936); H. V. Janson, *The Sculpture of Donatello* (Princeton, New Jersey, 1957); and B. A. Bennett and D. G. Wilkins, *Donatello* (Oxford, 1984). The last two authors favour a year between 1386 and 1390 for his birth.

[2] His inclusion among the Teenage Mutant Hero Turtles in the early 1990s suggests that his reputation is now on par with that of Leonardo, Michelangelo and Raphael.

[3] The wit commemorated by such anecdotes rarely survives retelling after five hundred years, but there is no reason to question the message.

[4] Much indirect evidence points to Donatello's life-long homosexuality, none more suggestively than one of the wings on Goliath's helmet snaking up and caressing (without any structural justification) the youthful David's thigh. Public attitudes to homosexuality seem to have been as confused in fifteenth-century Florence as they are in Europe and America today. Donatello (like Michelangelo after him) made no secret of his attachment to beautiful young apprentices – though he refused to have one even prettier than the current favourite with the oft-quoted phrase "the prettier, the sooner he will leave me" – but at least one offender was

figure. Until then, with almost every new work, he broke new ground and was acclaimed as the greatest innovator of the age.[5]

In his youth and middle age Donatello travelled widely to the brilliant and murderous courts of Renaissance Italy – to Mantua, Ferrara, Modena, Siena, Naples, and for a long and particularly fruitful sojourn to Padua. He probably spent a few months with Brunelleschi in Rome, digging for treasure. It was a good time to dig: half the surviving treasures of Antiquity, including the Apollo of Belvedere and Laocoön, were still lying under centuries of rubble or being used as building-blocks or door-stoppers. His emotional range continued to expand: by the time he reached his forties and fifties he could portray suffering and cruelty as well as tranquil contemplation and even that ultimate challenge, tormenting uncertainty. But perhaps he was happiest when he was creating little figures which expressed the joys, innocence and exuberance of childhood. His *putti* seem to be everywhere. The Prato pulpits and the choir galleries for the Duomo are entirely fashioned of them; but more often they are part of a supporting cast. Tottering they bear the crown of victory for St George, they sing and play music around the Virgin, they gather grapes in celebration of Judith. They also appear in quite unlikely places: on the episcopal staff of the meek and unhappy St Louis of Toulouse; on Goliath's helmet; on the saddle of the formidable Gattamelata; and, for the last time, above the solemn scenes of the San Lorenzo pulpits. Wherever they turn up, they are rumbustious, noisy and mischievous, quite unlike the vacuous little cherubs and *amoretti* of countless imitators for centuries to come.

Public taste in Florence began to change when he reached his late fifties; and there is nothing to suggest that he made any effort to chime in with changing trends. Piero de' Medici, Cosimo's son and heir, presented him with a vineyard (later exchanged for a modest annuity); but Piero's commission for a portrait bust went to the more fashionable Mono de Fiesole, and the younger Medicis raved about the sweet touch of Benozzo Gozzoli. Some time in his late sixties Donatello moved from Florence to Siena, a quieter and more conservative – or, as Florentines would have it, more backward – city.[6] There he petitioned the Balia to let him embellish the

burned at the stakes in Florence in Donatello's lifetime and in law sodomy was punishable with heavy fines or even death. But Florence was recognised as a centre of gay culture in the early Renaissance: in contemporary German "*Florenzer*" meant homosexual. See H. V. Janson, "La signification politique du David en bronze de Donatello", *Revue de l'art*, 39 (1968), p. 33.

[5] See above, Chapter 14, pp. 207–8.

[6] The antipathy was fully reciprocated: the Sienese regarded Florentines as arrogant and pushy. This makes Donatello's move, however close the two cities are geographically, even more mysterious. His motives both for the move or for his return have been the subject of a number of inspired guesses but have never been satisfactorily explains.

cathedral; but nothing of what he may have completed survives.[7] Then, for some reason not clear, he returned to Florence. He moved into a "poor little house" (as Vasari describes it), rented for him by the Opera del Duomo, near the nunnery of San Niccolò. Vasari also mentions an illness which incapacitated him from time to time, perhaps a series of minor strokes. Yet, it was during these last few years, partially crippled and ignored by Florentine society, that he reached his summit as an artist.

San Lorenzo's, one of Brunelleschis's simplest yet loftiest conceptions, was the parish church of the Medicis; and it is possible that Donatello's bronze reliefs were intended for a complex funerary monument to his greatest patron, Cosimo de' Medici.[8] Whatever their original purpose, they are now mounted on two sarcophagus-shaped pulpits on either side of the nave. The events of the Passion, except for the Last Supper, are portrayed on the left, facing the altar. The post-Passion miracles are on the right. The placing probably symbolises the passage from Death to Resurrection through the operation of the living Eucharist in the Mass. All uncertainties are forgotten when the reliefs are seen.

Both the Crucifixion and the Lamentation were scenes deeply engraved on Christian minds, in Donatello's day as they are today. They did not lend themselves to eccentricities. Nor did Donatello in his late seventies try to use them to stage a sensational comeback. Yet both scenes are representations of human emotions as can never have been seen before and have rarely been seen since. Many artists, all artists perhaps, faced with the task of portraying these events, must have asked themselves: how could they bear it? The Mother, Mary Magdalen, the disciples, the friends? How could they watch their Son, Teacher, Saviour and God suffer in agony hour after hour and die in front of their eyes? But accepting that they could and did, how could the experience be shown or even hinted at in a work of art? Two hundred years later Tintoretto would crown his labours in San Rocco's in Venice with a vast, volcanic vision. It is a shattering representation but not of this world. Of artists who tried to represent the happening as reality of human size, none have given proof that they had found the answer; but the aged and infirm Donatello came nearer to it than anyone else.

No rainbow Resurrection redeems the suffering as it does in Grünewald's

---

[7] V. Herzner, "Donatello in Sienna", *Mitteilungen des Kunsthistorischen Instituts in Florenz*, 15 (1971), p. 161.

[8] See V. Herzner, "Die Kanzeln Donatellos in San Lorenzo", *Münchener Jahrbuch der Bildenden Kunst*, 23 (1972), p. 101. Sadly, almost the whole of the original documentation relating to these masterpieces has been lost; but speculation relating to their projected purpose is searchingly reviewed by Irving Lavin in *Past-Present: Essays on Historicism in Art from Donatello to Picasso* (Berkeley, California, 1933).

great altar. Instead a bent, shrouded Christ ascends from Limbo, an exhausted traveller. The moment of hope comes only with *Pentecost*. Here the dying Donatello – he never himself finished the panel – proved that he was as much a master of expressing spiritual joy as he was at portraying grief. But again, there is no attention-grabbing gesture, not even a beatific smile. There is only the curly back of an otherwise featureless head as, overawed by the miracle, its owner presses it against the rough floor of the chamber. It is enough.

UCCELLO, Paolo (died in 1475, aged *c.* seventy-nine). Like Donatello, Uccello was a native of Tuscany and a pupil of Ghiberti's.[9] He became famous as a "perspectivist", one of Vasari's second wave of "illustrious painters" who raised the arts from "their medieval slough of barbarism".[10] But Vasari's praise was not unqualified: indeed, he was the first to strike that faintly patronising note that has stuck to the artist ever since. "Uccello's preoccupation with perspective and the truthful rendering of nature was estimable and instructive; but he sometimes tried too hard and the strain shows." [11] There may be some justice in this, even allowing for the revelatory impact of the new science on Uccello's generation.[12]

Uccello's fame now rests largely on three large panels, originally a single

[9] Monographs on Uccello include J. Pope-Hennessy, *Paolo Uccello* (London, 1969), and E. Faiano, *L'opera completa di Paolo Uccello* (Milan, 1971).

[10] G. Vasari, *La vite de' più eccellenti pittori, scultori ed archittetori*, edited by G. Milanesi, 9 volumes (Florence, 1906), ii, p. 104.

[11] Ibid., ii, p. 185.

[12] Both the theory and practice of perspective can nowadays be mastered in a few hours by any moderately intelligent art student; but its beginnings were immensely exciting and beset with controversy. All early systems were based on a single central vanishing point, other parallels being assumed to be parallel to the picture plane. Pictures entirely constructed on this principle depend for creating an illusion of reality on viewers remaining rooted to one spot and keeping their eyes at a certain level, conditions rarely fulfilled nowadays by gallery-goers. The system was soon refined to allow the use of two or more vanishing points to achieve uphill and downdale effects; and the exact representation of objects to scale was achieved by the introduction of measuring points. But no less important for the creation of an illusion is aerial perspective, the changes in tone, colour values and contrasts as objects recede from the spectator. It is mainly the lack of this element which separates Uccello's perspective from Bellini's. Let it be said, nevertheless, that when all the physical and mathe-matical rules of perspective have been rehearsed, and the subject has been dismissed as of no further scientific interest, much still remains a mystery. Congenitally blind individuals, for example, who gain their sight in late childhood experience great difficulties in relating their three-dimensional past experience, based on the size, shape and significance of objects, to the two-dimensional world they see. A particulary striking fact is the bigness spontaneously attributed to important objects; another is the incredulity at seeing small objects like a sharp needle capable of causing great pain. (Poets have of course long realised the power of "*kleine Dinge*".)

panoramic sequence, depicting episodes of what became know as the Rout of San Romano.[13] Belying its title, the engagement was of the utmost historical insignificance. Like most battles in early fifteenth-century Italy, it was fought by mercenary armies under the command of professional *condottieri* whose reputation and therefore livelihood depended on playing the game of war by the rules, with a minimum of damage and a maximum of *éclat*. The Rout made up for any dearth of blood and gore with pageantry, equestrian acrobatics and probably a phenomenal amount of noise. In the same spirit, Uccello used his commission to display his skill at foreshortening as much as for the commemoration of an historical event. Horses rear from every angle, banners unfurl, lances thrust and warriors crash to the ground. One can readily understand why, for a few years, the artist was highly popular; but acclaim for this kind of virtuosity is often short-lived. His old age is poorly documented but a letter to the taxation authorities survives from his seventy-sixth year. He described himself as old, infirm and unemployed, still capable of painting but unwanted. His wife was ill. Vasari confirms that the painter was destitute. None of this is reflected by the one work which survives from these years, *The Night Hunt* in the Ashmolean Museum in Oxford. It is a masterpiece.[14]

DELLA ROBBIA, Luca (died in 1482, aged eighty-two). Little is known about the life and personality of this great and for long undervalued artist;[15] but an early biographer described him as "learned and gentle".[16] He was born in Florence into a family of wool merchants and remained a local boy, becoming a celebrity, a syndic and eventually patriarch; never, so far as is known, venturing far beyond the frontiers of the republic.[17] His first major work was a commission for a sculpture in marble, the organ loft for Brunelleschi's new Duomo, and it was immediately acclaimed as a masterpiece; but his name and that of his numerous family is most closely associated with a ceramic ware, terracotta covered with coloured enamelled tin glazes, which he invented in his thirties.[18] Yet he always remained a sculptor rather than

[13] The panels got separated quite early on and are, in varying states of decay and restoration, in the National Gallery in London, the Louvre in Paris and the Uffizi in Florence.

[14] See above, Chapter 1, p. 11.

[15] An authoritative and highly dogmatic monograph of Luca is J. Pope-Hennessy's *Luca della Robbia* (London, 1965).

[16] Antonio Manetti in *De viri illustri di Firenze*, published in Florence thirty years after Luca's death.

[17] At the time of his birth the dyeing and processing of wool was still the basis of the city's wealth. Banking came a little later.

[18] There has been much argument how far Luca actually invented tin-glazed maiolica and

a potter: useful kitchen ware was never his main output and intially his technique was far from cheap.[19] His solemn blue and white Madonnas are among the most beautiful creations of the Florentine Renaissance, as is the fabulous ceiling of the Cardinal of Portugal's Chapel in San Miniato al Monte,[20] and his work at the pilgrimage church of Santa Maria Impruneta.[21] His compositions of tragic subjects, and his great Crucifixion, are impressive; but arguably they would be more so in an unglazed medium. His ware soon became eagerly sought after as far afield as the Netherlands and Portugal, as well as in most parts of Italy. In his last years he was the head of a flourishing workshop, almost a factory; and many younger della Robbias inherited his skill if not perhaps his inventive genius.[22] After his death the workshop continued to function under the direction of his gifted nephew, Andrea, until the latter's death in 1525. It then went into decline and seems to have closed sometime around 1540.

PIERO DELLA FRANCESCA (died in 1492, aged *c.* seventy-six). He was born in the small town of San Sepolcro (now called Sansepolcro) in Umbria, for which he seems to have retained great affection and where he eventually became a town councillor. Otherwise little is known about his life, though

how far he adapted existing techniques. Tin-glazed earthenware, some of it technically superb, had been imported to Italy from the Islamic East and Moorish Spain for at least two centuries; and some famous-to-be potteries were being set up in Urbino, Montelupo, Venice and elsewhere at the time della Robbia set up his own workshop in Florence; but to della Robbia glazed earthenware was as much an artistic medium as bronze or marble; and one only has to compare his deeply spiritual creations to the robust contemporary Florentine oak-leaf pharmacy jars manufactured for everyday use, or to a Montelupo charger of the period, to realise that Vasari was essentially right in hailing Luca as an "inventor" rather than as a "developer". Yet even today many find della Robbia's work difficult to classify. The eighteenth-century modellers in porcelain, like Kändler and Bustelli, or the flower painters of the faïence of Marseille and Strasbourg, were brilliant craftsmen, but they did not regard themselves as artists in the way della Robbia thought of himself as a sculptor.

[19] The cost of building a kiln and establishing the right firing procedure for ware as delicate as della Robbia's made the early products expensive as well as precious. Once the moulds were available and the technique established, mass production became relatively cheap.

[20] The church itself is a gem of Tuscan Gothic, its tiny graveyard affording a resting place to Walter Savage Landor as well as to Carlo Lorenzetti, creator of Pinocchio.

[21] The shrine owed its popularity not only to its closeness to Florence and its idyllic setting but also to its unique relic – a picture painted by the Evangelist St Luke himself and miraculously unearthed by a team of oxen ploughing in the neighbourhood. It is today as much a shrine to Luca della Robbia's genius as to that of St Luke.

[22] Andrea della Robbia, creator of the lovely maiolica plaques of foundling infants on the façade of the Spedale degli Innocenti, was already in his fifties when his uncle died. He himself died in 1525, aged ninety. The works of his sons, Giovanni and Girolamo, are difficult to identify individually.

he spent fruitful years in Florence and visited Padua and Rome.[23] It is uncertain how much he was appreciated as an innovative artist in his own lifetime outside his native city; after his death he was certainly virtually forgotten for the best part of four hundred years. Then, under the influence of Cézanne, Picasso and the Cubist experience, his art was rediscovered. He is now a cult figure, among the most popular of the Quattrocento. His vision was solemn, lucid and mathematical, impressive rather than endearing; and, like Cézanne at his best, he was a fine colourist. (He was never as bad as Cézanne at his worst.) Also, like Cézanne, he seems to have laboured for long, sometimes apparently for years, on some of his commissions. This makes the dating of his output difficult. *The Baptism* in the National Gallery in London is generally accepted as an early work, *The Madonna of the Duke of Urbino*, *The Flagellation* and the Brera *Madonna* are from his middle period. No late works are known. He may have gone blind in old age or he may have changed from artist to scientist.

BELLINI, Giovanni (died in 1526, aged *c.* ninety). He was the son and pupil of Jacopo and the half-brother of Gentile Bellini, both highly regarded painters in their lifetimes. Mantegna married his sister. Most biographies point to the influence of Tuscan artists – Uccello, Fra Filippo Lippi, Andrea del Castagno, Donatello and others – who worked in Venice or Padua at the time of Giovanni's apprenticeship;[24] but the art of all these seems restricted compared to Bellini's. This was true even of his early works. His *Agony in the Garden* was probably influenced by Mantegna; but, in contrast to Mantegna's interlocking forms and majestic architectural unity, Bellini achieved unity by means not seen in painting before. The light of dawn floods the landscape: the valleys are still shrouded in nocturnal shadows just as sleep still presses down on the three Apostles, but the sky in the east is already alight, and the rays of the sun touch cloud, turret and hilltop. Over the years light, colour and form would continue to fuse to create a setting that would perfectly match the mood and the theme. In the Brera *Pietà*, still executed in tempera, the dark blue and purple of the Virgin's habit are as part of the chill morning of desolation as the olive greens and umbers of the landscape

---

[23] Important and useful monographs on Piero include R. Longhi, *Piero della Francesca* (Florence, 1963); K. Clark, *Piero della Francesca* (London, 1969); and E. Battisti, *Piero della Francesca*, 2 volumes (Milan, 1971).

[24] Among noteworthy works on Bellini are R. Fry, *Giovanni Bellini* (London, 1899); G. Gronau, *Giovanni Bellini* (Stuttgart, 1930); R. Palucchini, *Giovanni Bellini* (Venice, 1949); G. Robertson, *Giovanni Bellini* (Oxford, 1968); Y. Bonnefoy and T. Pignatti, *Tout l'oeuvre peint de Giovanni Bellini* (Paris, 1975).

and the cool grey of the sky. Oil paints were probably introduced to Venice by the Neapolitan painter, Antonello de Messina, in the 1470s and provided scope for infinite gradations of tones, colours and textures. Bellini was for over forty years First Painter to the Most Serene Republic: it was probably in that capacity that he painted his portrait of Doge Leonardo Loredan, now in the National Gallery, London. He was widely revered as the greatest Madonna painter of his age, one of the greatest of any age. Little is known about his private life. During his last ten years his repertoire expanded and he painted some of his most beautiful as well as his most prophetic works, including *The Feast of the Gods, The Drunkenness of Noah,* his last altarpiece, dedicated to St Jerome, and the *Lady at her Toilet* (Plate 1). [25]

CRANACH, Lucas, the Elder (died in 1553, aged eighty-one). Cranach was born in the town of Kronach in upper Franconia, whence the name, but he is first recorded as working as a painter in Vienna in his thirties.[26] His passionate religious altar-pieces of that period, often distorted, aggressive figures appearing as part of the landscape, are regarded by many as his best. In 1504 he moved to Wittenberg as court painter to Frederick the Wise, Elector of Saxony, and remained in the town in the service of three successive Electors for most of his life. His religious paintings mellowed and became less compelling; but it was in Wittenberg (a city of which he became Burgo-master in 1537) that he formed close friendships with Luther, Melanchthon and other leading figures of the Reformation, and where he painted brilliantly characterised portraits of them. After the 1520s it becomes difficult to distinguish his autograph works from the output of a busy workshop, presided over by his two sons, Hans and Lucas the Younger, a fact which may account for his apparent decline in originality. No fully authenticated work of his own survives from his last years: the "self-portrait" in the Uffizi is thought by many (including the present writer) to be a filial tribute by the younger Lucas. The rather crude "late" woodcut illustrations of biblical texts are similarly probably the products of the workshop.

[25] See above, Chapter 21, pp. 294–97.

[26] The literature on Cranach includes M. J. Friedlander and J. Rosenberg, *Die Gemälde Lukas Cranachs* (Berlin, 1932); H. Posse, *Lucas Cranach der Ältere* (Vienna, 1942); and D. Koeplin and T. Falk, *Lukas Cranach: Gemälde, Zeichnungen und Druckengraphik* (Stuttgart, 1974).

MICHELANGELO BUONARROTI (died in 1564, aged *c.* ninety). His father was a magistrate but not rich; and he was apprenticed to the workshop of Domenico Ghirlandaio.[27] He spread his wings as an artist, philosopher and poet at the self-consciously brilliant court of Lorenzo de' Medici. After Lorenzo's death he moved to Rome where, at the age of twenty-three, he carved his first *Pietà*. He was then entrusted by Julius II della Rovere to decorate the ceiling of the chapel in the Vatican named after the first della Rovere pope, Sixtus IV. The completed work was acclaimed as one of the wonders of the age. Back in Florence he carved his marble *David*, probably the most admired and reproduced single sculpture in European art. His austere republican sympathies led him to take part in the defence of the city against his former patrons, the Medicis, as a builder of fortifications. The victorious Medicis forgave him and commissioned him to design their memorial chapel and the sculptured tombs of Giuliano and Lorenzo de' Medici in San Lorenzo's. He returned to Rome in 1534, where he intermittently worked on the colossal projected tomb of Julius II. The sublime *Moses* was the only major figure completed. He painted the huge *Last Judgement* on the altar wall of the Sistine Chapel.

His second surviving *Pietà*, a drawing, was dedicated to the formidably pious and intellectual lady, Vittoria Colonna, "the instrument of my moral rebirth and dispenser of divine Grace". It marked the end of his intense preoccupation with young male beauty and his celebration of his friend, Tommaso dei Cavallieri. (The early sonnets were not published till 1863. A bowdlerised version published in 1623 pretended that the beloved was a female.) At seventy-two he became chief architect to St Peter's and designed the mighty dome. None of the sculptural works of his last twenty years, including his last two *Pietàs* (or three; the authorship of one is doubtful), are finished; but to many they remain his greatest creations.[28] The death of Vittoria Colonna grieved him; but it also set him free from the stilted style favoured by her circle. In his late sonnets the stanzas roll forward with the freedom of Petrarch and yet with a grave and mounting cadence of irresistible power. They are the cries of anguish of a desperate soul who can no longer believe that his terrible sins can be forgiven but who yet continues to hope and pray. He died in Rome in the evening of 18 February 1564, in his ninetieth or ninety-first year, having worked on his last *Pietà* six days earlier. One

---

[27] Among modern works about the artist are A. Stokes, *Michelangelo* (New York, 1955); R. Wittkover, *The Divine Michelangelo* (London, 1964); C. de Tolnay, *Michelangelo: Sculptor, Painter, Architect*, 5 volumes (Princeton, 1971); L. Murray, *Michelangelo* (London, 1980); H. Hibbard, *Michelangelo* (2nd edn, London, 1985).

[28] See above, Chapter 20, pp. 283–85.

hundred and fifty years later his body was returned to Florence, as he had wished ("my soul to God, my body to Florence"). It rests in Santa Croce, the parish church of the quarter which he had always regarded as his own. Goethe among others regarded him as the supreme manifestation of the human spirit; and to many he remains the embodiment of the creative artist – solitary, single-minded, tormented, unsatisfied and undefeated.

TITIAN (Tiziano Vecellio) (died in 1576, aged *c.* ninety) (Plate 2). Born in the little town of Pieve di Cadore on the slopes of the Dolomites, he arrived in Venice in his late teens as an outsider.[29] His surpassing talent (which he was never at pains to hide) soon made him the favourite of the city's gilded youth. Circumstance and accident, especially the early death of Giorgione, his only potential rival in Venice, combined to establish his pre-eminence in the city. Unlike the great Michelangelo, he was a man of the world, a courtier and the head of a numerous and gifted if occasionally wayward family; and by the age of forty he was acclaimed as the greatest painter in Europe. Yet he never lacked critics. Vasari deplored that in Venice painters were taught to paint but not to draw. Whether creating Arcadias, recounting horror stories, recreating biblical scenes or painting allegories, he was as cavalier with his literary sources as he was with hallowed technical dos and don'ts. His *Sacred and Profane Love* (in reality probably the commemoration of the wedding of one of his patrons) became a Victorian favourite, though men usually regarded the naked beauty and women the overdressed lady as the sacred variant. His portraits were universally admired; and he was the first to paint children and youths (such as Admiral Pesaro's grandsons or fourteen-year-old Ranuccio Farnese) not as diminutive adults but as young characters. But the scarlet glow on the horizon of his grand equestrian portrait of the Emperor Charles V already presages more sombre times to come. He remained a revered patriarch in Venice in his seventies and eighties; but the cruel and often tortured autograph paintings of his old age were mostly dispatched to Philip II of Spain rather than installed in the palaces and churches of the city.[30] He died at the height of the devastating plague of 1576 and was buried in the church of the Frari. Some of his greatest and most tragic works, including the *Pietà*, the *Crowning with Thorns* and the Vienna *Nymph and Shepherd*, were found unfinished in his looted studio.[31]

---

[29] See H. Tietze, *Titian* (London, 1950); R. Palucchini, *Tiziano*, 2 volumes (Florence, 1969); H. Whethey, *The Paintings of Titian*, 4 volumes (London, 1969–1975); and C. Hope, *Titian* (London, 1980).

[30] Many were not even shown in Venice. See above, Chapter 2, p. 19; Chapter 12, pp. 183–84.

[31] See above, Chapter 23, p. 316 and n. 10.

BERNINI, Giovanni Lorenzo (died in 1680, aged eighty-six). Bernini was born in Naples but the family moved to Rome when he was five.[32] His father was an accomplished sculptor who gave his son a good grounding in his craft. Gianlorenzo's precocious brilliance was soon recognised; but it was the election of his friend and patron, Urban VIII Barberini, to the papacy in 1624 and his subsequent appointment as chief architect to St Peter's that opened the way to his most celebrated works: the colonnades of St Peter's Square, the papal tombs in St Peter's, the Cornaro Chapel and a series of great portrait busts. On his visit to Rome John Evelyn attended a function which he described as "a public opera by Bernini", for which Bernini "had painted the scenes, cut the statues, composed the music, writ the comedy and built the theatre". As perhaps the last in the line of "universal men", Bernini accepted Michelangelo as his model; but, unlike the Florentine master, he was an excellent organiser of a large workshop who never left anything unfinished: his accounts were models of clarity and he died in his own palazzo and bequeathed a fortune to his heirs. What Bernini and Michelangelo had in common were extraordinarily high standards: nothing shoddy ever emerged from their hands. Bernini probably lavished as much virtuosity on his festival decorations, fireworks, carnival floats and cata-falques as he did on the high altar of St Peter's; and he transformed Rome into a city of fairytale fountains as well as of Baroque churches and palazzi. His private life was and remains controversial; but even his enemies (who were numerous) never questioned his piety, his charm and his generosity; and his celebrated rages were as much admired as they were feared. He was fifty when he fell in love with Constanza Bonarelli, the wife of a studio hand. Casual affairs between the unmarried autocrat of the workshop and young women of no social consequence were probably the staple of the weekly confesssional; but this was no casual affair. Bernini laid aside pontifical commissions to carve a marble bust of his *inamorata*, now in the Bargello in Florence. It was his only uncommissioned portrait and it remains one of the glories of western art.[33] This was too much for his high ecclesiastical

---

[32] Two modern monographs dealing with Bernini's art and life, I. Lavin, *Bernini and the Unity of the Visual Arts*, 2 volumes (Oxford, 1980) and H. Hibbard, *Bernini* (London, 1965), supplement two vivid comtemporary accounts, F. Baldinucci, *Vita de Bernini*, translated by C. Enggass (Philadelphia, 1966), and Paul Fréart, Sieur de Chantalou, *Journal du voyage du Cavaliere Bernin en France*, edited by L. Lalanne (Paris, 1885).

[33] Though supposed to have been destroyed after the pope's intervention, it surfaced in the grand-ducal collection in Florence a century later. For long labelled *Portrait of an Unknown Woman*, it was as such that it enchanted John Ruskin on his first visit to Florence. Only during the First World War, when the Bargello was closed to visitors, did an unknown curator restore the work to the immortal memory of Constanza Bonarelli.

patrons: the Bonarellis were packed off to Urbino where Constanza soon died;[34] and a suitably virginal wife was found for the artist. The marriage was blessed with eleven children and he survived his wife by eleven years. Bernini was the greatest artist of the Counter-Reformation and a friend of the Jesuits; this probably accounts for his declining reputation after his death. It has still not fully recovered. But he continued to work to the end, and his last creations – the *Memorial to the Blessed Ludovica Albertoni*, the *Fonseca Memorial*, the *Chapel of the Holy Sacrament* in St Peter's, and, as an architect, the church of Sant' Andrea al Quirinale – are among his most ground-breaking and most inspired.[35]

CLAUDE GELEE, known as LORRAIN (died in 1682, aged eighty-two). Claude was born in the little village of Chamagne in Lorraine, not far from Arc, the birth-place of Joan, the Maid of Orleans.[36] He arrived in Rome at sixteen as an apprentice pastry cook and returned to his native land only once for a two-year stay; but he remained to the end of his life an expatriate Lorrainer. Only a few years separate his dates of birth and death from Bernini's, and for fifty years the two artists lived within shouting distance, working for the same patrons and probably patronising the same grocers. Yet their worlds hardly touched. Bernini was a public figure and as urban in his habits as his greatest patron was in name. Claude had no interest in politics, his religion was private and his heart was in the countryside. Bernini's monument is Baroque art everywhere in Europe. Claude's monument is the common perception of what is picturesque in the Mediterranean landscape: every gaudy travel brochure that advertises the bustle of a southern port or the distant prospect of a classical temple and a grove of cypresses pays unacknowledged tribute to him.[37]

His real education came from his rambles in the countryside. "He would lie in the fields before daybreak and sometimes till late at night studying the morning light and the evening sky", his friend Joachim von Sandrart wrote. Even at the height of his success, he would maintain that he was simply copying nature; no art was involved. More remarkably perhaps, he

[34] There is a hint of hyperthyroidism in the face and the full neck.

[35] See above, Chapter 19, pp. 272–76.

[36] The standard works on Claude are M. Roethlichsberger, *Claude Lorrain: The Paintings*, 2 volumes (Berkeley, 1961), and, by the same author, *Claude Lorrain: The Drawings*, 2 volumes (Berkeley, 1968). An informative modern monograph is H. Langdon, *Claude Lorrain* (London, 1989).

[37] This is sometimes turned upside down. Claude did not paint what was picturesque. What today is perceived as picturesque by holiday makers is as much conditioned by the paintings of artists like Claude as by the reality which they see.

may have believed this himself. Yet, within his chosen genre of landscape, he continued to develop throughout life; a slow progression but not that of a genius idiot. As he approached old age he penetrated more and more deeply into the Arcadian world of Virgil's *Aeneid*.[38] He was recognised as a master landscape painter even in his lifetime but his life style hardly changed. From his apprentice digs near the Spanish Steps he moved in his thirties to a still comparatively modest house in what is now the Via Babuino. In the Guild of St Luke (of which Bernini was life president) he rose to the somewhat dubious post of moral tutor to foreign apprentices. He himself seems to have lived in settled domestic sin with a woman from Lorraine known only as Marie. A much-courted young women known as Agnese, probably his daughter, made her appearance in the household when he was in his fifties. In his seventies he was joined by two nephews from Lorraine, the first an excellent business manager, the second an acclaimed cook. The doctor who attended him in his last illness was a Lorrainer, as was his nurse, the saintly Sister Paule. He was read to in their widely incomprehensible native tongue. A kinsman in holy orders brought the blessing of the Bishop of Nancy. When he died the two nephews composed the inscription over his grave in the French church of Santissima Trinità dei Monti: "To Claude Gelée Lorrain, born in Chamagne, a painter who excelled in representing the rays of the rising and setting sun over the landscape and who in this city where he practised earned high praise." [39] They could have added with no more than a touch of Baroque flourish that in his last landscapes he expressed like no other artist man's eternal longing for a vanished golden age.

DE LA TOUR, Maurice-Quentin (died in 1788, aged eighty-four). Had Maurice-Quentin de la Tour created his sparkling portraits in oils or in marble he would today be as celebrated as Ingres or Bernini. But during the Revolution David declared pastels to be frivolous, and it took fifty years and the dedication of the Romantics and the Impressionist for the medium to regain its popularity if not quite its prestige.[40] The artist was born in St-Quentin, a small market town in Picardy, and returned there to live the life of a harmless town idiot for the last thirty years of his life. But before his mind gave way his career had been dazzling.[41] At fifteen he ran away

[38] See above, Chapter 16, pp. 240–45.
[39] The church appears in the first landscape he painted in Rome.
[40] The life of Maurice-Quentin remains relatively unexplored. Monographs include A. Bernard and G. Wildenstein, *La Tour: la vie et l'oeuvre de l'artiste* (Paris, 1928); and C. Debrie, *Maurice-Quentin de La Tour* (St-Quentin, 1991).
[41] See also above, Chapter 4, pp. 55–56.

from home after some amorous escapade and for a short time worked as an engraver's apprentice in Paris. He then travelled to Holland and England, never staying in one place for long. At twenty he returned to France and, almost at once, found his artistic niche. The departure of Rosalba Carriera, the Venetian lady who may have invented and certainly popularised coloured chalks as a medium to rival oil paints and water colour, had left a gap. Though the technique looked easy (as it still does), it required very special skills. Maurice-Quentin seemed to possess them all: a quick grasp of character as reflected in a face and sometimes a pose and a gesture, a sharp eye directing a responsive hand, a natural sense of colour and composition, an engaging personality to gain the cooperation of his sitters – and of course that intangible something extra that, in any medium, raises great artists above the merely competent. His success was immediate. In a strictly ordered and hierarchical society where the classes rarely consorted except in a formal setting, Maurice-Quentin seemed to move from one circle to another with complete ease. Among his enthusiastic sitters were the King's legitimate family, the coterie around Madame de Pompadour, Paris's theatrical and intellectual salons, and his own class of craftsmen and artists. His portraits have the same ability to kindle the imagination as have Hals's portraits: one looks at the gracefully seated image of Madame de Pompadour, at that old reprobate the Maréchal de Saxe, at Rousseau, at Voltaire, at the immensely learned Duval d'Epinoy and many others, and feels that one has met them all. They are, it is true, almost all pleasant, witty, charming and usually pretty; but this was an age which unashamedly cultivated these excellent qualities, just as Hals's sitters cultivated *gravitas* and a certain ripe bonhomie. Marie Fel, his companion for many years, could be *la douce France* personified.[42] The colour schemes are invariable pleasing, the powder blues, dove greys and pinks somehow never becoming dull or cloying.

Yet there is no way of comparing Maurice-Quentin in youth and old age. In his forties he began to behave oddly, and, though Marie Fel kept up appearances as long as she could, by the mid 1750s there was no disguising that his mind was crumbling. Yet even in old age his brother's family and the citizens of St-Quentin seemed to cherish him, as they still do his memory.

[42] Marie Fel was the daughter of a famous organist and became a star of the Paris opera in 1734. She met Maurice-Quentin shortly afterwards and, despite her reputation (according to the Goncourts) of being something of a *femme fatale*, looked after him for many years with great devotion.

TURNER, Joseph Mallord William (died in 1851, aged seventy-six). Until recently Turner was more admired on the Continent than in England.[43] Despite the apparent British obsession with the weather, he never quite persuaded his countrymen to accept sunlight, rain, mist and fog as pictorial subjects as interesting as a horse, a nude, a country church or an apple. "Pictures of nothing and very like" was a typical contemporary comment (made by William Hazlitt in the *Examiner*); and for long the print industry sold a hundred Constables for every Turner. Doubts about Turner's artistic aspirations were compounded by a delicate distaste for his personality. Even John Ruskin, who ardently extolled the paintings, wrote about his character like a lord recommending an old retainer of questionable habits to another lord. One eminent Turner scholar suggested that "there seems to be no connection between the artist and the person". This is a travesty.

Turner flourished in an age whose eye-catching excesses seem to be more popular today than its achievements. Had he been a debauched Regency roué or an elegant rake, he would now be the loved and hated hero of television soap operas. Had he been a gentle but intermittently murderous psychopath, he would be held up as the victim of a mercenary society. But more typically, he was a self-made Englishman of the early Industrial Revolution, a member of the uncouth, pushy, hard-working, ambitious and generally unspeakable first generation whose descendents would soon blossom into the most couth, high-minded and self-satisfied class ever to set the tone of polite behaviour. The son of a barber and wigmaker in Covent Garden, he was highly gifted – one of the two genuine wonderchilds of English painting (Millais was the other) – but he had no other advantages by birth. He was a voracious self-educator and a lover (and writer) of Romantic poetry; but he was tongue-tied and, when he opened his mouth, his every syllable betrayed his lack of breeding. Though highly intelligent, the only *mot* of his on record is his reply at a dinner party to the question how he would define painting: "Well, it's a rum thing certainly." What made him the youngest associate fellow of the Royal Academy at twenty-two, the youngest fellow at twenty-five, the youngest professor at thirty and the richest painter in England in his thirties was hard work and single-minded ambition. Had he been a millowner or iron master, he would have been one of the small band of men who were transforming the face and social structure of England.

---

[43] The large and uneven Turner literature now includes several excellent works: A. J. Finberg, *The Life of J. M. W. Turner* (2nd edn, Oxford, 1961); L. Gowing, *Turner: Imagination and Reality* (New York, 1966); J. Walker, *John Mallord William Turner* (New York, 1976); A. Wilton, *Turner in his Time* (London, 1987); and A. Bailey, *Standing in the Sun: The Life of J. M. W. Turner* (London, 1998).

Though by his mid fifties Turner had achieved enough to establish himself as England's most successful painter, he had achieved nothing that would justify describing him today as one of its greatest. Had he then retired, his early watercolours would still be admired and a few of his oil paintings might be on view in Third World ambassadorial residences. The quality Sunday magazines would discover him from time to time and a little daringly call him the "English Delacroix". But he went on painting, though increasingly at odds with mid Victorian England. Copper plates were being superseded by steel, a quicker and cheaper method of engraving, which he hated. Public taste was changing. The grandiose and romantic were out; the cosy and the domestic were in. At Windsor Castle Mr Landseer was teaching the young Queen and her Consort, both seriously artistic, how to draw a stag. Her Majesty's humbler subjects preferred more cuddlesome pets but their sentiments were similar. The new art unions, selling the same engravings by the thousand, were a resounding success. Subscribers had a yearly chance to win an original oil in a raffle. The idea would have curdled Lord Egremont's blood; but Lord Egremont, like most patrons and cronies of Turner's youth, was dead. Even among connoisseurs Turner's stock was falling. But it was these inauspicious circumstances which propelled him to his artistic summit. For his last fifteen years he painted largely to please himself. His fantastic late seascapes and airscapes were products of frenetic activity and remain the essential Turner. Fifty years after his death the French Impressionists claimed him as their own and some of his last visionary landscapes are as close to abstract art as anything painted before the mid twentieth century. But *The Fighting Temeraire, Burial at Sea, Sun Setting over a Lake, Fingal's Cave* (the first Turner to cross the Atlantic), *The "Sun of Venice" Going to Sea* and *Rain, Steam and Speed* are impossible to categorise: they are Turner's unique visions of man and his artefacts clashing cataclysmically with the "elements". (Steam and smoke were elevated to this rank in the late paintings.)

Turner's private life scandalised mid Victorian society and he never received a public honour. For long he lived with the widow of a musician, Sarah Danby, by whom he had two daughters. Later her niece, Hannah, kept house for him. The infinitely accomplished and infinitely insufferable Elizabeth Rigby, later Lady Eastlake, thought that the whole menage was "exceedingly unsavoury". In his last years the hardworking and twice-widowed Sophia Booth looked after him in their house in Chelsea. His letters in old age to his few surviving friends are among his most cheerful, just as his paintings are his best. He faced the end stoically: he expected to die at the same age as his "Dad"; they were chips off the same block. He was buried with some pomp in St Paul's Cathedral; but at the Academy dinner that evening Lady

Eastlake summed up the general feeling: "Turner's life has been sordid in the extreme and far from respectable." [44]

INGRES, Jean-Auguste-Dominique (died in 1867, aged eighty-seven). Ingres was probably the greatest draughtsman of the nineteenth century, a good portraitist and an accomplished painter of nudes – but at best a mediocre painter of anything else.[45] But this is not how he saw himself. He especially hated people who praised his drawings at the expense of his paintings; and he was a dedicated hater. He elbowed his way to the graveside of the venerable Baron Vivant Denon (whose *fauteuil* at the Institut he was to inherit) and gave an impromptu oration: "Good, good, good! He is in it this time and this time he'll stay." Even his greatest triumphs were soured by the modest successes of others. Delacroix famously called him "a perfect expression of an imperfect intelligence".

The son of a Bohemian artist – his parents were separated – he was born in Montauban and started his artistic studies in nearby Toulouse. Later in Paris, as David's pupil, he won the Prix de Rome at the age of twenty-eight. On Napoleon's fall his stipend was stopped, one of the petty idiocies which made the Bourbon Restoration so unpopular. Thereafter his main source of income for some years came from quick portrait sketches, a genre he professed to hate. He drew hundreds, perhaps thousands: lost ones are still turning up. His sitters, in so far as they took the trouble to sit down on their way to more important social functions, were well-heeled tourists – mostly carefully chaperoned young ladies from England or honeymoon couples from German-speaking lands – or locally bred male dummies sporting operetta uniforms. He also drew a few established expatriates, perhaps in return for a square meal, and the occasional visiting celebrity, like Liszt and Paganini. There is not a dud among these sheets: the bodies breathe under the clothes, even the plainest faces are full of interest and the accessories – gloves, swords, parasols, books – are sketched in with throwaway brilliance.

Nothing in Ingres's oeuvre ever matched these sketches but some of his early nudes were compelling for a different reason. In his formal portraits the liberties he took with anatomy are concealed by sumptuous garments. In his nudes they are exposed – the extended back, the oddly sideways swell of a breast, the body tautly contracted and extended to suit his highly charged erotic sensibilities – often against a flat background. Yet such was his mastery

[44] Lady Elizabeth Eastlake, *Journals and Correspondence* (London, 1895), p. 321.

[45] Ingres never invited impartiality and the following monographs are partisan, either for or against: J. Cassou, *Ingres* (Brussels, 1947); J. Alazard, *Ingres and Ingrinisme* (Paris, 1950); G. Wildenstein, *Ingres* (London, 1954); R. Rosenblum, *Ingres* (London, 1967).

of line that one's eye accepts his vision as a kind of super-reality without noticing the abnormalities. But the springboard for his official rehabilitation in his thirties was an altar-piece, *The Vow of Louis XIII*, so feeble that it fails even to offend. It was the first of many such historicising and religious *tableaux*. Like a host of even less gifted purveyors of religious marshmallows, he went to great length to get his props right, consulting experts on medieval armour and Etruscan footwear; but his medieval knights and maidens are as redolent of Louis-Philippe and the Second Empire as Offenbach but without the wit.[46] He became a member of the Institut, a Grand Officer of the Legion of Honour, Director of the Ecole des Beaux-Arts and finally a Senator of the Empire. The influence he exercised on art teaching was dire. His insistence on the purity of line paralysed generations of artists whose soul was neither pure nor linear; and his obsession with drawing made art lessons in French lycées a horrible grind for a hundred years.

But his last formal portraits are in a class of their own. He unashamedly responded to qualities most artists profess to despise: the melancholy beauty of great wealth, the transcendent radiance of an ancient title, the inimitable poise bestowed by inherited power. He painted Elizabeth Rothschild (Betty to her friends) – born a Rothschild as well as married to one – at a time when the lustre of the name eclipsed that of most royal houses. The portrait is no Waldmüllerian confection; it is the beauty and animation of the face and the grace of the pose, not the beribboned satin dress and the famous jewellery, which draw attention to themselves. The Princesse de Broglie, his last society sitter (Plate 10), was twenty-eight and already known to be delicate. She died five years later from tuberculosis; and one remains haunted by the veiled tragedy framed in icy regal splendour.

Despite his tantrums and insinuations, perhaps there was more to Ingres than meets the eye. His two marriages were childless but idyllically happy; and his draughtsmanship was admired not only by *pompiers* but also by artists like Corot and Renoir. He equated *le dessin* with *la moralité*, perhaps rightly: both depend on drawing the line somewhere.

---

[46] Among apologists even for such horrors as *Christ in the Temple*, Richard Wollheim suggests that readers should bear in mind that the painting belongs to the Victorian age. See R. Wollheim, *Painting as an Art* (London, 1986), p. 248. But Victorian painting was not all bad, or at least not that bad.

COROT, Camille (died in 1875, aged seventy-nine). Corot was that rarity, a thoroughly nice genius.[47] He was born in Paris on the last day of Messidor in Year IV of the new revolutionary calendar (16 July 1796). The Revolution itself had only recently culminated in the Terror followed by a spasm of Counter-Terror; but historic convulsions left the Corot family unconvulsed. Camille's father was an industrious draper from Burgundy; his mother, who ran a fashionable milliner's shop in the family house overlooking the Quai Voltaire, came from the orderly Swiss city of Fribourg. Even as a young man Camille showed a gift for friendship – older people especially found his thoughtful cast of mind congenial – but his *amitiés sentimentales* never threatened to become *grandes passions.* Yet he was not a cold fish; only his passions were reserved for his art and for nature in her more placid moods. The former he was determined to pursue even against parental opposition. He was sixteen when the family acquired their country property in Ville d'Avray near Paris; and, though Camille loved travelling, especially to Italy, it was this house and the garden which for sixty years remained his deepest source of inspiration.

The aftermath of the Revolution of 1848 catapulted him to fame and fortune. The new-rich bourgeoisie which emerged as the real victors from the upheavals was extraordinarily crass; but their vulgarity created an insatiable demand for the trappings of eighteenth-century elegance. It was a demand which Corot was uniquely qualified to meet: his poetic landscapes harked back to Fragonard and Watteau without lapsing into kitsch. His countryside, his forests, his lakes, his distant towns and villages were harmonious, nostalgic, not without a touch of melancholy and devoid of extremes. The wind sometimes blows but it is a gentle breeze, the sun is just bright enough to warm the soul; clouds usually gather but they are never menacing. There are always figures in the landscape too: the red skirt of a peasant girl, the white shirt of a woodcutter, a painted cart or a dancing nymph add the last touch of refinement to the scene. It could have been – but almost never was – cloying or poeticising.

Affluence did not change his personality or way of life. He moved to a studio flat in the then fashionable Rue Paradis Poissonière but remained quiet, dignified, deliberate and pipe-smoking. His one extravagance, which he could now indulge, was personal generosity. An unsolicited gift saved the ailing and persecuted Daumier (whose political views Corot did not share) from being

---

[47] Among monographs and catalogues raisonnés some of the most important are H. Dumesnil, *Corot: souvenirs intimes* (Paris 1875); A. Robaut and E. Moreau-Nélaton, *Oeuvre de Corot,* 6 volumes (Paris, 1905); P. Dieterle, *Camille Corot* (Paris, 1964); G. Tinterow, M. Pantazzi and V. Pomarède, *Corot* (New York, 1996).

evicted from his studio. Lesser artists could always count on an indefinite loan. To his models he was a kindly uncle. Remarkably, his generosity was never resented by the recipients. Success also spawned an industry of forgeries – some astonishingly feeble and yet authenticated by museums – many of which found their final resting place in the Hollywood of the 1930s.[48]

Corot painted figures and nudes in all periods, bringing to them the same sensitivity and refinement that he did to his landscapes; but it was during his last ten years that not only his landscapes but also his figure paintings reached their summit. Among the former the *Belfry of Douai* was painted when he was in his mid seventies, while recovering from the hardships of the Siege of Paris. He bequeathed it to "le Museé", to form a pendant to his early *Cathedral of Chartres*.[49] Degas, a stern critic, regarded his last figure paintings, *The Lady in Blue*, as one of the masterpieces of the age. For long a pleasant air mystery surrounded the picture; even the omniscient Robaut seemed uncertain about the identity of the lady. In fact she was almost certainly the artist's favourite model, "la petite Daubigny", dressed in a slightly ill-fitting blue evening gown. She leans on a sideboard, her face half-turned to the viewer. She is in a *rêverie*, a state of mind soon to be destroyed by the telephone but which survives in a few great paintings (like Corot's), a few lines of poetry (like the Hungarian Vörösmarty's *A Merengöhöz*) and in a few bars of music (like Schumann's *Traumerei*).

MONET, Claude (died in 1926, aged eighty-six) (Plate 15). Though born in Paris, Monet spent his childhood in Rouen where his father was a house painter.[50] Around 1858 he met Boudin, who encouraged him to become an artist and introduced him to open-air painting. After two years' military service in North Africa (which cured him forever from hankering after military glory), he moved to Paris and, against parental opposition, enrolled in Charles Gleyre's atelier. On outings from there Impressionism was born.[51] No artist of the last 150 years has been so much written about and

[48] His signature, all capitals, was easy to forge and he often authenticated feeble copies by adding a few brushstrokes."Even poor forgers have to live."

[49] Even in this small respect Corot remained a child of the eighteenth century. The creation of the Musée National was one of the beneficial acts of the Revolution. It was soon to be universally known as the Louvre from the former royal residence where it was housed; but to its founders – and to Corot – it was always just "le Musée".

[50] Useful monographs include those by relatives and friends: G. Geffroy, *Claude Monet: sa vie et son oeuvre* (Paris, 1924); G. Clemenceau, *Claude Monet: The Water Lilies* (New York, 1930); L. Venturi, *Les archives de l'Impressionisme*, 2 volumes (Paris, 1939); J.-P. Hoschedé, *Claude Monet, ce mal-connu* (Geneva, 1960); R. Cogniat, *Monet and his World* (London, 1966); C. Joyes, *Monet at Giverny* (London, 1975).

[51] See above, Chapter 8, pp. 110–11.

commercially so exploited as Monet; and the survival of his reputation even among artists is a tribute to the robustness of his talent. Yet he was not particularly profound; indeed, his friend Cézanne came near the truth when he said that "Monet is just a pair of eyes; but, by God, what a pair of eyes!". But if Cézanne was near the truth, he was not quite there. Monet was also a charismatic leader of artists: it is impossible to imagine Impressionism triumphing without him. The name itself derives from one of his paintings, a harbour scene entitled *Sunrise: Impression*; it was derisively coined by the critic Leroy after the first exhibition of the group at the Galerie Nadar in 1874. Monet's faith in his own and his friends' artistic aims was as total as was his contempt for fossilised academic tradition. For nearly thirty years he was ignored or execrated by the art-political establishment; only the patronage of a few friends like Caillebotte and the faith of a few farsighted dealers like Paul Durand-Ruel made it possible for him to continue to paint and for his family to survive. But he never compromised. His series paintings of the 1880s and 1890s – the same view in different lights and atmospheric conditions of the *Gare St-Lazare, Haystacks* and *Rouen Cathedral* – remain the essence of Impressionism. His last paintings, created in Giverny in Normandy while his eyesight was deteriorating, transcend any such stylistic label.[52]

RODIN, Auguste (died in 1917, aged seventy-seven) (Plate 16). Rodin was born in Paris on the same day as Monet (12 November 1840); but the roots of both families were in Normandy.[53] This was to become an additional bond between the two men. Rodin's father was a low-grade official in the police and the artist's childhood was austere but not joyless. Educated by the Fathers of the Val de Grâce, the only subject at which he showed any promise was drawing; and at seventeen he was allowed to enrol in the Ecole de Dessin.[54] It was there that he first came across clay, a love at first sight. Only once thereafter did he hesitate in his resolve to become a sculptor. When his beloved older sister, Marie, a novice nun, died from peritonitis at the age of nineteen, he conceived the idea that it was his duty to take her place in holy orders. Fortunately both for European sculpture and for the continued holiness of any Order he might have entered, his instructing priest,

[52] See above, Chapter 15, pp. 222–30.

[53] An excellent monograph with a good bibliography is that by F. V. Grunfeld, *Rodin* (London, 1986). A good contemporary account is that by M. Tirel, *Rodin intime* (Paris, 1923).

[54] Every sizeable French city had one of these excellent institutions, teaching every aspect of the decorative arts, the bedrock of the French luxury industries. Dalou, Lhermitte, Cazin and Fantin-Latour were pupils in Paris, in addition to Rodin. But they were looked down upon by the dreary but prestigious Ecole des Beaux-Arts.

Father Pierre-Julien Eymard, recognised the transience of young Auguste's vocation and steered him back to his original course. (For this alone the Father deserved to be beatified by Pope Pius XI in 1929.) But it was a long haul. For the best part of fifteen years he slaved away at building sites and in monumental masons' yards at whatever carving or modelling job was going. Fortunately, in the Paris of Baron Haussmann no tenement was allowed to rise without a pair of titans propping up the arched portals and plaster swags of foliage dangling from windowsills. He always regarded it as a good training. During this period he also met Rose Beuret, his much-abandoned but never *completely* abandoned mistress and, in the last year of their lives, wife.

Between 1865 and 1872 he worked for the sculptor-entrepreneur Ernest Carrier-Belleuse.[55] During their stay in Brussels he modelled his first masterpiece and *succès de scandale, The Vanquished,* also known as *The Age of Bronze.* Others followed; and the outrage which greeted many of them helped to spread his fame. By the 1890 he was the most famous sculptor in France and probably the most famous Frenchman in Europe. He was also in the middle of his most torrid love affair. The beautiful Camille Claudel was a gifted sculptor as well as his mistress, muse and inspiration. The affair ended tragically for her; he would not abandon Rose entirely (or his innumerable other casual liaisons); and Camille was to die thirty years later in the public ward of a lunatic asylum, forgotten by all.[56] But the period was also his most prolific: in clay, bronze and marble he created a succession of great works – *The Kiss, The Thinker, Danaid, The Prodigal Son* and many others – portraying human passions and emotions with a directness and power not seen since Michelangelo.

In his sixties, while in the throes of another *grande affaire,* this time with the American-born Duchesse de Choiseul, he embarked on several new ventures, including the architectural exploration of French churches and cathedrals and a series of one-minute drawings.[57] His last years were overcast by the turmoil of the First World War and the efforts of his admirers to

[55] See above, Chapter 15, pp. 219–20.

[56] Camille's brother, Paul, Catholic poet, dramatist, ambassador, academician and prince of phoneys, never tired of accusing Rodin of abandoning his sister. In fact, Rodin made several attempts to communicate with her, whereas Paul, already moving in exalted circles where sisters in lunatic asylums might cause embarrassment, refused to have anything to do with her until she was safely dead. Yet people who visited her maintained that she was far from hopelessly insane. The truth about the tragedy will probably never be known; but, though he never pretended to be a pillar of virtue, Rodin was a kindly man who did not lack compassion.

[57] See above, Chapter 16, pp. 238–40.

secure his estate for a future Musée Rodin.[58] But he went on working to the end and his last portrait busts are among his best. Like many artists to whom creating likenesses comes easily, he himself never thought much of them; but his bust of his friend, the great chemist Berthelot, is brilliant; and that of the middle-aged Duchesse explains her appeal better than words ever could.

NOLDE, Emil (died in 1956, aged eighty-nine). Nolde's name at birth was the Danish-sounding Hansen; he adopted the name of his native town in 1902 to affirm his Germanness.[59] For generations his forebears were Friesian farmers, German-speaking and Protestant. The future artist, a younger son, was apprenticed to a carpenter in Flensburg where he taught himself to paint. In 1890 he moved to St Gallen in Switzerland to teach at the School of Industrial Design. He published a series of humorous postcards of Swiss moutains, the financial success of which enabled him to travel and to broaden his artistic horizons. Among modern writers Nietzsche made a deep impression on him, as did Ibsen; but he would always feel insecure among academics and the literati. He married a cultivated but highly strung Danish opera singer, Ada Vestrup, who soon suffered her first nervous breakdown and who remained a semi–invalid for most of the rest of her life. Nolde remained devoted to her. In 1909 he began his series of paintings on biblical and religious themes, mingling ecstatic fervour with brutal sensuality, followed by a series on the theme of the dance in both its secular and its religious associations. He was present at the birth of German Expressionism, joining Die Brücke in Dresden and exhibiting with Der Blaue Reiter in Munich and the *Neue Sezession* in Berlin. In 1914, on a journey organised by the German Imperial Colonial Office to the Far East and Oceania, he had a chance to study the native art of people virtually untouched by European civilisation. This made a deep impression on him.

The postwar atmosphere of moral and material collapse in Germany favoured the Expressionists: their often apocalyptic pictorial language suddenly began to resemble everyday reality. This was reflected in their new name, *Die Neue Sachlichkeit* or "New Objectivity". As one of the founding fathers, Nolde became a revered figure. Early National Sociaslism, with its mystical verbiage of blood, soil and spiritual renewal, appealed to him (as it did to many other Expressionist artists); and he joined the Party and

---

[58] See above, Chapter 18, pp. 262–65.
[59] Monographs include W. Haftmann, *Emil Nolde* (London, 1959); H. Fehr, *Emil Nolde: ein Buch der Freundschaft* (Cologne, 1960); M. Urban, *Emil Nolde: Werkverzeichnis der Gemälde*, 2 volumes (London, 1990). The last volume of his autobiographical writings is E. Nolde, *Reisen, Ächtung, Befreiung* (5th edition, Cologne, 1993).

welcomed the advent to power of Hitler. Disillusionment soon followed. Hitler, a third-rate artist himself, hated Expressionism; and Nolde figured prominently at the exhibition of Degenerate Art (*Entartete Kunst*) staged in Munich in 1936. A prohibition on any artistic activity soon followed. The artist, now a non-person, and his wife, withdrew to their isolated house at Seebüll on the North German Plain. There he spent the war years secretly creating hundreds, perhaps thousands, of "Unpainted Pictures" (*Ungemalte Bilder*). To many they remain not only unique but also his most striking and individual contribution to modern art.[60] After the war he became an international celebrity. Ada died in 1946 and he married the daughter of a friend, Jolanthe Erdman. After his death the house in Seebüll became the home of the Nolde Stiftung, dedicated to the display of his works and the study of his art.

KOLLWITZ, Käthe (died in 1945, aged seventy-eight). Käthe Kollwitz was born Käthe Schmidt in Königsberg, then the capital of East Prussia, the city of Kant, now Russianised as Kaliningrad.[61] Her family were devout nonconformist Lutherans; and her passionate socialism always retained a strong Christian element. She was courageous and compassionate, one of the few artists who could make her art a vehicle of her political beliefs without either suffering. She had started studying art in Berlin when she met Karl Kollwitz, a district physician in a poor working-class area. Karl's practice provided her with inspiration and models at a time when most middle-class women had little contact with the industrial proletariat. Her first successful graphic works were a series of drawings and engravings, loosely based on the historic events which inspired Gerhardt Hauptmann's *The Weavers*, a landmark play of the 1890s.[62] Other series followed, paintings and carvings as well as graphics, depicting the tragic lives of the urban poor, especially of women and children, as searing today as they must have been when first shown. Her

---

[60] See above, Chapter 19, pp. 276–77.

[61] There is now a significant literature on Käthe Kollwitz and she has a devoted following even in England, where she was for long excruciatingly patronised. Monographs include U. M. Schneede, *Käthe Kollwitz: das zeichnerische Werk* (Munich, 1989); E. Prelinger (ed.), *Käthe Kollwitz* (London, 1992); E. E. Jansen, *Ernst Barlach – Käthe Kollwitz: Geschichte einer verborgenen Nähe* (Berlin, 1988). Some and some of her own writings and letters have been published: K. Kollwitz, *Bekenntnisse* (Leipzig, 1981); and K. Kollwitz, *Diary and Letters*, translated by R. and C. Winston (Chicago, 1988).

[62] Hauptmann's early plays with their social and political message had a revolutionary impact similar to those of Ibsen's. *The Weavers*, one of the most powerful, describes the ill-fated revolt of the Silesian Weavers in 1844. The performance so moved Kollwitz that she abandoned her series illustrating Zola's *Germinal* to embark on her first masterpieces.

elder son Peter was killed on the Western Front in 1914. The granite momorial she sculpted to stand on his grave is arguably the greatest in a genre whose tragic message tended to overwhelm even brilliant artists.

The 1920s were artistically her most creative period. She became well-known, though she never sought the limelight or joined vocal art-political groupings. Her husband too continued to practise, declining promotions which would have removed him from contact with his patients. The sculptor Ernst Barlach became one of their close friends. She never entertained any illusions about the Nazis and many advised her and her husband to emigrate. She refused for fear that it might bring retaliation on her family. In 1938 she was expelled from all artistic organisations and teaching posts. Karl died in 1939. She was forbidden to maintain a studio or to sell her work. Examples of her earlier creations in public collections were removed. Many were never to be recovered. Her grandson, another Peter, was killed on the Russian Front in 1943. Her flat, with all her graphic material, plates and small sculp-tures, perished in one of the Allied air raids on Berlin a few months later. She was evacuated to Saxony, where she died in 1945. She was one of the greatest artists of the twentieth century; but too few of her late works survive to serve the immediate purpose of this book.

BONNARD, Pierre (died in 1947, aged eighty). Bonnard's father was a senior civil servant, his mother the daughter of a banker, and he was educated at one of France's most prestigious schools, the Lycée Louis-le-Grand in Paris (as had been Degas and, before Degas, Robespierre).[63] Discretion tinged with subtle irony was bred into him. After a trial period as a civil servant, he embarked, a little hesitantly, on a career as an artist. At the Académie Julian he met Edouard Vuillard, Ker-Xavier Roussel, Maurice Denis and Paul Sérusier, young men from a similar background. The group adopted the name of "Nabis" or Prophets, though their resemblance to such patriarchal figures as Elijah or Job was remote. They cultivated a flat, essentially decor-ative style, influenced by Japanese prints and the art of Gauguin, seen to best advantage in brilliant theatrical works, prints and book illustrations. Bonnard's prize-wining poster for *France-Champagne* led to his friendship with Félix Fénéon, secretary to the influential *Revue Blanche* to which the Nabis continued to contribute. (It also prompted Bonnard's friend Henri de Toulouse-Lautrec, by then firmly ensconced in the brothels of Montmartre,

[63] Good monographs, including several by members of the related Terrace family, are R. Cogniat, *Bonnard* (Milan, 1968); A. Terrace, *Bonnard* (Paris, 1988); N. Watkin, *Bonnard* (London, 1994); M. Terrace, *Bonnard: du dessin au peinture* (Paris, 1996); T. Hyman, *Bonnard* (London, 1998).

to try his hand at posters.) At twenty-six he met Marie Boursin (who preferred to call herself Marthe de Méligny), who became his muse and model and, eventually, wife. She was pretty in a birdlike way, clinging, demanding and vulnerable. His friends saw her as a millstone; but catering to her whims became one of his life's fulfilments. It was to alleviate her chronic *atopie*, a fashionable form of allergy, that the couple moved from Veronnet in Normandy to Le Cannet in the South of France. His mastery of light and colour had by then earned him fame and the classification as a Post-Impressionist ("post" in this case meaning late rather than after). His work was also frequently described as *intimiste*, a tradition essentially French and bourgeois which linked him to Chardin. He objected to neither pigeon-hole, though, by the 1930s, his shimmering surfaces were entirely his own. Becoming a celebrated international artist, he travelled widely (though usually summoned back by a telegram from Marthe), exhibited in many cities in Europe and the United States and received the Carnegie Medal and other accolades. His favoured subjects were his everyday milieu of solid middle-class comfort – a well-laid breakfast table, a cultivated garden, Marthe in the bath, Marthe at her toilet, Marthe looking at herself in the mirror. During the war years he hardly moved out of his villa.[64] In 1942 Marthe died and, grief-stricken, Bonnard wrote to Matisse that without her his career as an artist had come to an end. But it had not. His next and last five years became his golden age, not only because yellows and whites, often set against a bluish darkness, became dominant colours in many of his still lives, land-scapes and self-portraits but because the very weaknesses of his style – or what to many appeared as weaknesses – now became his strengths. "I'm only just beginning to to understand what it is to paint", he confided in the much younger painter, Bazaine.[65] The tentativeness of his touch now imparted to his vision a kind of quivering and yet unalterable rightness, the uncertainty and diffidence with which he seemed to approach the ever-changing visible world now became positive virtues, the dissolved blurs of colours a celebra-tion of natural beauty. At the same time, in the fashionable art world of the postwar years of *marxisant* existentialism, dominated by Picasso's ever-innovative genius,[66] his art was to many almost an irritant. Bonnard accepted this. "They don't much like me: I understand that. That's what happens to each passing generation." [67] On his last visit to Paris in 1946, staying at the Hôtel Terminus near the Gare St-Lazare, a haunt of commercial travallers,

[64] A rather unattractive house with a superb view called Le Bosquet. Bonnard painted in the entrance hall or dining-room; he never had a proper studio.

[65] Quoted by Hyman, *Bonnard*, p. 202.

[66] Matisse esteemed Bonnard highly but Picasso could not abide him.

[67] Quoted by Hyman, *Bonnard*, p. 204.

he drew from his window the teeming Place du Havre. The sheet has the same tremulous beauty as the last drawings of Claude and even of Michelangelo. His last painting, a small canvas of the almond tree under his window bursting into bloom after a long hard winter, is the final triumph of a sensuous and yet refined vision. But he was never satisfied. Contemplating the ostensibly finished painting from his sickbed in January 1947, already too weak to get up unaided, he asked his nephew, Charles Terrace, to let him make a few alterations. "The green on the patch of ground to the left is all wrong. What it needs is a touch of yellow." [68] Terrace made the changes under his direction. Four days later he slipped away, perhaps content at last.

MATISSE, Henri (died in 1954, aged eighty-five). Matisse's father was a modestly prosperous grain merchant in Bohain-en-Vermondois in Picardy: there was no tradition of art or Bohemianism in the family. [69] Henri, a second son, studied law and practised as a solicitor's clerk before announcing his intention of becoming an artist. This, he would often explain to Anglo-Saxon friends, was no more "eccentric" in France than to decide to become a butcher, doctor or teacher; but the normality of the decision depended on pursuing one's training at the Ecole des Beaux-Arts in Paris and then cultivating a traditional style. Matisse never did either. The paternal allowance was soon stopped and Matisse made his living copying Bouchers and Fragonards in the Louvre and painting miles of laurel leaves around the cornices of the Grand Palais for the stupendous Exposition Universelle of 1900. Mme Matisse's successful millinery salon also helped. The artistically explosive first decade of the twentieth century saw him leading a group of young artists, soon to be dubbed "*les Fauves*" (or wild beasts), exploring vivid primary colours and wildly distorted forms. To the incomprehension, indeed disgust, of respectable critics, these found unexpected favour with patrons from the edge of civilisation. Two Muscovite merchants, Sergei Ivanovich Shchukin and Ivan Morosov, actually commissioned for their own homes (inhabited by their wives, children and servants as well as by the deluded collectors themselves!) huge canvases representing Dance, Music and other subjects, "an excuse for painting prancing naked women in vivid orange"; and rich Americans, with suspiciously German-sounding names like Stein, clearly had more money than sense buying other works no less deranged.

Matisse was too old for the trenches in 1914 but for him too the war years

[68] Ibid., p. 205.
[69] The large Matisse literature includes A. C. Barnes, *The Art of Henri Matisse* (New York, 1933); P. Reverdy and G. Duthuit, *The Last Works of Henri Matisse* (New York, 1954); J. Flam, *Matisse: A Retrospective* (New York, 1968); F. Gilot, *Matisse and Picasso*, translated by N. A. Talese (London, 1990).

were a watershed. He discovered the Midi, made new friends and lost old
ones. With bourgeois certainties in ruins, the 1920s saw the savages of
yesteryear embraced by respectable society; and during the doom-laden 1930s
Matisse's "escapist art" – he never painted anything gloomy or sad – gave
the gallery-going public an illusion of Arcadia just round the corner. (It was
also the heyday of Hollywood glitz.) There were exhibitions of his work in
Europe and the United States, forays into stage designs (as for Diaghilev's
staging of Stravinski's *Le chant de Rossignol*), major commissions (like the
murals for the Barnes Foundation building in Merion, Maryland) and travels
to exotic places. He received the Carnegie Medal and sat on the jury which
awarded one to Picasso. During the Second World War he settled in unoc-
cupied France, while Mme Matisse and their daughter Marguérite got busy
in the Resistance. Matisse did not approve of such provocation and the
marriage, long floundering over his serial infidelities, came adrift. He had
his more private trials: a routine abdominal operation in 1942 led to a
deep-vein thrombosis in the leg and a pulmonary embolus which almost
killed him; and its after-effects made it difficult for him to walk for the rest
of his life. But, together with Picasso, who spent most of the war years in
Paris, he emerged into the postwar world as one of the grand old men of
European art. Decorations and gold medals rained on him and prices paid
for his casual doodles began their giddy upward spiral. The little Dominican
chapel which he decorated in Vence was consecrated to tourism with three
stars from Michelin a year before it was consecrated to God by the Bishop
of Nice. Artistically he continued to advance. For generations artists had
been taught how to achieve harmony by allowing one colour or hue to
dominate. Matisse (in John Berger's eloquent phrase) "clashed his colours
like cymbals and the effect was like a lullaby"."But", as he himself put it in
an interview on his eighty-first birthday, "it took me sixty years to organise
my brain." In his last years there was a joyous outpouring of great works –
*The Pool, Snail,* the last *Blue Nude* and dozens of others – the creative
exuberance of childhood harnessed by the wisdom of old age.

# Index of Works of Art

A list of the whereabouts of works of art mentioned in the text specifically or in general terms.

ABBREVIATIONS: Accademia (Gallerie dell' Accademia, Venice); Bargello (Museo Nazionale del Bargello, Florence); National Gallery (National Gallery, London); Louvre (Louvre, Paris); Uffizi (Uffizi, Florence); Prado (Museo del Prado, Madrid); Musée d'Orsay (Musée d'Orsay, Paris); Munch Museum (Munch Museum, Oslo; Municipal Museum, Oslo); Pompidou (Musée Nationale d'Art Moderne; Centre Georges Pompidou, Paris); Guggenheim New York (Solomon R. Guggenheim Museum, New York); Metropolitan Museum (Metropolitan Museum of Art, New York).

ADLER, Jules (1875–1952)
*The Strike at Le Creusot* (Musée des Beaux-Arts, Pau)
*The Weary* (Musée Calvet, Avignon)

BASTIEN-LEPAGE, Jules (1848–1884)
*The Little Pedlar* (Musée des Beaux-Arts, Tournai)

BAZILLE, Jean-Frédéric (1841–1870)
*Renoir* (Musée d'Orsay)

BELLINI, Giovanni (*c.* 1430–1516)
*Agony in the Garden* (National Gallery)
*The Drunkenness of Noah* (Musée des Beaux-Arts, Besançon)
*The Feast of the Gods* (National Gallery of Art, Washington DC)
*Lady at her Toilet* (Kunsthistorisches Museum, Vienna)
*Madonna with Angels* (Frari, Venice)
*Madonna Enthroned from San Giobbe* (Accademia, Venice)
*Madonna with Standing Child* (Accademia, Venice)
*Pietà with Virgin and St John* (Pinacoteca di Brera, Milan)
*St Jerome Altar-piece* (San Giovanni Crisostomo, Venice)

BERNINI, Gianlorenzo (1598–1680)
*Baldacchino* (St Peter's Rome)
*Blessed Ludovica Albertoni* (San Francesco a Ripa, Rome)

*Cappella del S. Sacramento* (St Peter's, Rome)
*Constanza Bonarelli* (Bargello)
*Cornaro Chapel* (Santa Maria della Vittoria, Rome)
*Fonseca Memorial* (Fonseca Chapel, San Lorenzo in Lucina)
*Self-Portrait (1620)* (Galleria Borghese, Rome)
*Self-Portrait (1665)* (drawing) (Royal Collection, Windsor Castle)
*Tomb of Alexander VII* (St Peter's, Rome)
*Tomb of Urban VIII* (St Peter's, Rome)

BONNARD, Pierre (1867–1947)
*Almond Tree in Flower* (Pompidou)
*The Breakfast Table* (Tate Modern, London)
*Le Cannet, 1945* (Private Collection)
*Corner of Table* (Pompidou)
*Nude in the Bath, 1937* (Petit Palais, Paris)
*Self-Portrait, 1945* (Private Collection, New York)

BOUGUEREAU, Adolphe William (1825–1905)
*The Birth of Venus* (Musée d'Orsay)

CARRIERA, Rosalba (1675–1757)
*Louis XV* (Zwinger Gallery, Dresden)
*Portrait of a Lady* (Galleria Estense, Modena)

CASSATT, Mary Stevenson (1844–1926)
*The Bath* (Art Institute, Chicago)

CHAMPAIGNE, Philippe de (1602–1674)
*Richelieu* (Louvre)

CHARDIN, Jean-Baptiste-Siméon (1699–1779)
*Basket of Wild Strawberries* (Private Collection)
*The Buffet* (Louvre)
*The Cellar Boy* (Hunterian Art Gallery, University of Glasgow)
*Mme Chardin* (Louvre)
*Good Education* (Museum of Fine Arts, Houston)
*Jar of Olives* (Louvre)
*Lady Taking Tea* (Hunterian Art Gallery, University of Glasgow)
*The Morning Toilet* (Nationalmuseum, Stockholm)
*The Rayfish* (Louvre)
*Saying Grace* (Louvre)
*Self-Portrait at the Easel* (Louvre)
*Self-Portrait* (Louvre)
*The Scullery Maid* (Hunterian Art Gallery, University of Glasgow)

DAGNAN-BOUVERET, Pascal-Adolphe-Jean (1852–1929)
*Brittany Pardon* (Metropolitan)
*Horses at the Watering Trough* (Musée d'Art et d'Histoire, Chambéry)

DAVID, Jacques-Louis (1748–1825)
*Amor and Psyche* (Cleveland Museum of Arts)
*Andromache Mourning Hector* (Louvre)
*Antiochus and Stratonice* (Ecole des Beaux-Arts, Paris)
*The Battle between Mars and Minerva* (Louvre)
*Belisarius Begging for Alms* (Musée des Beaux-Arts, Lille)
*Bonaparte Leading his Troops across the Alps* (Malmaison, Musée Nationale)
*Bonaparte, 1793* (Louvre)
*Comte de Turenne* (Ny Carlsberg Glypthotek, Copenhagen)
*Coronation of Napoleon* (Louvre)
*Distribution of the Eagles* (Louvre)
*Emmanuel-Joseph Sieyès* (Fogg Art Museum, Cambridge, Massachusetts)
*The Lictors Carrying the Bodies of Brutus's Sons* (Louvre)
*Louise Pastoret* (Art Institute, Chicago)
*Marat Assassinated* (Musées Royaux des Beaux-Arts de Belgique, Brussels)
*Marie-Antoinette on the Way to the Scaffold* (Bibliothèque Nationale, Paris)
*Monsieur et Madame Pécoul* (Louvre)
*The Oath of the Horatii* (Louvre)
*Pauline Jeanne Jeanin and her Daughter* (Snite Museum, University of Notre Dame)
*The Sabine Women* (Louvre)
*Self-Portrait* (Uffizi)
*Télémache et Eucharis* (Paul Getty Museum, Malibu, California)
*Thermopylae* (Louvre)
*Venus and the Graces Disarming Mars* (Musées Royaux des Beaux-Arts, Brussels)
*Zénaïde and Charlotte Bonaparte* (Paul Getty Museum, Malibu, California)

DEGAS, Hilaire Germain Edgar (1834–1917)
*Absinthe (Au Café)* (Musée d'Orsay)
*Ballet Rehearsal* (Louvre)
*The Bath* (Art Institute, Chicago)
*Dancer* (sculpture) (Tate Modern)
*Dancer on Stage* (pastel) (Louvre)
*Woman Combing her Hair* (Musée d'Orsay)
*Women Ironing* (Musée d'Orsay)

DELLA ROBBIA, Luca (1400–1482)
*Lady's Portrait Bust* (Bargello)
*Stemma of the Duke of Anjou* (Victoria and Albert Museum, London)

GOYA y Lucientes, Francisco José de (1746–1828)
  *Agony in the Garden* (Escuolas Pias de San Antonio, Madrid)
  *Aun Aprendo* (Still I'm Learning) (Prado)
  *Autumn, Summer* and *Winter* (Prado)
  *Black Paintings* (Prado)
  *Blind Guitarist* (Prado)
  *Brigands Stripping a Woman* (illustration to de Sade?) (Private Collection, Madrid)
  *Caprichos*, series of etchings (plates in British Museum, London)
  *Carlos IV and his Family* (Prado)
  *The Clothed* and *The Naked Maya* (Prado)
  *Dead Turkey* (Prado)
  *Disasters of War*, series of etchings (plates in British Museum, London)
  *Don José Pio de Molina* (Collection Oskar Reinhart, Winterthur)
  *Francisco Bayeu* (Museo Provinciale de Bellas Artes, Valencia)
  *Godoy as Commander in the War of the Oranges* (Real Academia de Bellas Artes de San Ferdinando, Madrid)
  *Golden Bream* (Houston Museum of Fine Arts)
  *Javier* (Collection de Noailles, Paris)
  *Josefa* (Prado)
  *Last Communion of St Joseph of Calasance* (Escuolas Pias de San Antonio, Madrid)
  *Leandro Fernandez de Moratin* (Museo de Bellas Artes, Bilbao
  *Mariano* (Private Collection, Madrid)
  *2 May, 1808* and *3 May, 1808* (Prado)
  *The Milkmaid of Bordeaux* (Prado)
  *Monk Talking to an Old Woman* (miniature) (University Museum, New Jersey)
  *Pieces of Rib, Loin and Head of Mutton* (Louvre)
  *Self-Portrait with Dr Arrieta* (Institute of Art, Minneapolis, Minnesota)
  *Tauromachia* (series of etchings) (plates in the British Museum, London)
  *Tiburcio Pérez* (Metropolitan)
  *Time (Old Crones)* (Musée des Beaux-Arts, Lille)
  *Woodcocks* (Meadows Museum, Dallas)

GRECO, EL (Doménikos Theotokopoulos) (1541–1614)
  *The Fifth Seal of the Apocalypse* (Metropolitan Museum)
  *Laocoön* (National Gallery, Washington DC)
  *View of Toledo* (El Greco Museum, Toledo)

GREUZE, Jean-Baptiste (1725–1805)
  *Broken Pitcher* (Louvre)
  *Grandfather Explaining the Bible to his Family* (Louvre)
  *Paralytic Nursed by his Children* (Hermitage, St Petersburg)

*George Washington* (Capitol, Richmond, Virginia)
*Madame Houdon* (Louvre)
*Marquis de Lafayette* (Capitol, Richmond, Virginia)
*Mirabeau* (Louvre)
*Napoleon (1807)* (Musée des Beaux-Arts, Dijon)
*Rousseau* (Louvre)
*Thomas Jefferson* (Boston Museum of Fine Arts)
*Voltaire* (sitting) (Comédie Française, Paris)
*Voltaire* (standing) (Pantheon, Paris)

HUNT, William Holman (1827–1910)
*The Light of the World* (Keble College, Oxford)
*The Scapegoat* (Lady Lever Art Gallery, Port Sunlight)

INGRES, Jean-Auguste-Dominique (1780–1867)
*Antiochus and Stratonice* (Musee Condé, Chantilly)
*Baronne James (Betty) de Rothschild* (Private Collection)
*Bonaparte as First Consul* (Musée d'Armes, Liège)
*Comte Amadé de Pastoret* (Louvre)
*Grande Odalisque* (Louvre)
*Madame J.-A.-D. Ingres, née Delphine Ramel* (Oskar Reinhart Collection, Winterthur)
*Madame J.-A.-D. Ingres, née Madeleine Chapelle* (Bührle Collection, Zurich)
*Napoleon on the Imperial Throne* (Musée de l'Armé, Paris)
*Niccolò Paganini* (Louvre)
*Princesse de Broglie* (Metropolitan Museum)
*Self-Portrait at Twenty-Four* (Musée Condé, Chantilly)
*Self-Portrait at Seventy-Nine* (Fogg Art Museum, Cambridge, Massachusetts)
*The Vow of Louis XIII* (Musée Ingres, Montauban)

KANDINSKI, Vasili (1866–1944)
*Around the Circle* (Guggenheim, New York)
*Arrow* (Öffentliches Kunstmuseum, Basel)
*Autumn in Bavaria (1908)* (Pompidou)
*Bleu de Ciel* (Pompidou)
*Brown Elan* (Maeght Collection, Paris)
*The Circle and the Square* (Pompidou)
*Composition IV* (Kunstsammlung Nordheim-Westfalen, Düsseldorf)
*Contact XIV* (Pompidou)
*Green Band* (Maeght Collection, Paris)
*Red Accent* (Guggenheim, New York)
*Red Square, Moscow* (State Tretyakov Gallery, Moscow)
*Reciprocal Accord* (Pompidou)
*Soft Hard* (Guggenheim, New York)

Several copies of Maillol's statues exist. Bronze nudes, the property of the French state, are on permanent display in the Jardin des Tuilleries, Paris. A comprehensive collection is shown, together with smaller terracottas, in the Fondation Maillol, Paris.

MALEVITCH, Kasimir Severinovich (1878–1935)
*Suprematism* (Stedelijk Museum, Amsterdam)

MANTEGNA, Andrea (*c.* 1431–1506)
*Agony in the Garden* (National Gallery)

MATISSE, Henri (1869–1954)
*Blue Nude* (Private Collection)
*La Danse* (Hermitage, St Petersburg)
*Sorrow of the King* (Pompidou)
*Snail* (Tate Modern, London)

MEISSONIER, Jean-Louis-Ernest (1815–1891)
*1814* (Louvre)

MELENDEZ, Luis (1716–1780)
*Dead Turkey* (Prado)
*Self-Portrait* (Louvre)

MICHELANGELO BUONARROTI (1475–1564)
*Bearded Slave and Awakening Slave* (Galleria dell'Accademia, Florence)
*David* (Galleria dell' Accademia, Florence)
*Medici Tombs* (Medici Chapel, San Lorenzo, Florence)
*Moses* (San Pietro in Vincoli, Rome)
*Pietà* (1498) (St Peter's, Rome)
*Pietà* (for Vittoria Colonna) (drawing) (British Museum)
*Pietà* (1540) (Museo dell' Opera del Duomo, Florence)
*Pietà* ("Rondanini") Castello Sforzesco, Milan)

MILLET, Jean François (1814–1874)
*The Gleaners* (Louvre)

MONET, Claude (1840–1926)
*Doges' Palace* (Brooklyn Museum, New York)
*Gare St-Lazare* (series) (various museums, including Art Institute, Chicago)
*Haystacks* (series) (various museums, including Musée d'Orsay)
*Impression: Sunrise* (Musée Marmottan, Paris)
*Poplars* (series) (various museums, including Musée d'Orsay)
*Rouen Cathedral* (series) (various museums, including Tate Modern, London)
*Waterlilies* (last series) (Orangerie, Paris)

*La Grenouillère* (Oskar Reinhart Foundation, Winterthur)
*Gabrielle and Jean* (Musee d'Orsay)
*La Loge* (Courtauld Instute of Art Gallery, London)
*Mme Charpentier and her Children* (Metropolitan Museum)
*Maternité* (Museum of Fine Arts, St Petersburg, Florida)
*Les Parapluies* (National Gallery)
*Piazza San Marco, Venice* (Institute of Art, Minneapolis, Minnesota)
*Venus Victrix* (sculpture) (Maison des Collettes, Cagnes)

REPIN, Ilya Efimovitch (1844–1930)
*Return of the Exile* (Tretyakov Gallery, Moscow)
*Volga Boatmen* (Russian Museum, St Petersburg)

RIPPL-RONAI, Jozsef (1861–1927)
*Banyuls* (National Gallery of Art, Budapest)

RODIN, Auguste (1840–1917)
*The Age of Bronze* (*The Vanquished*) (Place Rodin, Paris)
*Berthelot* (Musée Rodin, Paris)
*Balzac* (Boulevard de Montparnasse, Paris)
*Burghers of Calais* (Musée Rodin, Paris)
*La Duchesse de Choiseul* (Musee Rodin, Paris)
*L'homme qui marche* (Musée des Beaux-Arts, Besançon)
*The Kiss* (Tate Modern, London)
*"One-Minute Drawings"* (Musee Rodin, Paris)
*St John the Baptist* (Musée Rodin, Paris)
*The Thinker* (*The Great Shade*) (Villa des Brillants, Meudon)
*Victor Hugo* (Palais Royale, Paris)

There are replicas of most of Rodin's Work (150 of *The Age of Bronze*) in addition to the original castings or marbles. The Musée Rodin in Paris has replicas of most works, as well as drawings; the Tate Modern in London has an excellent collection. There is also an interesting Rodin Museum in Philadelphia.

SZINYEI-MERSE, Pál (1845–1921)
*Autumn* (Private Collection)
*May Picnic* (National Galley of Art, Budapest)

THORMA, János (1870–1937)
*The Sufferers* (Hungarian National Gallery, Budapest)

TINTORETTO (Jacopo Robusti) (1518–1594)
*Adoration of the Shepherds* (Scuola Grande di San Rocco, Venice)
*Crucifixion* (Scuola Grande di San Rocco, Venice)

*Deposition* (San Giorgio Maggiore, Venice)
*The Last Supper* (San Giorgio Maggiore, Venice)
*Old Senator* (National Gallery of Ireland, Dublin)
*The Origin of the Milky Way* (National Gallery)
*Paradise* (Palazzo Ducale, Venice)
*St Mark Rescuing a Slave* (Accademia)
*Self-Portrait in Old Age* (Louvre)

TITIAN (Tiziano Vecellio) (*c.* 1487–1576)
*Allegory of Wisdom* (triple portrait of Titian, Orazio Vecellio and Marco Vecellio) (National Gallery)
*Annunciation* (San Salvatore, Venice)
*Assumption of the Virgin* (Frari, Venice)
*The Crowning with Thorns* (Alte Pinakothek, Munich)
*Diana of Actaeon* (National Gallery)
*Diana and Callisto* (National Gallery of Scotland, Edinburgh)
*Equestrian Portrait of Charles V* (Prado)
*The Flaying of Marsyas* (Statnzamek, Kromeriz, Czech Republic)
*Gerolamo and Francesco da Pesaro* (Private Collection)
*Man with the Blue Sleeve* (National Gallery)
*Martyrdom of St Lawrence* (Iglesia Vieja, Escorial, Spain)
*Nymph and Shepherd* (Kunsthistorisches Museum, Vienna)
*The Pardo Venus* (Louvre)
*Paul III Farnese with his Two Grandsons* (Museo di Capodimonte, Naples)
*Pietà* (Accademia)
*Presentation of the Virgin* (Accademia)
*Ranuccio Farnese* (National Gallery of Art, Washington, DC)
*The Rape of Europa* (Isabella Stewart Gardner Museum, Boston)
*The Rape of Lucretia* (Fitzwilliam Museum, Cambridge)
*"Sacred and Profane Love"* (Galleria Borghese, Rome)
*St Mary Magdalen* (Palazzo Pitti, Florence)
*Self-Portrait, c.* 1550 (Staatliche Gemäldegalerie, Berlin)
*Self-Portrait, c.* 1560 (Prado)
*Venus and Adonis* (Prado)

TURNER, Joseph Mallord William (1775–1851)
*The Fighting Téméraire* (National Gallery)
*The Harbour of Dieppe* (Frick Collection, New York)
*Music at Petworth* (Tate Gallery, London)
*Rain, Steam and Speed* (National Gallery)
*Snowstorm* (Tate Gallery, London))
*Ulysses Deriding Polyphemus* (National Gallery)
*Venice* (water-colours) (Turner Collection, Tate Gallery, London)

UCCELLO, Paolo (1397–1475)
*The Deluge* (Chiostro Verde, Santa Maria Novella, Florence)
*The Night Hunt* (Ashmolean Museum, Oxford)
*The Rout of San Romano* (National Gallery, Uffizi, Louvre)
*St George and the Dragon* (National Gallery)

VERONESE, Paolo (Paolo Caliari) (*c.* 1528–1588)
*The Rape of Europa* (Palazzo Ducale, Venice)

VIGEE-LEBRUN, Marie-Elisabeth-Louise (1755–1842)
*Countess Golovin* (Barber Institute of Art Gallery, Birmingham)
*Queen Marie-Antoinette with her Children* (Château de Versailles)

# Index